Palgrave Studies in Impact Finance

Series Editor
Mario La Torre
Sapienza University of Rome
Rome, Italy

The *Palgrave Studies in Impact Finance* series provides a valuable scientific 'hub' for researchers, professionals and policy makers involved in Impact finance and related topics. It includes studies in the social, political, environmental and ethical impact of finance, exploring all aspects of impact finance and socially responsible investment, including policy issues, financial instruments, markets and clients, standards, regulations and financial management, with a particular focus on impact investments and microfinance.

Titles feature the most recent empirical analysis with a theoretical approach, including up to date and innovative studies that cover issues which impact finance and society globally.

More information about this series at
http://www.palgrave.com/gp/series/14621

Satyajit Bose • Guo Dong • Anne Simpson

The Financial Ecosystem

The Role of Finance in Achieving Sustainability

Satyajit Bose
Columbia University
New York, NY, USA

Guo Dong
Columbia University
New York, NY, USA

Anne Simpson
CalPERS
Sacramento, CA, USA

ISSN 2662-5105   ISSN 2662-5113   (electronic)
Palgrave Studies in Impact Finance
ISBN 978-3-030-05623-0   ISBN 978-3-030-05624-7   (eBook)
https://doi.org/10.1007/978-3-030-05624-7

Cover illustration: © Satyajit Bose

This Palgrave Macmillan imprint is published by the registered company Springer Nature Switzerland AG.
The registered company address is: Gewerbestrasse 11, 6330 Cham, Switzerland

JANUARY
2021

COLIN —

WITH THANKS +

APPRECIATION FOR

S.B. dedicates the book to Tripti and Satyakam.
G.D. dedicates the book to his grandfather.
A.S. dedicates the book to Eden, Frances, and Eve.

THE WONDERFUL

WORK YOU LEAD

IN THIS ARENA.

HERE'S TO A NEW

YEAR OF HOPE +

OPPORTUNITY ON

PURPOSE.

Anne

Preface

We have developed the material in this book from teaching, research, and practical experience in sustainable investing especially in the last seven years. In 2013, the Robert F. Kennedy Center for Justice and Human Rights collaborated with the Earth Institute at Columbia to develop a six-day intensive training workshop for investment analysts and managers from institutional investors, foundations, endowments, pension funds, sovereign wealth funds, consultants, investment managers, and interested non-profit organizations. Part of the motivation for the development of the workshop was the high interest among institutional investors for comprehensive overview, greater depth, and technical training in new methods of due diligence, portfolio screening, and data sources for an investing strategy that integrated the assessment of environmental and social impact. The aftermath of the global financial crisis of 2007–2008, when many institutional investors experienced unanticipated sharp declines in asset values and levels of funding, served as a catalyst for an integrative and wide-ranging search for sources of unexpected systemic risk and sustainable return. The workshop subsequently inspired many years of research, discussion, teaching, and codified practice in this field that has come to be known as sustainable finance.

The writing of a book is a fortunate by-product of a vibrant ecosystem of ideas. We have been lucky to be part of thoughtful communities of practice and scholarship. We have many kindred souls to thank. First, this book would never have come to fruition without Steve Cohen's early and continuous encouragement. Similarly, Qian Jing was an unfailing sounding board for many ideas. Our colleagues at the Research Program on

Sustainability Policy and Management at the Earth Institute and at CalPERS provided inspiration, interdisciplinary perspectives, and unfailing moral support. The faculty and students at the Sustainability Management and Environmental Science & Policy programs at Columbia seeded a large portion of the ideas articulated in the book. The co-Chairs, rapporteurs, and members of the Columbia University Seminar on Sustainable Finance #783 created a fertile ground for the cross-pollination of a range of concepts from ecology, economics, engineering, environmental science, finance, law, political science, and sociology. We are grateful to Andrea Armeni for reading multiple drafts of the impact investing chapter and for his constructive comments and to Simiso Nzima for kindly and patiently reading the entire manuscript and providing critical corrections. We are especially appreciative of the thorough research assistance of Olin Berger, Boris Lebedev, Liao Xiaoyu, Qin Ling, Debasmita Sarkar, and You Simiao. We wish to acknowledge the quiet efficiency, global reach, and able support of Columbia University Libraries, including especially the Interlibrary Loan division, who never failed to oblige requests for the most arcane sources.

We especially wish to thank the following individuals for inspiration, animated discussions, wise counsel, and support during the years this book took root and grew: Chris Agnos, Kristina Alnes, Janice Hester Amey, Chaarvi Amit Badani, Frank Barbarino, Matias Bendersky, Haben Berhe, Agustina Besada, Dazzle Bhujwala, Eron Bloomgarden, Travis Bradford, Allison Bridges, Arnaud Brohe, Vonda Brunsting, William Burckart, the late Sir Adrian Cadbury, Helen Chaitman, Jenny Chan, Tony Colman, Todd Cort, Robert Costanza, Mark Cox, Stephen Davis, James Dearborn, Kelsie DeFrancia, Ruth DeFries, Nancy Degnan, Lynn Forester de Rothschild, Maria Julia Diaz Ardaya, Daniel Ding, Hervé Duteil, Prajit Dutta, Robert Eccles, Michael Eckhart, Bill Eimicke, Paul Ellis, Jonas Englund, Scott Fisher, Vicky Flores, Steve Freedman, Steve Godeke, Marcie Frost, Vicky Galeano, Alyson Genovese, Emanuele Gerratana, Dan Giuffrida, Linda Giuliano, Adela Gondek, Bernardo Guillamon, James Hawley, Geoff Heal, Davida Heller, Marc Henry, Susan Holgate, Bert Hunter, Bruce Kahn, Urvashi Kaul, Kerry Kennedy, Dinah Koehler, Cary Krosinsky, Rina Kupferschmid, Sophie L'Helias, Allison Ladue, Rob Lake, Manu Lall, Linda-Eling Lee, Arthur Lerner-Lam, Marc Levy, Ma Lei, Parisa Mahdad, Hayley Martinez, Priya Mathur, Christoph Meinrenken, the late Don Melnick, Teri Mendelsohn, Bhakti Mirchandani, Thomas Murtha, Yu Meng, Alison Miller, Hayley Mole, Robert Monks, Dennak

Murphy, David Ng, Dan O'Flaherty, Amie Patel, Maneesha Patel, Radhika Patel, William Patterson, Marivi Perdomo Caba, Julie Pertuiset, Charlotte Peyraud, John Plender, Jeffrey Potent, Curtis Probst, Olga Puntus, Roy Radner, Jenik Radon, Fiona Reynolds, Bridget Realmuto, Rod Richardson, Ailsa Roell, Gema Sacristan, Ashley Schulten, Aniket Shah, Courtney Small, Jason Smerdon, Song Mingyuan, Art Small, Robert Smith, Amy Springsteel, Nina Sun, Sun Zhe, Tian Tuo, Tian Xiaolei, Bruce Usher, Louise Venables, Kurt Vogt, Wang Anyi, Wang Jun, Jason Wingard, Lynnette Widder, Donald Wissell, Zhang Yong, and Richard Zimmerman.

We are very grateful to our sage and patient editors: Mario La Torre, Tula Weiss, Sophia Siegler, and Ruth Noble. We are fortunate to have had so many illuminating teachers who corrected our early errors. Despite all the help we have received from our ecosystem, there undoubtedly remain many errors of omission and commission in this work. We are solely responsible for them. We apologize in advance to those whose writings we may have inadvertently missed in our efforts to compress a complex and nuanced literature into a concise and coherent narrative. We also make the following important disclaimer: This book was written by Anne Simpson in her personal capacity. The opinions expressed are her own and do not necessarily reflect the view of her current employer, the California Public Employees' Retirement System.

Finally, we express our deepest gratitude to our families for supporting this endeavor over many years.

New York, NY, USA   Satyajit Bose
New York, NY, USA   Guo Dong
Sacramento, CA, USA   Anne Simpson
June 2019

CONTENTS

ABOUT THE AUTHORS

Satyajit Bose is Associate Professor of Practice at Columbia University, where he teaches sustainable investing, cost-benefit analysis, and mathematics and serves as Associate Director of the Program in Sustainability Management. He is also Co-Chair of the University Seminar in Sustainable Finance, a forum for faculty and finance practitioners to discuss and research methods to use the financial system, with the help of technology, innovative design, and disruptive change, to mobilize capital for sustainable development and widespread beneficial impact. He was previously the Faculty Director of the joint Earth Institute-RFK Compass Education Program which trained institutional investors how to incorporate environmental, social, and human rights, as well as corporate governance issues as integral elements of risk mitigation and return optimization.

Guo Dong is Associate Research Scholar and Associate Director of the Research Program on Sustainability Policy and Management at Columbia University's Earth Institute. He teaches courses on Microeconomics and Quantitative Methods for masters students in Columbia's School of International and Public Affairs. His expertise lies in impact and evaluation methods and his research interests include sustainability metrics, sustainable development, environmental policy, and Chinese education.

Anne Simpson is Director of Board Governance and Strategy at the California Public Employees Retirement System (CalPERS), where she led the development of the fund's sustainable investment strategy, and previously headed the corporate governance program. Anne is a member of the SEC's Investor Advisory Committee, and the Leadership Council of the RFK Center for Justice and Human Rights. She serves on the Senior Advisory Board at the Center for Responsible Business, in the Haas School, Berkeley, California.

Anne writes in a personal capacity and the opinions expressed are the author's own. They do not necessarily reflect the views of her current employer, CalPERS.

LIST OF FIGURES

LIST OF TABLES

CHAPTER 1

The Role of Finance in Achieving Sustainability

The field of finance is a large and diverse ecosystem and the role of the financial sector in the broader economy and the environment can sometimes seem complex and opaque. In the United States, the portion of 2014 GDP attributable to the finance, insurance, and real estate sector was approximately 20%, which is the largest contribution of any sector tracked by the Bureau of Economic Analysis.[1] What role does the financial sector perform in the economy? The efficiency of capital allocation presupposes the long-run sustainability of the natural and human ecosystems within which economic activities occur, yet how do the activities of the financial sector affect the sustainability of the social and environmental systems upon which the economy depends? When so eminent an authority as Pope Francis issues an encyclical listing finance and the pursuit of profit among the causes of the present ecological crisis, one might wonder whether the financial system can play a beneficial role in the environment.[2] At a very simplified level, financial institutions exist to channel efficiently the savings of households to productive investment opportunities, to businesses, governments, and entrepreneurs looking for capital. But what if those investments have the unfortunate side effects of polluting waterways, dispersing toxic substances into the air or disturbing the balance in fragile ecosystems? What if the products and processes created by those investments hasten disease or even death in customers, employees, and communities?

Financial markets are the primary source of signals used to direct investment and economic activity in a capitalist global economy. The flows of

© The Author(s) 2019
S. Bose et al., *The Financial Ecosystem*, Palgrave Studies in Impact Finance, https://doi.org/10.1007/978-3-030-05624-7_1

capital controlled by the financial sector are larger than those available for sustainable development from governments and multilateral agencies as well as those available for philanthropic activities. Hence the potential impacts (for good or ill) of private financial decision-making on the health of the broader ecosystem are significantly larger than choices made by aid agencies or philanthropic organizations. For example, total annual development aid in 2013 amounted to approximately $150 billion. In the same year, portfolio flows of equity and debt capital to emerging economies amounted to $214 billion.[3] If we were to list countries by their nominal 2017 GDP in the same table as companies by their revenue, the largest company by revenue, Walmart, with $486 billion in net sales, would rank 24th, just behind Sweden and before Poland. A small change in the character of private financial flows or corporate behavior has the potential to be perhaps even more transformative than directed aid or philanthropy.

THE ROLE OF FINANCE

It is clear that the role of the financial sector in the economy, and therefore in the environment, is large. But what is that role? Why is the financial sector useful to the economy? Can it play a role in achieving sustainability of the natural and social ecosystem? The role of financial markets and institutions within the economy is commonly understood as follows. There are three broad functions that an established financial system provides for economic activity. First, the financial sector facilitates efficient resource allocation, spatially and across time, in an uncertain environment. Second, through the mechanisms of risk-pooling and sharing, the financial system allows savers with diverse investment horizons and risk appetites to find appropriately productive investments while paying acceptable transaction costs. Third, a critical but sometimes forgotten role of financial markets is to provide signals of spatially and temporally varied scarcity and abundance so as to guide optimal decentralized decision-making. Let's examine each of these three roles in greater detail.

The Resource Allocation Role

For any system to minimize waste, its resources must be allocated to their most valued use. For the financial sector, capital is an important and scarce resource which needs to be deployed in activities which generate the highest possible risk-adjusted return. Therefore, for the individual owner of capital, failing to maximize risk-adjusted return consistently is tantamount to a relative loss of wealth. Due to uncertainty about the future, it is not a trivial problem to guide capital from owners to the best investments. An allocator of capital must deploy her assets before she knows what the investment return will be, and her assessment of risk at the time of deployment is most likely inaccurate and will almost certainly change over the life of the investment. The complexities of assessing risk and estimating return support the development of specialized skills to aid the activity of allocating capital, ensuring that there is a role for a formal industry of asset managers to whom can be outsourced, at varying levels of aggregation, the mundane but critically important task of ensuring that current wealth is preserved and enhanced.

For society as a whole however, what is true of the individual owner of capital is not necessarily true in aggregate. For example, an investor in corporate bonds may suffer losses because the bond issuer unexpectedly uses the proceeds of issuance to buy back stock, increasing the credit risk of the bonds and leading to price depreciation of the bond in the medium term. Because the share buyback risk was unanticipated by the bondholder, the investor may have diverted capital from other investments with a higher risk-adjusted return in order to purchase the bond. In evaluating the impact on society, we must consider that the bondholder's avoidable loss may be offset by an unexpected gain for the shareholders who sell their stock to the company. For society, the net impact of the incorrect risk assessment may be negligible.[4] This is likely to be true for any transient or unsystematic errors of risk assessment or institutional failures. There is however a real loss to society from a systematic failure to protect bondholder interests, for example, if weak creditor protections reduce investor appetite for bonds.[5] The loss to society occurs because future bond investors either demand a higher compensation for their risk or eschew investments in some issuers or jurisdictions altogether. Such high-risk premiums or a refusal to invest will prevent otherwise productive investments from being financed.

An important societal role of the financial sector is to provide a low-cost method of channeling capital to productive investment opportunities. If this role cannot be fulfilled efficiently, a society cannot fund new capital formation and innovation, virtually ensuring the moderation and elimination of future wealth enhancement opportunities. In the context of natural ecosystems, the financial sector can play a crucial role of financing promising investments in preserving natural capital or remediating degraded ecosystems, or directing investment toward attaining social goals, while preserving the discipline of metrics-based selection and quantitative evaluation. Direct investments in preserving natural capital are often referred to as 'green infrastructure financing' or 'conservation finance' (see Chap. 13), while investment in enterprises with both social and financial goals is sometimes described as 'impact investing' (see Chap. 11). These two subsectors of the financial system are illustrations of the potentially beneficial resource allocation role that finance can play in the natural ecosystem.

The Risk Transfer Role

In Shakespeare's *Hamlet*, when Laertes takes leave of his father Polonius to return to his studies, Polonius advises his son: "Neither a borrower nor a lender be; for loan oft loses both itself and friend." It is impossible for an investor to heed this exhortation in its entirety, for the *raison d'être* of finance is the ubiquitous mismatch between investment capacity and financing need. Since it is so rare that a factory owner looking to expand or an entrepreneur growing his business has access to all the capital he needs in his own resources, the financial sector performs the critical role of matching borrowers and lenders, capital users and investors. The second part of Polonius's exhortation contains an important warning for the investor: it is unwise to lend to a friend since both loan and friend may be lost together. In modern finance terms, this is a warning to diversify away from investments which are too close in other ways. For example, it might be imprudent to have a significant portion of your retirement assets invested in the stock of your employer, as discovered by employees in Enron Corporation in November 2001.[6] The financial sector plays a critical role in facilitating the diversification of investments by matching borrowers and lenders by their risk tolerances, investment horizons, and liquidity needs rather than by ties of friendship or ethnic origin or common interest.

Economic theory posits that most individuals are risk-averse, as a consequence of which insurance increases well-being. Most people are willing to pay for at least some form of insurance, whether it is for the contents of their home or their level of health. Households faced with many unpredictable risks must keep a significant portion of their wealth in liquid assets, reducing their ability to invest in long term, typically higher return opportunities. There is macroeconomic evidence suggesting that insurance market activity contributes to economic growth not just through its contribution to GDP, but also by providing risk transfer and indemnification services, which allow households to mobilize their savings into higher return investments.[7] Since pooled risks are easier to predict, the insurance premiums required of large, diversified pools of exposure are lower than those of less diversified risks.

Financial intermediaries allow households to invest in diversified investment opportunities, for example, through mutual funds. By pooling capital from many investors and allocating the pooled capital to a basket of investment opportunities, financial intermediaries allow households to invest a greater portion of their wealth in less liquid assets. There are two sustainability challenges where the diversification and risk transfer role of intermediation is potentially transformative. The first is the financing and securitization of improvements to commercial and residential buildings that increase energy efficiency (see Chap. 12). The second is the financing of innovation and new technologies necessary to effect a transition to a renewable energy economy (see Chap. 14). A related issue is whether calls for divestment from fossil fuel companies make sense on financial grounds alone, which some investors have argued.

The Decentralized Signaling Role

The signaling role of financial markets is perhaps the one that is least replicable by other institutions. As Friedrich Hayek pointed out in his 1945 article "The Use of Knowledge in Society", the truly difficult societal problem that a rational economic system must solve is not so much how to allocate scarce resources, but rather how to utilize all the knowledge in society, which necessarily exists in dispersed form in the minds of disparate individuals who cannot be made to aggregate their information.[8] Hayek argued that prices are signals of relative scarcity or abundance: it is only by observing the relative prices of different commodities that an entrepreneur learns what productive capacity is in demand and requires investment. The subsequent actions of the profit-seeking entrepreneur relieve the scarcity and reduce the relative price differential. In Hayek's formulation, without the information carried by the price system, we would not know what was scarce and what was abundant.

An established view in financial theory dating from Hayek's paper is that financial markets are efficient aggregators of the private information and beliefs of market participants and the resulting prices embed more information than may be present in expert forecasts. An oft-cited example of this principle is the argument suggested by Roll (1984) that the traded prices of frozen concentrated orange juice futures carry better information about the likelihood of frost in Central Florida (the primary growing area for the underlying commodity) than the expert forecast of meteorologists at the National Weather Service.

This capacity of distributed information, appropriately assembled, to predict better than expert prophesies is seen in other spheres. Weather forecasts today are rarely produced by a single model; they are weighted averages (technically ensembles) of a number of underlying 'expert' models combined with real-time updates of the forecast errors observed from geographically distributed weather stations. Google, whose index-based search algorithm largely supplanted the human knowledge-inspired, hierarchical category-based search engine Yahoo, is a case in point. Perhaps the information aggregation problem will eventually be solved by the advent of social networks and the possibilities of massive computational power. However, it is likely that the information aggregation role of financial markets will always be relevant.

An important insight embedded in Hayek's argument is the fallibility of the expert (or the central planner in his words). The complexity of the real world will always trump the most sophisticated model. Hayek argued that a rational economic system must allow scope for small-scale, local experimentation. Indeed, the system must incorporate incentives and rewards for successful distributed initiatives (as the price system does). There are two areas where the fallibility of the expert and this signaling role of financial markets can advance distributed efforts to achieve sustainability. In some forms of responsible investing in public equity markets, investors who are not experts at investment management choose social or environmental themes or parameters for their portfolio, such as a minimum environmental, social, and governance (ESG) score or a refusal to include tobacco stocks. In Chap. 12, we examine the extent to which this type of investing, facilitated by modern technological platforms, can affect incentives for sustainable corporate behavior. In Chap. 15, we consider the significant advances made by the cooperative movement and distributed social entrepreneurship in alleviating poverty where centrally directed aid programs of much greater scale have failed.

WHAT IS SUSTAINABILITY?

Two related and fundamental concepts utilized in financial systems are those of the *stock* and the *flow*. The stock is an asset or a liability, which represents a reckoning at a point in time, an accumulation of past flows, or an estimate of future flows. The flow is periodic, a somewhat continuous stream of services or money. An asset is anything that can be used to generate a future flow of goods or services (a *real* asset) or claims on goods and services (a *financial* asset). An example of this relationship between a stock and a flow is seen in the valuation principle embedded in the common dividend discount method of stock valuation:

Value of stock at time 0 = Expected present discounted value
of flows of future dividends

Another instructive example is the valuation of future liabilities. Under the Statement of Financial Accounting Standard No. 143, the asset retirement obligation for companies engaged in resource extraction is to be recorded as a liability (or a *negative* asset). The obligation is measured as the expected present discounted value of future cash outflows necessary to remediate a current extraction site such as an oilfield or fracking well (FASB, 2001):

Value of asset retirement   = Expected present discounted value
obligation at time 0   of flows of future expenses to return
                                an extraction site to its pre-extraction state

The concepts of *stocks* and *flows* are essential to any precise discussion of the notion of 'sustainability'. For example, one oft-quoted definition of 'sustainable development' is the one proposed by the Brundtland Commission in their 1987 report entitled *Our Common Future*: "Sustainable development is the kind of development that meets the needs of the present without compromising the ability of future generations to meet their own needs."[9] This definition could be recast as follows: sustainability implies that the magnitude of current flows of goods and services cannot impair the stock of wealth from whence future flows of goods and services will come. An alternative formulation of this type of sustainability is embedded in the Hartwick rule: rents earned from resource extraction must be invested in other forms of capital and should not be consumed.[10] The financial interpretation of the Hartwick rule states that cash inflows from liquidations of capital (which cannot be repeated) should always be invested rather than consumed. The underlying logic is to keep assets as assets and consume only that which represents the periodic flow of benefits. In other words, eat only the fruit of the apple tree, and do not cut down the tree for firewood. If you must cut down the tree, then use the wood to build another long-lived asset, such as a barn.[11] Sustainability, in this interpretation, is synonymous with the repeatability of flows of benefits.

At a societal level, our measurement systems are more adapted to quantifying flows than stocks. For example, the most common measure of success for national economies is gross domestic product, a flow concept. Very few countries publish national balance sheets, whereas almost all countries and many sub-national regions, metropolitan areas, and cities produce GDP statistics. Hamilton and Hepburn (2014) argue that the societal obsession with flows is not inevitable, citing the observation of J.R. Hicks that Keynesian demand management practices increased the immediate utility of flow measurement. They also point out that wealth (which is the related stock concept) is at best only partially measured. Among the components of wealth, quantifications of natural and human capital fall far short of the measurement of produced capital. This is a deplorable state of affairs since Hamilton and Liu (2014) argued that human capital in particular represents a very significant portion of overall wealth in the developed world (Fig. 1.1).

One reason that wealth is less likely to be measured than flows of benefits is that there is less uncertainty involved in the quantification of flows than in the measurement of stocks. This is because the measurement of stocks requires an assessment of future flows and the capitalization of those future uncertain amounts into a stock value, using a discount rate which may itself be uncertain. At a societal level, it can be argued that wealth is nothing more than the capitalized value of the flow of future benefits, so the difficult task is to measure future flows and discount them. An individual investor attempting to value his asset has the option to compare his estimation of the present value of future flows with the amount that another investor might be willing to pay to purchase the asset, which might incorporate the other investor's beliefs about future flows. He is able to infer others' valuations by examining the transaction prices or the

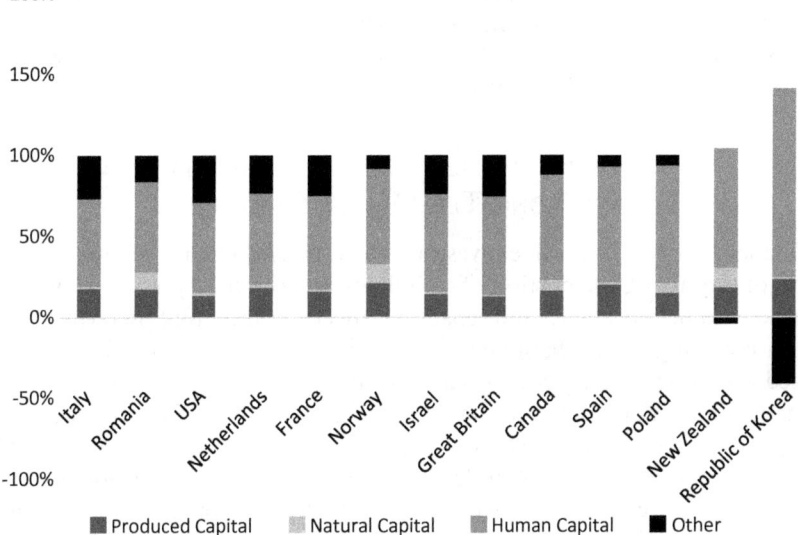

Fig. 1.1 Wealth decomposition, 2005. (Source: Author calculations with data from Hamilton and Liu (2014). Notes: Countries listed in ascending order by % of wealth attributable to human capital)

bid and ask prices of comparable assets (see Chap. 6). This ability to compare the contemporaneous assessments of others with our own idiosyncratic forecasts helps to triangulate and anchor valuations of assets at the individual level. When we try to value a societal asset, such as the monetary value of all ecosystem services in the world, the problem becomes less grounded by market transactions.[12] At the societal level, to a large extent, we lose the reference point provided by other actors' financial bids and transactions. This reduces the level of current consensus around valuations of stocks of wealth, making it more difficult for governments to construct useful balance sheets. Nevertheless, the challenges to valuation caused by reduced consensus are not insurmountable, and must be faced in almost all interactions between financial practice and efforts to advance sustainability.

In our effort to assess the sustainability or repeatability of flows, we must be careful to identify all flows, including the services received from natural, human, and intangible capital. The second section of the book

(Chaps. 3, 4, 5, 6, 7, 8, 9, and 10) is an extended tour of the analytical foundations of sustainable finance which lays out the trenches that one must inhabit in order to develop a fluency in the measurement and valuation of the services of natural and human capital.

The Equivalence of Sustainability and Long-Term Value Creation

Financial analysts and value investors relish the challenging but rewarding job of estimating the portion of cash flows experienced by a company that is likely to be repeatable, and separating this from the cash flows which are non-recurring.[13] The discipline of determining which flows can be capitalized and which merely added is an essential part of their training.[14] Given the formulae that relate repeatable flows to valuations of stocks, financial analysts, in attempting to compute fundamental value, are constantly evaluating the sustainability of underlying flows. For example, analyst reports are often concerned with what they call the 'quality of earnings', that is, the extent to which earnings and profitability flow from the ongoing operations of the underlying business rather than one-time gains realized from asset or reserve liquidations. In this sense at least, financial valuation analysis is very close to the concept of sustainability underlying the Hartwick rule.

The preceding discussion of valuation analysis leads us to one possible meaning of sustainability in finance: the practice of identifying repeatable sources of value. This practice, married with the principle of arbitrage, is the basis for value investing. The value investor's art consists of identifying flows of benefits whose value other market participants do not currently recognize, where there is a reasonable likelihood that within the investment horizon, such value will become monetized. What does sustainability mean in the context of finance? It means identifying the repeatable sources of return through a holistic understanding of the notion of capital, one that includes natural and human capital in addition to produced capital. How does this understanding of sustainability create opportunity? By isolating undervalued sources of return which might be expected to be more widely valued in future. How can this sustainability approach mitigate risk in the management of assets? This perspective facilitates the avoidance of investments where short-term returns are generated by the unsustainable liquidation of capital (broadly defined), reducing the risk of asset impairments when those returns can no longer be repeated.

The Principles of Responsible Investment

The United Nations sponsored Principles of Responsible Investment (UNPRI or PRI) were launched at the New York Stock Exchange in 2006 by the then UN Secretary General, Kofi Annan, flanked by a group of 100 founding investors. The founders boldly announced:

> We believe that an economically efficient, sustainable global financial system is a necessity for long term value creation. Such a system will reward long-term, responsible investment and benefit the environment and society as a whole. The PRI will work to achieve this sustainable global financial system by encouraging adoption of the Principles (of Responsible Investment) and collaboration on their implementation; by fostering good governance, integrity and accountability.

In the wake of the global financial crisis, which significantly diminished the assets of PRI signatories and rendered many pension funds under-funded for the decades to come, the PRI subsequently added a wider ambition to take on the responsibility for the daunting task of ensuring the sustainability of the financial system itself. This new goal exhorted signatories to "address obstacles to a sustainable financial system that lie within market practices, structures and regulation". The founding of the PRI reflected a recognition by global investors that their decisions had profound impact, for good or ill, both of which could rebound on investors to their detriment or to their advantage.

The PRI incorporates two intertwined beliefs. First, the founders declared that the integration of environmental, social, and governance (ESG) considerations into financial decision-making would be of mutual benefit to investors seeking long-term risk-adjusted returns as well as to a wider set of stakeholders seeking to ensure that finance is aligned with the broader interests of society at large. This perspective is founded upon the understanding that the fortunes of finance and society are interdependent. Second, the founders of the PRI also articulated a new understanding of their own investment obligations. The inclusion of ESG in investment choice is not merely an instrument to be used for the ultimate goal of seeking financial return, but also an implied mandate in the discharge of their legal duties to invest on behalf of others in alignment with the common good.

"As institutional investors, we have a duty to act in the best long-term interests of our beneficiaries. In this fiduciary role, we believe that environmental, social and corporate governance (ESG) issues can affect the performance of investment portfolios (to varying degrees across companies, sectors, regions, asset classes and through time)." The PRI founders had a vision of the financial system which captured sustainability as both an opportunity and a necessity for long-term value creation.

Long-Term Value Creation Is *Ex Ante* Unpopular
The value investor's perspective is necessarily contrarian. J.M. Keynes, who was an early champion of value investing over momentum strategies, said that the long-term investor must be 'eccentric, unconventional, and rash'. As the fiduciary for the King's College endowment, he believed in the importance of equities as a new asset class for long-horizon investors such as endowments. He allocated a far higher proportion of the endowment to this 'speculative' asset class than was common for foundations and endowments of that time. The King's College endowment under Keynes management was able to avoid the losses of the 1929 stock market crash. He subsequently experienced losses in 1930, 1931, 1938, and 1940 but was able to rack up an average annual outperformance of 8% versus the UK equity index over a 24-year investing run. Such significant outperformance of the benchmark can only come from making different investment choices than the average investor.

The Time Horizon and Principal-Agent Problems

In attempting to identify and assess the value of natural and human capital in her investments, the value investor must necessarily be eccentric. The frameworks, information sources, and due diligence processes she must rely upon are likely to differ to a large extent from the inputs of the valuation models used by the broader marketplace. As with any contrarian investment, and even more so in this case, the horizon within which there might be broad recognition of the hidden value of investments in human and natural capital may be excruciatingly long. As noted by Keynes and others, this point limits sharply the kinds of opportunities which are appropriate investments for the value investor.[15] The value investor must balance the possibility of outsize gains derived from being different and right in the long run against the possibility of tracking error resulting from being different in the short run. Since the investment decision is often made by a manager rather than an owner, this trade-off is also connected to at least two principal-agent problems.

First, the investment manager is often compensated for short-term performance and cannot usually be penalized for long-term underperformance. The owner, on the other hand, wants to prevent long-term asset impairment, even at the cost of short-term underperformance. A second incarnation of this principal-agent problem appears in the relationship between the shareholder and the corporation. Although in theory the corporation is managed in order to maximize value for the shareholder, this may not be the case in practice. Robert Monks has referred to this problem as that of 'the ownerless corporation', and more generally the mechanisms designed to address it are part of the sub-field of finance known as 'corporate governance'[16] (see Chap. 3 for detailed discussion of corporate governance). These incentive alignment problems are at the heart of challenges in realizing the value of long-term sources of return.

Faced with incentive alignment problems, the rational principal's response is often to monitor a range of performance metrics of the agent. Long-term institutional investors recognize that ranking investments using single measures of risk-adjusted return, such as the Sharpe ratio, or short-term measures of corporate performance, such as quarterly earnings per share, is an ineffective and potentially dangerous strategy. Hence, there is an increasing interest in broadening the range of performance metrics, both for investment managers and for corporations.

SUSTAINABLE FINANCE

After the global financial crisis in 2007–2008, the pursuit of financial profit alone is viewed by many as unsustainable and detrimental to long-term societal interest. There appears to be steady and inexorable growth in Google searches for 'impact investing', 'ESG investing', and 'social finance'. We will label the intentional efforts to use and influence the financial system to mobilize capital for sustainable development and widespread social benefit the field of 'sustainable finance'. The rise of sustainable finance is a natural corollary of some significant recent phenomena:

1. The Citizen Investor and the Intergenerational Transfer of Wealth
   The financial wealth of working people, embodied in pension funds, insurance company reserves, and monetizable household wealth, has become a significant portion of global assets under management, creating demand for bespoke investment products catering to the values of specific demographic groups of investors (Davis, Lukomnik, &

Pitt-Watson, 2006). Trade union concern for the stewardship of capital and the entry of sovereign wealth funds as significant pivotal investors has created the conditions for an explicit articulation of investment goals beyond pecuniary return. The imminent intergenerational transfer of wealth from the 'baby boomer' generation to their heirs in Organisation for Economic Cooperation and Development (OECD) countries has also led to vocal demands for an investment management industry catering to the combination of investment and 'purpose' (Accenture, 2015).

2. Power of Corporations relative to Regulators

   The scale and power of corporations dwarfs the resources available to the governments of most countries to regulate the societal impact of corporate activity. The calls of civil society upon governments to address the Sustainable Development Goals (SDGs) (United Nations General Assembly, 2015) are accompanied by a recognition that they cannot be implemented without a concurrent partnership with and concerted pressure upon the private sector. The apparent impotence of most governments in the face of the power of corporations drains the credibility of any effort at sustainable development that does not include the corporate sector as a driving force. The use of concerted social media campaigns to influence corporations can be a more potent, immediate tool than political advocacy (Heimans & Timms, 2018). Since the power of finance to shape corporate behavior looms large after the global financial crisis, it is natural for many observers to consider the potential role of the financial system in advancing some of the goals of environmental regulation.

3. Concern with Planetary Boundaries

   There is a growing recognition that the unprecedented scale of human economic activity has caused stresses on natural ecosystems. These include global warming, fresh water scarcity, the diminished availability of arable land in the face of increasing global population, the collapse of pollinating insect colonies, plastic pollution and the degradation of fish stocks in the oceans, and the potentially adverse impact of endocrine disruptors on human reproductive systems. The possibility that anthropogenic activity has already breached four out of nine planetary boundaries[17] and is in danger of breaching others infuses an urgency into calls for the financial system to be an immediate and active contributor to broad-based efforts to address sustainability. On the other hand, the risk that breaches of these planetary boundaries would cause the impairment of financial assets is of concern to investment analysts (Linnenluecke, Birt, Lyon, Sidhu, & Walsh, 2015).

4. The Search for an Ethical Grounding for Environmental Protection
The receding of agriculture from the working lives of the vast majority of people in the OECD countries and the increasing urbanization of the global population has eliminated the palpability of the human connection with nature for much of the world. Some scientists and environmentalists have searched for a source of moral fervor that could fuel an urgent battle to limit anthropogenic environmental impact.[18] The ethical commandments of many world religions offer philosophies of the stewardship of nature that are potential allies in the quest for sustainable development. A Christian articulation of these commandments is given by Pope Francis (2014). A concordance between moral concepts and environmental SDGs from an Islamic perspective is given in Shaikh (2018).

Sustainable finance encompasses a number of related trends within the financial ecosystem. These include dramatic growth in responsible and impact investing (see Chaps. 10 and 11), the advent of innovative financing methods to fund the transition to a global low-carbon economy (Chaps. 13 and 14), and global and decentralized efforts to design financial mechanisms and institutions to ensure the sustainability of natural and human ecosystems (Chaps. 12 and 15).

CONCLUDING REMARKS

Long-term asset owners and managers, while seeking high risk-adjusted returns and efficiently allocating scarce financial capital to the highest value economic activities, have the essential and formidable role of ensuring the sustainability of return. Long-term return depends on a number of sources of intangible value, including returns facilitated by well-conserved natural capital and consenting stakeholders. The persistence of return requires healthy ecosystems, nutrient-rich soils, sources of clean water and clean air, and the absorptive capacity of the environment near industrial sites as well as satisfied consumers, motivated employees and investors eager to provide capital. Generally accepted financial accounting methods are ill-equipped to provide clear signals of the risks and opportunities created by scarce natural and human capital. In this next chapter, we will discuss the nature of the financial ecosystem and its role in allocating capital to highest-valued uses, matching savers and investors, and crucially, generating accurate signals of scarcity in the face of planetary boundaries. By drawing parallels between natural and financial ecosystems and reviewing a taxonomy of players in the global financial market, we will highlight the specific capacities of components of the financial sector to improve the sustainability of the broader ecosystem.

Notes

1. Author calculation using Table 6.1D National Income without Capital Consumption Adjustment by Industry released by the Bureau of Economic Analysis. Based on average of seasonally adjusted quarterly data for 2014.
2. See Pope Francis (2014).
3. See Institute of International Finance (2014).
4. Indeed, an implication of the Miller-Modigliani proposition is that the total value of bondholder and stockholder claims cannot change as a consequence of changes in leverage effected at fair value. See Miller and Modigliani (1961).
5. The question of whether creditor rights are systematically weak in a specific jurisdiction or simply temporarily being restructured due to unforeseen events is a difficult one to resolve, as illustrated in the context of sovereign bonds by recent litigation and controversy around the restructuring of Argentine bonds. See Eavis and Stevenson (2014).
6. See Oppel Jr. (2001).
7. See Arena (2008) for a cross-country empirical study of 55 developed and developing countries.
8. See Hayek (1945).
9. See World Commission on Environment and Development (1987).
10. See Hartwick (1977).
11. A farmer would point out that apple wood does not make good barn timber, but I hope she will indulge the metaphor.
12. See Costanza et al. (1997) and its update (Costanza et al., 2014) for a commonly cited and often contested attempt at this type of societal valuation.
13. See, for example, chapter 5 of Greenwald, Kahn, Sonkin, and Biema (2001).
14. For example, see chapters 2–5 of Penman (2011) for a method of determining which cash flows are repeatable using information embedded in accrual accounting.
15. See Shleifer and Vishny (1997) for a recent statement of this point.
16. See Chapter 1 of Monks and Minow (2011).

17. See Rockström et al. (2009).
18. See pages 18–23 of Daly (1996) for a description of this search and its obstacles.

References

Accenture. (2015). *The "Greater" Wealth Transfer: Capitalizing on the Intergenerational Shift in Wealth*. Retrieved from https://www.accenture. com/us-en/~/media/Accenture/Conversion-Assets/DotCom/Documents/ Global/PDF/Industries_5/Accenture-CM-AWAMS-Wealth-Transfer-Final-June2012-Web-Version.pdf

Arena, M. (2008). Does Insurance Market Activity Promote Economic Growth? A Cross-Country Study for Industrialized and Developing Countries. *The Journal of Risk and Insurance, 75*(4), 921–946. http://onlinelibrary.wiley. com/journal/10.1111/%28ISSN%291539-6975/issues

Costanza, R., dArge, R., deGroot, R., Farber, S., Grasso, M., Hannon, B., ... vandenBelt, M. (1997). The Value of the World's Ecosystem Services and Natural Capital. *Nature, 387*(6630), 253–260. https://doi.org/10.1038/387253a0

Costanza, R., de Groot, R., Sutton, P., van der Ploeg, S., Anderson, S. J., Kubiszewski, I., ... Turner, R. K. (2014). Changes in the Global Value of Ecosystem Services. *Global Environmental Change-Human and Policy Dimensions, 26*, 152–158. https://doi.org/10.1016/j.gloenvcha.2014.04.002

Daly, H. E. (1996). *Beyond Growth: The Economics of Sustainable Development*. Boston, MA: Beacon Press.

Davis, S., Lukomnik, J., & Pitt-Watson, D. (2006). *The New Capitalists: How Citizen Investors Are Reshaping the Corporate Agenda*. Boston, MA: Harvard Business School Press.

Eavis, P., & Stevenson, A. (2014, July 31). Argentina Finds Relentless Foe in Paul Singer's Hedge Fund. *New York Times*. Retrieved from http://dealbook.nytimes. com/2014/07/30/in-hedge-fund-argentina-finds-relentless-foe/?_r=0

FASB. (2001). Statement of Financial Accounting Standards No. 143: Accounting for Asset Retirement Obligations Norwalk, CT. *Financial Accounting Standards Board*. Retrieved from https://www.fasb.org/jsp/FASB/Document_C/Docu mentPage?cid=1218220124991&acceptedDisclaimer=true

Greenwald, B. C. N., Kahn, J., Sonkin, P. D., & Biema, M. v. (2001). *Value Investing: From Graham to Buffett and Beyond*. Hoboken, NJ: John Wiley & Sons, Inc.

Hamilton, K., & Hepburn, C. (2014). Wealth. *Oxford Review of Economic Policy, 30*(1), 1–20. http://oxrep.oxfordjournals.org/content/by/year

Hamilton, K., & Liu, G. (2014). Human Capital, Tangible Wealth, and the Intangible Capital Residual. *Oxford Review of Economic Policy, 30*(1), 70–91. http://academic.oup.com/oxrep/issue

Hartwick, J. M. (1977). Intergenerational Equity and the Investing of Rents from Exhaustible Resources. *American Economic Review, 67*(5), 972–974. http://www.aeaweb.org/aer/

Hayek, F. A. v. (1945). The Use of Knowledge in Society. *American Economic Review, 35,* 519–530.

Heimans, J., & Timms, H. (2018). *New Power: How Power Works in Our Hyperconnected World—And How to Make It Work for You.* New York, NY: Doubleday.

Institute of International Finance. (2014). *Introducing the IIF Portfolio Flows Tracker.* Retrieved from Washington, DC: https://www.iif.com/system/files/PF_0314_4.pdf

Linnenluecke, M. K., Birt, J., Lyon, J., Sidhu, B. K., & Walsh, K. (2015). Planetary Boundaries: Implications for Asset Impairment. *Accounting and Finance, 55*(4), 911–929. https://doi.org/10.1111/acfi.12173

Miller, M. H., & Modigliani, F. (1961). Dividend Policy, Growth, and the Valuation of Shares. *Journal of Business, 34,* 411–433.

Monks, R. A. G., & Minow, N. (2011). *Corporate Governance* (5th ed.). Hoboken, NJ: John Wiley & Sons.

Oppel Jr., R. A. (2001, November 22). Employees' Retirement Plan Is a Victim as Enron Tumbles. *New York Times.* Retrieved from http://www.nytimes.com/2001/11/22/business/employees-retirement-plan-is-a-victim-as-enron-tumbles.html

Penman, S. (2011). *Accounting for Value.* New York, NY: Columbia University Press.

Pope Francis. (2014). Laudato Si' [Encyclical Letter on Care for Our Common Home], Vatican City. Retrieved from http://w2.vatican.va/content/francesco/en/encyclicals/documents/papafrancesco_20150524_enciclica-laudato-si.html#_ftn87

Rockström, J., Steffen, W., Noone, K., Persson, Å., Chapin Iii, F. S., Lambin, E. F., ... Foley, J. A. (2009). A Safe Operating Space for Humanity. *Nature, 461,* 472. https://doi.org/10.1038/461472a

Roll, R. (1984). Orange Juice and Weather. *American Economic Review, 74*(5), 861–880. http://www.aeaweb.org/aer/

Shaikh, S. A. (2018). Exploring the Significance of Islamic Environmental Ethics for Fostering Sustainable Environment. *Journal of Islamic Banking & Finance, 35*(1), 55–67.

Shleifer, A., & Vishny, R. W. (1997). The Limits of Arbitrage. *Journal of Finance, 52*(1), 35–55. http://onlinelibrary.wiley.com/journal/10.1111/%281SSN%291540-6261/issues

United Nations General Assembly. (2015). *Transforming Our World: The 2030 Agenda for Sustainable Development.* Retrieved from http://www.undocs.org/A/RES/70/1

World Commission on Environment and Development. (1987). *Our Common Future.* Retrieved from Oxford: http://www.un-documents.net/our-common-future.pdf

CHAPTER 2

The Financial Ecosystem

In Chap. 1, we outlined the three traditional roles of the financial sector: allocation of scarce capital to its highest-valued use, the matching of savers to investors, and the generation of the most accurate possible signals of scarcity and abundance. As a corollary to these functions, we would like the financial sector to advance the sustainability of the natural and social ecosystems upon which economic activity depends. For example, the allocation of capital to its highest-valued use implies that portfolio construction by asset managers would need to incorporate the importance of natural capital in facilitating the future flow of benefits from all forms of capital. Similarly, the matching of savers to investors includes addressing the broader investment goals of the citizen investor: the socially responsible investor, the trade union pension fund, faith-based investors, and the sovereign wealth fund that incorporates non-pecuniary motives within its investment strategy. The generation of accurate signals of scarcity and abundance must incorporate a recognition of the planetary boundaries that limit the sustainability of certain types of economic activity. These are formidable responsibilities for any actor.

So far, we have referred to our actor as the 'financial sector', but we must pause now to describe this actor in some detail. What is the financial sector? Who are its constituent entities? How do they interact with each other? What would it mean for this financial ecosystem to contribute to the sustainability of other systems? What motivates the individuals who own, control, manage, and work in this ecosystem? What are the personal

© The Author(s) 2019
S. Bose et al., *The Financial Ecosystem*, Palgrave Studies in Impact Finance, https://doi.org/10.1007/978-3-030-05624-7_2

and institutional horizons, both temporal and spatial, that inspire and constrain their behavior. In short, do they have the inclination and resources to discharge the awesome responsibility we have so casually thrust upon them? To address these questions, we must examine the nature of the financial ecosystem and review a taxonomy of players in the global financial market.

The range of modern financial intermediaries is nearly infinite and displays a continuous capacity to adapt to environmental and regulatory shocks to the system, as well as to shape the nature of future shocks. In Chap. 1, we argued that there are similarities between the concept of sustainability embodied in the Hartwick rule and financial analysts' efforts to identify the portion of periodic cash flows that is likely to be repeatable. Here we approach our review of the financial ecosystem with a belief that it is fruitful to draw similar parallels between natural ecosystems and the financial one. We believe that it is informative to view the financial ecosystem in a systems context, using insights from the fields of ecology and cybernetics and gathering what statistics are available on the systemic scale of flows and stocks of financial, physical, human, and natural capital.[1]

THE CIRCULAR FLOW OF INCOME

There is a long, but sparse history of efforts to view the financial ecosystem within a physical systems context. What does the financial ecosystem do for the physical ecosystem? Why do financial intermediaries exist? We take the view that financial intermediaries are indispensable agents that assist in the transformation of unconsumed income into productive investments. This is perhaps a quaint view: that the role of the financial ecosystem is to channel the savings of households into productive investment opportunities. It is a variant of a view, commonly articulated in introductory textbooks of economics and referred to as the circular flow of income.

The notion of the circular flow of savings originates at least as far back as Richard Cantillon's 1755 *Essai sur la nature du commerce en general.*[2] It is usually portrayed as the flow of income back and forth between households and firms and forms the basis of the national income identities. Here we modify the circular flow of income to focus in on the circular flow of savings (which is income that is not expended in the period in which it is earned). Figure 2.1 highlights two aspects of the circular flow: the role of the financial ecosystem and the traditional role of government in protecting natural capital.

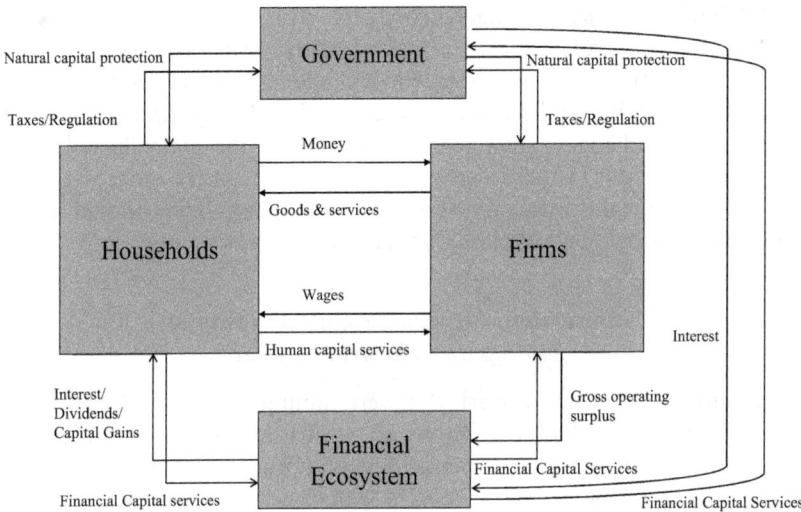

Fig. 2.1 Savings cycle. (Source: Authors)

Across disciplines, circular flows or cycles are often a defining feature of sustainability. Sustainability is generally associated with stable systems or steady states. We would not characterize an exponentially growing or rapidly collapsing dynamical system as sustainable. Systems of circular flows, with balanced injections and leakages, maintain a stable scale and may be expected to be sustainable if the environment within which the system operates is itself stable. It is for this reason that the circular flow of savings is a useful tool for our analysis of the interaction between the financial sector and the sustainability of natural and human ecosystems. If the flow of savings within the system is characterized by excess leakage or injection, the system is likely to become unstable.

The study of natural ecosystems is replete with cyclical systems, such as the carbon cycle, the hydrological cycle, the nitrogen or phosphorus cycles. The materials flows within these cycles are facilitated by a number of key ecosystem services.[3] The Circular Economy model of systems design popularized by the Ellen MacArthur Foundation is inspired in part by natural ecosystem services in a process labeled biomimicry.[4] Stable circular flows in natural systems require the decentralized management of nutrient cycling processes by countless organisms, which respond to positive and negative feedback loops. There exist few species whose activity could destabilize the entire planetary ecosystem. This is because the scale of impact of any individual species is limited by the collective physical power of the few members of the species who are able to communicate with each other. Humans, having harnessed energy that has the potential to facilitate planetary scale damage, are a notable exception to this generalization.[5] In the context of the financial ecosystem, a similar capacity exists with systemically important financial intermediaries and large institutional investors making investment choices that have planetary scale impact.

Interactions Between the Circular Flow of Savings and Natural Capital

A key question that must be asked in determining the sustainability of the circular flow of savings is the following: to what extent does the enhancement in the value of financial capital depend upon changes in the value of other forms of capital? In principle, it should not be possible to increase the value of financial capital without also increasing the value of other forms of capital. This is because financial capital represents claims on future benefits from other forms of capital. In theory, the value of financial capital cannot rise if the present value of the sum of future benefits from physical, natural, and human capital falls. In practice, the current value of financial capital is merely the current estimate of future values using a limited set of techniques. The current estimate will differ from the actual present value for many reasons, not least that financial decision-makers may be mistaken in their estimate of future value because of their unfamiliarity with emerging techniques of valuation in other fields.

Consider that global GDP amounted to approximately $68 trillion in 2011 in 2010 dollars. This amount includes the value of services from physical and human capital to the extent that such services are transacted at market prices. A commonly cited attempt to value global ecosystem services in monetary terms in the same year (Costanza et al., 2014) estimates that they amounted to approximately $130 trillion in 2010 dollars.[6] This would imply that the value of natural capital amounted to approximately 1.9× the value of physical and human capital, assuming that the discount rate to value the cash flows from all types of capital were the same. In 1997, the value of global GDP was $45 trillion, while that of global ecosystem services was $48 trillion, implying a ratio of 1.1×. This increase in relative valuation occurred in the context of decreases in the availability of certain biomes whose perceived value per hectare rose sharply between 1997 and 2011.

In particular, global recognition of the increased value of tidal marshes, mangroves, coral reefs, and tropical forest for the global ecosystem drove a significant portion of the increase in relative valuation. If we believe both estimates of GDP and ecosystem service value, then the value placed on ecosystem services as a proportion of the value placed on other forms of capital has increased significantly between 1997 and 2011. The estimates in Costanza et al. (2014) are constructed from 320 studies using a range of environmental valuation methods: revealed preference and contingent valuation (see Chap. 6 for a detailed discussion of these methods). While these methods are partially anchored to market values through the mechanism of revealed preference, they may diverge significantly from values placed on related assets by financial markets.

For an asset manager concerned with relative valuation trends, the conclusion to be drawn is that non-market signals of relative scarcity are signaling a sharp increase in the relative value of natural capital. By definition, such increase in relative value is not currently captured in market values. We would expect the financial ecosystem to search for market instruments which capture the increased value of scarce biomes over time, bidding up their prices, consequently reducing the gap between the value assigned to such biomes by financial markets and non-market methods. In our review of the taxonomy of financial players, we will attempt to identify appropriate actors who might fulfill this role.

In his testimony to the U.S. Senate in 1933, Marriner Eccles stated:

> It is utterly impossible, as this country has demonstrated again and again, for the rich to save as much as they have been trying to save, and save anything that is worth saving. They can save idle factories and useless railroad coaches; they can save empty office buildings and closed banks; they can save paper evidences of foreign loans; but as a class they can not save anything that is worth saving, above and beyond the amount that is made profitable by the increase of consumer buying. It is for the interests of the well to do—to protect them from the results of their own folly—that we should take from them a sufficient amount of their surplus to enable consumers to consume and business to operate at a profit. (U.S. Senate Committee on Finance, 1933)

Eccles was referring to the tendency of savers to limit their foresight to the form of their investments without considering whether their actions might limit the utility of those very same investments. He was advocating against saving too much in the form of physical and financial capital, lest that puritan strategy lead to low remuneration for human capital services, with consequent reduction in the value of physical and financial capital. This is what has come to be known as the Keynesian approach to macro-economics. Today, we must use a version of this logic to consider the interaction between physical capital and natural capital.

As a group, the financial ecosystem can fulfill the promises embedded in financial instruments only by investing the savings that it handles into productive real investments in physical, human, or natural capital. Any single intermediary can invest in financial assets, but the ecosystem as a whole cannot increase total financial wealth without simultaneously increasing the sum of present values of physical, human, and natural capital. Financial assets, from any asset class, are claims on the same economic system. In the long run, their value is impacted by interactions between the value of physical, natural, and human capital.

Accepting this relationship implies re-interpreting modern portfolio theory. It is no longer sufficient to invest in the total stock market or the total bond market or any index of total financial wealth unless such index incorporates an appropriate set of claims on the services provided by human and natural capital. It also implies that some ecological risks are non-diversifiable.

PLANETARY BOUNDARIES

The physical limits to the scale of economic activity are not known with certainty. However, nine 'planetary boundaries', consisting of maximum prudent levels of specific global environmental variables, have been proposed (Rockström et al., 2009). These define a safe operating space for human life and arise from the planet's biophysical processes. The boundaries consist of thresholds in parameters related to the following:

1. atmospheric carbon dioxide concentration
2. the rate of biodiversity loss
3. the rate of nitrogen extracted from the atmosphere for human use and the amount of phosphorus run-off into the oceans
4. the concentration of atmospheric ozone
5. ocean acidification
6. global freshwater use
7. the proportion of global land cover converted into cropland
8. atmospheric aerosol loading

9. chemical pollution (such as the concentration of persistent organic pollutants, plastics, endocrine disrupters, heavy metals, and nuclear waste in the planetary environment).

Herman Daly, in critiquing the absence of planetary boundaries in the neoclassical growth paradigm, notes the physical limits to growth were always a defining feature of classical economics, as embodied in Malthus's iron law of wages and Ricardo's law of diminishing marginal returns to land brought into cultivation (Daly, 1996). Daly argues that neoclassical growth theory assumes that non-physical parameters (such as the level of technology, individual preferences over goods and services, and the distribution of wealth and income) are exogenous[7] and prescribes adjustments in physical variables, such as the amount of goods and services to be produced (with consequent implications for environmental variables). A modeling choice that considers non-physical variables as exogenous parameters and physical ones as endogenous is incapable of incorporating signals of scarcity generated by physical parameters, unless the non-physical parameters happen fortuitously to reckon for such scarcity.[8] This form of theory, he argues, leads to unchecked economic growth, delinked from any physical limits. The prescriptions of such a theory will sooner or later come up against the ecological limits of the finite global environment, with adverse, possibly catastrophic consequences.

A financial intermediation process that ignores planetary limits would fail in its role of providing society with accurate signals of scarcity and abundance. For example, an investment strategy that did not incorporate the potential risk of fossil fuel reserves becoming unusable due to future regulatory action related to climate change would significantly underprice the capital deployed in this highly capital-intensive sector[9] (this is commonly referred to as the financial valuation impact of stranded assets in the fossil fuel sector). Proponents of incorporating planetary boundaries into the investment decision-making process call for a recognition of the necessity of targeted growth to meet the basic needs of the poorest segments of the global population.

A recent articulation of Daly's position, incorporating the resource extraction and increased efficiency necessary to meet a minimum suite of social needs while remaining within ecological limits is to be found in the concept of 'doughnut economics' (Raworth, 2012). Raworth describes a visual framework, shaped like a doughnut, which delineates a space bounded by an outer and inner circle, which represent physical planetary boundaries and minimum social requirements for inter alia income, equity, resilience, and voice. Another insightful articulation of the principles of a regenerative economy is laid out by John Fullerton (Fullerton, 2018). Fullerton is focused on incorporating patterns and principles observed in natural ecosystems into the financial ecosystem. He lists eight principles of a regenerative financial system, which include a holistic view of wealth, empowered participation, robust circulatory flow, and the honoring of community and place.

A Taxonomy of the Financial Ecosystem

The financial ecosystem comprises a diverse and amorphous collection of financial intermediaries and institutional investors along with a number of supporting actors: exchanges, data providers, and regulatory agencies. Here we describe the constituent parts and interconnecting functions within what we have hitherto called the 'financial sector' and view finance as an ecosystem. We briefly review a descriptive list of members of the financial ecosystem in Table 2.1.

Our list differs somewhat from other such lists[10] in two ways. Firstly, we attempt to categorize the elements in our list by their function in the ecosystem rather than by their nominal descriptions, even though that means that some entities appear in multiple categories. For example, we refer to 'deposit-taking intermediaries' rather than commercial banks. The categorization by function is an essential feature of cybernetics and systems theory.[11] Secondly, we do not make much of the commonly cited difference between regulated and unregulated institutions, or banks and 'shadow banks'. Since we are approaching the financial ecosystem from a systems perspective, we must choose to view the 'regulator' as an endogenous part of the system, and cannot rely on the distinction between say hedge funds as 'unregulated' or 'lightly regulated' deposit-accepting institutions and commercial banks as regulated institutions. The plasticity and adaptability of financial institutions and the web of interconnections among them behoove us to at least make an effort to look for deeper parameters (Lucas, 1976) than those imposed by a changing regulatory environment.

An important benefit of our approach is to highlight the lacunae in the reporting of statistical information about the ecosystem. Since the collection of consistent statistical information is usually the outcome of regulatory directive, the scale of lightly regulated activities such as the acceptance of assets under management by hedge fund managers is not as comprehensively or consistently reported as the scale of deposits in regulated

Table 2.1 Taxonomy of financial ecosystem

Category	Function	Examples
Savers	Choose to limit current expenditure below current receipts in order to fund future cash-flow requirements	Households
Shareholders	Advance cash to a company in return for a residual claim to the assets of that company	Households, pension funds, sovereign wealth funds, foundations, endowments, commercial banks (in civil law countries)
Liquidity providers	Advance cash in return for a future promise to return such cash along with interest, with or without collateral	Savers, insurance providers, credit card companies, mortgage lenders, capital market underwriters, payday lenders, pawn-brokers
Insurance providers	Accept periodic contributions of cash from households in return for a promise to provide lump-sum or periodic contributions of cash in the advent of need	Pension funds, insurance companies
Deposit-taking intermediaries	Accept cash from households with the purpose of storing and enhancing the value of such cash in the future	Commercial banks, savings and credit associations, credit unions, money market fund managers, mutual fund managers, private equity fund managers, venture capital fund managers, hedge fund managers
Brokers and lawyers	Act as an agent on behalf of borrowers, lenders, shareholders, and firms in return for a fee or a bid-ask spread	Brokerages, investment banks, securities lawyers
Consultants	Provide advice to savers or borrowers in return for a fee	Financial consultants, mergers & acquisitions advisory firms
Payment facilitators	Facilitate the payment of pre-determined amounts of cash between parties	Digital payments networks, credit card companies, Western Union, SWIFT, commercial banks
Supporting institutions	Facilitate standardization of contracts, provide verification of information, provide privacy to transactors and other supporting roles that do not involve the provision of capital or direct advice	Exchanges, peer-to-peer lenders, information providers, custodians, nominee or professional director services, rating agencies, auditors
Regulators	To design and administer rules intended to enhance the net social benefits of the financial ecosystem	National and supra-national agencies

Source: Authors

thrifts. Similarly, statistics on the carbon emissions impact of portfolio construction choices are far less understood than the expected loss in bank capital from a 100 basis point upward shift in the US Treasury yield curve.

In addition to the flows of goods, services, and labor in return for revenue and wages that occurs between households and firms, Fig. 2.1 portrays savings flowing from households, via the financial ecosystem, to firms and governments. The financial ecosystem receives the use of the savings of households in return for a promise to return the value of those savings at a future date along with compensation for the use of such savings, in the form of interest, dividends, capital gains, or other forms of capital service compensation.

Financial intermediaries, directly or indirectly, invest those savings in firms and sovereigns. Those firms hope to use these savings (or capital) to create goods, services, or new capital with an aggregate value greater than the sum of the inputs used to create them. It is only through the process of value-enhancing creation that financial intermediaries can make good on their promises to deliver both principal and capital charge to their lenders. In addition to firms, a key recipient of the use of capital is the government sector, both domestic and foreign. Sovereign debt outstanding represents approximately 30% of all debt outstanding. Financial intermediaries, and households, provide capital voluntarily to governments upon the belief that by and large governments have staying power and will in future be able to both redeem principal and make interest payments. In theory, sovereign debt issued by governments that control significant natural capital assets such as the Amazon rainforest, with periodic cash flows linked to the ecosystem services provided by such natural capital, could act as a financial ecosystem generated signal of relative scarcity. Chapter 13 details an example of Debt for Nature swaps that could evolve to become such a signal of natural capital scarcity.

The portrayal of the circular flow of savings in Fig. 2.1 serves to place the financial ecosystem within the broader economic system, but it occludes much of the complexity inside the financial ecosystem. Figure 2.2 displays our view of the financial ecosystem in a little more detail. We have also constructed the categories of financial institutions listed in Table 2.1 based on a list of critical functions that the financial system must provide. There is not a one-to-one correspondence between particular financial institutions and a specific category. There are many types of intermediary which fall into multiple categories. For example, a typical large bank such as JPMorgan Chase has subsidiaries which facilitate payments, accept

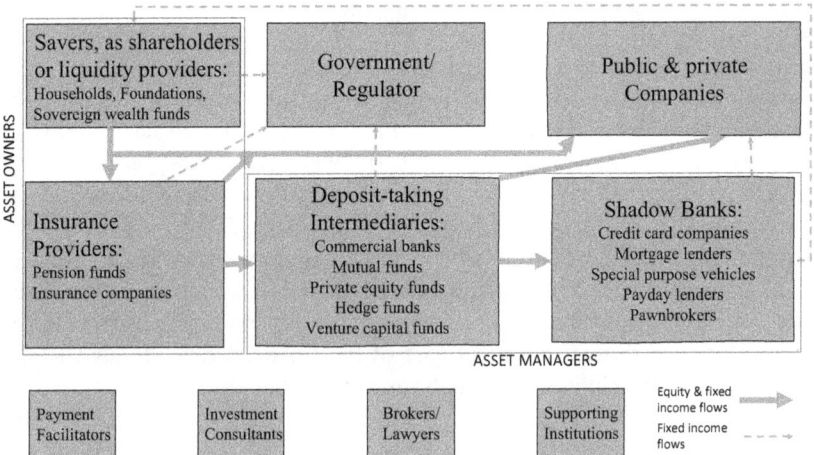

Fig. 2.2 Savings flow through the financial ecosystem. (Source: Authors)

deposits, act as broker, provide advice, act as shareholder, and provide liquidity. Even a structurally simple institution such as a pension fund, in our categorization, acts as an insurance provider, shareholder, and liquidity provider. Conversely, our categorization places hedge funds and commercial banks within the same functional category of deposit-taking intermediary.

Savers

The structural savers in the financial ecosystem are households, foundations, endowments, and sovereign wealth funds. Savers actively choose to limit current expenditure at a level below current receipts with the intention of preserving and enhancing the value of the residual for use in a future period. As a group, households are net savers, though there may be many classes of households that are net borrowers. In Fig. 2.2, we note that many households may rely on net borrowings from the shadow banking sector (in the form of student loans, credit card debt, and mortgage borrowings). Foundations and endowments are conceived as net savers, being required to maintain positive net worth. In principle, governments with continuing budget surpluses are savers also, but this is the exception rather than the norm. Most governments operate with a deficit, financed by fixed income borrowing ultimately from savers.

Shareholders

The flows of savings within the ecosystem occur in the form of equity provided by shareholders or owners and fixed income flows supplied by liquidity providers. Fixed income has always commanded larger flows of savings than equities. Indeed, in the early twentieth century, equities were an emerging asset class—most conservative endowments chose to invest primarily in fixed income (Chambers & Dimson, 2013). However, the lower magnitude of equity value belies their importance in the flow of capital, as they are the only instrument associated with ownership. Fixed income flows rarely stand on their own. Equity flows often do. Hence, shareholders represent a critical part of the financial ecosystem—the system could in principle operate without any fixed income flows, but ownership is essential. The owner is the only stakeholder that has the nominal responsibility of preserving the residual value of the investment (Berle and Means). The separation between the nominal responsibility of preserving residual value and the actual discharge of this responsibility through control is discussed in Chap. 3.

Liquidity Providers

The uncertainty of future cash flows from any investment creates a need for the provision of liquidity without an associated ownership interest. Uncertain returns imply that an investor may be willing to fund a portion of the investment for a fixed return if it is quite likely that such fixed return will be achieved. The owner and controller of the project may agree to such an arrangement if her estimate of future return is higher than the liquidity provider's, resulting in an appropriate sharing of the future return. The overlapping, but divergent estimates of future return between the liquidity provider and the shareholder create the conditions for both parties to jointly fund a project. Since there is always a chance that the project will lose a significant portion of the fixed income investment, some liquidity providers may require collateral as an imperfect guarantee of the expected return.

Liquidity providers facilitate investment in projects where all investors do not agree on the potential range of future values. They allow a project to proceed even if capital belonging to ready owners is insufficient. Liquidity providers, assuming that the owners are over-optimistic, but nevertheless believing in some potential return from the project, are willing to lend on condition that they are given a priority over the cash flows generated by the project. The existence of liquidity providers improves the chances of any project being financed. It is in this sense that debt can provide a real societal benefit.

Insurance Providers

The insurance provider accepts funds from savers, called premiums, and generally promises to return an augmented amount of those funds if some contingency occurs (for example, if the beneficiary lives past retirement age and meets certain vesting requirements, in the case of a pension fund). Insurance providers are generally obliged to protect the interests of their beneficiaries by a restrictive form of contractual obligation, known as fiduciary duty. Insurance providers, along with foundations, endowments, and sovereign wealth funds, are referred to as institutional investors. Different institutional investors may specialize in different types of investment opportunities. For example, a property & casualty insurance company is likely to invest in relatively liquid investments with a comparatively greater allocation to fixed income securities, given the uncertain timing of their liabilities. On the other hand, pension funds can generally predict the timing of their expected future cash outflows with relative certainty, given demographic information about their beneficiaries. Hence, they are in principle able to pursue longer-term investment objectives.

Deposit-Taking Intermediaries

The deposit-taking intermediary, such as a commercial bank, accepts funds and generally promises to return an augmented amount of those funds at a future date.[12] The difference between insurance provision and deposit acceptance generally has implications for the level of discretion over assets that the intermediary receives. The insurance provider is often what is referred to as an 'asset owner', while the deposit-taking intermediary is often an 'asset manager' (see below). The date of payment by the insurance provider is more uncertain than in the case of the commercial bank. Given imperfect information about future cash flows, both deposit-taking intermediaries and insurance providers must search for productive investment opportunities and screen out projects likely to dissipate capital. In addition to searching and screening, these two financial intermediaries engage in efforts to transform the attributes of cash flows resulting from their investments into those which match the risk appetite, desired term structure, holding size, currency exposure, and other attributes desired by the depositor or the insured party.

Insurance providers and deposit-taking intermediaries perform the core function of transforming current monetary savings of households into assets designed to support monetary expenditure in future periods when current monetary income may be diminished. Within the deposit-taking intermediary classification, private pools of capital such as hedge funds, private equity managers, and venture capital firms represent alternative methods of channeling savings to productive investment opportunities. We will examine the specific roles that each of these investment vehicles might feasibly play in advancing sustainability in subsequent chapters (Chaps. 10 and 14).

Delegation of the Management of Assets Within this category of intermediary, a distinction is drawn between *'asset owners'* and *'asset managers'*. Pension funds, sovereign wealth funds, insurance companies, foundations, endowments, and family offices are asset owners insofar as they retain full discretion over the funds or premiums they have received from households and delegate limited control to asset managers. Asset owners do not earn fees related to the investment performance of the underlying assets—the cost of provision of services by asset owners is borne out of investment performance but is not usually explicitly tied to the size of or return on those assets. Asset owners generally delegate control over a subset of their assets to managers who earn fees related to the size of and return on such assets. Asset owners can generally reverse such delegation at will.[13] The relationship between an asset owner and asset manager can be characterized as a principal-agent relationship, much like the relationship between shareholder and management. The asset owner has ultimate control over its assets, while the manager generally has day-to-day control and far better information about those assets. Typically, the larger asset owners (pension funds, insurance companies, and sovereign wealth funds) fall into the insurance provider category, while asset managers fall into the deposit-taking intermediary category.

In the context of sustainability, the difference in objectives and incentives between asset owners and managers implies that any effort to incorporate environmental or social considerations into investment choice must be appropriately outlined and tested both at the asset owner and at the asset manager levels. The information asymmetry between the two actors implies that it is not sufficient for asset owners to incorporate sustainability into their investment strategies—manager efforts must also be verified to the extent feasible. See Chap. 10 for a more detailed discussion of this critical issue.

Payment Facilitators

We list payment facilitators as important members of the ecosystem, but our focus on them will be limited, given our interest in the long-term consequences of investment. Payment facilitators are essential to the efficient transfer of value in the short term, but their real-time nature reduces the importance of their role in the process of preserving and enhancing the long-term value of capital.

We have chosen to focus on the flow of savings through the ecosystem, rather than income. Therefore, we are limiting our analysis to the part of the financial ecosystem whose primary focus is on the long-term storage of purchasing power in monetary form. We exclude from our analysis the review of that part of the ecosystem designed to facilitate the payments system. Historically, the payments system and the storage of savings have been intimately connected because a payment provider can very easily become a deposit-taking intermediary if the payers and receivers do not immediately withdraw cash balances intended for payment in the near future. The recent emergence of digital payment technologies has begun to sever the link between these two functions. For example, payment networks such as PayPal and Square in the United States and AliPay and WeChat Pay in China obviate the need for bank involvement in large parts of the payment chain. We recognize that there are synergies between the two functions, so one might expect both traditional financial institutions and digital payment networks to evolve similarly in form and substance. However, since our focus is on the long horizon impacts of investing choices, the immediate nature of payments reduces its relevance to our analysis.

Investment Consultants

The information asymmetry between asset owners and managers has created a niche for a variety of consultants. These range from individuals who advise the mass affluent on their retirement investment strategies to large advisory firms that significantly influence all major investment choices made by their client asset owners. Investment choices recommended by advisory firms have the potential to affect the environmental and social impact of trillions of $ in assets. Many savers, both modestly wealthy households and large pools of savers' capital, such as pension funds and insurance companies, rely on the advice of consultants to such an extent that it would be naïve to suggest that the saver was doing any financial decision-making.

Brokers and Lawyers

Brokerage and legal services are essential to the unimpeded flow of savings within the ecosystem. Brokers and lawyers act as agents on behalf of savers, insurance providers, and financial intermediaries in return for a fee or a bid-ask spread. Improvements in efficiency in the provision of brokerage and legal services can sharply increase the flow of savings through the financial ecosystem, reducing transaction costs and resultant leakage.

Supporting Institutions

The financial ecosystem could not function without a diverse array of supporting institutions that help to reduce information asymmetry, limit counterparty risks, and provide trusted execution of transactions. These include accountants, centralized exchanges, due diligence providers, interdealer networks, custody and storage providers, and depository trust monopolies.

Governments and Regulators

What is the role of governments in the circular flow of savings? The common role assigned to government intervention in economic theory consists of the addressing market failure, or providing services which cannot be efficiently provided by firms. These functions include the provision of public goods such as the supervision of market mechanisms, the pricing of externalities, and the enforcement of contracts. In the context of sustainability, the standard economic theory assigns the responsibility for the protection of natural and human capital to the government. These functions can be subsumed into the role of the regulator, broadly defined to include both supervision and control of the financial system as well as the broader ecosystem.

Within the financial ecosystem, the explicit goal of the regulator has hitherto consisted of ensuring the flow of savings through the system and limiting the extent of recurring financial crises. In theory, the regulator must design and administer rules that are expected to increase the net societal benefits of the financial ecosystem. In practice, the discipline of cost-benefit analysis (see Chap. 6) is not explicitly employed in financial regulation as it is in fiscal regulation in a number of countries.

Ashby's textbook on cybernetics defines the nature of good regulation in a system thus: "an essential feature of the good regulator is that *it blocks the flow of variety from disturbances to essential variables*" (emphasis in the original).[14] Let us translate it into contemporary language. Ashby defines a good regulator as one who prevents the natural volatility in state variables caused by shocks ('disturbances') from allowing a set of essential variables to diverge outside their acceptable limits. This means that a good regulator prevents information from propagating through the system. For example, Ashby states: "the unskilled hunter or earner, in difficult times, will starve and will force his liver and tissues (the essential variables) to extreme and perhaps unphysiological states, the skilled hunter or earner will go through the same difficult times with his liver and tissues never taken to extremes." Similarly, Ashby argues that a good air conditioner should operate in such a way that the occupant of the room does not know that it is getting warmer outside: "the good conditioner blocks the flow inwards of information about the weather".

Taking Ashby's definition, we might be tempted to think that a good regulator is one who does not let external pressures influence the conditions felt by internal parties. However, this is clearly a faulty approach for the regulation of the financial ecosystem. Ashby wrote his textbook as a way to teach students of biological organisms how good machines are designed. Neither machines nor the parts of biological organisms have any consciousness, or the ability to second-guess the regulator. Unlike the liver and tissues, the CEO of any financial intermediary who comes to know that the government will attempt to shield the intermediary from the adverse effects of any volatile shock will immediately jettison his prudence. Ashby's definition of a good regulator is not 'incentive compatible', in the language of mechanism design, a more recent incarnation of cybernetics which takes into account the pitfalls of moral hazard. Mechanism design and incentive compatibility were innovations on cybernetics first outlined by Leonid Hurwicz in 1960.[15] Unlike cybernetics, which is focused on the design of automatons incapable of consciousness, mechanism design attempts to account for the pitfalls for system design dug by the human's unfortunately ingenious capacity to behave in a strategic way.

Incentive compatibility implies that those agents (such as bank CEOs as well as central bank regulators) whose actions cause variation in risk within the system must be given contracts that vary their compensation accordingly. Put differently, in Ashby's colorful analogy, if the hunter's liver were a conscious being, a well-regulated system would force the liver to experience some pain in lean times, so that it might choose the behaviors necessary to avoid or minimize such lean times.

INTERACTIONS IN THE FINANCIAL ECOSYSTEM

In Chap. 1, we noted that the scale and strength of smaller governments are dwarfed by those of larger multinational firms. Hence, it would be naïve to imagine that governments alone might have the capacity to address the awesome responsibility that economic theory thrusts upon them: that of protecting the natural and human capital upon which the continued circular flow of savings depends. Our study of Ashby's definition of a good regulator highlights another limitation of relying on government as sole regulator: a regulator that attempts to eliminate feedback loops within the system might exacerbate the impact of shocks. Insuring too well will generally increase the incentives for excessive risk-taking.

The financial ecosystem is characterized by what has been called 'a tangle of interconnections' that are thought to increase its fragility.[16] In a perhaps prescient article in a periodical not commonly read by economists, May, Levin, and Sugihara (2008) argue that "the increasingly complicated and globally interlinked financial markets are no less immune to ... system-wide threats". They argue that it is fruitful to explore parallels between the financial ecosystem and systems thinking in ecology, engineering, and related fields. They highlight an alarming conclusion of a collaborative report (Kambhu, Weidman, & Krishnan, 2007) prepared by the US National Academies and Federal Reserve Bank of New York. The report, prepared as part of a conference to stimulate fresh thinking on systemic risk, points out that the resources allocated to the analysis of drivers of systemic risk is a miniscule portion of that spent on evaluating risks for individual actors.[17] May et al. argue that an analogous situation has occurred in the field of fisheries management: significant research resources have been committed to species-by-species management, with relatively little study of the interconnections between species.

This is not a surprising phenomenon to observers of the financial ecosystem. In Chap. 1, we noted in our discussion of the principal-agent problem that the investment manager is rewarded for short-term outperformance, and crucially, cannot be penalized for long-term underperformance. Almost all risk managers are employees of individual firms and they are incented by the financial performance of single firms. They are generally not penalized for the underperformance of the system, on the assumption that they have limited control over it and hence could not influence it for better or worse. Faced with competing demands on their time and intellectual capacity, such risk managers have no incentive to devote more than passing attention to systemic sources of risk. The only risk managers whose job description might incorporate systemic risk are employed by central banks and regulators. While their efforts at researching and disseminating the nature and drivers of systemic risk are laudable and precious indeed, they fall short of the relentless and diverse efforts at draconian control that a risk manager must employ to prevent crises in times of excessive exposure. We know of no examples where the compensation of employees of regulating bodies is linked to the systemic performance of the financial ecosystem.

There are precious few attempts to map the interconnections between different types of financial intermediaries and the flows of savings within the financial ecosystem. After the financial crisis of 2007–2008, the Office of Financial Research, a US government agency formed as a response to the crisis, undertook the mapping of the financial system to show how risks can emerge and spread throughout the system (Bookstaber & Kenett, 2016). Bookstaber and Kenett construct an illuminating map of the financial system as a multi-layered network, disaggregating the activities of a 'typical bank/dealer' into prime broker, financing desk, trading desk, derivatives desk, and the bank's corporate treasury.[18] They argue that a single-layer network cannot adequately represent the financial system because there are multiple types of flows within the network. They point out that many single participants, such as Bear Stearns before the crisis, in acting as a large bank or dealer, while simultaneously running hedge funds, can represent a node that controls flows of cash assets, collateral, and funding. These interconnections between nodes can imply that an impairment in the value of assets, which appear to be a small proportion of overall wealth, such as subprime mortgages in the United States, can trigger systemic crises. The mechanism of magnification generated by a system of repackaging and leveraging renders relatively insignificant assets into exposures that are a large multiple of the underlying assets.

To what extent might changes in the natural ecosystem induce unanticipated changes in the valuations of systemically important financial assets? What would be the impact of widespread adoption of carbon prices, which would reduce the value of equity and fixed income claims on fossil fuel reserves? Which companies depend most on the widespread availability of single-use plastics for the viability of their business model? What financial instruments are linked to the activities of companies that produce endocrine disruptors most likely to be accused of widespread damage? To answer these questions requires incorporating planetary boundaries into any analysis of financial risks and opportunities. It also requires measuring and disclosing new data, so that financial analysts can make appropriately informed choices. The Task Force on Climate related Financial Disclosure (TCFD) represents the broadest effort to encourage disclosure on the first planetary boundary, that of climate. Each of the nine planetary boundaries require similar efforts to gather and interpret data that can inform whether any particular investment choice moves the planetary ecosystem away from or closer to the boundary.

CONCENTRATION IN THE FINANCIAL ECOSYSTEM

Among the listed functions of financial intermediaries, there are very few, chief among them that of acting as regulator, that a large bank does not have the capacity to perform in some measure. The stocks and flows of capital controlled by such large banks are enormous. For example, the total assets on the balance sheet of JPMorgan Chase & Co. amounted to $2.6 trillion on June 30, 2018, and the notional amount of derivatives contracts outstanding at that date was $57.3 trillion.[19] The latter amount is a more accurate reflection of the stocks of capital influenced by JPMorgan because large banks routinely utilize derivatives contracts to earn returns on assets which do not appear on their balance sheets.[20] This amount compares to the global total notional amount of derivatives contracts of $576.4 trillion.[21] Derivatives notional exposure is typically a multiple of the value of related financial capital; for example, the total global private and public debt is estimated to be $164 trillion in 2016, implying that derivatives exposure is more than 3× debt outstanding.[22] Within the United States, the top four banks account for approximately 90% of all derivatives exposure (Office of the Comptroller of the Currency, 2017).

This level of concentration within the derivatives ecosystem is usually a fact that is cited as one of concern—for example, because of the disruptive potential of the failure of any single systemically important bank. However, a would-be sustainable finance analyst might also draw a hopeful conclusion: that if a feasible method of using the capital allocation power of banks to enhance ecosystem service protection can be devised, it can be implemented by just a handful of decision-makers. This is in stark contrast to the level of consensus that was necessary to arrive at the formulation of the Sustainable Development Goals in 2016 (see Chap. 1). Having achieved that consensus, to the extent that their implementation depends on action by the largest financial intermediaries, the challenge of coordination is significantly reduced.

As a group, the largest financial intermediaries control a very significant portion of global assets under management. For example, the top 50 asset managers (a subset of the deposit-taking intermediary classification) and the top 500 asset owners (a subset of the insurance provider category) control over $40 trillion in assets under management in 2017 (AOD Project), which would amount to approximately one-fifth of all financial assets under management (UNEP). A concerted effort to address planetary boundaries in the portfolio construction process initiated by the largest asset owners would be felt throughout the financial ecosystem, forcing asset managers to consider ways in which the related risks and opportunities might be incorporated into their investment process. Once some asset managers had begun to routinize such procedures, it is likely that such procedures would be adopted or adapted by others if they appeared to aid asset growth.

The founding signatories to the PRI, which included both asset owners and managers, were responsible for approximately $600 billion in assets. The drafters of the principles represented a wide section of the international investment community, including ethical investment managers such as Domini Social Investments, faith-based asset owners such as the United Methodist Church, and activist investment managers such as Hermes, owned by British Telecom Pension Fund. These boutique investment managers were joined by geographically dispersed institutional investors in control of the largest global asset portfolios, including the California Public Employee Retirement System (CalPERS), the pension funds of New York City public employees, Stichting Pensioenfonds ABP, Norges Bank Investment Management, Daiwa Asset Management, and the

Government Pension Fund of Thailand. By the time the PRI was launched, this group had swelled to 100, increasing the breadth and depth of the founding signatories to include the largest asset owner in Latin America, Previ, and its counterpart on the African continent, the Government Pension Fund of South Africa, as well as a broad range of investment managers and pension funds from around the world. By 2018, the PRI signatory base had grown to nearly 2000 investors responsible for over $70 trillion in assets under management.

Drafting Signatories of the Principles of Responsible Investment, 2006 (to be Checked)
BT Pension Scheme, UK
Caisse des Dépôts et Consignments, Canada
California Public Employees Retirement System (CalPERS), USA
Canada Pension Plan Investment Board, Canada
Connecticut Retirement Plans and Trust Funds, USA
Daiwa Asset Management Co. Ltd., South Korea
Domini Social Investments, USA
Folksam, Sweden
Fonds de réserve pour les retraites, France
Wespath Investment Management, United Methodist Church, USA
Stichting Pensioenfonds ABP, Netherlands
Government Pension Fund of Thailand
Hermes Pensions Management, UK
Munich Reinsurance AG, Germany
New York City Employees Retirement Fund, USA
International Finance Corporation, World Bank Group
PREVI, Brazil
PGGM Investments, Netherlands
Public Sector Superannuation Scheme, Australia
Norwegian Government Pension Fund, Norway
TIAA CREF, USA
United Nations Joint Staff Pension Fund
Universities Superannuation Scheme, UK

Asset Owner Effort to Identify Systemically Important Carbon Emitters

A number of asset owners, in collaboration with the carbon emissions data provider CDP, launched the ClimateAction100+ initiative. This is a five-year initiative launched in December 2017 to engage with the largest corporate carbon emitters. As of September 2018, approximately 300 asset owners with $31 trillion assets under management had signed on to the initiative. The initiative is an effort to routinize the investor commitment set out in the Global Investor Statement on Climate Change to "work with companies in which we invest to ensure that they are minimizing and disclosing the risks and maximizing the opportunities presented by climate change and climate policy".

The companies identified as systemically important carbon emitters were selected from the MSCI ACWI, an index of global stock market returns. The initially chosen 100 companies have the highest combined direct and indirect scope 1, 2, and 3 emissions, according to CDP estimates. According to CDP, these 100 companies are responsible for up to two-thirds of annual industrial greenhouse gas emissions.

The initiative also identified a set of companies believed by representatives of the asset owners to represent important drivers of the transition to clean energy. Together, these companies represent the portfolio of issuers that are likely to experience the largest relative gains or losses from widespread adoption of carbon pricing.

CONCLUDING REMARKS

An understanding of the financial ecosystem and its place within planetary boundaries enriches our understanding of the traditional role of finance within society. It allows the financial analyst to ask questions which operate at the frontier between the financial ecosystem and societal efforts to attain sustainability. There are currently a number of proposals to redesign the financial system to increase its contribution to sustainability. For example, the United Nations Environment Programme (UNEP) and the World Bank have jointly produced a report entitled "Roadmap for a Sustainable Financial System". The European Union High Level Expert Group on

Sustainable Finance has issued a report entitled "Financing a Sustainable European Economy". Both these reports outline laudable prescriptions that an all-powerful regulator might be able to impose on a large, variegated, cross-border financial ecosystem. Unfortunately, the distributed nature of the financial ecosystem with decision-makers subject to varying jurisdictions implies that the prescriptions of a single regulator are likely to remain ineffective. There are valuable efforts to codify sustainable financial practice, most notably in the taxonomies of sustainable investing activity prepared by the People's Bank of China (Sandalow, 2018) and the European Union's expert group (EU Technical Expert Group, 2019). These can serve as useful guidelines within their own jurisdictions, and can act as an example for other jurisdictions if they are persuasive to investors on their own merits.

The essence of financial decision-making is that effective solutions are designed in a decentralized way, tailored to the particulars of cash-flow expectations, maturity, volatility, and other sources of both financial and ecosystem risk. In this context, it is our belief that a roadmap of solutions or a prescriptive design for a new financial ecosystem would amount to hubris. A roadmap or a new architecture would be useful only to those precious few global decision-makers who might have the power to re-shape the financial ecosystem. We are doubtful that any such powerful decision-maker exists. We conclude with the hope that an understanding of the financial ecosystem and its linkages with the global environment will allow financial analysts to identify pressure points in the existing financial ecosystem and facilitate the disciplines of risk identification and the search for opportunities. A future financial ecosystem must be able to fulfill its properly conceived roles: to allocate scarce capital to its highest social value, to match investors in search of a broad range of financial, physical, human, and natural returns with appropriate risk-adjusted investment opportunities, and to generate signals of scarcity in the context of planetary boundaries.

NOTES

1. See Meadows (2008) for a basic introduction to the language and tools of systems analysis. See Zigrand (2014) for a review of the uses of systems thinking in the context economic and financial systems. In particular, Zigrand details the meaning of the word "system", differentiates the concept from "aggregate", discusses the history of systems ideas within economics and outlines the value of studying economic systems *qua* systems.

2. In his 1758 manuscript *Tableau Économique,* Francois Quesnay presents the circular flow as the movement of agricultural surpluses through the economy in the form of rent, wages, and purchases of manufactured goods. Hayek (1931) notes that this is a systematization of Cantillon's thought outlined in *Essai.* Note that Cantillon died 20 years before the 1755 publication of his *Essai.*

3. Such as nutrient cycling or erosion control (services that limit leakages of nitrogen, phosphorus, or water) or soil formation or seasonal floods where flood channel capacity is available (services that limit injections of nitrogen, phosphorus, or water). For a detailed description of these environmental cycles and associated ecosystem processes, see chapters 7–17 of Hassan, Scholes, and Ash (2005).

4. See pp. 26–27 of Ellen MacArthur Foundation (2013) for the intellectual antecedents of the Circular Economy concept and Benyus (1997) for examples of natural phenomena that inspired successful innovations.

5. This is the rationale for labeling the geological period since the Industrial Revolution the "Anthropocene" (Crutzen, 2002).

6. The global value of ecosystem services in 2011 in 2007 dollars was estimated by Costanza et al. (2014) to be $125 trillion per year. This figure is converted to 2010 dollars using the US GDP deflator.

7. An exogenous variable is one whose behavior is not modeled within the system being described. Conversely, endogenous variables are those whose behavior is explained by the model.

8. In neoclassical growth theory, if humans with significant purchasing power happen to value coral reefs (exogenous individual preferences and the distribution of endowments), then an impending destruction of coral reefs would be prevented by increases in the value assigned to coral reefs by the market. However, if humans with significant wealth are not persuaded that coral reefs are scarce, then the financial ecosystem has no reason to prevent their destruction. The physical scarcity of coral reefs will count for nought in the face of the non-physical parameter of their relative lack of popularity.

9. See Meinshausen et al. (2009) for an analysis that concluded that only a small fraction of the existing global fossil fuel reserves could be burned in any scenario intended to limit increases in global mean temperature increases to 2 °C above pre-industrial levels. See Griffin, Jaffe, Lont, and Dominguez-Faus (2015) for an analysis of the impact on stock prices of US fossil fuel companies as this information diffused through financial markets.

10. There are numerous descriptive lists of financial intermediaries. See, for example, Investopedia (2012) for a quick introduction. For detailed descriptions and a more commonly cited categorization, see Chapter 2 of Greenbaum, Thakor, and Boot (2016). An early effort to describe the range of financial actors who need to be pressed into the quest for eco-efficiency and sustainability was presented by Schmidheiny and Zorraquin (1996).

11. In his chapter on "The Determinate Machine" in the classic textbook on cybernetics, Ashby (1956) argues that there is an 'exact parallelism' between the properties of functions (which he calls 'transformations') and the 'properties of machines and dynamic systems'. Ashby states: "It should be noticed that the definition [of a system] refers to a way of behaving, not to a material thing."

12. Note that the future date may be the next date, automatically rolled over, as is the case with demand deposits.

13. In recent years, there has been a trend towards in-sourcing of investment management among large asset owners.

14. Section 10/6 of Ashby (1956).

15. See Chapter 9 of Mirowski and Nik-Khah (2017).

16. On page xvi of Financial Crisis Inquiry Commission (2011), the Financial Crisis Inquiry Commission refers to 'a tangle of interconnections' as a factor in precipitating the credit crisis in September 2008.

17. See page 72 of Kambhu et al. (2007).

18. See Fig. 1 of Bookstaber and Kenett (2016).

19. JPMorgan Chase & Co. (2018). Form 10-Q for the quarterly period ended June 30, 2018.

20. Note that due to differences in allowable netting of exposures in US GAAP versus IFRS, US banks such as JPMorgan Chase subject to US GAAP have comparatively lower assets on the balance sheet for a given level of risk exposure than international banks subject to IFRS.

21. This amount is derived from the Bank of International Settlements data as the sum of OTC derivatives and exchange-traded futures and options. OTC derivatives amounted to $531.9 trillion for H2 2017 as per Table D5 of the BIS derivatives statistics. Exchange-traded contracts amounted to $44.5 trillion for March 2018 as per Table D1. See BIS (2018).

22. The bulk of derivatives exposure comprises interest rate swaps, with smaller proportions relating to foreign exchange contracts, commodities, and equities. Hence, the relationship between total debt and debt-related derivatives is greater than 3×.

References

Ashby, W. R. (1956). *An Introduction to Cybernetics*. London, UK: Chapman & Hall Ltd.

Benyus, J. M. (1997). *Biomimicry: Innovation Inspired by Nature* (1st ed.). New York, NY: Morrow.

BIS. (2018). *BIS Statistics Explorer: Derivatives Statistics*. Retrieved from https://stats.bis.org/statx/toc/DER.html.

Bookstaber, R., & Kenett, D. Y. (2016). *Looking Deeper, Seeing More: A Multilayer Map of the Financial System*. Retrieved from Washington, DC: https://financialresearch.gov/briefs/2016/07/14/multilayer-map

Chambers, D., & Dimson, E. (2013). Retrospectives: John Maynard Keynes, Investment Innovator. *Journal of Economic Perspectives, 27*(3), 213–228.

Costanza, R., de Groot, R., Sutton, P., van der Ploeg, S., Anderson, S. J., Kubiszewski, I., ... Turner, R. K. (2014). Changes in the Global Value of Ecosystem Services. *Global Environmental Change-Human and Policy Dimensions, 26,* 152–158. https://doi.org/10.1016/j.gloenvcha.2014.04.002

Crutzen, P. J. (2002). Geology of Mankind. *Nature, 415,* 23. https://doi.org/10.1038/415023a

Daly, H. E. (1996). *Beyond Growth: The Economics of Sustainable Development.* Boston, MA: Beacon Press.

Ellen MacArthur Foundation. (2013). *Towards the Circular Economy.* Retrieved from https://www.ellenmacarthurfoundation.org/assets/downloads/publications/Ellen-MacArthur-Foundation-Towards-the-Circular-Economy-vol.1.pdf

EU Technical Expert Group on Sustainable Finance. (2019). *Taxonomy Technical Report.* Retrieved from https://ec.europa.eu/info/sites/info/files/business_economy_euro/banking_and_finance/documents/190618-sustainable-finance-teg-report-taxonomy_en.pdf

Financial Crisis Inquiry Commission. (2011). *The Financial Crisis Inquiry Report: Final Report of the National Commission on the Causes of the Financial and Economic Crisis in the United States.* Washington, DC: Government Printing Office. Retrieved from https://www.govinfo.gov/content/pkg/GPO-FCIC/pdf/GPO-FCIC.pdf

Fullerton, J. (2018). *Finance for a Regenerative World.* Retrieved from http://capitalinstitute.org/wp-content/uploads/2018/11/Regen-Finan-RVSD-Interactive_FINAL2.0.pdf

Greenbaum, S. I., Thakor, A. V., & Boot, A. W. A. (2016). *Contemporary Financial Intermediation.* Amsterdam, The Netherlands: Elsevier.

Griffin, P. A., Jaffe, A. M., Lont, D. H., & Dominguez-Faus, R. (2015). Science and the Stock Market: Investors' Recognition of Unburnable Carbon. *Energy Economics, 52,* 1–12. https://doi.org/10.1016/j.eneco.2015.08.028

Hassan, R., Scholes, R., & Ash, N. (Eds.). (2005). *Ecosystems and Human Wellbeing: Current State and Trends* (Vol. 1). Washington, DC: Island Press.

Hayek, F. A. V. (1931). Richard Cantillon. *Journal of Libertarian Studies, VII*(2), 217–247.

Investopedia. (2012). *Types of Financial Institutions and Their Roles.* Retrieved March 28, 2012, from @Investopedia. https://www.investopedia.com/walkthrough/corporate-finance/1/financial-institutions.aspx

Kambhu, J., Weidman, S., & Krishnan, N. (2007). *New Directions for Understanding Systemic Risk A Report on a Conference Cosponsored by the Federal Reserve Bank of New York and the National Academy of Sciences.* Washington, DC: National Academies Press.

Lucas, R. E. (1976). Econometric Policy Evaluation: A Critique. *Carnegie-Rochester Conference Series on Public Policy*, *1*, 19–46. https://doi.org/10.1016/S0167-2231(76)80003-6

May, R. M., Levin, S. A., & Sugihara, G. (2008). Complex Systems: Ecology for Bankers. *Nature*, *451*(7181), 893–895. https://doi.org/10.1038/451893a

Meadows, D. H. (2008). *Thinking in Systems: A Primer* (D. Wright Ed.). White River Junction, VT: Chelsea Green Publishing.

Meinshausen, M., Meinshausen, N., Hare, W., Raper, S. C. B., Frieler, K., Knutti, R., … Allen, M. R. (2009). Greenhouse-Gas Emission Targets for Limiting Global Warming to 2 °C. *Nature*, *458*, 1158. https://doi.org/10.1038/nature08017. https://www.nature.com/articles/nature08017#supplementary-information

Mirowski, P., & Nik-Khah, E. (2017). *The Knowledge We Have Lost in Information: The History of Information in Modern Economics*. New York, NY: Oxford University Press.

Office of the Comptroller of the Currency. (2017). *Quarterly Report on Bank Trading and Derivatives ACtivities*. Retrieved from Washington, DC: https://www.occ.treas.gov/topics/capital-markets/financial-markets/derivatives/dq217.pdf

Raworth, K. (2012). *A Safe and Just Space for Humanity: Can We Live Within the Doughnut?*. Retrieved from https://oxfamilibrary.openrepository.com/bitstream/handle/10546/210490/dp-a-safe-and-just-space-for-humanity-130212-en.pdf;jsessionid=614768142ECA717378881105A7F34D94?sequence=13

Rockström, J., Steffen, W., Noone, K., Persson, Å., Chapin Iii, F. S., Lambin, E. F., … Foley, J. A. (2009). A Safe Operating Space for Humanity. *Nature*, *461*, 472. https://doi.org/10.1038/461472a

Sandalow, D. (2018). *Guide to Chinese Climate Policy 2018*. New York: Columbia University Center for Global Energy Policy. Retrieved from https://energypolicy.columbia.edu/sites/default/files/pictures/Guide%20to%20Chinese%20Climate%20Policy%207-27-18.pdf

Schmidheiny, S., & Zorraquin, F. J. (1996). *Financing Change: The Financial Community, Eco-Efficiency, and Sustainable Development*. Cambridge, MA: MIT Press.

U.S. Senate Committee on Finance. (1933). *Investigation of Economic Problems; Hearings Before the Committee on Finance*. 72nd Congress. Washington, DC: United States Government Printing Office.

Zigrand, J.-P. (2014). *Systems and Systemic Risk in Finance and Economics*. London, UK: LSEPS Systemic Risk Centre.

CHAPTER 3

Governing the Corporation

Introduction

The modern corporation is ubiquitous. The size, scale, and global control of resources of the largest corporations make their operations of profound importance to society. Corporations are significant sources of employment, essential goods and services, investment returns for pension funds, critical contributors to governments' tax bases, and wellsprings of research, innovation, and creativity. As we note in Chap. 1, the scale and power of corporations dwarfs the resources available to the governments of most countries to regulate the societal impact of corporate activity. Based on a ranking of the 100 largest global economic entities compiled by the non-governmental organization Global Justice Now, 69 are corporations and just 31 are countries (Inman, 2016). The ranking lists countries and corporations by their revenue. At 10th place, Walmart, the largest corporation by revenue, outstrips the revenues of Australia, South Korea, and India. Apple and BP outstrip the government revenues of Switzerland, Norway, and Russia.

Given the relative scale of the corporate sector, it is a truism to state that the activities of companies will shape the quality and sustainability of the natural environment, for good or ill. The calls of civil society upon governments and supra-national bodies to address the SDGs are accompanied by a recognition that they cannot be implemented without a concurrent partnership with and concerted pressure upon the corporate sector. The relative impotence of the vast majority of governments in the

© The Author(s) 2019
S. Bose et al., *The Financial Ecosystem*, Palgrave Studies in Impact Finance, https://doi.org/10.1007/978-3-030-05624-7_3

face of the power of large corporations renders ineffective any effort at sustainable development that does not include the corporate sector as a driving force.

Companies have contributed to extraordinary advances in human welfare in many parts of the world. Global progress in eradicating extreme poverty and improving health, nutrition, education, and life expectancy has, in many cases, been achieved through the success of companies. As governments struggle to harness the resources to fund developmental efforts, companies are expected to play an increasingly important role. The Sustainable Development Goals alone require $70 trillion in investment, an amount far exceeding the discretionary budgets of all governments, but approximately equal to the current market value of the equity in publicly listed companies.

The Organisation for Economic Cooperation and Development (OECD), an international organization for wealthy countries, was one of the earlier supra-national organizations to recognize the importance of the private sector to developmental priorities. In 1998, the OECD convened a taskforce to develop global principles to guide policy makers on best practices in corporate governance. The Principles of Corporate Governance, which resulted from this effort, recognizes the importance of the corporation to social and economic well-being:

> Over the past decade, the world has witnessed a significant transformation in the role of the private sector in economic development and job creation. As more and more countries have adopted market-based approaches to economic policy, awareness of the importance of private corporations for the welfare of individuals has increased.
>
> Corporations create jobs, generate tax income, produce a wide array of goods and services at reasonable prices, and increasingly manage our savings and secure our retirement income. (Organisation for Economic Cooperation and Development, 1999)

However, many observers have raised concerns that company activity strains the natural environment by overreaching our planetary boundaries, depleting scarce common resources, contributing to growing inequality with soaring executive pay, and meager rewards for overworked employees, as well as appalling working conditions in outsourced supply chains. Other charges include private commandeering of social necessities such as water supplies, production of endocrine disrupters that adversely impact human fertility, pesticides that stress pollinating insects and addictive drugs such as opioids, and the marketing of food that causes ill health, such as high-sugar-, fat-, and salt-laden snacks that trigger obesity, heart disease, and diabetes.

The political economy of the influence of business on regulation was laid out by George Stigler, who argued that the formidable powers of the state to tax, subsidize, and regulate represent an unavoidable temptation for powerful corporate interests to capture (Stigler, 1971). More recently, the concept of 'regulatory capture' describes the process through which corporate special interests shape the nature of state intervention within industry (Dal Bo, 2006). The social effect of corporate political activity is a sharply debated topic in the United States, especially in the wake of the 2010 Supreme Court ruling on the *Citizens United* versus *Federal Election Commission* case, which eased limits on corporate political expenditure. Corporate lobbying has been demonstrated to be effective in reducing tax rates and facilitating tax avoidance (Minnick & Noga, 2017). Corporate funding appears to affect the language and thematic content of polarizing debate on climate change (Farrell, 2016). Concerns have been voiced that corporate political activity might be directed at preventing legislation to address air pollution or that the dissemination of 'fake news' through unregulated, corporate-controlled social media will corrode democratic discourse.

Is the company a curse or cure to society? Yes and, at times, both. Corporate governance, which is the study of how corporations are owned and controlled, is a critical tool for any investor interested in enhancing the sustainability of social and natural ecosystems. Investors provide a significant portion of the funding for companies, and thereby have the ability to influence directly how companies conduct their affairs. In the modern corporation, that influence is constrained by other stakeholders, the most powerful among which is the state. The history of the corporate form reveals that large corporations have always been closely aligned with state purposes.

Inventing the Corporation: A Brief History

The ubiquity of the modern corporation may make its current form and function seem inevitable. It is not. The role of the corporation, the responsibilities of management and shareholders, and the division of labor, rights, and duties were finely negotiated in entirely political circumstances.

The word 'corporation' is rooted in the Latin word *corpus* for body, or in this case, a body of many individuals acting as one. The early corporation had two defining features: *legal personhood* and *centralized management*. Legal personhood implies that the corporation has the right to own property, receive gifts, enter into contracts, petition, or be sued. In the context of commerce, legal personhood facilitates a partitioning of the assets of the corporation from the assets of its members, a critical innovation for the proper functioning of business credit. In particular, the concept of 'forward partitioning' (Mahoney, 2000) or 'entity shielding' (Hansmann, Kraakman, & Squire, 2006) refers to rules that protect the entity's assets from the claims of the creditors of an owner.[1] Centralized management means that the corporation must have well-defined decision-making authority. There must be one or more persons who have the ability to commit the entity to enter contracts or make certain routine decisions without first consulting all its members. Centralized management reduces the transaction costs incurred by continuous collective decision-making, but also gives birth to the essential problem of corporate governance: that of ensuring a congruence of interest between owner and manager. Versions of the corporate form with these two attributes were being used in India from the ninth-century BCE. Examples include guilds of artists and craftsmen, municipal and political groups known as *sreni*, which conducted trade as separate legal persons, maintaining a strict separation of the assets of the corporate entity and its members using detailed accounting practices (Khanna, 2005). Since the second-century BCE, Roman law recognized similar corporate forms (with legal personhood and centralized management) for non-commercial purposes. These included inter alia municipalities (*municipia*), associations and guilds (*collegia*), and charitable organizations (*piae causae*). A de facto commercial entity with effective asset partitioning and a form of limited liability without legal personhood existed under Roman law in the form of an enterprise managed by a co-owned slave, the *negotiatio per serves communes* (Abatino, Dari-Mattiacci, & Perotti, 2011).

Across medieval Europe, public institutions such as churches and local governments became incorporated, including the Papacy and the Corporation of London (both of which continue to this day). The common form of entity for commercial enterprise was the partnership, which is a legal agreement between individuals intending to conduct activities in order to make a profit. The oldest industrial corporation in the world is considered to be Stora Kopparberg Bergslags Aktiebolag, which began as a copper mine in Falun, Sweden, and received its charter of incorporation from King Magnus Eriksson in 1347, after having operated for decades or perhaps centuries before in unincorporated form (Time, 1963). As the largest copper supplier in medieval Europe, Stora Kopparberg helped to make the Swedish state a rising European power by the time King Gustavus Adolphus entered the Thirty Years' War (1618–1648).

VOC and the Advent of Permanent Capital

The rise of the corporation as a dominant form for organizing economic activity came with the mercantile era in Europe. Global trade, and ulti-mately, the business of empire, was conducted through companies. The modern corporation added three innovations to legal personhood and centralized management: *permanent capital, easy transferability of owner-ship*, and *limited liability*. Permanent capital offers a company continuity, allowing its existence to continue well beyond the lifespan of its founders, unlike a partnership. Permanent capital allows the company the ability to change its line of business, as circumstances require or allow.

The Dutch East India Company, *Vereenigde Oost-Indische Compagnie* (VOC), chartered in 1602, was the earliest example of a company with permanent capital. In 1602, the VOC was chartered with an unusually long ten-year term, which in 1612 was made permanent. Permanent capital means that the company is not bound to liquidate at a fixed time in the future and shareholders do not have the unilateral right to the return of capital. Without this attribute, the company could not invest in long-term infrastructure of its own that was outside the reach of its owners. Investments in long-term infrastructure within reach of local shareholders existed before the advent of the VOC. Stora Kopperbarg is one such example. Another consists of the wheat mills in Toulouse in the fourteenth century (Bris, Goetzmann, & Pouget, 2015). Previous commercial voyages were financed by general partnerships, with each financing limited to a particular voyage. The capital raised was invested in the ships and inventory, with a liquidation and settlement of accounts occurring upon the completion of each voyage. Permanent capital facilitated the VOC's investments in forts and ware-houses in far-flung Indonesia (Dari-Mattiacci, Gelderblom, Jonker, & Perotti, 2017). The work of Dari-Mattiacci et al. demonstrates that perma-nent capital is the critical innovation that dramatically increased the powers of the modern corporation over its predecessor. The VOC's rival, the English East India Company (EIC), chartered two years before the VOC, continued to operate using the traditional cycle of liquidation and refinancing of individual voyages until 1657. The VOC's mercantile ambitions to control trade with Asia via the Cape of Good Hope necessitated military operations to eliminate the rival incumbent: the Portuguese. It defeated the Portuguese in battle to allow trade with the Moluccan Islands and bring spices back to Europe. Dari-Mattiacci et al. argue that the VOC's lead in locking up capital gave it a decisive advantage over the Portuguese and the English, allowing it to invest in a far larger fleet and long-term infrastructure in Asia, facilitating the waging of continuous war to protect its trade.

The other two innovations that characterize the modern corporation (easily transferable shares and limited liability) developed earlier but became essential appurtenances of VOC's permanent capital. Permanent capital, by locking in shareholders' funds, sharply increases the potential for shareholder losses due to managerial indiscretion. While transferable shares existed before the VOC, actual transfers were relatively infrequent, being limited to situations where a partner died or needed to exit his investment. The VOC issued paper certificates to its shareowners and maintained a transparent share register, which enabled trading on the Amsterdam Stock Exchange. The unusually long term of the equity investment in the VOC made share trading an essential facility for the viability of locked-in capital. Those shareowners were also granted limited liability, that is, their potential liability to creditors of the company in the event of company failure was limited to the extent of their investment, rather than their entire assets. Limited liability breaches an essential principle of Roman law: *cuius commoda eius et incommoda* meaning he who profits from an activity must also bear its losses. Limited liability has a long history, being a feature of slave-run enterprises in Roman times, as well as the Byzantine *chreokoinonia*, the Jewish *'isqa*, the Islamic *qirad*, and the eleventh-century Italian *commenda* (Hillman, 1997). Abatino et al. argue that the limited liability of the Roman slave-managed enterprise never developed into modern corporate form due to the deeply-held Roman prohibition against the externalization of losses that is enshrined in the principle of *cuius commoda*. Today, the concept of limited liability remains contested. It has been lauded as an ingenious invention that contributed to human progress on par with the steam engine.[2]

The lock-in of capital by the VOC led to shareholder abuse. The company initially kept its accounts secret from minority shareholders and refused to pay dividends, or paid in the form of surplus nutmeg, as noted by Davis, Lukomnik, and Pitt-Watson (2006). Davis et al. state that the VOC saw the first recorded instance of investor protest, with Isaac Le Maire challenging the company in 1609 for its 'absurd and impertinent' management and for its squandering of shareholder capital. Le Maire's protest calling for the protection of shareholder interests had little impact on the VOC because it was dominated by the Dutch Estates General, the legislative body and the highest political power in the newly independent country (Gelderblom, de Jong, & Jonker, 2011).

Why did the Dutch Estates General allow the VOC the luxury of permanent capital in 1612? Gelderblom, de Jong, and Jonker (2013) demonstrate that the VOC petitioned for this unusual dowry because by 1609 its coffers were depleted by the waging of war, rendering it impossible to remain solvent if it had to wind up in 1612 as per its original charter. The VOC had spent significant portions of shareholder capital on military resources at the behest of the fledgling Dutch state which needed protection of its interests from Spanish incursions. In turn, the state could not afford to let the company fail: the VOC's military infrastructure in Asia would be too dangerous in the hands of another power. Thus, the innovation of permanent life, which had been hitherto reserved for public purposes, was extended to a commercial enterprise which undertook the public purpose of nurturing a young state seeking to cement its independence from Spain. In this sense, the VOC should be viewed more as a public-private partnership rather than solely as a commercial, profit-maximizing company.

EIC and the Imperial Corporation

This commingling of public and private purposes has always been a feature of the history of the largest corporations. The VOC example demonstrates the obverse of the point made by Stigler: the formidable powers afforded by the far-flung resources and networks of transnational corporations represent an unavoidable temptation for state co-option and expropriation. While the VOC engaged in military actions on behalf of the Dutch state to protect and expand its trade, the English East India Company (EIC) eventually ceased all commercial operations and effectively became a territorial power.[3] Like the VOC, it began as a spice trader, with its employee Sir Thomas Roe, who was also simultaneously the James I's ambassador, concluding a trading agreement with the Mughal emperor Jahangir (or more likely with his empress Nur Jahan) in 1618.[4] Unlike the VOC, in the early decades, it had few standing military investments, establishing its first fort in Madras in 1639. During the seventeenth century, the EIC was a minor military power, repeatedly defeated in battles in South Asia (Roy, 2011). More than a century later in 1757, the EIC's employee, Robert Clive won a decisive battle[5] against the governor of Bengal, the richest province in the Mughal empire, which led to the company receiving the tax farming rights to the province in 1765. These rights proved far more lucrative than its previous commercial operations, ushering in what Nick Robins referred to as the 'Bengal bubble' (Robins, 2012), a doubling of the company's stock price between 1757 and 1769. The Company leadership melded a dual role of managing an empire and maximizing revenue. Stern (2011) has argued that even in the seventeenth century, the Company saw "their settlements in Asia not as mere trading factories, but as colonial plantations, and their role as a government in Asia…the Company sought within them to cultivate law, jurisdiction, and a robust civic life that could in turn ensure an active, obedient, and virtuous body of subjects and, in a sense, citizens." Its husbandry over the population had limits. According to Mughal practice, the acquisition of the tax farming rights made the Company responsible for the welfare of Bengal province. This meant in particular the management of water and grain supplies and the provision of famine relief when necessary. However, when famine hit in 1770, the Company's relentless pursuit of profit ensured that relief efforts were meager at best. The Company's refusal to ease tax burdens ensured that its revenue from the province in 1770–1771 did not decrease despite the large proportion of barren lands (Sur, 1976). Estimates of the dead ranged from 3 to 10 million, likely one-third of the population of Bengal.

The Company's excesses during the famine drew eloquent critique from contemporary observers in England, with Edmund Burke prosecuting Warren Hastings, the Governor-General in India, in his 1785 impeachment. Adam Smith argued in *The Wealth of Nations* that the EIC's monopoly control and revenue extraction had led to falling wages of common people and turned a dearth into a famine. The famine led to tighter oversight of the Company's activities by the English state, and expanded the scope of Company operations to include management of granaries, embankments, and water tanks (Jonsson, 2010). Nevertheless, famines remained a feature of British India (both during Company rule and under the British government) and only ended after independence in 1947. Amartya Sen has demonstrated that the critical governance device that prevents famine is democratic accountability, a feature absent from both Company and British government rule in India (Sen, 1983).

Speculation and the Pause in Incorporation

In the early years of the eighteenth century, the French and British governments conceived similar schemes to securitize existing government debt using corporations. The South Sea Company (SSC), founded in 1711 in London, was granted a monopoly to trade in South America, a continent under Spanish control, in return for assuming the government's debts incurred during the War of Spanish Succession (1701–1714). Since Spain was at war with Britain, the monopoly had no economic value unless the war ended and Spain improbably recognized the monopoly right of the British company. Early shares were issued to many politicians and courtiers, with no money down, financed by the Hollow Sword Blade Company, an affiliated bank. The public was encouraged to invest in shares of the company through the machinations of insiders, newspapers and pamphlets, and conversations between stock-jobbers and the literati in the new coffeehouses (Dale, 2004). The British Crown would pay interest on the debt assumed by SSC, which would in turn fund a dividend on the shares. The SSC pushed through special interest legislation on June 11, 1720, that subsequently came to be known as the 'Bubble Act', which sought to outlaw corporations other than those that had been chartered before June 24, 1718 (which included the EIC, the Bank of England and the SSC) (Harris, 1994). The intent of the Act was to prevent other smaller (and perhaps fraudulent) companies from issuing shares to the general public. When the bill was being discussed in early June, the share price of SSC reached £750, five times its value in January. Following the Act, the price rose further in June and July to above £1000 when many well-informed investors sold (Kindleberger, 1996). The crash began in August and continued through the autumn, with the price ending below £200 by the end of the year. The SSC's sovereign debt securitization scheme was inspired by a similar plan conceived by John Law in France, who founded the Compagnie de l'Occident and, subsequently, the Compagnie des Indes and sold shares on credit provided by his Banque Generale. John Law's plans rescued the French Regency under the Duc d'Orleans from financial ruin wrought by war and court extravagance of Louis XIV. The proceeds of the share issuance were used to reduce and restructure the French government's debt. Both speculative bubbles made early purchasers rich and bankrupted late investors, especially the less-connected smaller merchants who constituted the emerging middle class. In both cases, the state remained the considerable beneficiary, with sharp reductions in government debt and debt service obligations. Peter Garber shows that the debt conversions allowed the SSC to acquire 80–85% of the public's holdings of government debt (Garber, 2000). After the collapse of the SSC, much of the government debt owned by SSC was transferred by Parliament to the Bank of England. The so-called Bubble Act required all future companies to have a Royal Charter, consolidating the Crown's control of the economy and sharply curtailing the formation of new joint-stock companies for a century. In France, in 1721, the government restructured the claims of holders of shares in the Compagnie des Indes so that, ultimately, 27% of the original sovereign debt was extinguished (Velde, 2016). It is hard to avoid the impression that both the French and British Crowns benefitted significantly from the speculative bubbles, at the expense of smaller investors. While the VOC and the EIC can be viewed as semi-public enterprises with both commercial and government purpose, the SSC and the Compagnie des Indes had dubious commercial value. In retrospect, they are most appropriately viewed as attempts to utilize the corporate form to restructure and securitize government debt. Investors in both countries licked their wounds, sharply curtailing risk tolerance in financial investments for nearly a century.

The Anglo-American Proliferation of Corporations in the Nineteenth Century

In the nineteenth century, the corporate form was taken from its core role in mercantile trading and the building of Empire, to become a commonplace feature of the civilian economy. The company was adapted for a mass market, through the introduction of cheap, accessible registration and limited liability for investors. The growth of business activity sparked by the American Revolution and the aftermath of the Industrial Revolution in Britain was contemporaneous with the ease of company registration, common access to the privilege of limited liability and the consequent proliferation of corporations.

Widespread Access to the Corporate Form in the United States
The aftermath of the 1720 speculative bubbles cemented the idea of the British corporation as privileged monopoly available only to a narrow aristocratic elite, closely aligned with the state. Starting in the 1790s, in the United States, the privileges of incorporation became widely accessible. The new republic, lacking a sovereign, had no legitimate way of limiting corporate charters to the few: it had to extend the corporate privilege to any white male that demanded it. US states chartered some

26,000 corporations between 1790 and 1860 (Wright & Sylla, 2011). It is estimated that by 1830, the United States had 15 times more corporations per capita than Britain did. Wright and Sylla argue that the explosion of corporations in the United States over such a long period indicates that corporate governance must have been sufficiently protective of shareholder interests that it allowed such dispersed corporate capital raising to grow so large. They argue that widespread access to the corporate form is one of the features that contributed to rapid economic growth and the transformation of the United States from a weak and peripheral new state to a global power within a century. What is intriguing about this period is that government regulation of managerial malfeasance was non-existent: there was no securities regulator such as the Securities & Exchange Commission (SEC). A number of corporate governance innovations were common in US companies of the time. These included checks and balances built into corporate charters and bylaws, widespread share trading and dividend expectations, stockholder monitoring and activism, and a free press that reported on stock trading. In addition, one-fifth of early companies employed the so-called prudent mean-voting rule, first proposed by Alexander Hamilton. The prudent mean-voting rule would give the shareholder one vote per share for the first two shares, one vote for every two shares for the next eight shares, one vote for four shares for the next 20 shares and so on, reducing the marginal votes per share for the large shareholders. This non-linear voting rule helped to balance the interests of the smallest and largest shareholders.

Joint-Stock Companies in Britain

A confluence of political and economic influences led to the widening of access to the corporate form in Scotland and England in the nineteenth century. Adam Smith in 1776 and, subsequently, David Ricardo and James Mill had attacked the monopolies granted to the EIC. The interests of industrialists and private traders wishing to trade directly with India and China coincided with the views of the political economists who wrote in favor of free trade. Perhaps the loss of the American colonies served as a warning to the British government of the danger of potential losses that might result from continued support of sclerotic monopolies in overseas trading, marine insurance, and banking. There was concern in Parliament to find ways to expand financial capital to fund the growing demands of imperial expansion. There was also a keen observation of the revolutionary upheaval in Europe: as the working classes became concentrated in urban centers during the Industrial Revolution, there was much need for investment in public works, such as water, sanitation, and housing to avert proletarian mutiny.

Between 1807 and 1825, more than 600 joint-stock companies were promoted in London. While some of these were domestic railway and dock companies, many others were established to invest in mines and plantations in the newly independent Latin American colonies of Spain. The legal personhood of joint-stock companies was tenuous under restrictive interpretations of the 'Bubble' Act of 1720. In 1825, the 'Bubble' Act was repealed, allowing the Crown to grant charters for companies without specific Acts of Parliament for each new company. The repeal eased the process of obtaining state-sanctioned legal personhood, but did not grant limited liability. In 1826, the monopolies in marine insurance and banking were eliminated (Harris, 2000). The 1844 Joint-Stock Companies Act allowed easy incorporation and transferable shares. Between 1826 and 1844 in Britain, relaxed regulations on the formation of joint-stock banks with wide ownership allowed the formation of 120 banks in Britain, some with more than a thousand shareholders. These banks distinguished themselves from private banks, formed before 1826 when a maximum of six shareholders were allowed. Private banks were viewed as being accessible to a connected elite that was already affluent, while the joint-stock banks were likely to receive deposits and lend to a wider segment of middle-class society (Alborn, 1998). By the middle of the nineteenth century, joint-stock banks had largely supplanted private banks.

Limited Liability as the Antidote to Communism

Throughout the first half of the nineteenth century, debates raged on the advantages and disadvantages for society of extending limited liability to the mass of new joint-stock companies. Adam Smith and the early political economists had viewed limited liability as an evil that reduced the zeal with which owners would manage the efficiency of their enterprises. Samuel Jones-Lloyd, a Manchester banker and proponent of the Currency School, responding to the Mercantile Law Commission's request for his views on the subject in 1853, wrote:

> Any relaxation of [unlimited liability] must of necessity tend to cause a diminution of the caution with which concerns are undertaken, of the anxious vigilence with which they are conducted, and the resolute effort with which difficulties are encountered and overcome, without which we should be exposed far more than at present to the evils of inconsiderate enterprise and reckless speculation. (Quoted in Hunt (1936))

On the other hand, the corporation with limited liability was also viewed as a way to spread wealth and extend the fruits of commercial activity beyond a narrow moneyed elite, at a time when continental Europe was beset by revolution. It was argued that if working people could be persuaded to invest their savings in companies, they would thereby assign their future well-being to capitalism, and stay loyal to free enterprise, rather than responding to the call of the Communist Manifesto, the English translation of which was published in 1850. That same year saw the appointment of a Parliamentary select committee on investments for the savings of the middle and working classes. In the previous decades, new legislation protected and encouraged the formation of savings banks, friendly societies and benefit-building associations, life insurance, and deferred annuities. The report of the select committee opined: "the man who has invested a portion of his earnings in securities, to the permanence and safety of which the peace and good order of society are essential, will be a tranquil and conservative citizen…to have saved money and invested it securely, is to become a capitalist; it is to have stepped out of the category of the proletaires; and to have deserted the wide and desolate multitude of those who *have not* for the more safe and reputable companionship of those who *have*" (Greg, 1853).

The Committee's report held up many local projects as examples of good investments for middle-class savings—waterworks, lodging houses for workmen, baths, and wash houses. John Stuart Mill gave evidence to the Committee in favor of limiting liability in 1850:

> There is no way in which the working classes can make so beneficial a use of their savings both to themselves and to society, as by the formation of associations to carry on the business with which they are acquainted.…The great value of limitation of responsibility as related to the working classes would not be so much to facilitate the investment of their savings, not so much to enable the poor to lend to the rich, as to enable the rich to lend to the poor. (Quoted in Hunt (1936))

Mill was arguing that the limitation of liability allowed the wealthy to invest alongside the working classes without fear of risking their entire fortunes on socially beneficial infrastructure. Richard Cobden, the Manchester manufacturer who had fought for free trade against import duties on wheat, argued that limited liability would facilitate the marriage of skill and capital and that this had already led to commercial prosperity in France and America. The Select Committee also argued that charters should be available at a far more reasonable cost in the future (one for a workman's housing project had cost upwards of £1000), recommending the emulation of the American and Canadian system of granting charters to all applicants as a public right. The subsequent Committee of 1851 reiterated the views of its predecessor that restraints should be removed, which prevented those of moderate means from "taking shares in investments with their richer neighbours, as thereby their self respect is upheld, their industry and intelligence encouraged, and an additional motive given to preserve order and respect for the laws of property".

The supporters of limited liability won their victory in 1855 with the passage of the Limited Liability Act, which extended the privilege to joint-stock companies with more than 25 members. The new law led to a vast expansion in enterprises incorporated with limited liability – 2500 companies with paid up capital of £30 million (equivalent to £90 billion today).

The Problem of Dispersed Ownership and the Advent of the Universal Owner

The proliferation of corporations that raise capital from dispersed shareholders gave rise to the separation of ownership and control in the modern Anglo-American corporation. In their now classic work, Adolf Berle and Gardiner Means drew a parallel between workers who gave up control of the product of their labor in return for fixed wages and shareholders who gave up control of their corporations to become mere recipients of 'the wages of capital' (Berle & Means, 1932). The control of the corporation, nominally owned by shareholders passed to professional managers, giving rise to the 'ownerless corporation' and the central problem of agency theory: how to align the incentives of owner and manager:

> When the owner was also in control of his enterprise he could operate it in his own interest and the philosophy surrounding the institution of private property has assumed that he would do so. This assumption has been carried over the present conditions and it is still expected that enterprise will be operated in the interests of the owners. But have we any justification for assuming that those in control of a modern corporation will also choose to operate it in the interests of the owners? The answer to this question will depend on the degree to which the self-interest of those in control may run parallel to the interests of ownership and, insofar as they differ, on the checks on the use of power which may be established by political, economic or social conditions. (Berle & Means, 1932)

Berle and Means challenged the assumption that owners of private property in the form of shares in corporations would efficiently manage such property for their own good, never mind the good of society as a whole. Dispersed ownership created a collective action problem, a form of the tragedy of the commons. Each individual rational shareholder has little incentive to monitor small holdings, essentially allowing the managers of the company to follow their own path, unrestrained:

> Where ownership is sufficiently sub-divided, the management can thus become a self-perpetuating body even though its share is negligible. This form of control can properly be called 'management control'. Such management control, though resting on no legal foundation, appears to be comparatively secure where the stock is widely distributed. (Berle & Means, 1932)

The liquidity of the stock market can serve to reinforce the security of errant management, since it is always less costly for the individual shareholder to liquidate her investment in a particular stock than to push for change in management.

The pooling of savings into institutional holdings in the late twentieth century in the Anglo-American markets has mitigated, to some extent, the collective action challenge. The holdings of the largest publicly-traded companies have become concentrated in a relatively small number of fiduciary institutions. For these institutional owners, it is not feasible to trade in and out individual stocks given their relative size in the marketplace: a large institutional investor would need to execute an exit or entry over time and with circumspection in order to prevent market participants from front-running their trades. Since liquidation is a costly strategy for large institutions, they are forced to own a significant portion of the universe of available stocks for the long term. Being unable to switch nimbly into alternative investments, a large institutional owner is effectively a 'universal owner' (Hawley & Williams, 2000). A universal owner must necessarily focus on the governance of the overall market, not just the governance of individual companies, as their returns are largely driven by market returns not individual holdings. The boxed section below provides some examples of universal owner efforts to overcome the collective action challenge of dispersed ownership.

Universal Owners Overcoming Barriers to Collective Action

The last 30 years have seen significant progress by investors attempting to overcome the collective action challenge which dispersed ownership presents. A wide array of national and regional investor groups have recognized the need to pool resources, compare notes, and coordinate their governance activity both in engaging companies, voting their shares and advocating for reforms with regulators. Examples include the International Corporate Governance Network, the US-based Council of Institutional Investors, the Asian Corporate Governance Association, the Australian Council of Superannuation Investors, Brazil's Institute for Corporate Governance and also its Association of Capital Markets Investors (AMEC). In the UK, the Pensions & Investment Research Consultants (PIRC) was founded by public sector pension funds. The movement for shareholders to take responsibility for their position as corporate owners was galvanized by the formation of the PRI (as discussed in Chap. 2).

These membership groups reflect the shift in capital markets from individual to institutional holdings—pension funds, insurance companies, mutual funds, and sovereign wealth funds. The pooling of savings into institutional holdings mitigates the collective action challenge to the extent that institutional owners recognize that, given their relative size in the marketplace, it is not feasible to trade in and out individual stocks. Being forced to own a significant portion of the universe of available stocks, and being unable to switch to alternative investments, a large institutional owner is effectively a 'universal owner'.

OTHER MODELS OF CORPORATE OWNERSHIP

This separation of ownership and control in the United States, Britain, the Netherlands, Australia, and Canada is a relatively unusual phenomenon. In most other markets, ownership and control is not quite so separated: it remains conjoined through family-controlled business groups (in continental Europe, Latin America, and south Asia), state ownership (in China, Russia, and France), control of proxy voting by banks (Germany), and cross-shareholding within inter-firm networks such as the Japanese *keiretsu* and the Korean *chaebol*.

Ownership of the largest publicly-traded firms outside of the Anglo-American countries tends to be more concentrated, often in the hands of a small group of wealthy families or the state (La Porta, Lopez-de-Silanes, & Shleifer, 1999). About half of the 100 largest corporations in Germany are owned by a majority owner (Fohlin, 2005). In France, self-financing from their retained earnings by corporations is the favored source of investment capital over equity issuance and bank borrowing (Murphy, 2005). The same was true of the Netherlands in the late nineteenth century (de Jong & Roell, 2005). This type of financing tends to increase concentration of ownership by a few large corporations and wealthy families rather than dispersing ownership to the broad public. In continental Europe, pyramidal[6] groups are a common method of ensuring control by insiders that is greater than equity ownership. In Japan and South Korea, the *keiretsu* and chaebol systems consist of cross-shareholding by related firms so that a group of related managements can vote *en bloc*, if necessary. In China, despite the rise of giant technology companies such as Tencent and Alibaba in the private sector, the state still owns and controls many of the largest corporations, including the second largest corporation in the world by revenue, the State Grid Corporation of China.

Many of the jurisdictions outside the Anglo-American countries are characterized by a civil law framework, which originated from Roman codification of laws, supplemented by discussions of natural law and the Napoleonic codification of rights and responsibilities after the fall of the *ancien regime* in France. The English system of common law, on the other hand, is determined by judicial decisions and judicial interpretations of statute. The civil law framework prevails in most jurisdictions outside the Commonwealth countries. Latin America received the civil law framework courtesy of Spanish and Portuguese colonial rule. Russia, China, South Korea, and Japan adopted the clarity of the civil law framework over common law when they instituted modern legal frameworks in the nineteenth and twentieth centuries.[7] In markets where ownership and control did not separate, which are largely civil law countries, there is an array of protections for minority shareholders, which acknowledge that with closer ownership and control by the majority shareholder, the group needing protection is the minority investor. A taxonomy of systems of corporate governance has been proposed that eschews the civil/common law distinction and instead uses other dimensions such as the prevailing concept of the firm, the board system, the identity of the salient stakeholders and the importance of stock markets in the national economy (Weimer & Pape, 1999). Weimer and Pape argue that four systems of governance emerge from their taxonomy: the Anglo-Saxon, the Germanic, the Latin, and the Japanese systems. Among these, the shareholder primacy, common law approach is exceptional and limited to the Anglo-Saxon system.

Examples of statutory minority safeguards include Sweden's provision for minority shareholders to form a nominating committee to select board members, Russia's cumulative voting rules, Italy's *vota lista*, which allows minority investors to appoint their own board directors and Brazil's fiscal council, which allows minority investors to effectively form an audit committee to scrutinize company accounts when trouble is suspected. In continental Europe, the concentration of ownership is combined with an explicit partnership between management and organized labor. Writing about Sweden, Peter Hogfeldt notes that "previous adversarial relations between capital and labour have given way to a corporatist society where heavily entrenched private ownership of the largest listed firms coexists and cooperates with labor unions whose members enjoy strong employee protection and are represented on the board"(Hogfeldt, 2005). In Germany, corporations have been required to have dual boards (a supervisory and a management board) since the Company Law of 1870, to protect minority shareholders and the public from self-serving insiders.

THE PURPOSE OF THE CORPORATION

The purpose and social role of the corporation has been at the heart of public debate and private commentary since its inception. We have seen that the corporation has always had to negotiate private and public goals. The history of the corporate form demonstrates the linkages between political power, imperial expansion, class conflict, and corporate activity. The long-term and global scale of influence facilitated by the seventeenth-century corporations with access to legal personhood, centralized management, permanent capital, transferable shares, and limited liability allowed two peripheral European countries (the Netherlands and England) to displace the then regional hegemons (Spain and France). The speculative joint-stock companies of 1720, the proliferation of limited liability companies in the nineteenth century and the concentrated ownership, corporatist economies of continental Europe were responses to specific challenges of excessive government debt, urban infrastructure needs, and class conflict. The nature of corporate influence on society was not determined by any inherent qualities in the corporation's structure. The corporation's purpose was defined and redefined in different settings. This exemplifies the maxim that 'the company is a creature of statute, not of nature' (Charkham & Simpson, 1999).

A little considered example is the change in the purpose of the corporation in Germany introduced before World War II by the Third Reich to allow the regime to take control of the country's industrial base, without incurring the costs of having to nationalize ownership. The Nazi regime introduced a new definition of corporate purpose via its Shareholder Rights Act of 1937. This dissolved any obligation of the company to serve its shareholders, and instead introduced the *Führerprinzip*, effectively, loyalty to the Fuhrer, Adolf Hitler, as the new corporate purpose of industry. The Nazis abolished shareholder voting rights, and introduced new forms of governance control through proxy voting rights residing in the banks. Through their control of the banks, the Third Reich could then control German industry (Morck, 2006).

The opposite view to the *Führerprinzip* is the shareholder manifesto laid out by the storied Chicago economist, Milton Friedman, who championed the virtues of profit as defining the purpose of the corporation. Friedman's position is laid out in an essay entitled "The Social Responsibility of Business is to Increase its Profits", published in the *New York Times* magazine in 1970:

> In a free enterprise, private-property system, a corporate executive is an employee of the owners of the business. He has direct responsibility to his employers. That responsibility is to conduct the business in accordance with their desires, which generally will be to make as much money as possible while conforming to the basic rules of the society, both those embodied in law and those embodied in ethical custom. (Friedman, 1970)

Friedman's proposition is generally interpreted to support profit maximization at the expense of ethics. Nevertheless, in admitting that the pursuit of corporate profit requires attention to the basic rules of society, in both law and ethical custom, even Friedman's essay can be interpreted to support corporate social responsibility as a prerequisite for sustainable profits. Colin Mayer makes an eloquent case for the need to overturn Friedman's narrow conception of the purpose of corporation as a profit-maximizing entity. Mayer notes that "in marked contrast to the Friedman conception of the firm, not only were social and public considerations incorporated in corporate purpose from the outset, they were interwoven in a fusion of commercial and community in a single corporate form" (Mayer, 2018). He points out that the English and Italian words for company originate from cum *panis* or 'sharing bread together', a decidedly social act.

Certain social enterprises in the United Kingdom and in the United States have chosen to incorporate as community interest companies or benefit corporations (Cho, 2017). These corporate forms are recent innovations, which explicitly include a social purpose in the company's formation documents. The benefit corporation retains a statutory right to prioritize its responsibilities to employees, communities, and customers over its nominal owners, the shareholders. Over 30 US states have adopted this voluntary provision, and more than 5000 private companies have incorporated as benefit corporations.

The two main bodies of corporate law—common and civil—have also had bearing on the purpose of the corporation. Typically, common law countries have given primacy to the interests of shareholders, whereas civil law countries have given broader responsibilities of corporations to serve a broader range of interests, which may include employees or wider society. Despite the difference in emphasis between common law and civil law jurisdictions, there has been a global convergence in corporate governance practice. The pressure to serve shareholder interests has been seen to create a dialectic need to attend the interests of other stakeholders. Likewise, stakeholder focused jurisdictions recognize that they must meet shareholder expectations in order to be able to access the financial capital they need for growth. The global principles developed by the OECD on corporate governance, and their extension to emerging markets by the IFC are an example of this convergence (see below).

The purpose of the corporation is influenced by the legal framework, by government, by investors and companies themselves, through the adoption of governing documents that specify its mission for its shareholders and stakeholders.

CORPORATE GOVERNANCE IN THE FINANCIAL ECOSYSTEM

We saw in Chaps. 1 and 2 that the financial ecosystem plays a critical role in society: to ensure the efficient allocation of resources, to match savers with investment opportunities and to provide accurate signals of scarcity. The efficient governance of the corporation is critical to all three of these functions.

Resource Allocation Investors are the ultimate allocators of financial capital. They must choose to invest in companies that are efficient in their use of capital and divest from those which are likely to deplete it. If investors are unwilling or unable to manage their corporate investments in accordance with their long-term interest, there is no guarantee that their capital will continue to grow. A good corporate governance regime reduces the costs of monitoring and managing their investments in companies, facilitating efficient resource allocation.

Matching A good corporate governance regime ensures that a saver is safely able to invest in a range of assets other than sovereign debt, which was the primary asset class of choice before the advent of corporations. Even when investing in corporations became widespread, initially the largest investments were in the form of debt. We noted in Chap. 2 that equities as a widely held asset class is a recent phenomenon, less than a century old. Savers today invest directly in companies through equity and debt investments in public and private markets, and indirectly via limited partnerships that finance corporate structures. A good corporate governance regime allows savers a wider assortment of issuers, maturities, risk profiles, and geographies to invest in than would be possible if corporations could not be trusted to invest financial capital in accordance with investor expectations. This diversity of investment choices benefits the saver, by allowing a tighter congruence between saving horizon and investable opportunity.

Signals of Scarcity A reliable corporate governance framework reduces friction between the signals of scarcity observed by a company and those seen by investors in the public marketplace. If copper becomes scarce relative to demand, we would expect the price of copper to rise. One might also expect that the share prices of copper miners would rise in tandem. However, this would only happen if investors could reasonably expect that managements of copper mining companies would efficiently utilize their windfall profits from high copper prices. If management pursues inefficient acquisitions or rewards themselves with outsized bonuses, there is no reason to expect that cash flows to shareholders would rise. A good corporate governance regime ensures that signals of scarcity observed by a few insiders can be quickly transmitted to a wider public.

Hence, the governance of the corporation matters for the financial eco-system because it determines how efficiently this powerful method of organizing economic activity will transmit cash flows and information within the ecosystem. How companies are governed is an issue of impor-tance, not just to investors but also to society more broadly. The OECD Principles of Corporate Governance note that

> A good corporate governance regime helps to assure that corporations use their capital efficiently. Good corporate governance helps, too, to ensure that corporations take into account the interests of a wide range of constitu-encies, as well as of the communities within which they operate, and that their boards are accountable to the company and the shareholders. This, in turn, helps to assure that corporations operate for the benefit of society as a whole. (*Organisation for Economic Cooperation and Development*, 1999)

In the preface to the World Bank's 2000 report on Corporate Governance, Sir Adrian Cadbury provided an inclusive definition: "Corporate gover-nance is concerned with holding the balance between economic and social goals and between individual and communal goals...the aim is to align as nearly as possible the interests of individuals, corporations and society" (Iskander & Chamlou, 2000). Recent regulatory proposals for corporate governance reform are even more explicit about the need to include the broad interests of society in the corporate governance framework. The 2018 European Commission explicitly recognizes the wider social and economic impact of companies, and sets out an extensive range of pro-posed reforms, including recognizing the social purpose of companies, the duties of their owners to ensure that companies 'do no harm', with pro-posed standards and reporting requirements to allow regulators and stakeholders to ensure alignment of interest between companies and soci-ety. An echo of this concern in Europe is heard across the Atlantic in The Accountable Capitalism Act, proposed by Senator Elizabeth Warren, who wrote that a short-term focus on profit maximization by companies was undermining the US economy's ability to invest in productive growth and to ensure that workers were properly rewarded. The bill proposed that companies with revenues over $1 billion should require a federal charter, beyond their state level incorporation. That federal charter would give employees the right to elect 40% of the directors, and introduce a new hurdle of approval before political donations could be made by companies (Warren, 2018).

What are the precise constituent parts of society that we must consider? In addition to shareholders, corporate governance affects liquidity providers such as bond-holders, employees, regulators, customers, and the communities in which the corporation operates.

Shareholders As we noted in the taxonomy of the financial ecosystem in Chap. 2, shareholders advance cash to a company in return for a residual claim on the assets of the company. Their share of the company is called 'equity', originating in the idea that the voting rights of control over the company they receive are generally allocated in proportion to their investment. Equity investors do not have specified contractual rights to any returns on their investment, but they are entitled to any residual dividend that management may choose to declare after other claims on the company's assets have been timely met. Typically, the shareholders have the right to cease the company's operations, to amend its governing documents and upon dissolution, divide the remaining assets. With variations in different markets, shareholders also have a range of supplementary rights, which can include the ability to call special meetings in between the required annual general meetings, to make corporate decisions by written agreement, to file proposals for fellow shareholders to vote upon, which may be binding or advisory in directing the board in a particular course of action, amend the charter, and to approve certain transactions. Examples here include approve the issuance of new shares, which may dilute the holdings of the existing shareowners, capital issuance, plus, in some cases, significant mergers and acquisitions, policy on compensation for the board and senior executives, and, even in some jurisdictions, political donations above a certain threshold (for example, over £200 in the UK).

Corporate Boards Shareholders delegate the oversight of the company to boards of directors. These directors are held accountable by investors, who have voting rights as shareholders and can thereby vote them into office, or as needed, replace them. In the United States, United Kingdom, and other countries with common law frameworks (including the Commonwealth nations of Canada, Australia, and former British colonies of Asia and Africa), there is one board of directors. In other markets, there are dual boards: one being supervisory and comprising both investors and employees of the company, and a subordinate management board which has executive rather than oversight responsibilities. The two-tier system is common in civil law countries, such as in continental Europe.

Liquidity Providers The corporate governance regime sets out rules for debt holders, whose rights are specified by contract (for example to receive interest payments over a particular period of time) and translate into governance rights of control in certain situations, for example, bankruptcy with a lien or right of possession of certain assets to act as collateral for their loan.

Regulators In theory, regulators must design and administer rules that are expected to increase the net societal benefits of the corporate governance regime. Securities regulators impose requirements of disclosure and rules governing the offering and trading of securities. In the context of banks, regulators are more interventionist, imposing capital adequacy requirement, 'fit and proper' tests for bank directors, and in the case of the European Union, caps on financial institution bonus arrangements, with an eye to concerns about incentives for excessive risk-taking. This recognition of the need for special regulation of companies which pose 'systemic risk' sets the stage for considering other issues where companies approach and strain planetary boundaries. One example is climate change, where the Financial Stability Board, representing the world's central bankers, established a Taskforce to consider the need for disclosure of risks presented by climate change in order that these could be managed and mitigated in asset portfolios. The disclosure regime resulted in recommendations from a Taskforce on Climate Financial Related Disclosure, which are further discussed in Chap. 7.

Employees and Other Stakeholders The corporate governance regime in common law countries imposes few duties on the corporation with regard to employees and other stakeholders, other than those set within the general legal framework. The civil law jurisdictions do impose a requirement for employee participation on boards, recognizing that employees represent a constituency with an interest in the long-term survival of the company. Our review of the history of the EIC demonstrated that communities in which a large multinational corporation operates generally do not have much influence on the governance of that corporation. The relationship between corporate financial performance and stakeholder relations is further discussed in Chap. 8.

Corporate Governance in the Circular Flow of Savings

As noted in Chap. 1, today, much of the world's largest corporations are owned by the citizen investor, represented by pension funds, insurance companies, mutual funds, and sovereign wealth funds. This is a fairly recent portfolio trend for investors. Until the 1960s, equities were not widely held by institutional investors. Pension funds and insurance companies relied initially on sovereign bonds, and then on corporate bonds, before venturing into equities. Pension funds provide one of the largest sources of finance and, in their search for investment returns, invest in companies. Investment returns are often the largest source for pension payments, one example being CalPERS, the largest defined benefit fund in the United States, which relies upon investment returns to pay two thirds of pension benefits. This illustrates the circular flow of savings described in Chap. 2: pensions represent the savings of employees, which are then advanced to companies which generate wages for other employees and also investment returns for the pension fund. Recognizing the circulation of savings helps us to understand the importance of the efficient functioning of the corporate governance regime for the financial ecosystem: corporate governance is valuable not so much to plutocratic providers of vast amounts of capital, but to employees and small entrepreneurs who are investing their life-savings. If these savers are unable to invest in companies because of poor governance, then their options become limited, forcing them to accept meager returns from government debt or bank deposits. The plutocratic capitalists can dispense with good corporate governance—they have the option to invest in their own companies where the governance problem is non-existent.

Natural Limits to the Rigidity of a Corporate Governance Regime

An additional stakeholder in this process is the corporation itself, or more precisely its proximate decision-makers, corporate management. Rigid standards of corporate governance and investor activism impose significant monitoring and disclosure costs on management. If the costs of raising capital from public markets exceed its benefits, management will consider alternative sources of finance. Indeed, there has been a dramatic decline in the number of publicly listed companies worldwide.[8] In particular, there is a significant decline in the number of smaller, growth-oriented companies choosing to access the public equity markets in the form of initial public offerings.[9] Abundant capital, little regulation, and the absence of agency costs in the private markets can make this the more attractive alternative. In addition, a focus on short-term returns on the part of many public markets investors forces management to focus on quarterly goals at the expense of longer-term strategy, hurting both management and long-term investors. The uniformity of corporate governance rules in public markets makes them more burdensome for smaller companies (Organisation for Economic Cooperation and Development, 2015). This phenomenon should act as a judicious constraint on corporate governance requirements for listed companies: the would-be market designer must consider the costs and benefits of each additional monitoring and disclosure requirement. The OECD report notes that the proportion of revenue that stock exchanges earn from listing fees has declined significantly also—this phenomenon suggests that we cannot blame the drop in initial public offerings on higher listing fees. Hence, there is a natural limit to the extent of monitoring that shareholders or any other stakeholder can expect to be effective. In any ecosystem, the stability of a bilateral relation is determined by the availability of exit options. Just as the shareholder can avail herself of an easy exit through a sale of shares in a liquid public market, management can choose to tap alternative sources of financing and take the company private. There are, however, some companies which are harder to take private than others. The largest companies and those with low or unstable cash flows relative to market value are least likely candidates for private financing. Happily, these are also the companies where good corporate governance can have the most social value.

An additional rationale for limiting the power of shareholders over management arises from essential features related to a company's purpose. For example, Reuters, the financial news provider, has issued a Founders Share with significant voting rights to a private company to ensure that Reuters cannot be acquired by any party that may seek to acquire the company in order to influence its reporting. Many founder-dominated companies employ similar share-class discrimination to retain founder control far in excess of their economic ownership (examples include Google, Facebook, and Amazon). There is of course a significant difference between protecting the codified mission of a corporation and the idiosyncratic interests of its all too human founders. Loyalty to the former is principled. Loyalty to the latter is tyranny. Founder shares designed to protect the precise social purpose of a corporation enhance the diversity of the corporate ecosystem, allowing principled corporate behavior to persist even when it is challenged by concentrated economic power. Founder shares meant to protect the narrow interest of individuals, however important such individuals may be to the genesis of that corporation, merely perpetuate the tyranny of precedence.

GLOBAL CONVERGENCE IN CORPORATE GOVERNANCE

The geographic distribution of capital needs and capital supply is not generally aligned: economies with significant wealth available for deployment are not necessarily those which are hungry for capital. Hence, there is a critical need to reduce cultural barriers to cross-border investment. Cross-country differences in corporate governance standards are a form of cultural barrier, which impedes flows of capital and hampers its efficient allocation.

An important initiative in aligning global standards of corporate governance and in balancing the interests of all stakeholders originates with the OECD, which predated and also informed its Ministerial advice. In 1997, the OECD commissioned a Business Sector Advisory Group with representatives from the United States, the United Kingdom, France, Germany, and Japan to consider whether there were common principles across industrialized markets—regardless of whether they were civil or common law countries, or had dispersed or concentrated ownership. The group compared notes, and worked over many months, to conclude that, indeed, all governance systems may reflect the particular legal, economic, and cultural setting. However, across markets, there were four principles that needed to guide corporate governance: transparency, accountability, fairness, and responsibility. The resulting report was a seminal document in global corporate governance and set the stage for harmonizing expectations in different markets. A core section of the report set out a discussion on corporate purpose as follows:

> In the production of goods and services, corporations serve as an efficient instrument of cooperation among all the required resource providers, such as suppliers of capital, labour, intellectual property and various professional skills.

By hosting relatively durable relations, corporations also form social networks. Long term cooperation and resulting mutual dependencies among owners, managers, employees, suppliers, consumers, local communities, etc, create loyalties, expectations and understandings that go beyond pure market interaction. (Quoted in Charkham and Simpson (1999))

The language of the OECD Principles (see box) was crafted to be inclusive of the shareholder primacy model of the common law country members of the OECD—notably the United States and the United Kingdom, as well as the stakeholder model of civil law countries, such as Germany, France, and Japan. The Principles garnered wide attention in the wake of the 1998 Asian financial crisis, which challenged the prevailing Washington Consensus at the World Bank and International Monetary Fund that the economic and social development of emerging markets would be best accomplished by privatizing state enterprises and liberalizing cross-border financial capital flows. The rapid growth based on this model was dubbed the Asia Miracle, reflected in a World Bank report of the same title. Devastatingly, in the summer of 1998, the miracle was transformed into the Asia crisis. Reflecting on the impact of the Asia crisis on regional economies, currencies, and even far-flung hedge funds in New York, James Wolfensohn, then World Bank President, commented that "the governance of companies is now as important to the world economy as the government of countries" (*The Economist*, Review 1998).

> **Balancing Shareholder and Stakeholder Interests**
> The OECD developed and promulgated its Principles of Corporate Governance using the Business Sector Advisory Group's report as a foundation. The OECD provided guidance for member states to balance shareholder and stakeholder interests, ensure timely and accurate disclosure, and require active board oversight, as follows:
>
> I. *The Rights of Shareholders*: The corporate governance framework should protect shareholders' rights.
> II. *The Equitable Treatment of Shareholders*: The corporate governance framework should ensure the equitable treatment of all shareholders, including minority and foreign shareholders. All shareholders should have the opportunity to obtain effective redress for violation of their rights.

(continued)

(continued)

III. *The Role of Stakeholders in Corporate Governance*: The corporate governance framework should recognize the rights of stakeholders as established by law and encourage active co-operation between corporations and stakeholders in creating wealth, jobs, and the sustainability of financially sound enterprises.

IV. *Disclosure and transparency*: The corporate governance framework should ensure that timely and accurate disclosure is made on all material matters regarding the corporation, including the financial situation, performance, ownership, and governance of the company.

V. *The Responsibilities of the Board*: The corporate governance framework should ensure the strategic guidance of the company, the effective monitoring of management by the board, and the board's accountability to the company and the shareholders.

The response was to address the governance deficit by establishing a new partnership between the World Bank, in the form of a Global Corporate Governance Forum, later integrated into the IFC—with Roundtables established to develop and adapt the OECD Principles to local market conditions, and develop white papers for reform. Subsequent to the publication of the OECD Principles, there has been a worldwide effort to codify national standards of corporate governance. The European Corporate Governance Institute maintains a repository of national codes and updates (European Corporate Governance Institute, 2019). There is some evidence that, during this period, corporate governance standards improved and converged in the majority of developed and emerging economies (De Nicolo, Laeven, & Ueda, 2008; Claessens & Yurtoglu, 2013).

Concluding Remarks

The scale and impact of corporate activity makes corporations indispensable partners in any effort to advance the sustainability of the global ecosystem. Our review of the history of the corporation demonstrates that the special privileges of the corporate form arose from links between public purpose and corporate activity. The twentieth-century nostrum that the purpose of corporations is above all to make profits for its shareholders, if necessary, at the expense of other stakeholders turns out to be a relatively new concept. There is growing pressure for companies to meet the wider needs of society—from the acknowledgment of the value of stakeholder focused corporate governance regimes, the advent of benefit corporations and investor efforts to measure the environmental and social impact of corporate activity. A key challenge for sustainable finance lies in shaping corporate governance cultures, along with advances in financial analytics, environmental pricing, instrument structuring, sustainability-aware security selection, and risk management to monitor and manage corporate impact on the environment and society.

An essential dimension of the corporate governance framework is corporate reporting, which is the channel through which owners and other stakeholders can check whether management is an effective steward of the capital invested in the corporation. The disclosure framework, parameterized by accounting and verification standards and norms of transparency, ensures that investors and society have a true and fair picture of the financial circumstances. The next chapter considers the significant value as well as the limitations of the existing financial accounting system for incorporating the management of human and natural capital within resource allocation. While there is considerable information on a company's reliance on natural and human capital available to the careful analyst of accounting information, there is also a need to supplement the view available from accounting statements with non-financial information. In addition, questions remain as to the content, reliability, optimal timing of, and time horizon of the reporting framework, which will be discussed in the next chapter.

NOTES

1. Hansmann et al. (2006) argue that entity shielding is an innovation that can only arise from the law, whereas limited liability, a more celebrated form of asset partitioning, can be implemented through the operation of contracts. Mahoney (2000) argues that entity shielding can and indeed did arise from contracts: "For most of the seventeenth and eighteenth centuries, the separate personality of business organizations survived in practice despite judicial and legislative attempts to undermine it."

2. Reflecting on the success of the English experiment to expand cheap company registration and invite a wider participation by offering limited liability in the late nineteenth century, *The Economist* commented that "the economic historian of the future may assign to the nameless inventor of the principle of limited liability, as applied to trading corporations, a place of

honour with Watt and Stephenson, and other pioneers of the industrial revolution. The genius of these men produced the means by which man's command of natural resources was multiplied many times over; the limited
liability company the means by which huge aggregations of capital required
to give effect to their discoveries were collected, organised and efficiently
administered." *The Economist*, December 18, 1926—quoted in Hunt
(1936).

3. See Bowen (2000) for a short history of the Company, written to com-
memorate the 400th anniversary of its founding.
4. Lal (2018) notes that it took Roe a long time to understand that he had to
negotiate with Nur Jahan as the effective ruler and not Jahangir. There is no
record among the extensive documents of the Mughal court that Jahangir
ever met Roe, or that he granted any trading privileges to him or the EIC.
5. The outcome of 1757 battle of Plassey was sealed by bribery and duplicity
rather than military prowess. It has been described as 'a transaction' rather
than a battle.
6. Pyramidal groups are an affiliated group of companies, controlled by an
apex shareholder through direct and indirect control holdings. Very often,
pyramidal groups allow one company or family to control an empire of companies with a relatively small portion of the invested capital of the companies
within the group. See section I.C of La Porta et al. (1999) for examples of
pyramidal groups.
7. Some markets have layers of both civil and common law frameworks,
explained by the history of waves of colonization bringing different legal
systems to bear (Indonesia and the Philippines being examples of countries
where such complexities apply).
8. Between 1976 and 2016, the number of listed companies per capita in the
U.S. dropped from 23 to 11. See Doidge, Kahle, Karolyi, and Stulz (2018)
for a detailed analysis of this phenomenon.
9. The share of equity capital raised through initial public offerings of $100
million or less in advanced economies fell steadily from 21% in 1994–2000
to 11% in 2014 (Organisation for Economic Cooperation and Development,
2015).

References

Abatino, B., Dari-Mattiacci, G., & Perotti, E. C. (2011). Depersonalization of
Business in Ancient Rome. *Oxford Journal of Legal Studies, 31*(2), 365–389.
https://doi.org/10.1093/ojls/gqr001
Alborn, T. L. (1998). *Conceiving Companies: Joint-Stock Politics in Victorian
England*. London, UK: Routledge.
Berle, A. A., & Means, G. C. (1932). *The Modern Corporation & Private Property*.
New York, NY: Macmillan.

Bowen, H. V. (2000). 400 Years of The East India Company. *History Today, 50*(7), 47.

Bris, D. L., Goetzmann, W. N., & Pouget, S. (2015). *The Development of Corporate Governance in Toulouse: 1372–1946* (NBER Working Papers: 21335). National Bureau of Economic Research, Inc. Retrieved from http://www.nber.org/papers/w21335.pdf

Charkham, J., & Simpson, A. (1999). *Fair Shares: The Future of Shareholder Power and Responsibility*. New York, NY: Oxford University Press.

Cho, M. (2017). Benefit Corporations in the United States and Community Interest Companies in the United Kingdom: Does Social Enterprise Actually Work? *Northwestern Journal of International Law and Business, 37*(1), 149–172.

Claessens, S., & Yurtoglu, B. B. (2013). Corporate Governance in Emerging Markets: A Survey. *Emerging Markets Review, 15,* 1–33. https://doi.org/10.1016/j.ememar.2012.03.002

Dal Bo, E. (2006). Regulatory Capture: A Review. *Oxford Review of Economic Policy, 22*(2), 203–225. https://academic.oup.com/oxrep/issue

Dale, R. (2004). *The First Crash: Lessons from the South Sea Bubble*. Princeton, NJ: Princeton University Press.

Dari-Mattiacci, G., Gelderblom, O., Jonker, J., & Perotti, E. C. (2017). The Emergence of the Corporate Form. *Journal of Law, Economics, and Organization, 33*(2), 193–236. https://academic.oup.com/jleo/issue

Davis, S. M., Lukomnik, J., & Pitt-Watson, D. (2006). *The New Capitalists: How Citizen Investors Are Reshaping the Corporate Agenda*. Boston, MA: Harvard Business School Press.

de Jong, A., & Roell, A. (2005). Financing and Control in the Netherlands: A Historical Perspective. In R. K. Morck (Ed.), *A History of Corporate Governance Around the World: Family Business Groups to Professional Managers* (pp. 467–506). Chicago, IL: University of Chicago Press.

De Nicolo, G., Laeven, L., & Ueda, K. (2008). Corporate Governance Quality: Trends and Real Effects. *Journal of Financial Intermediation, 17*(2), 198–228. http://www.sciencedirect.com/science/journal/10429573

Doidge, C., Kahle, K. M., Karolyi, G. A., & Stulz, R. M. (2018). *Eclipse of the Public Corporation or Eclipse of the Public Markets?* (NBER Working Papers: 24265). National Bureau of Economic Research, Inc. Retrieved from http://www.nber.org/papers/w24265.pdf

European Corporate Governance Institute. (2019). *Codes*. Retrieved from https://ecgi.global/content/codes

Farrell, J. (2016). Corporate Funding and Ideological Polarization About Climate Change. *Proceedings of the National Academy of Sciences of the United States of America, 113*(1), 92–97. https://doi.org/10.1073/pnas.1509433112

Fohlin, C. (2005). The History of Corporate Ownership and Control in Germany. In R. K. Morck (Ed.), *A History of Corporate Governance Around the World: Family Business Groups to Professional Managers* (pp. 223–277). Chicago, IL: University of Chicago Press.

Friedman, M. (1970, September 13). Social Responsibility of Business Is to Increase Its Profits. *New York Times Magazine*, 32.

Garber, P. M. (2000). *Famous First Bubbles: The Fundamentals of Early Manias.* Cambridge, MA: MIT Press.

Gelderblom, O., de Jong, A., & Jonker, J. (2011). An Admiralty for Asia. Isaac le Maire and Conflicting Conceptions About the Corporate Governance of the VOC. In J. Koppell (Ed.), *The Origins of Shareholder Advocacy* (pp. 29–60). New York, NY: Palgrave Macmillan.

Gelderblom, O., de Jong, A., & Jonker, J. (2013). The Formative Years of the Modern Corporation: The Dutch East India Company VOC, 1602–1623. *Journal of Economic History, 73*(4), 1050–1076. http://journals.cambridge.org/action/displayBackIssues?jid=JEH

Greg, W. R. (1853). *Essays on Political and Social Science, Contributed Chiefly to the Edinburgh Review.* London, UK: Longman, Brown, Green, and Longmans.

Hansmann, H., Kraakman, R., & Squire, R. (2006). Law and the Rise of the Firm. *Harvard Law Review, 119*(5), 1335–1403.

Harris, R. (1994). The Bubble Act: Its Passage and Its Effects on Business Organization. *Journal of Economic History, 54*(3), 610–627. http://journals.cambridge.org/action/displayBackIssues?jid=JEH

Harris, R. (2000). *Industrializing English Law: Entrepreneurship and Business Organization, 1720–1844.* Cambridge, UK: Cambridge University Press.

Hawley, J. P., & Williams, A. T. (2000). *The Rise of Fiduciary Capitalism: How Institutional Investors Can Make Corporate America More Democratic.* Philadelphia, PA: University of Pennsylvania Press.

Hillman, R. W. (1997). Limited Liability in Historical Perspective. *Washington & Lee Law Review, 54*, 615–627.

Hogfeldt, P. (2005). The History and Politics of Corporate Ownership in Sweden. In R. K. Morck (Ed.), *A History of Corporate Governance Around the World: Family Business Groups to Professional Managers* (pp. 517–579). Chicago, IL: University of Chicago Press.

Hunt, B. C. (1936). *The Development of the Business Corporation in England 1800–1867.* Cambridge, MA: Harvard University Press.

Inman, P. (2016, September 12). Study: Big Corporations Dominate List of World's Top Economic Entities. *The Guardian.* Retrieved from https://www.theguardian.com/business/2016/sep/12/global-justice-now-study-multinational-businesses-walmart-apple-shell

Iskander, M. R., & Chamlou, N. (2000). *Corporate Governance: A Framework for Implementation.* Washington, DC. Retrieved from http://documents.worldbank.org/curated/en/810311468739547854/pdf/multi-page.pdf

Jonsson, F. A. (2010). Rival Ecologies of Global Commerce: Adam Smith and the Natural Historians. *American Historical Review, 115*(5), 1342–1363.

Khanna, V. S. (2005). *The Economic History of the Corporate Form in Ancient India.* Retrieved from Available at SSRN: https://ssrn.com/abstract=796464

Kindleberger, C. P. (1996). *Manias, Panics, and Crashes: A History of Financial Crises* (3rd ed.). New York, NY: Wiley.

La Porta, R., Lopez-de-Silanes, F., & Shleifer, A. (1999). Corporate Ownership Around the World. *Journal of Finance, 54*(2), 471–517. http://onlinelibrary.wiley.com/journal/10.1111/%28ISSN%291540-6261/issues

Lal, R. (2018). *Empress: The Astonishing Reign of Nur Jahan.* New York, NY: W. W. Norton.

Mahoney, P. G. (2000). Contract or Concession? An Essay on the History of Corporate Law. *Georgia Law Review, 34*(2), 873–893.

Mayer, C. (2018). *Prosperity: Better Business Makes the Greater Good.* Oxford, UK: Oxford University Press.

Minnick, K., & Noga, T. (2017). The Influence of Firm and Industry Political Spending on Tax Management Among S&P 500 Firms. *Journal of Corporate Finance, 44,* 233–254. http://www.sciencedirect.com/science/journal/09291199

Morck, R. K. (2006). *A History of Corporate Governance Around the World: Family Business Groups to Professional Managers.* Chicago, IL: University of Chicago Press.

Murphy, A. E. (2005). Corporate Ownership in France: The Importance of History. In R. K. Morck (Ed.), *A History of Corporate Governance around the World: Family Business Groups to Professional Managers* (pp. 185–219). Chicago, IL: University of Chicago Press.

Organisation for Economic Cooperation and Development. (1999). *OECD Principles of Corporate Governance.* Paris, France: OECD Publishing.

Organisation for Economic Cooperation and Development. (2015). *Growth Companies, Access to Capital Markets and Corporate Governance: OECD Report to G20 Finance Ministers and Central Bank Governors.* Paris, France: OECD Publishing.

Robins, N. (2012). The Corporation that Changed the World: How The East India Company Shaped the Modern Multinational. *Asian Affairs, 43*(1), 12–26. https://doi.org/10.1080/03068374.2012.642512

Roy, K. (2011). The Hybrid Military Establishment of the East India Company in South Asia: 1750–1849. *Journal of Global History, 6*(2), 195–218. https://doi.org/10.1017/S1740022811000222

Sen, A. (1983). *Poverty and Famines: An Essay on Entitlement and Deprivation.* Oxford, UK: Oxford University Press.

Stern, P. J. (2011). Soldier and Citizen in the Seventeenth-Century English East India Company. *Journal of Early Modern History, 15*(1/2), 83–104. https://doi.org/10.1163/157006511X552769

Stigler, G. J. (1971). The Theory of Economic Regulation. *Bell Journal of Economics and Management Science, 2*(1), 3.

Sur, N. (1976). The Bihar Famine of 1770. *Indian Economic & Social History Review, 13*(4), 525–531.

Time. (1963). The Oldest Corporation In the World. *Time, 81*(11), 98.

Velde, F. R. (2016). What We Learn from a Sovereign Debt Restructuring in France in 1721. *Economic Perspectives, 40*(5), 1–17.

Warren, E. (2018, August 14). Companies Shouldn't be Accountable Only to Shareholders. *Wall Street Journal.*

Weimer, J., & Pape, J. C. (1999). A Taxonomy of Systems of Corporate Governance. *Corporate Governance: An International Review, 7*(2), 152.

Wright, R. E., & Sylla, R. (2011). Corporate Governance and Stockholder/Stakeholder Activism in the United States, 1790–1860: New Data and Perspectives. In J. Koppell (Ed.), *Origins of Shareholder Advocacy.* New York, NY: Palgrave Macmillan.

CHAPTER 4

Accounting for Sustainability: Frameworks for the Aggregation of Financial and Non-financial Metrics

As we note in Chap. 3, an essential pillar of corporate governance is accurate and timely disclosure, which enables investors to check whether management is an effective steward of the capital invested in the corporation. Corporate disclosure, parameterized by financial accounting standards, ensures that investors and society have a true and fair picture of corporate financial activity. Financial accounting is used to record, summarize, and report the monetary transactions of a business operation or an organization in any given period, and it is a form of communication between management and owners of a company. The summary impact of financial transactions is revealed in financial statements such as an income statement or a balance sheet. These statements are often compiled by certified accountants and are based on established principles designed to depict a comprehensive picture of a company's financial situation. In theory, these statements should allow investors to estimate accurately the financial value of their interest in a given entity. In addition to investors, other external stakeholders, such as employees, suppliers, consumers, regulators, and broader civil society, routinely rely on financial statements to form a partial picture of corporate financial health.

The broader environmental and social impact of corporate activity has not hitherto been the subject of financial reporting practices. As we noted in Chap. 1, the Principles for Responsible Investment articulate a belief in the value of integrating environmental, social, and governance considerations in financial decision-making. Long-term investors are incorporating

© The Author(s) 2019

S. Bose et al., *The Financial Ecosystem*, Palgrave Studies in Impact Finance, https://doi.org/10.1007/978-3-030-05624-7_4

non-financial indicators such as carbon emissions intensity, energy efficiency, employee turnover, and brand loyalty to assessments of company value, innovative capacity, and alignment with the common good. In addition, the number of environmentally conscious consumers is increasing and consumer loyalty to a particular brand often depends upon the brand's social and environmental awareness. Internally, company employees (especially millennials) are demanding a corporate culture that is environmentally and socially friendly. The increasing discussion of broader measures of success, such as the triple bottom line, and efforts to weave sustainability into the daily operation of organizations has heightened the profile of beneficial social impact as an important corporate objective. Finally, modest pressure from some regulatory institutions to analyze the risks of climate change and extreme weather on corporate balance sheets has led to investor interest in greater disclosure on the local impact of global climate trends on corporate assets and supply chains. There is thus widespread interest in revising accounting and disclosure frameworks to track quantitative measures of non-financial performance and incorporate geospatially specific analysis of climate-related risks and opportunities. Both the largest corporations and smaller enterprises have sharply increased their reporting of non-financial performance through the issuance of corporate sustainability reports and disclosure regarding corporate responsibility efforts.

The Measurement of Earnings and the Rate of Return

Dating back to the earliest recorded historical periods, accounting is a social practice that developed so that economic activity could be recorded and summarized for the benefit of governments, wealthy families, and other stakeholders. Indeed, the earliest known written texts dating back to 3200 BC consist of accounting records (Provasi & Farag, 2013). Sequences of pictographs, found on clay tablets in Uruk in modern-day Iraq, have been deciphered to be lists and amounts of goods taken out and distributed to workers. With the development of agriculture, human beings, for the first time, were able to accumulate stores of goods. Trade emerged, giving rise to the need for record keeping. When recorded inventories first appeared in Mesopotamia around 4000 BC, they were used to count things in the form of object-specific 'concrete counting'. For example, one character or object denoted five apples; another character denoted five pears. Given the numerous types of goods to count, such as food, clothing, shelter, and labor, this method became cumbersome over time, and the lack of abstract numbers became a real problem.

A system with abstract numbers developed gradually in conjunction with the development of writing in many distinct civilizations and then spread rapidly as trade and commerce flourished. Large agricultural societies grew into empires, which were funded by the collection of taxes. Egyptian bookkeepers started to keep a record of inventories for the royal families using bone labels around 3000 BC. Soon wealthy families of other societies also began keeping records of inventories to reflect what they owned and owed. One primitive technique of record keeping was to knot a cord; this later evolved into drawing inscriptions on clay tablets.

It was not until the end of the fifteenth century that the double-entry bookkeeping, as we know it today, was developed. Luca Pacioli, an Italian monk, published a textbook in 1494 that demonstrated how double-entry bookkeeping could effectively separate out the resources of an entity from any claim on those resources by other entities. He essentially devised a balance sheet with separate entries for 'credit' and 'debit', which serves as the foundation for today's financial accounting system. Pacioli is often credited as the father of modern accounting, though his system is exclusively focused on record keeping rather than the computation of periodic profit, return analysis, or asset valuation. Pacioli's system was developed for Venetian traders and small businesses, as owners were heavily invested in understanding the current health of their businesses.

Double-entry bookkeeping by itself is not sufficient to compute the rate of return on invested capital. For this calculation, it is also essential that the accounting system record interim net profits by incorporating periodic evaluations of assets, most notably inventory, and record a charge for the depreciation of assets. The accounting records of the East India Company (EIC) facilitated such calculation of interim rates of return; the system of double-entry bookkeeping maintained by the VOC did not (Robertson & Funnell, 2012). The computation of a rate of return on invested capital has been described as the sine qua non of capitalism, since without it, it makes no sense to speak of a system where capital is a factor of production and receives a return. Capitalism can be described as a practice that strives to continually expand a stock of wealth by searching for the maximum rate of return on the disembodied factor of production we call capital. Only a system that calculates periodic net income and maintains a continual record of capital employed can facilitate such a practice.[1]

With the rise of the corporate economy and the dispersed ownership of large scale business enterprises in the nineteenth century described in Chap. 3, the provision of financial statements to absentee shareholders and creditors became routine. The accounting profession, its standards, and the use of auditors developed in the late nineteenth and early twentieth centuries. The audit profession developed to serve owners' needs to check management performance. The separation of ownership and control mirrored the bifurcation of accounting into financial accounting and managerial accounting. Not only did owners and those working for the corporation need a reliable internal accounting system to track the embedded costs of inventory in various stages of the manufacturing process but external investors, such as shareholders and bondholders, needed to be informed in a concise manner of the summary financial impact of periodic corporate activity. Audits were not required, but were voluntarily paid for by owners to guard against management fraud.

The increased complexity of business and financial activities called for standardized accounting principles as well as dedicated accounting professionals. The second half of the nineteenth century saw the formation of groups of accounting professionals: the Institute of Accountants in Glasgow (1854), the Institute of Chartered Accountants of England and Wales (1880), the Société Académique de Comptabilité in France (1881), and the American Association of Public Accountants in the United States (1887). The accounting bodies generally created and administered certification tests for the admission of prospective accountants into the profession.

In the United States, before 1934, accounting disclosure requirements were set by the stock exchanges and could differ significantly across exchanges. In 1917, the American Institute of Accountants collaborated with the Federal Trade Commission to develop guidelines for accounting and auditing procedures, but there was no regulatory requirement for companies to follow such guidelines (Moonitz, 1970). In 1934, following the 1929 stock market crash and the subsequent Great Depression, the US Congress established the SEC in an effort to restore public trust in the financial markets. The SEC was vested with the authority to determine required accounting methods and minimum levels of corporate financial disclosure. In 1939, under pressure from the SEC's Chief Accountant, the Committee on Accounting Procedure (CAP) of the American Institute of Accountants began to issue Accounting Research Bulletins, which subsequently formed the basis of what is today referred to as generally accepted accounting principles (GAAP) (Zeff, 2005). The CAP is the predecessor of the Financial Accounting Standards Board (FASB) formed in 1973. The GAAP formalized and standardized financial accounting practices in the United States, with variants being adopted in national jurisdictions globally. The primary focus of GAAP was to increase the quality of reported earnings and its components (Ely & Waymire, 1999). Accounting earnings forecasts are routinely prepared by investment analysts, and the price-earnings ratio is the most frequently cited valuation multiple. Management compensation routinely depends on accounting earnings. The singular focus of GAAP, of financial observers, and of incentive compensation plans on earnings makes this particular metric a high-stakes performance measure. In the terminology of principal-agent theory, earnings are the basis of *high-powered incentives.* High-powered incentives are performance-based compensation plans where an agent's pay increases sharply with the measure of performance (in this case, earnings).[2]

LIMITATIONS OF THE FOCUS ON ACCOUNTING EARNINGS

Modern-day accounting practices based on these principles call for companies to produce four types of external financial statements. These are the *income statement,* the *balance sheet,* the *cash flow statement,* and the *shareholders' equity statement.* The income statement, also known as the profit and loss statement, summarizes a company's profitability during a given period by reporting revenues, cost of sales, and operating expenses, such as salaries, utility bills, and rents. Balance sheets reflect the financial condition of a company at a point in time, listing its assets, liabilities, and shareholders' equity: essentially what the company owns and owes. A balance sheet is also referred to as the statement of financial condition. The cash flow statement summarizes the major categories of cash inflows and outflows experienced by the company within a given period, typically due to operating, investing, and financing activities. The stockholders' equity statement describes the changes in the equity position of the company's shareholders in the same period as the income and cash flow statements.

The system of double-entry bookkeeping, by requiring two equal and opposite entries for every transaction and by linking accounts of stocks and flows, constrains in a mechanical way any effort to fraudulently overstate assets or earnings. A fraudulent increase in earnings, if the accounts are to remain in balance, must be accompanied by a corresponding increase in assets or reduction in liabilities. The balances in the asset and liability accounts are verifiable at any point in time. Asset overstatement is relatively easy to discover, since an auditor can in principle verify the existence and valuation of everything listed as an asset. Liability understatement is more difficult to detect, since the auditor must imagine possible unstated liabilities and check if they have been incorporated in the accounts. The former task starts from a defined list of assets; the latter involves starting from an infinite range of possibilities. This need to start from an infinite range of possibilities to verify that liabilities have not been understated implies that it is ultimately impossible to provide complete assurance on the integrity of any balance sheet.[3] These conclusions can be viewed as implications of Alan Turing's theorem stating that there exists no general algorithm that can ensure that every possible pair of computer programs and program inputs will halt execution (Turing, 1937, 1938). Another related implication of this Theorem is that it is impossible to design a virus checker that can detect any possible virus. Similarly, no set of rules can ensure that accounting fraud is eliminated.

Incentives for Earnings Management

Predictably, the establishment and subsequent refinement of GAAP did not eliminate financial accounting scandals and crises. Corporate management often has an incentive to manage earnings and to delay or conceal bad news. Most cash and stock incentive compensation plans for corporate management depend on accounting results. This can create an incentive for management to overstate current period financial profitability at the expense of future period earnings or by understating liabilities, which in turn creates a market for innovative financial products that facilitate such window-dressing behavior (Imhoff Jr., 2003). More generally, high-powered incentives induce slanted presentations of accounting data and even in some cases outright accounting fraud (Admati, 2017). Auditors provide little comfort to investors in this context. One observer states: "Auditors are supposed to be watchdogs, but ... they sometimes looked like lapdogs—more interested in serving the companies they audited than in assuring a flow of accurate information to investors" (Ronen, 2010).

For example, the infamous bankruptcy of Enron was the result of many years of financial window dressing. The Texas-based natural gas and electricity giant was once the seventh-largest company in the United States and was named by Fortune Magazine as America's most innovative company for six years (Dobson, 2006). In late 2001, it was revealed that the

Enron management, in collusion with the company's auditor Arthur Andersen, had committed financial fraud using convoluted financial transactions, accounting loopholes, fake trades by shell companies and special purpose entities, all designed to hide the company's ballooning liabilities, overstate current profitability, and convert cash flow from financing into cash flow from operations (Smith, 2011).

The Curious Case of the Scallop Exodus

In early 2018, Dalian Zhangzidao Fisheries Group, one of the China's largest seafood producers, announced that it had experienced a net loss of CNY 629 million (USD 96 million) for calendar year 2017. The announcement was unanticipated as the first three quarters of the year had been profitable. Dalian Zhangzidao claimed that they had experienced an 'abnormal inventory' of their scallops and as a result was recording a CNY 578 million inventory impairment. In a statement, the company explained that the irregular temperature change in the Northern Yellow Sea coupled with an insufficient level of biological fodder led to a decrease in the stocks of scallops. Dubbed the 'scallop exodus' by the media, the incident generated much publicity, with the public and some investors accusing the company of financial fraud. An investigation by China's Security Regulatory Commission is underway, and analysts suggest it is common for the industry to engage in fraudulent activities and manipulation of their accounts in the absence of a standardized inventory assessment mechanism in the Chinese agriculture sector (Li, 2018).

In what appeared to be a comparatively simple accounting fraud, the SEC in 2002 alleged that Waste Management Inc. (North America's largest waste treatment and environmental services company) and its auditor (Arthur Andersen) had perpetrated accounting fraud between 1992 and 1997. In the 20 years from 1971 to 1991, Waste Management had grown exponentially and expanded its revenue by nearly 470 times from $16 million to more than $7.5 billion (Securities and Exchange Commission, 2002). However, to overstate current profit, the company's senior management began to inflate salvage values of their assets by extending the useful lives of trucks, landfills, and other equipment. Furthermore, company officials avoided recording some of the expenses associated with failed projects and bribed their auditor to overstate fraudulently the company's equity value.

Another well-known financial fraud case was that of Lehman Brothers, whose bankruptcy in September 2008 is the largest in history and triggered the sub-prime mortgage financial crisis and the subsequent Great Recession. All of these cases involve blatant manipulation of corporate financial statements, often involving collusion with company auditors. In the case of Lehman Brothers, the investment bank manipulated its balance sheet by treating large amounts of repurchase agreements (a form of short-term loan) as sales, which allowed the company to exclude the related liabilities and also to use the cash from the 'sales' to retire other collateralized debt securities (Markham, 2015; Valukas, 2010). This fraudulent operation significantly reduced Lehman Brothers' leverage ratio and misled investors into believing that its financial health was better than in reality.

The Decision-Theoretic Basis for Integrating ESG Information

These cases demonstrate that the overstatement of current earnings and the corresponding overstatement of assets or the understatement of future liabilities is a common type of accounting fraud. It should not be surprising that when accounting earnings is by far the most important metric of success, then unscrupulous management might be expected to attempt to distort that very metric, by managing or manipulating accounting earnings. It is a well-established tenet of principal-agent theory that high-powered incentives increase the likelihood of fraud (Jacob & Levitt, 2003). In the presence of asymmetric information about the level of managerial effort, the principal can improve her welfare by conditioning agent compensation on as many different metrics of success as possible. A corresponding principle in decision theory states that combining multiple forecasts (generated by different analysts, experts, or models) leads to significantly improved forecast accuracy (Clemen, 1989). The principle of averaging many diverse predictions to produce more accurate estimates is the basis of many forecasting algorithms in climate and meteorology forecasting, real-time macro-economic forecasting, electricity demand forecasting, and psychiatric diagnosis. Therefore, investors should expect to improve their monitoring of corporate management by combining standard accounting information with a diverse array of other metrics of success. These other metrics have been called *non-financial* information, *environmental, social, and governance* (or 'ESG') indicators and *sustainability* indicators. In principle, transparency on other metrics could discourage the manipulation of a single high-stakes metric of success by increasing the probability that the manipulated metric would look incongruous next to the many other disclosed metrics. As noted by Justice Brandeis, "Sunlight is said to be the best of disinfectants; electric light the most efficient policeman" (Brandeis, 1914).

Measurement of Externalities

Financial statements have hitherto been designed to elucidate the financial health of a company and give investors the means to measure the current monetary earnings of a company. The origins of financial accounting as a system for monitoring the private interests of owners of firms imbue the discipline with a narrow focus on *monetary* and *private* costs and benefits. This is demonstrated by a consideration of the difference between the *accounting* and *economic* concepts of profit. Accounting profit consists of the monetary value of revenue earned by the entity less monetary expenses incurred by the entity. The measurement of accounting profit ignores any notion of the opportunity cost of capital—the value of alternate uses of financial, human, or natural capital. The concept of economic profit, on the other hand, is calculated with an allowance for the opportunity cost of financial and human capital (although not for natural capital).[4] Furthermore, traditional financial accounting does not recognize the economic concept of an *externality*, that is, the costs and benefits incurred by an unrelated third party as a side effect of a transaction between two parties. Accounting for externalities is at the heart of measuring the societal impact of corporate activity. There is a small sub-field within accounting science known as social and environmental accounting that seeks to broaden the focus of accounting principles to include opportunity costs and externalities (Bebbington & Larrinaga, 2014). An important area within this sub-field is the study of *full cost accounting*, which is an attempt to incorporate the estimated monetary value of pollution resulting from corporate activity in accounts measuring environmental resources maintained by the corporation (Atkinson, 2000). There are precious few examples of true cost accounts maintained by actual corporations. A notable example is the Environmental Profit and Loss Account published by Kering Corporation, a European luxury goods conglomerate, which estimates the monetary value of the societal loss resulting from the air pollution, solid waste generation, water usage, and other forms of natural capital depletion in the supply chain of its luxury brands. This is a remarkably forthright analysis, since it is not in the obvious interest of Kering to compute and reveal the external costs that its supply chain imposes on society. Kering's continued commitment to this level of transparency is perhaps an indication of the willingness of some corporate decision-makers to move beyond the dialogue of shareholder value to societal value and systemic boundary concerns. We describe the construction and implications of Kering's externality accounting in detail in Chap. 7.

Broadening of Performance Metrics by Investors and Other Stakeholders

As we noted in Chap. 1, the scale and power of corporate activity implies that any serious effort to enhance the sustainability of natural and human capital must incorporate an assessment of the linkages between corporate activity and the broader ecosystem. A range of stakeholders, including consumers, employees, suppliers, civil society, and regulators demand information on the non-financial impact of corporate activity. Investors, as suppliers of capital, have a special role to play insofar as they can allocate capital to corporate activities that minimize adverse impact or facilitate innovation that pushes away planetary boundaries. Investment strategies that integrate environment, social, and governance (ESG) factors have grown dramatically in recent years. ESG integration is the driving goal of the PRI (see Chap. 1), which has experienced a sharp rise in the number of signatories. In particular, investors with longer term horizons, such as pension and sovereign wealth funds, insurance companies, foundations, and endowments have been prominent among asset owners focused on the integration of ESG information in security selection. Large institutional investors such as Japan's Government Pension Investment Fund (the largest pool of retirement savings in the world), the Norwegian Future Fund (the largest sovereign wealth fund), and CalPERS (the largest asset owner in the United States) have actively embraced and incorporated ESG strategies into their investment portfolios. The amount of assets invested with socially responsible principles rose to more than a quarter of total assets under professional management (Global Sustainable Investment Alliance, 2019). In 2017, amongst the 250 largest corporations by revenue, 93% issued corporate responsibility reports that include non-financial data. This proportion is up from 35% in 1999 (KPMG, 2017). The European Union requires large public-interest companies with more than 500 employees to disclose certain non-financial information on environmental and social impact of corporate activity. The EU non-financial reporting directive (Directive 2014/95/EU) applies to approximately 6000 companies, including publicly listed companies, banks, and insurers (European Union, 2014).

SUSTAINABILITY MEASUREMENT

The demand for the monitoring and assessment of quantitative non-financial metrics of corporate economic activity parallels global calls for sustainable development. As noted in Chap. 1, one reasonable interpretation of sustainability is the identification and protection of the sources of repeatable flows of benefits. In the context of finance, a holistic understanding of the drivers of the sustainability of cash flows implies integrating reporting on the levels of natural and human capital that facilitate long-term returns. At a broad level, there is a commonality between the calls of civil society for sustainable development, that is, the balancing of economic growth and environmental and social objectives, and the interest of corporate investors in avoiding companies that generate short-term returns from the unsustainable liquidation of natural and human capital. Furthermore, our recognition of the advent of the citizen investor and dispersed ownership (described in Chaps. 1 and 3) suggests that viewing investors as primarily owners of and lenders to companies is a woefully incomplete description. The investor constituency now intersects far more broadly than in previous centuries with the consumer, employee, and community constituencies. In this section, we will find it productive to describe frameworks for sustainability measurement that were created in the context of corporate activity and shareholders, as well as sustainable development and a broader cross-section of stakeholders.

SUSTAINABILITY FRAMEWORKS AND STANDARDS

There are myriad frameworks and standards proposed and developed by various organizations and researchers, which are qualitative categorizations of the components of sustainability used to group and isolate related quantitative indicators. One of the earliest, and still highly influential frameworks to incorporate non-financial measures of performance into the evaluation of corporate activity is the Triple Bottom Line (Elkington, 1998), inspired by the concept of sustainable development. John Elkington argued that corporations should measure their net performance in the following three 'bottom lines': the financial 'profit and loss' account, the social 'people' account, and the environmental 'planet' account. Measuring sustainability based on these three categories does not imply that corporations maximize returns on all three dimensions, but rather that the social, environmental, and economic performance of an entity is summarized with a selected set of indicators. The Triple Bottom Line represents one of the most widely accepted frameworks to evaluate an institution's performance in sustainable development.

GRI: Stakeholder Reporting

Perhaps the most common example of a Triple Bottom Line categorization of non-financial information are the reporting standards developed by the Global Reporting Initiative (GRI), which was founded by the Coalition for Environmentally Responsible Economies (CERES), the United Nations Environmental Program, and the Tellus Institute in 1997. In 2016, GRI launched its global standards for sustainability reporting, based on its 4th version of reporting guidelines launched in 2013. The GRI Standards include 6 standards guiding reporting on economic performance, 8 standards on environmental performance, and 19 standards on social performance (see Table 4.1).

GRI Standards are designed to guide the voluntary preparation of sustainability reports, which are generally published annually, separately from regulatory quarterly, half-yearly, and annual filings required by securities regulators. GRI is by far the most widely adopted framework for sustainability reporting. Its database lists nearly 6988 sustainability reports for 2016, of

Table 4.1   GRI global topic-specific standards

Economic standards:	Social standards:
Economic performance	Employment and labor-management relations
Market presence	Occupational health and safety
Indirect economic impacts	Training and education
Procurement practices	Diversity and equal opportunity
Anti-corruption	Non-discrimination
Anti-competitive behavior	Freedom of association and collective bargaining
	Child labor
Environmental standards:	Forced or compulsory labor
Materials	Security practices
Energy	Rights of indigenous peoples
Water and effluents	Human rights assessment
Biodiversity	Local communities
Emissions	Supplier social assessment
Waste	Public policy
Environmental compliance	Customer Health and Safety
Supplier environmental assessment	Marketing and Labeling
	Customer privacy
	Socioeconomic compliance

Source: Adapted from www.globalreporting.org/standards

which 4534 (65%) are prepared according to GRI guidelines. The intended audience of the GRI consists of a broad range of stakeholders, including investors, consumers, employees, and civil society. GRI's mission is "to empower decisions that create social, environmental and economic benefits for everyone" (GRI, 2019). This focus on a range of stakeholders arises from GRI's origins within the United Nations dialogue around sustainable development. Investors are not a privileged stakeholder in that discourse.

An example of an issue that demonstrates GRI's focus on the broad range of stakeholders is its current draft Standard on disclosure on Tax and Payments to Governments. In a detailed account of the available methods of valuing intellectual capital and allocating it to tax-advantaged jurisdictions, Wiederhold (2014) demonstrates how multinational companies can drastically and legally reduce their tax burden. In a study of French firm-level data on arms' length and intra-firm export prices, Davies, Martin, Parenti, and Toubal (2018) demonstrate that tax avoidance through transfer pricing between affiliates of the same multinational group is economically significant. They note that export prices for intra-firm exports of differentiated products (whose market prices are harder to verify) are significantly lower for exports to tax haven destinations, whereas such destinations do not influence export prices for arms-length transactions. If a multinational exports to an affiliate in a tax haven at an artificially low price, it can deflate profits in the exporting (high-tax) country and inflate profits in the importing tax haven jurisdiction. Their work suggests that the manipulation of internal transfer pricing is largely a phenomenon for large firms. They note that the majority of tax losses for the French government are driven by the exports of approximately 450 multinationals resident in France or owned by a French group to 10 tax haven jurisdictions. GRI's draft standard, which is expected to be promulgated by the end of 2019, would require public country-by-country reporting of taxes paid by a multinational corporation. Such disclosure would sharply increase transparency for taxing jurisdictions and has the potential to discourage aggressive tax avoidance. In theory, tax avoidance benefits shareholders and certain accounting and tax advisory professionals, but adversely affects the funds available for public infrastructure and social welfare, hurting almost all other stakeholders. It can be argued that universal owners (see Chap. 3) have a collective incentive to minimize the adverse effects of aggressive tax avoidance since they bear a significant share of the burden of externalities that cannot be ameliorated due to precarious government financing. It is worth noting that the shareholder-focused accounting frameworks (IIRC and SASB) discussed below have so far failed to propose any standard on tax transparency.

IIRC: Integrated Reporting for Investors

The Integrated Reporting framework developed by the International Integrated Reporting Council (IIRC) aims to "improve the quality of information available to providers of financial capital to enable a more efficient and productive allocation of capital". Unlike the GRI, the IIRC explicitly targets providers of financial capital, while recognizing that there are multiple forms of capital. It aims to "enhance accountability and stewardship for the broad base of capitals (financial, manufactured, intellectual, human, social and relationship, and natural) and promote understanding of their interdependencies" (IIRC, 2013). The IIRC was originally convened in 2010 by the Accounting for Sustainability project (A4S) of the Prince of Wales Charities and the GRI, drawing on the earlier work of A4S and the King reports on corporate governance in South Africa.

The IIRC framework is significantly more difficult to apply than the GRI Standard, being principle-based and requiring a re-evaluation of the organization's 'business model' and how it creates value using the six types of capital outlined in the framework. The framework's articulation of the importance of six different types of capital is unique and shows promise that it might recognize the importance of different stakeholders in the value creation process. However, the IIRC's 2013 standard has been criticized for its privileging of financial capital, its focus on providers of financial capital to listed companies, and its exclusion of context-based sustainability considerations (McElroy & Thomas, 2017). Outside of South Africa, the adoption of the IIRC framework has lagged far behind that of GRI. Based on the authors' analysis of information available at the Corporate Register,[5] the number of organizations using the IIRC framework for its sustainability report was approximately 15% of the number of organizations using GRI Standards. According to data from the Corporate Register, the only country where the IIRC framework is more widely adopted than GRI is South Africa, likely because the Johannesburg Stock Exchange has required integrated reporting for its listed companies since 2009. It is important to note that the GRI Standard and the IIRC framework are not mutually exclusive choices, but are complementary tools. A corporation may use the IIRC framework to select the key performance metrics while using the GRI Standard to guide the calculation of the selected metrics. Even in South Africa, companies which are required to use the IIRC framework often use the GRI Standard to compute their non-financial metrics. Based on the data available from the Corporate Register, it is not possible to identify the proportion of reporters who use both IIRC and GRI.

SASB: Focus on Materiality

In contrast to the GRI and in common with the IIRC, the Sustainability Accounting Standards Board (SASB) in the United States has adopted a focus on investors as the primary audience.[6] The SASB Foundation was formed in 2011 by Jean Rogers, under the patronage of Michael Bloomberg, former Mayor of New York city and founder of the Bloomberg information service. Its mission is "to establish disclosure standards on sustainability matters that facilitate communication by companies to investors of decision-useful information" (SASB, 2018). In November 2018, SASB issued 77 different standards covering the minimum sustainability reporting requirements for industries in 11 different sectors.

SASB has emphasized the notion of 'financial materiality', meaning that its standards focus on sustainability matters that are "reasonably likely to have a material impact on financial performance or condition". SASB has chosen, through its multi-stakeholder process of standards creation, to identify the specific sustainability issues that are material to each of 11 sectors for which it has issued standards. SASB has developed the SASB Materiality Map to codify its assessment of materiality by sector and sustainability issue. The delineation of materiality by sector can be justified: for example, carbon emissions from fuel combustion are likely to be a more material issue for the transportation sector than it is for the financial sector. In this vein, according to the Map, business ethics is likely to be a material issue for more than 50% of the industries in the financials and healthcare sectors. It is likely to be a material issue for less than 50% of the industries in the extractives and mineral processing, infrastructure, resource transformation, services and transportation sectors. It is likely not to be a material issue in the consumer goods, food and beverage, renewable resources and alternative energy, and technology and communications sectors. This *ex ante* determination of what issue might be material to what industry is meant to ease the analytical burden on corporations and investors. The Materiality Map reduces the work of an investment analyst, who can now rest assured that she need only limit her due diligence to the reduced set of issues for any specific industry. This is in contrast to the GRI, which does not make any pronouncements on materiality, leaving the identification of material issues to the corporate report issuer or other stakeholders.

The codification of materiality can go a little too far. In a world of disruptive change for many industries, the hope that certain issues could be identified as negligible through a cumbersome and occasional process of standard-setting is ambitious at best. As outlined in its Materiality Map, SASB determined that business ethics issues are not likely to be material for the technology and communications sector. SASB defines 'business ethics' as "the company's approach to managing risks surrounding ethical conduct of business, including fraud, corruption, bribery and facilitation payments, fiduciary responsibilities, and other behavior that may have an ethical component". A casual internet search for 'technology industry fraud' conducted in January 2019 returned two relevant links within the first five search results. The first was an industry report from Ernst and Young on increasing fraud risks in the IT sector in India. The second was an article from the Seattle Times about a Redmond CEO charged with obtaining fraudulent visas for employees sub-contracted to various technology companies (Lerman, 2018). Perhaps the Materiality Map is a little too optimistic about the potential risks of questionable business ethics in the technology sector.

The relatively recent inception of the SASB standards implies that it is too early to judge whether they will be as widely adopted as the GRI framework. Their focus on the investor will undoubtedly limit the possibility of garnering the universal legitimacy that a stakeholder-focused initiative such as the GRI can aspire to.

IRIS: Simplified Metrics for Impact

The Impact Reporting and Investment Standards (IRIS) is a catalogue of performance metrics that many impact investors use to measure social, environmental, and financial performance. It was developed by the Global Impact Investing Network (GIIN), which was convened by the Rockefeller Foundation in 2009. In 2011, 29 impact investors signed a letter of support for the IRIS framework, committing to using the framework for the performance measurement of their own funds. The impact investing community is significantly smaller than the global listed equity marketplace (see Chap. 11), so that an initiative supported by 29 organizations in this community carries significantly more weight than it would in the listed equities marketplace. ImpactBase, the database of impact data prepared in accordance with the IRIS standard, contains social, environmental, and financial performance metrics for 5000 organizations that are beneficiaries of impact investing funds.

B Impact and Future Fit: SME Assessment

The GRI, IIRC, and SASB frameworks are targeted toward large corporations. The IRIS has been designed for recipients of impact investing funds, which tend to be small enterprises and community organizations. Two other frameworks, the B Impact and the FutureFit Benchmark, are designed for small and medium size enterprises. The B Impact framework is used as the basis for certification by B Labs as a B corporation. The Global Impact Investing Rating System (GIIRS) rates impact funds that invest in companies that have been rated according the B Impact framework. The FutureFit Benchmark is a publicly available guideline designed for firms to self-assess the fitness of their mission and operations for a systemically sustainable future.

Climate-Related Frameworks

There are a number of frameworks for climate-related indicators such as the Climate Disclosure Standards Board (CDSB), the Carbon Disclosure Protocol (CDP), the recommendations of the Taskforce on Climate-related Financial Disclosure (TCFD), and the declarations of the Natural Capital Protocol. While these climate-related frameworks will be described in detail in Chap. 7, a key distinction should be drawn between efforts that aim to measure the environmental impact of corporate activity such as the early versions of CDP and efforts to measure the impact of changes in environment and climate on corporate balance sheets and financial performance (such as the TCFD).

Other Frameworks

A number of other frameworks deserve mention, even though they are not specifically designed for the financial ecosystem. Most frameworks we have described so far consist of lists of indicators or principles, without attempting to model the relationships between different state variables within the social and natural systems in the world. An early framework for sustainable development indicators which incorporates linkages between indicators is the pressure-state-response (PSR) framework developed by the OECD. The PSR framework lays the groundwork for many subsequent sustainability measurement models by describing the process in which human activities create particular pressures on the social and natural environment, eliciting responses from societal, economic, and environmental agents (Singh, Murty, Gupta, & Dikshit, 2009). The PSR model delineates how people influence their surrounding environment and how the environment reacts. Organizations were able to use this model to measure the impact of their actions on the environment, and to evaluate the impact of different management response options. The PSR model was later revised to the more comprehensive driver-pressure-state-impact-response (DPSIR) model. An exploration of the DPSIR framework is fruitful for evaluating the relative impacts of mitigation and adaptation on climate-induced changes in financial performance.

Frameworks have also been developed to provide qualitative evaluation of composite environmental, social, and economic indicators. For example, the Barometer of Sustainability (Prescott-Allen, 1995) was developed to evaluate simultaneously the environmental and social aspects of sustainability. The Ecological Footprint (Wackernagel & Rees, 1998) computes the putative area of land needed to produce enough food, water, and energy and to dispose of waste that would be required for a person, a product, or a city. The Eco-Efficiency Framework, first outlined in Schmidheiny and Zorraquin (1996), was developed by the World Business Council on Sustainable Development (WBCSD) to assist large corporations investing in developing countries to maximize the efficiency of their use of environmental resources.

Societal Broadening of Performance Metrics: From MDGs to SDGs

In parallel with investor initiatives to broaden performance metrics of companies, the United Nations (UN) has pursued a process of expanding the quantitative measures of social and environmental performance, culminating in the development of the Sustainable Development Goals (SDGs) in 2015. Led by the UN, representatives from 196 member states joined together to create a framework for governments, the private sector, and civil society to promote and catalyze sustainable development. The SDGs were an expansion from the earlier Millennium Development Goals (MDGs) established in 2000, which comprised eight goals with specific targets to be achieved in 2015 (see Table 4.2). The richer nations were to provide funds through international organizations such as the World Bank and the IMF to assist poorer nations in achieving these goals. Progress on the MDGs was limited. The poverty alleviation target (cut extreme poverty[7] by half from its 1990 level) was achieved largely due the progress made by South and East Asian countries, specifically China and India, whereas progress in sub-Saharan African countries was limited. China and India were not significant recipients of foreign development funds. Nepal and Bangladesh saw significant improvements in child mortality.

In 2015, the UN replaced the MDGs with the SDGs. The SDGs are more expansive, universal, and ambitious. Perhaps most significantly, the SDGs are designed to specifically emphasize development goals that encompass a broader range of performance categories. The SDGs encour-

Table 4.2   MDGs and achievement status by 2015

	Goal	Major achievement as of 2015
MDG 1	Eradicate Extreme Poverty and Hunger	Globally, number of people living in extreme poverty reduced by half
MDG 2	Achieve universal primary education	Global number of out-of-school children reduced by half
MDG 3	Promote gender equality and empower women	90% of countries have more women in parliament
MDG 4	Reduce child mortality	Global child mortality rate reduced by half
MDG 5	Improve maternal health	Global maternal mortality ratio reduced by 45%
MDG 6	Combat HIV/AIDS, malaria, and other diseases	Global antiretroviral therapy treatment expanded 17 times from 2003 to 2014
MDG 7	Ensure environmental sustainability	91% of global population has improved drinking water access
MDG 8	Develop a global partnership for development	Financial assistance from developed countries increased by 66%

Source: Adapted from United Nations (2015)

age nations and private actors to conceptualize the triple bottom line of people, profit, and planet and strive for economic growth that balances social and economic development with environmental sustainability. As Table 4.3 illustrates, the SDGs added economic goals that were absent in the MDGs. While the MDGs largely focused on social development, the SDGs include many goals related to environmental sustainability.

Recognizing the complex nature of sustainable development, the SDGs expanded upon the eight MDGs and now include 17 comprehensive goals, with distinct additions such as clean water, innovation and infrastructure, sustainable cities, climate action, and peace. The MDGs called for assisted development of the poorer nations by the richer ones. Acknowledging that many development issues transcend national boundaries and equally affect all nations, the SDGs are universal and ask that all countries work to achieve the same goals locally. This eliminates the patronizing tone of the North-South dichotomy of the MDGs. Unlike the MDGs that were intended to spur government actions, the SDG framework presupposes that businesses, government, and civil society are all responsible for progress on the goals. The business sector was far more involved in the formulation of the SDGs than in the MDGs and many observers argue that the private sector can bring innovation, responsive-

Table 4.3   MDGs and SDGs comparison

	MDGs (2000–2015)	SDGs (2016–2030)
# of goals	8	17
Targets	21	169
Indicators	60	230
Origin	2000 Millennium summit	2012 Rio+20
Created by	UN secretariat	UN member states
Scope	Developing countries	International
Theme	Anti-poverty	Sustainable development
Economic goals		SDG 8: Decent work and economic growth
		SDG 9: Industry, innovation, and infrastructure
Social goals	MDG1: Eradicate extreme poverty and hunger	SDG1: No poverty
	MDG4: Reduce child mortality	SDG2: Zero hunger
	MDG5: Improve maternal health	SDG3: Good health and well-being
	MDG6: Combat HIV/AIDS, malaria, and other diseases	
	MDG2: Achieve universal primary education	SDG4: Quality education
	MDG3: Promote gender equality and empower women	SDG5: Gender equality
		SDG 10: Reduced inequalities
Environment goals	MDG7: Ensure environmental sustainability	SDG 6: Clean water and sanitation
		SDG7: Affordable and clean energy
		SDG 11: Sustainable cities and communities
		SDG 12: Responsible consumption and production
		SDG 13: Climate action
		SDG 14: Life below water
		SDG 15: Life on land
Governance goals	MDG8: Develop a global Partnership for Development	SDG 16: Peace and justice strong institutions
		SDG 17: Partnership for the Goals

Note: Broadly categorizing the goals into economic, social, environment, and governance spheres of development is the work of the authors, and is for the benefit of comparing the two sets of goals. Some of the goals could have fallen into multiple categories

Source: Adapted from United Nations (2015)

ness, efficiency, and targeted skills to the achievement of the goals (Scheyvens, Banks, & Hughes, 2016). For example, the SDGs strongly recommend that the private sector participate in developing effective energy efficiency programs, producing green products and technology, and promoting green supply chains. Crucially, the process of formulating the SDGs focused on the participation of broad segments of civil society in a wide swathe of countries. The two-year process included UN efforts to crowdsource new ideas from the poorest and most vulnerable segments of society in public consultations and multi-stakeholder engagement with civil society, generating unprecedented and widespread legitimacy for the formulated Goals (Carpentier, 2018).

SDG Indicators

As outlined in Chaps. 1 and 3, the scale and power of the largest corporations are greater than the capacities of many nations. Directing some of this power toward achieving SDG targets could have significant impact if private companies make genuine efforts to align their activities with the SDGs. In theory, the private sector can go beyond creating jobs and fueling economic growth to take on more responsibility in promoting international sustainable development. To this end, the GRI, the UN Global Compact, and WBCSD have developed the SDG Compass, which provides a five-step approach to align business strategies with the SDGs: (1) understanding the SDGs; (2) defining priorities; (3) setting goals; (4) integrating; and (5) reporting and communicating. Although the Compass focuses primarily on multinational corporations, it also encourages smaller companies to develop their own SDG-aligned plans. Business toolkits, standards, and assessment frameworks from third party organizations such as those described above can assist companies in achieving each of the 17 goals. The SDG Compass website listed 58 such tools in February 2019, including inter alia the Aqueduct Water Risk Atlas, the Corporate Human Rights Benchmark, the Food Loss and Waste Protocol, the Global Protocol on Packaging Sustainability, the ISO 14000 family of standards on environmental responsibility and the Bribe Payers Index. While the range of categories of concerns covered by the SDGs appears broad, their universal legitimacy is enhanced by incorporating the concerns of a comprehensive cross-section of constituencies.

The Statistics Division of the Department of Economic and Social Affairs of the UN maintains a list of 232 official indicators that measure progress on the SDGs. In addition, the Compass maintains an inventory of indicators produced by other organizations, such as GRI or the World Bank, which align with specific SDGs. This inventory facilitates the categorization of performance on specific metrics into one of the 17 SDGs. In theory, companies can use these indicators to compare their progress to the SDGs. Some organizations (such as GRI, CDP, and Oxfam) publish their own guides that teach companies how to incorporate the goals and targets into their business operations and how to assess performance using SDG-aligned indicators.

At the national level, the SDGs present an internally consistent and widely acknowledged framework to measure progress on multiple dimensions. In principle, a wide range of stakeholders could also interrogate corporate performance on specific SDGs and related indicators that are congruent with national goals. By creating a common set of metrics for governments and corporations, the SDGs have facilitated the possibility of an internally consistent dialogue on performance measurement that includes governments, corporations, and civil society. For example, assessments of ESG performance that measure the isolated contribution of a single corporation's economic activity to the social and natural ecosystem can now be placed in the context of broad progress at the national or regional level. This is no mean achievement. The facilitation of a meaningful dialogue on quantifiable performance measurement between the international development community and socially responsible investors is a significant prerequisite for any real and accountable collaboration between governments, business, and civil society. The simultaneous expansion of salient performance metrics by investors and international development organizations and their alignment has the potential to facilitate constructive dialogue and cross-sectoral critique.

Critique of the SDGs

The SDGs provide a common vision and actionable goals, measurable indicators and wide legitimacy. However, they are subject to a number of critiques. UN resolutions are not legally binding—they may evolve into a sort of 'soft' law if many jurisdictions pass national legislation that encapsulates some of the content of the resolutions. The SDGs have no legal import; private sector actors are encouraged to participate on a voluntary basis and there is no requirement for independent verification of performance. The purpose of the SDG Compass is to make it easier for companies to adopt the framework, but no national government has any regulations governing corporate declarations regarding their own SDG performance.

It has been argued that goals and targets are formulated in an isolated and sometimes contradictory way. For example, Goals 8 (decent work and economic growth) and 12 (responsible production and consumption) are likely to be in conflict, especially when the former is relatively well measured, while the latter is not precisely defined (Koehler, 2015). Another critique emphasizes that although the indicator list is comprehensive, no composite indicators are privileged, nor is there any consensus on a common weighting scheme, leaving too much leeway for variation in emphasis (Sachs, 2015). On the one hand, companies can enjoy flexibility in setting their own priorities and matching them to the SDGs. However, diversity makes it difficult to standardize and compare performance across companies and hold companies accountable.

Furthermore, indicators may not be specific enough. For example, SDG 7.2 *Affordable and Clean Energy* states that by 2030, the share of renewable energy in the global energy mix has to 'increase substantially', but there is no specific quantitative goal. Participants are encouraged to achieve as many goals as possible, but the multitude of goals reduces accountability because no single actor can be responsible for progress on more than a few goals. If all the goals are equally important, companies can be expected to choose the indicator or target that is the most convenient and the easiest to achieve, ensuring that the hardest goals would see little progress.

Concluding Remarks

The origins of the financial accounting system as a tool to help owners of firms determine whether management is an effective steward of capital limits the focus of financial accounting to the relatively narrow concerns of investors. While indicators of sustainability at the issuer level have the potential to improve capital allocation choices for investors, they are also important metrics of success and intermediate progress for a broader range of stakeholders focused on universal sustainable development. Quantitative metrics of sustainability are able to transform a vast amount of information about our complex environment into concise, policy-applicable, and decision-relevant information. We have described a number of structured frameworks that limit and categorize the universe of metrics, as well as those that incorporate inter-relationships between metrics of systemic drivers and responses. There is some likelihood of coalescence between frameworks in the near future, although the investor-focused and stakeholder-focused approaches do not share a common vision.

Decision-makers in the financial ecosystem can view the multiplicity of frameworks and metrics as an obstacle or an opportunity. Many bemoan the lack of standardization in definitions of sustainability and the consequent leeway in its measurement. The next chapter on financial markets and signals of scarcity outlines the value of diverse approaches to capturing and responding to measures of sustainability performance. Adaptability and evolution of frameworks and composite indexes of sustainability is essential because the collective understanding of sustainability remains in flux. This evolution calls for flexibility in indicator selection, with thoughtful approaches to index construction, standardization, weighting, and aggregation methods. The variation in the choice of composite indicators also affects the relationship with financial performance, which we delve into in the next chapter.

NOTES

1. Double-entry bookkeeping has been credited by some to be the essential progenitor of capitalism, most notably by Werner Sombart, though this is a somewhat debunked view (Yamey, 1994).
2. The term 'high-powered incentive' in this context was coined by Williamson (1984).
3. Note that by the same logic, it is impossible to verify that assets in the balance sheet have not been understated. To check that assets are not omitted in the accounts, the auditor must imagine an infinite range of possibilities and check if all the corresponding assets have been incorporated.
4. In general, economic analysis assumes that wages are an accurate estimate of the opportunity cost of leisure, which is the resource expended when labor is utilized in the production of goods and services.
5. The Corporate Register maintains maps that list the number of organizations using the IIRC framework and the GRI framework for their corporate responsibility reports. Maps are available at http://www.corporateregister.com/frameworks/gri/ and http://www.corporateregister.com/frameworks/iirc/. For 24 countries accessed in January 2019, the number of organizations using IIRC was 15% of the number of organizations using GRI.
6. In January 2014, the IIRC and SASB signed a memorandum of understanding "to more closely collaborate to advance the evolution of corporate disclosure and communicate value to investors".
7. Extreme poverty is defined by the UN as living on $1.25 or less a day.

REFERENCES

Admati, A. R. (2017). A Skeptical View of Financialized Corporate Governance. *Journal of Economic Perspectives, 31*(3), 131–150. https://doi.org/10.1257/jep.31.3.131

Atkinson, G. (2000). Measuring Corporate Sustainability. *Journal of Environmental Planning and Management, 43*(2), 235–252. https://doi.org/10.1080/09640560010694

Bebbington, J., & Larrinaga, C. (2014). Accounting and Sustainable Development: An Exploration. *Accounting, Organizations and Society, 39*(6), 395–413. https://doi.org/10.1016/j.aos.2014.01.003

Brandeis, L. D. (1914). *Other People's Money: And How the Bankers Use It.* New York, NY: F.A. Stokes.

Carpentier, C. L. (2018). How United Nations Reform Can Support a Reimagined Democracy. *Reimagining Democracy.* Retrieved from www.civicus.org website: https://www.civicus.org/index.php/re-imagining-democracy/overviews/3513-how-united-nations-reform-can-support-a-reimagined-democracy

Clemen, R. T. (1989). Combining Forecasts: A Review and Annotated Bibliography. *International Journal of Forecasting, 5*(4), 559–583. https://doi.org/10.1016/0169-2070(89)90012-5

Davies, R. B., Martin, J., Parenti, M., & Toubal, F. (2018). Knocking on Tax Haven's Door: Multinational Firms and Transfer Pricing. *Review of Economics and Statistics, 100*(1), 120–134. http://www.mitpressjournals.org/loi/rest

Dobson, J. (2006). Enron: The Collapse of Corporate Culture. In P. H. Dembinski, C. Lager, A. Cornford, & J.-M. Bonvin (Eds.), *Enron and World Finance: A Case Study in Ethics* (pp. 193–205). London, UK: Palgrave Macmillan UK.

Elkington, J. (1998). Partnerships from Cannibals with Forks: The Triple Bottom Line of 21st-Century Business. *Environmental Quality Management, 8*(1), 37–51.

Ely, K., & Waymire, G. (1999). Accounting Standard-Setting Organizations and Earnings Relevance: Longitudinal Evidence from NYSE Common Stocks, 1927–93. *Journal of Accounting Research, 37*(2), 293–317. https://doi.org/10.2307/2491411

European Union. (2014). Directive 2014/95/EU. *European Union.* Retrieved from https://eur-lex.europa.eu/legal-content/EN/TXT/PDF/?uri=CELEX:32014L0095&from=EN

Global Sustainable Investment Alliance. (2019). *Global Sustainable Investment Review 2018.* Retrieved from http://www.gsi-alliance.org/wp-content/uploads/2019/06/GSIR_Review2018F.pdf

GRI. (2019). *Chief Executive.* Retrieved from https://www.globalreporting.org/information/about-gri/governance-bodies/secretariat/Pages/CE-Office.aspx

IIRC. (2013). *The International <IR> Framework*. Retrieved from http://integratedreporting.org/wp-content/uploads/2015/03/13-12-08-THE-INTERNATIONAL-IR-FRAMEWORK-2-1.pdf

Imhoff, E. A., Jr. (2003). Accounting Quality, Auditing, and Corporate Governance. *Accounting Horizons, 17*, 117–128. https://doi.org/10.2308/acch.2003.17.s-1.117

Jacob, B. A., & Levitt, S. D. (2003). Rotten Apples: An Investigation of the Prevalence and Predictors of Teacher Cheating. *Quarterly Journal of Economics, 118*(3), 843–877. https://academic.oup.com/qje/issue

Koehler, C. (2015). Seven Decades of 'Development', and Now What? *Journal of International Development, 27*(4), 733–751.

KPMG. (2017). *The Road Ahead: The KPMG Survey of Corporate Responsibility Reporting 2017*. Retrieved from https://assets.kpmg/content/dam/kpmg/xx/pdf/2017/10/kpmg-survey-of-corporate-responsibility-reporting-2017.pdf

Lerman, R. (2018). Redmond CEO Charged with Fraud on More than 100 H-1B Visa Applications. *The Seattle Times*. Retrieved from https://www.seattletimes.com/business/technology/redmond-ceo-charged-with-fraud-on-more-than-100-h-1b-visa-applications/

Li, J. (2018). Something Fishy as Chinese Company Blames 'Disappearing' Scallops for Looming US$114 Million Loss. *South China Morning Post*. Hong Kong. Retrieved from https://www.scmp.com/business/china-business/article/2131453/something-fishy-chinese-company-blames-disappearing-scallops

Markham, J. W. (2015). *A Financial History of Modern US Corporate Scandals: From Enron to Reform*. London, UK: Routledge.

McElroy, M. W., & Thomas, M. P. (2017). With the Changing of the Guard at the IIRC, a Challenge to Richard Howitt. *SB Communications Weekly*, 1–1.

Moonitz, M. (1970). Three Contributions to the Development of Accounting Principles Prior to 1930. *Journal of Accounting Research, 8*(1), 145–155. https://doi.org/10.2307/2674722

Prescott-Allen, R. (1995). *Barometer of Sustainability; A Method of Assessing Progress Toward Sustainable Societies*. Victoria, BC: PADATA.

Provasi, R., & Farag, S. (2013). Accounting in Ancient Times: A Review of Classic References. *Accounting & Financial History Research Journal*, (5), 68–87.

Robertson, J., & Funnell, W. (2012). The Dutch East-India Company and Accounting for Social Capital at the Dawn of Modern Capitalism 1602–1623. *Accounting, Organizations and Society, 37*(5), 342–360. https://doi.org/10.1016/j.aos.2012.03.002

Ronen, J. (2010). Corporate Audits and How to Fix Them. *Journal of Economic Perspectives, 24*(2), 189–210. http://www.aeaweb.org/jep/

Sachs, J. D. (2015). Goal-Based Development and the SDGs: Implications for Development Finance. *Oxford Review of Economic Policy, 31*(3–4), 268–278.

SASB. (2018). *Mission.* Retrieved from https://www.sasb.org/governance/

Scheyvens, R., Banks, G., & Hughes, E. (2016). The Private Sector and the SDGs: The Need to Move beyond 'Business as Usual'. *Sustainable Development, 24*(6), 371–382.

Schmidheiny, S., & Zorraquin, F. J. (1996). *Financing Change: The Financial Community, Eco-Efficiency, and Sustainable Development.* Cambridge, MA: MIT Press.

Securities and Exchange Commission. (2002). *Complaint in SEC vs. Buntrock, D. L., Rooney, P. B., Koenig, J. E., Hau, T. C., Getz, H. A., & Tobecksen, B. D. United States District Court for the Northern District of Illinois Eastern Division.* Retrieved from https://www.sec.gov/litigation/complaints/complr17435.htm

Singh, R. K., Murty, H. R., Gupta, S. K., & Dikshit, A. K. (2009). An Overview of Sustainability Assessment Methodologies. *Ecological Indicators, 9*(2), 189–212.

Smith, D. J. (2011). Hidden Debt: From Enron's Commodity Prepays to Lehman's Repo 105s. *Financial Analysts Journal, 67*(5), 15–22.

Turing, A. M. (1937). On Computable Numbers, with an Application to the Entscheidungsproblem. *Proceedings of the London Mathematical Society, Series 2, 42*, 230–265. https://doi.org/10.1112/plms/s2-42.1.230

Turing, A. M. (1938). On Computable Numbers, with an Application to the Entscheidungsproblem. A Correction. *Proceedings of the London Mathematical Society, s2, 43*(1), 544–546. https://doi.org/10.1112/plms/s2-43.6.544

United Nations. (2015). Millennium Development Goals Report 2015. *United Nations Publications.* Retrieved from https://www.undp.org/content/dam/undp/library/MDG/english/UNDP_MDG_Report_2015.pdf

Valukas, A. R. (2010). *Lehman Brothers Holdings Inc. Chapter 11 Proceedings Examiner's Report.* Retrieved from https://web.stanford.edu/~jbulow/Lehmandocs/menu.html

Wackernagel, M., & Rees, W. (1998). *Our Ecological Footprint: Reducing Human Impact on the Earth* (Vol. 9). Gabriola Island, BC: New Society Publishers.

Wiederhold, G. (2014). *Valuing Intellectual Capital; Multinationals and Taxhavens.* New York, NY: Springer Science.

Williamson, O. E. (1984). The Incentive Limits of Firms: A Comparative Institutional Assessment of Bureaucracy. *Weltwirtschaftliches Archiv, 120*(4), 736–763.

Yamey, B. (1994). Accounting in History. *The European Accounting Review, 3*(2), 375–380. https://doi.org/10.1080/09638189400000025

Zeff, S. A. (2005). The Evolution of U.S. GAAP: The Political Forces Behind Professional Standards—Part 1: 1930–1973. *CPA Journal, 75*(1), 18–27.

CHAPTER 5

Signals of Scarcity and Financial Performance

INTRODUCTION

In Chap. 1, we noted Hayek's point that market prices play the essential role of aggregating decentralized information about scarcity and abundance into widely available signals (Hayek, 1945). Viewed from the perspective of systems thinking, a set of interconnected and related markets with prices that respond to changes in relative scarcity represents the most important technology in the financial ecosystem. Hayek marvels that inter-related markets for a commodity such as tin could facilitate coordination in the plans of dispersed individuals separated by geography. If a new use were discovered for tin, or if a previously reliable source of supply were no longer available, the consequent increase in the price of tin would be sufficient information to induce many dispersed consumers of tin to economize its use. Hayek's concern is to highlight the "unavoidable imperfection of man's knowledge and the consequent need for a process by which knowledge is constantly communicated and acquired". The system of market prices is that very process by which particular knowledge is aggregated into general signals, which then cause dispersed decision-makers to make plans and engage in economic activities, which tend to dampen relative scarcity and abundance. In systems thinking, this process would be characterized as a negative feedback loop. The information aggregation function of the price system is enabled by two distinct processes: dispersed individual plans by uncoordinated decision-makers and a widely available *output of* and *input into* dispersed planning that we call the market price.

© The Author(s) 2019
S. Bose et al., *The Financial Ecosystem*, Palgrave Studies in Impact Finance, https://doi.org/10.1007/978-3-030-05624-7_5

In the box below, we discuss a simple example where the system of interconnected prices allows dispersed action to efficiently address relative scarcity: demand response management in electricity grids.

Electricity Demand Response

Generated electricity is the ultimate perishable commodity. Methods of storing electricity in batteries and hydro-electric reservoirs remain relatively expensive or are limited by location-specific geographical features. In order to meet demand and simultaneously avoid excess generation, electricity grids need to equate electricity demand and supply on a near continuous basis. When electricity demand rises sharply within a short space of time, such as on a hot August afternoon in New York City, grid operators need to be able to request increases in electricity supply and/or decreases in electricity demand in real time. Requesting increases in supply necessitates asking just a few operators of generation capacity. Unfortunately, most sources of electricity require more than a few hours to be dispatched (or brought online) or are subject to intermittency. The major source that can be quickly dispatched, called a peak load plant, is usually a natural gas turbine. Peak load plants provide the option to meet demand in near real time. Since peak load plants cost more per unit of electricity generated than base load plants, they are not utilized all the time. Their use is limited to those times when electricity demand rises and threatens to outstrip supply. The limited capacity utilization implies a low return on the fixed costs of operating a peak load plant. Since peak load plants are capital intensive, their low utilization means that it would rarely be profitable to invest in a peak load plant if it could earn revenue only on the few days it generated power for the grid. For such plants to be profitable, they would have to receive additional payments for maintaining generation capacity, leading to increases in overall electricity costs for all users.

Demand response is a Hayekian solution that can reduce or eliminate the need for peak load plants. Demand response schemes are conceived on the premise that a significant portion of electricity utilization during peak load times has low value to the user: consumers may be willing to turn off some appliances or reduce demand for a relatively small monetary inducement. The scheme offers a portfolio

(*continued*)

(continued)
of the larger electricity users' incentives to reduce electricity consumption when total grid demand approaches capacity. The dispersed conservation by many users is much cheaper than maintaining one or two rarely utilized peak load plants. The inducement to dispersed action requires that users face a variation in price that is linked to the social cost of instantaneously delivered electricity. Demand response allows each consumer to determine whether it is worth it for her to reduce the load she imposes on the grid, rather than leaving the choice to a central grid operator. Without demand response, the grid operator could choose to shut down supply to parts of the grid in an indiscriminate way (a process called load shedding) without considering the variation in the instantaneous economic value generated by different types of electricity consumption. For demand response to be effective, the price variation or related incentives must be sensitive to the expected changes in demand, much as a market price might be. Demand response is Hayekian insofar as it obviates the need for the grid operator to know which customers are using electricity for low-value activities when the system is capacity constrained. A fuller explanation of demand response and related mechanisms is available in Chapter 9 of Bradford (2018).

The example of electricity demand response above illustrates a very simple and clear application of Hayek's insight on the function of the price mechanism: temporary scarcity can be alleviated by distributed conservation measures coordinated by an incentive system such as the price mechanism, which eliminates the fool's errand to gather dispersed information in the mind of a central decision-maker. The mechanism rewards foresight on the part of a consumer of electricity who chooses to pre-pone or postpone high-load activities with low economic value outside the peak period. This reward system induces behavior that minimizes social scarcity. Decentralized efforts at arbitrage are rewarded by lower electricity costs for some and higher system availability for all. Can we expect that the financial ecosystem can evolve a set of mechanisms that minimize the scarcities created when planetary boundaries are in danger of being breached? The scarcities associated with planetary boundaries (see Chap. 2) have vastly greater dimensionality than the problem of diurnal peaks in electricity demand.

Some planetary scarcities may be related to single metrics (such as the amount of unrecycled plastic), while others have a range of underlying physical causes which have yet to be identified (such as the collapse of pollinating insect colonies). The economics textbook solution to most such problems is the regulatory imposition of a Pigovian tax or the assignment of property rights to scarce common resources. These mechanisms are theoretically effective and efficient in situations of complete information, which almost never applies. Hayek's study of the importance of knowledge and its partial and subjective nature implies that the regulatory solution can at best be incomplete. Moreover, our review of the relative power of the largest corporations and governments (see Chaps. 1 and 3) suggests that it is naïve to assume that lobbying and regulatory capture cannot erode the potential power of regulations to restrain corporate activity. In an early articulation of this view, Schmidheiny and Zorraquin (1996) wrote "the market is a tougher master than a government, which can be lobbied and influenced". They state that "a number of corporate directors, although they would rarely admit it, actually favor government regulations over market instruments. They have learned to deal with the former but not the latter".

THE PROBLEM OF ANALYTICAL MONOCULTURES

What kinds of market instruments could reward the dampening of scarcity in the context of planetary boundaries? In Chap. 4, we describe the decision-theoretic rationale for expanding the range of relevant metrics beyond solely financial ones. The lesson we learned is that a single metric cannot suffice as a driver of decisions that have any hope of advancing sustainability. Sustainability is multi-dimensional, and the prices at which its different dimensions can be translated into monetary value remain indeterminate. Revealed preference methods can signal non-market values to the would-be arbitrageur who might consider searching for biomes that are likely to become scarce, or are likely to be seen to become scarce. If there is reason to expect that non-market values might eventually translate into market values, then an investor who cared only about financial return and not a whit about the broader ecosystem is incented to search for and conserve those assets which might serve as sinks for increasingly abundant pollutants, even if those assets are not currently recognized as valuable. This is the process of entrepreneurial discovery that Israel Kirzner refers to as "the natural alertness to possible opportunities (or the danger of possible disaster) which is characteristic of human beings" (Kirzner, 1997). As we briefly mention in Chap. 1, the frameworks, information sources, and due diligence processes that such an investor must rely upon are likely to differ to a large extent from the inputs of the valuation models used by the broader marketplace. This creates the risk that the investor will need to wait an excruciatingly long time before other market participants recognize the inherent value of such scarce biomes. Richard Bronk, in a reassessment of Hayek's position on the wisdom of prices, notes that financial markets have a tendency to develop "homogenous frames of reference, widespread conventional opinions and analytical monocultures" (Bronk, 2013). At the conclusion of a three-year multi-disciplinary study of 118 financial traders in four major financial institutions operating in London, Fenton-O'Creevy, Nicholson, Sloane, and Willman (2005) note that amongst traders, "there is always the danger of groupthink, collusive relationships that yield support without critical analysis". Fenton-O'Creevy et al. recommend institutionalized diversity of experience, knowledge, and approach and a culture of open dialogue among traders to counteract this danger. In an anthropological study of employees in the financial services sector in New York, Ho (2009) contrasts the euphoria embedded in the dramatically rising stock prices of corporations such as AT&T, when they announced layoffs of tens of thousands of employees with the downsizing-induced worker trauma in New Jersey where AT&T had significant operations. If the financial ecosystem is to evolve into a mechanism that rewards intertemporal arbitrage seeking to conserve assets rendered scarce by planetary boundaries, the analytical approaches and common measures of performance have to be broadened.

By what means can the financial ecosystem broaden its frames of reference, or diversify beyond analytical monocultures? Is it feasible to institutionalize Hayek's insight that local, particular knowledge creates systemic value within a financial sector that is globalized and measured on a single metric of success; financial return evaluated in periods that last as long as nanoseconds in the geological timescale. Frames of reference are notoriously difficult to legislate. Regulation can drive action, but the only tool available to a government interested in the task of changing hearts and minds is propaganda, which becomes ineffective, nay counterproductive, the moment it is seen to be propaganda. Frames of reference must be fashioned from an iterative process that incorporates dispersed experimentation, diversity of perspectives and a system-wide messaging mechanism that facilitates widespread and diverse evaluation of the results of such experimentation. In his bestseller, James Surowiecki writes: "If one virtue of a decentralized economy is that it diffuses decision-making power (at least on a small scale) throughout the system, that virtue becomes meaningless if all the people with power are alike…or they become alike through imitation" (Surowiecki, 2004). Surowiecki cites the work of psychologist Irving Janis, who argued that homogenous groups are more likely to fall prey to groupthink because they are naturally more cohesive than diverse groups, rendering them more likely to be insulated from dissenting views. In the context of the financial ecosystem, what are those dissenting views that need expression within the conventional frames of reference? Our review of sustainability accounting frameworks in Chap. 4 points to the wide range of stakeholders of the firm as the pool from which to seek out a range of perspectives. We noted that the investor-focused frameworks that ultimately privilege the shareholder cannot hope to assume the mantle of broad legitimacy that a stakeholder-focused framework can. Legitimacy is the natural reward of broad representation—cognitive diversity in the decision-making process increases the likely range of stakeholders who accept that the decision is sound. In principle then, the broad range of sustainability metrics of interest to stakeholders can serve as the field in which to search for additional metrics of performance. These metrics may not immediately impact shareholder returns so long as the analytical monocultures persist, but it behooves the alert investor to consider them in her capital allocation process.

The counter-argument, grounded in the dominant narratives of shareholder value and financial accounting, emphasizes the shareholder's limited role: that of maximizing shareholder value. This narrative argues that surely, the innocent shareholder with diversified holdings, with such little influence even on the companies she owns, cannot be responsible for addressing the external impacts of corporate activity on an inchoate mass of consumers, employees, suppliers, communities, and the environment. This logic points to government action as the only legitimate regulator of the adverse impacts of externalities. Unfortunately, regulatory action in this area has been slow, and is likely to continue to lag behind efforts from other stakeholders, particularly investors, consumers, and employees. An important concept to internalize in this regard is the intellectual barrenness of the view that social and environmental problems must be addressed either by firms or the state. Such a view denies the power and agency of other forms of constraint systems that often regulate much better. This argument has been the subject of the research of Elinor Ostrom et al. In her Nobel acceptance speech, Ostrom lays out evidence of the crowding out of decentralized monitoring activities caused by blunt and ineffective regulation by a centralized state (Ostrom, 2010). Dispersed ownership, as well as the central tenet of the factor models that underlie return and risk attribution in empirical finance, militate against the possibility of earning significant returns from careful due diligence on individual securities. True believers of the capital asset pricing model, which is the foundation of factor models, predict that the assumption of idiosyncratic risk cannot be rewarded by excess return in the marketplace. This belief limits the propensity of many investment analysts to examine the environmental, social, and governance risks and opportunities that affect individual issuers in their portfolios. The belief that risk is attributable solely to portfolio-level risk factors such as market risk, firm size risk, or momentum risk crowds out the incentive to examine the local and specific circumstances of any individual issuer. In addition, this approach denies the possibility that stakeholders other than dispersed owners might have useful information and perspectives on the functioning of a corporation in the broader ecosystem. This crowding out is isomorphic to the crowding out described by Ostrom.

Broadening the range of metrics that an investor considers has the potential to square this circle, linking the concerns of stakeholders with those of stockholders. Perhaps a continuum can be discerned between the broader sustainable development agenda, a state's role in regulating markets, and the objectives of responsible shareholders who profess focus on ESG performance. This continuum could be the basis of a grand coalition of parties incorporating a broader set of performance measures, effectively becoming a diverse set of perspectives converging to society as a whole. In order for this broadening strategy to be effective, investors and other stakeholders need enhanced and targeted disclosure on the sustainability impacts of corporate activity. An example of the need for nuanced and targeted indicators is presented in the context of metrics ranking the sustainability of electric vehicles and related investor action in the box below.

Acting on the Wrong Metric?

Electric vehicles (EVs) are widely viewed as clean transportation alternatives to conventional gasoline-powered cars because they do not have tailpipe emissions. Although the production of car batteries may impact the environment, the use phase still causes the majority of the impact (Meinrenken & Lackner, 2015). Many countries in hoping that the use phase impact of EVs could be kept smaller than internal combustion engine vehicles (ICEVs) provide incentives for the adoption of electric vehicles. China, Europe, and the United Kingdom have announced plans to ban new ICEVs by 2030.

Life cycle analysis (LCA) computes the emissions and toxicity potential generated by products during their manufacture, use, and recycling phases. EVs generally have more intensive environmental impact than ICEVs during the manufacture stage. In an award-winning life cycle analysis of generic EVs and ICEVs matched in size, researchers estimated that ICEVs had lower global warming potential, lower human toxicity potential, lower freshwater eco-toxicity potential, lower mineral depletion and lower freshwater eutrophication in the production phase (Hawkins, Singh, Majeau-Bettez, & Strømman, 2013). In the use phase, if the electricity generated to recharge the batteries of EVs is primarily coal-based, then EVs effectively generate higher carbon emissions than ICEVs. The size of the vehicle and the source of electricity are pivotal in determining whether EVs are actually cleaner than some ICEVs. A much-read Financial Times article notes that large EVs with longer ranges such as the Tesla Model S P100D, which require much larger batteries, have higher lifecycle carbon emissions than small ICEVs such as the Mitsubishi Mirage if driven in the Midwest United States, a region with significant coal-generated electricity. Driven in that region, the Tesla would emit 226 grams of CO_2 equivalent per km traveled over its life. This compares to 385 grams for an equivalent sized BMW 750i xDrive ICEV and 192 grams for the compact Mitsubishi (McGee, 2017). The article also notes that EV batteries require significant amounts of cobalt, the majority of which is procured from the Democratic Republic of Congo under lax environmental and ethical standards.

(*continued*)

(continued)

These analyses suggest that the tailpipe carbon emissions per car are not the appropriate metric to rank the sustainability of cars. In studying the introduction of more and more electric vehicles into system-wide fleet, Meinrenken and Lackner (2015) found that if the battery is small, then the environmental impacts per mile driven are smaller than ICEVs, but in which case the cars cannot be used much, so the system-wide benefits are negligible; if the batteries are very large, then most trips can be done on EVs, but the impacts per mile driven are actually larger than ICEVs. Therefore, the optimum range depends on a range of factors such as grid mix, average trip distance between charges, the energy density of the battery, and car weight, etc. In a study evaluating the benefits of weight reduction for cars, Serrenho, Norman, and Allwood (2017) estimate that fostering vehicle weight reduction could lead to greater cumulative emissions reductions until 2050 in Great Britain than those obtained by incentivizing a fast transition to electric drivetrains, unless there is extreme decarbonization of the electricity generation mix. Incorporating car weight rewards the efforts of those users who for reasons of thrift or concern for their environmental footprint, gravitate toward smaller EVs or ICEVs. In addition to carbon emissions, an evaluation of the non-carbon impacts of EVs relative to ICEVs is warranted. Users and investors who are aware of and care about the potential toxicity and ethical violations in the extraction and disposal of cobalt, lithium, and rare earth metals essential to current EVs need more information to make the correct choice between alternate methods of reducing their use of scarce environmental resources.

Electric vehicles represent a promising disruptive technology, which, along with significantly decarbonized generation, can reduce overall emissions of many local and global pollutants. Responsible sourcing, cobalt recycling, and research and development of alternative materials for cathodes in batteries are exactly the dispersed activities that should be encouraged to ensure that this carbon-reduction strategy does not create other sustainability challenges. Only a policy of choosing and rewarding the correct metrics of performance can push back planetary boundaries. Grassroots investor action in the

(continued)

(continued)

financial ecosystem has the potential to respond more nimbly and in a more targeted way than government policy. Trilllium Asset Management Corporation, as a Tesla shareholder, lead-filed a proxy resolution, which notes that Tesla does not substantively report on a range of environmental health and safety issues, including the 'life cycle benefits of its products'. The resolution calls for Tesla to publish comprehensive annual sustainability reports rather than sporadic blog posts to address these issues (ICCR, 2019). The Transition Pathway Initiative, established by the Church of England Investing Bodies and the UK Environment Agency Pension Fund and supported by many major asset owners, ranks Tesla at the lowest possible score on its "management of greenhouse gas emissions and of risks and opportunities related to the low-carbon transition" (Transition Pathway Initiative, 2017).

The promise of targeted investment and security selection by investors incorporating signals of scarcity is only feasible if the shareholder, whose primary interest is financial return, is not hurt by the integration of non-financial metrics into the capital allocation process. This caveat causes us to review what is known about the relationship between corporate sustainability performance (CSP) and corporate financial performance (CFP) later in the chapter. Before we turn to financial performance, we briefly examine the state of regulation requiring corporate disclosure on sustainability performance.

THE STATE OF REGULATORY INITIATIVES

Globally, there has been a dramatic increase in requirements for non-financial disclosure in the last 25 years. The Reporting Exchange, an initiative of the World Business Council on Sustainable Development (WBCSD) has developed a free online tool[1] to collate corporate sustainability disclosure-related regulations around the world. In February 2019, the tool listed over 1100 reporting requirements from nearly 70 countries. This number has grown from less than 100 requirements in 1992 (WBCSD, 2018a). The list is not comprehensive since it is a non-profit-led effort that relies on contributions from civil society, moderated by staff members from the Reporting Exchange. The coverage of regulations is deep for the Americas, Europe, Eastern and Southern Asia, and Australasia. Coverage of countries in Africa and the Middle East, with the exception of South Africa, Nigeria, and Israel, is more sparse. Nevertheless, The Reporting Exchange is the most comprehensive collation of reporting regulations on sustainability reporting available in one place. The database lists 730 environmental, 555 social, 346 governance, and 208 economic reporting requirements. These include mandatory, comply or explain, and voluntary reporting requirements. The database lists requirements from government regulators as well as listing requirements for stock exchanges. The Reporting Exchange notes that both developed and developing countries have significant reporting requirements, with developed countries having a relatively greater emphasis on governance than developing economies. A significant difference in emphasis between developed and developing economies is that in developing economies, disclosures are less likely to be required by stock exchanges. In addition, they are less likely to be provided in broadly available reports to the general public and more likely to involve reporting directly to the regulator (WBCSD, 2018b). These two characteristics make corporate sustainability disclosures less easily available to investors in emerging markets.

Datamaran, an ESG research provider that uses natural language processing (NLP) to identify sustainability risks and opportunities in electronic texts (including annual reports and regulations), has published a report detailing its analysis of the increase in ESG regulations in the United Kingdom, Canada, and the United States (Datamaran, 2018). NLP has the advantage of being less labor-intensive than civil society volunteer efforts, but it is harder to transcend language barriers with this technology. Other NLP data providers include RepRisk and TruValue Labs, both of which have expanded their search to a few languages other than English. A significant opportunity remains to use NLP to track sustainability disclosures in Mandarin, Japanese, Korean, and Arabic, as many companies with primary disclosures in these languages often do not translate their reports into English, French, and Spanish, where significant NLP search algorithms have already been deployed.

Amongst OECD countries, the reporting requirement with the widest applicability is the European Union's Non-Financial Reporting Directive (2014/95/EU), which requires large and public interest companies to disclose their management and performance on a range of social and environmental issues. This directive has been translated into legal requirements in the member countries of the EU. Consequently, approximately 6000 companies are required to publicly disclose information on environmental protection, diversity, and human rights. Since 2010, China has also sharply increased reporting requirements for companies on environmental issues, especially emissions of air and water pollutants. The United States, with the largest capital market in the world, remains a jurisdiction with relatively limited disclosure requirements for non-financial reporting.

The Sustainable Stock Exchange (SSE) initiative, launched in 2009 by the United Nations, has been instrumental in widening the range of exchanges instituting sustainability disclosure requirements for listed companies, especially in developing economies. In June 2019, the SSE listed 88 partner stock exchanges, with more than 51,000 listed companies with a market capitalization of $86 trillion. Of these, 16 stock exchanges with 15,000 listed companies, with a market capitalization of $16 trillion, require ESG reporting as a listing rule. In addition, 36 stock exchanges also maintain sustainability-related indexes (SSEI, 2019).

The Financial Performance of Corporate Sustainability

The advent of new reporting requirements governing non-financial disclosure has increased the salience of the link between corporate sustainability performance (CSP) and corporate financial performance (CFP). The relationship between a range of measures of CSP[2] and measures of CFP has been the subject of study in over a thousand different academic papers, dating back to at least 1972. Although there is overwhelming evidence of a broadly positive correlation, there are specific proxies where there is no relationship and a few where there is a negative relationship.

Meta-analyses and Surveys

There have been sufficient numbers of studies investigating the CSP-CFP relationship that academics have been able to perform statistically valid meta-analysis of these studies, that is, compute the average strength of the estimates of the relation across different studies. Most recently, Busch and Friede (2018) conduct a second-order meta-analysis, which is an aggregation of the results of other meta-analyses. Busch and Friede find a highly significant, positive, robust, and bi-directional relationship between different measures of corporate environmental and social performance and corporate financial performance. Intriguingly, their results are stronger for corporate social reputation than for corporate social disclosure. This is gratifying, since it suggests that disclosure is not sufficient to correlate with better financial performance—actual improvements in reputation validated by others is associated with improved financial performance. The Busch and Friede results are stronger for financial operating performance than for market performance. This is perhaps to be expected, since the analytical frameworks employed in financial valuation are yet to fully integrate ESG factors. Firms are likely to need to experience accounting profits from sustainability investments for some time before investors give the issuers credit for such investments. The weakest CSP-CFP relationship occurs for companies deemed sustainable on the basis of inclusion in a socially responsible mutual fund. It appears that inclusion in socially responsible mutual funds is a weak signal of corporate financial performance. This is consistent with other studies, which find that many mutual funds labeled as socially responsible often have portfolio holdings indistinguishable from other funds not labeled as sustainable (Utz & Wimmer, 2014).

Surprisingly, the Busch and Friede study find that papers published in journals focused on social issues find a weaker CSP-CFP relation than studies published in general management journals. This would imply that journals focused on ESG issues are not skewing the strength of the relationship. This is important because the Busch and Friede analysis confirms the results of an earlier meta-analysis which concluded that social responsibility (and to a lesser extent environmental responsibility) is likely to pay off financially (Orlitzky, Schmidt, & Rynes, 2003). Another meta-study has similarly found that corporate carbon performance has a positive relationship with financial performance (Busch & Lewandowski, 2017).

In addition to meta-analyses that measure quantitatively the average strength of the published relationships, there are a number of survey papers that document the relationship at the level of specific proxies for CFP or CSP. A commonly-cited survey used by practitioners is Clark, Feiner, and Viehs (2015). Clark et al. compile the results of 200 papers that are a mix of academic studies, industry articles and newspaper reports, and categorize the studies into performance on the 'E', 'S', and 'G' dimensions. They state that 90% of the studies demonstrate that improved sustainability practices reduce the cost of capital for companies, 88% of studies show that improved ESG performance are related to improved operational performance and 80% of studies show that higher stock price return is associated with good sustainability practices.

Selected Individual Studies

The link to a lower cost of capital is a double-edged sword: the dominant analytical framework of the capital asset pricing model in financial valuation declares that stocks with a lower cost of capital should experience lower returns. Some researchers have built on this logic to argue that stocks of companies considered social pariahs such as adult entertainment, alcohol, gambling, nuclear power, tobacco, and weapons (often referred to as 'sin' stocks) should demonstrate higher returns than stocks of companies deemed to be socially responsible. In a study of US stocks between 1965 and 2006, Hong and Kacperczyk (2009) find that sin stocks are less likely to be held by institutional investors, less likely to receive analyst coverage and more likely to outperform the broad market benchmark. However, in a more recent study of matched portfolios of sin stocks and socially responsible stocks, Lobe and Walkshäusl (2016) find no compelling evidence that sin stocks or socially responsible stocks outperform or underperform each other. As suggested by Busch and Friede, studies of the socially responsible mutual funds demonstrate a weak relationship to financial performance. In a study of matched ethical and non-ethical European funds, Kreander, Gray, Power, and Sinclair (2005) find that there is no discernible difference in performance between the two types of funds. In a comparison of the performance of SRI indices against matched non-SRI indices Schröder (2007) finds no difference in risk-adjusted performance, although there is greater risk (and therefore greater return) in SRI indices. Other studies have shown that companies which adopted sustainability policies significantly outperformed other companies on sales growth, return on assets, and stock market price over a 10-year time horizon (Jong, Paulraj, & Blome, 2014) and a 16-year time horizon (Eccles, Ioannou, & Serafeim, 2014). Additional studies finding stock return outperformance associated with corporate social responsibility include Borgers, Derwall, Koedijk, and ter Horst (2013), Cai and He (2014), Jiao (2010), Kempf and Osthoff (2007), and Trudel and Cotte (2009). We discuss the conclusions of a selection of these studies related to stakeholder relations in Chap. 8.

On the other hand, corporate case studies of sustainability-driven innovation do not demonstrate financial returns in the short run (Marcus, 2015), and many others have found an inconsistent relationship between corporate social performance and corporate financial performance (Barnett, 2014; Flammer, 2015; Kitzmueller & Shimshack, 2012). Given the variety of proxies for corporate social performance and the confounding factors, this is perhaps not surprising. Without adequate controls, we cannot know whether the above relationships are driven by sustainability factors or result from differences in governance structure, stakeholder engagement strategy, and/or the level of transparency (Esty & Cort, 2017).

It is important to understand that studies on the link between ESG and financial performance often measure different things. Perhaps it is reasonable to assume that some elements of sustainability are connected to financial returns, while other elements are not. For example, "end of pipe" practices focused on lowering or "cleaning" undesirable process outputs (as opposed to re-engineering the system creating these outputs) are shown to have a negative relationship to economic performance. Input-based practices (those involving changes made to the materials used prior to their input into a system) are shown to have no significant relationship to economic performance (Wagner, 2005). However, sustainability management, which focuses on process innovation, is more environmentally successful and is shown to have a significant positive influence on financial performance indicators (Wong, Lai, Shang, Lu, & Leung, 2012). The environmental metrics most likely to have a positive, significant impact on firm performance were recycling, waste reduction, remanufacturing, environmental design, and surveillance of the market for environmental issues (Montabon, Sroufe, & Narasimhan, 2007).

Input efficiency can lead to financially beneficial results by decreasing costs, while "green" products generate their financial benefit in higher sales growth through improved consumer loyalty. The pedigree of such products must be well known by customers in order for a company to take full advantage of this demand. In a related study, increased customer satisfaction stemming from the "green reputation" of a company was shown to influence economic performance to a larger degree than the overall corporate reputation of the firm (Tang, Lai, & Cheng, 2012). This also points to the importance of market awareness of sustainable activities since, as a subset of an overall reputation, a "green reputation" must be actively promoted in order to be distinguishable from that of the company as a whole. Studies showing that environmental strategy integration is most strongly linked to enhanced firm image and market performance further strengthen the argument for the importance of "green reputation" regarding firm performance (Wagner, 2007).

Studies have also found a trend for the market to penalize large, profitable firms lacking CSR programs, while supporting similar firms that maintain CSR programs (Lourenço, Branco, Curto, & Eugénio, 2012). These results are closely linked to firm reputation and shareholder communication, as market penalization likely stems from stakeholders punishing a firm that is obviously capable of implementing CSR, but refuses to do so. Indeed, there is no short-term benefit in being a firm with a highly rated CSR program, but in the long term such a firm performs better financially (Lin, Yang, & Liou, 2009). This strengthens the argument for the indirect influence of CSR on firm performance, rather than direct, quantifiable benefits.

Lastly, the majority of studies evaluating the sustainability/financial performance relationship focus on short-term time frames, which may miss the greater benefit of these programs. Environmental sustainability is inherently related to a long-term time frame, diminishing the significance of the short term. Similarly, many investment strategies are focused on quarterly reports—a display of 'short-termism'—which presents a time frame too short to account for many forms of benefits arising from sustainability programs. Sustainability programs are sometimes avoided due to implementation costs, though perceived costs in the short term may develop into long-term benefits, as such benefits may only accrue gradually over time (Claver, López, Molina, & Tarí, 2007; Mollet, von Arx, & Ilic, 2013). Without considering the full time frame required to adequately study the effects of a sustainability program, there exist the risks of either assessing a program's value inaccurately or lauding sustainability programs, which may turn out only to be an instance of 'green washing'.

THE FINANCIAL CASE FOR SUSTAINABILITY WITHIN CORPORATIONS

This section presents the financial arguments, which are in some cases theoretical, for the integration of sustainability into organizational operations within companies. We divide the arguments into three parts: those related to cost efficiency, revenue generation, and the impact on intangible factors.

Cost Efficiency

The promotion of cost reductions is one of the most obvious arguments for sustainability within companies, especially within the frame of rising resource costs. A number of studies relating input efficiency to financial performance are surveyed in Bose and Springsteel (2017). Studies find that investment in energy efficiency is connected to higher productivity in manufacturing industries (Bergmann, Rotzek, Wetzel, & Guenther, 2017). As might be expected, increasing energy prices affect the costs of agricultural products more significantly than other inputs as well as impacting relevant labor demand (Moss, Livanis, & Schmitz, 2010). A key tenet of sustainability is the more efficient usage of inputs. The lower the amount of inputs needed to produce the same outcome will be sure to benefit a company's bottom-line, regardless of industry sector.

Perhaps the most common example associated with this concept is that of energy efficiency, as in the less energy one uses the less one has to buy. Similarly, increases in efficient uses of materials allows for lower amounts of materials purchased. However, the actual cost reductions from energy reductions have been shown to vary based upon factors such as the price of energy and the magnitude of the rebound effect (decreases in price leading to increases in usage) (Chu & Sappington, 2013), while some management within certain companies does not believe energy costs compose a significant enough portion of overall business costs to merit the cost of efficiency upgrades (Pellegrini-Masini & Leishman, 2011). Such variations in savings accrued make sector specific considerations highly important when determining the end cost or benefit of a particular efficiency program.

Many of the cost reductions associated with sustainability programs maintain a less direct effect on financial performance compared to those associated with decreases in energy or materials used. Examples of such indirect cost reductions include supply chain risk mitigation, penalty avoidance, and decreases in the cost of capital and labor via heightened company reputation.

Costs associated with human resources can be mitigated through the development of sustainability programs that improve the attractiveness of a company. In a 2012 study conducted by Net Impact, 45% of students surveyed responded that they would take a 15% pay cut in order to work for a company making a social or environmental impact. The same study found that workers able to make a social or environmental impact at their job were twice as likely to report high levels of job satisfaction (Zukin & Szeltner, 2012). Similarly, multiple studies exist detailing the beneficial effects of "green" buildings on employee productivity. A 2003 report to California's Sustainable Building Task Force estimated the productivity benefits of silver level LEED certification to be over $36 per square foot and over $55 per square foot for gold and platinum LEED certifications (Kats, Alevantis, Berman, Mills, & Perlman, 2003).

Increasing environmental awareness has led to the growth and development of a growing number of governmental regulations on private industry. The threat of punitive governmental measures is responsible for much of the rise in sustainable operations, such as ecosystem services accounting; private firms may no longer pollute or misuse common resources without fear of repercussions. However, such "regulatory avoidance" is generally associated with reactionary measures and minimum sustainable performance, as firms are largely extrinsically motivated to mitigate risk via compliance. Intrinsically motivated firms are more likely to integrate sustainability programs into strategic practices for the sake of long-term profit strategy related to consumer and/or investor demand (Moore, De Silva, & Hartmann, 2012).

Financial and environmental risk mitigation is an outcome of many sustainability programs. ESG considerations are shown to benefit a firm through increasing its ability to access capital, mitigate operational risk, and manage its liabilities (Bancilhon, 2012). The linkage of sustainability to financial risk mitigation may be more suitable for discussion regarding firm reputation (addressed below), as the increased ability to access capital has been linked to the increased reputation of a firm, which is associated with, but not directly generated by, ESG or CSR performance.

Revenue Generation

Sustainability programs produce a variety of outcomes ranging from the tangible to the intangible, and the environmentally to socially focused. Each of these outcomes affects financial performance differently and achieves various results. There could be drivers of economic success arising from sustainable practices, such as competitive advantage, reputation development, and the growth of mutually beneficial partnerships (Mollet et al., 2013). Also frequently noted are benefits related to enhanced customer or employee satisfaction and overall firm reputation (Wagner & Schaltegger, 2004). Many of these performance indicators fall within the same firm attribute, which can more clearly describe how specific outcomes related to sustainability generate financial gain.

Firms implementing sustainability programs often receive the benefit of reputations as leaders in their fields and/or as environmentally and socially conscious businesses. Growing consumer/investor demand for such consciousness, paired with increasing demand for transparency of business practices, has heightened the role of reputation as an indirect driver of economic performance. Due to methodological inconsistencies across studies and the diversity of businesses and sectors analyzed, definitive linkages between reputation and economic performance have not yet been proven, though there are multiple generalizations that appear commonly enough to be worth consideration.

Within sectors that generate relatively large amounts of pollution, strong environmental performance does not lead to firm differentiation even though it relates to cost competitive advantages (Lucas & Noordewier, 2016). The inverse of this relationship has been found for low polluting companies; they do not enjoy cost advantages from polluting less, but do achieve differentiation from their competition (López-Gamero, Molina-Azorín, & Claver-Cortés, 2009). This finding implies that, when it is considered easily avoidable, polluting has strong negative effects on a company's reputation but that stakeholders tend to be more lenient in their judgment when pollution is considered an unavoidable outcome of business.

Market awareness of sustainability practices is an easily discernible influencer of firm reputation, as actions must be publicly known in order to affect reputation. Such market detection was found to be especially influential regarding the linkage of "product stewardship" (re-designing a product to make it more efficient or environmentally friendly) to financial benefit (Wong et al., 2012). This makes logical sense as "green" products generate their financial benefit via consumer demand. As previously mentioned, green reputation could matter more to the economic performance of firms than their overall corporate reputation. The development of a "green reputation" may very well be a benefit of sustainable practices that is more financially beneficial than other, more easily quantified, outcomes. For example, the main benefits to firms that account for ecosystem services are considered to be brand value and competitive differentiation, not those benefits arising from a more responsibly maintained ecosystem. However, such findings also reflect the influence of a short time frame of benefit consideration and it is possible that the direct benefit of ecosystem services accounting would be more prominent in long-term considerations.

Innovation is a frequently cited benefit arising from sustainability programs. The necessity to develop new production processes or design new products leads to long-term benefits through forced firm development. Studies on firms in the manufacturing industry have found that the development of sustainability within supply chains is linked to the ability to exploit valuable new market opportunities (Rao & Holt, 2005). Promotion of CSR programs has also been shown to have a positive effect on a firm's research and development, which is proposed to equate to future financial gain (Lioui & Sharma, 2012). Innovation and R&D prepare a company for future changes to the marketplace and allow them to act on future opportunities, allowing firms to better access the long-term benefits achieved through the short-term costs related to sustainability.

Intangible Factors

One of the most studied effects of firms' CSR programs relates to their effect on positive stakeholder and regulator interactions (Epstein & Roy, 2001). Firms putting significant effort into their CSR programs have been shown to increase the quality and consistency of their shareholder dialogue (Moore et al., 2012). Results from other CSR studies recommend that companies with strong ESG considerations can benefit by communicating their performance to their investors as this serves to enhance firm reputation (Roy & Gitman, 2012). Increased shareholder reputation gains further significance from reports that find that, of all ESG-related programs implemented by a group of firms, only those with community-based factors had a significant effect on increases in firm profitability (Mollet, von Arx, and Ilić, 2013).

Besides investors, other stakeholders such as limited partners and consumers are increasingly demanding that corporations consider ESG factors. For example, consumers have become increasingly aware of environmental issues, and the growing demand for sustainable goods and services is a strong motivator for many private firms to develop sustainable products. The indirect benefit of customer attraction attributed to environmentally friendly material use perfectly describes the tendency for sustainability programs to provide indirect value to a firm. Such indirect value arises from the generation of "intangible" benefits, which cannot easily be measured, but which affect firm performance.

An example of this indirect influence is the effect of employee satisfaction on financial performance. When customer satisfaction is used as a mediator, a study has found a significant indirect relationship between employee satisfaction and financial performance (Chi & Gursoy, 2009). Another study hypothesizes that employee satisfaction increases firm value, but only after it is manifested in a tangible outcome (Edmans, 2011). Other studies agree with such assertions, promoting the concept that there is rarely a direct relationship between individual characteristics of sustainability programs and financial performance, but instead that a firm's intangible resources moderate the relationship between these factors (Surroca, Tribó, & Waddock, 2010). However, this hypothesis may be dependent on the time frame used for financial considerations.

Other studies have more clearly delineated the positive tangibles stemming from sustainability programs to include elements such as improved research and development (Lioui & Sharma, 2012). Apart from innovation, tangibles are also often linked to sustainability programs on technology, human capital, and reputation, and while the intangible outcomes of sustainability programs often cannot be directly linked to financial performance, the tangible benefits they help generate are shown to improve firm performance (Surroca et al., 2010).

Concluding Remarks

Expanding the range of metrics beyond financial indicators is likely to lead to improved capital allocation. There is overwhelming evidence that many measures of sustainability performance are associated with improved financial performance, especially operating performance. Efficient energy and resource use constitute the "low hanging fruit" of sustainability-integrated capital allocation. A number of sustainability measures are only related to long-term outperformance. There has not been significant evidence that corporate social performance is detrimental to corporate financial performance. A great number of theoretical as well as empirical studies have shown that many aspects of ESG have positive impact on firm value.

In addition, current research points to multiple indirect effects of sustainability that can improve financial performance. It is reasonable to assume that the support for these influences will only become clearer as further research analyzes longer timelines and growing environmental constraints. Consumer and investor demand for social and environmental accountability is rising and the external scrutiny of company reputations is arguably at an all-time high. Companies implementing ESG programs now are mitigating current risks while preparing for an uncertain future. Given the proven relationship between corporate sustainability performance and financial return, it is highly likely that it will pay the investor to incorporate non-financial metrics that measure the impact on planetary boundaries into the security selection process. In the next chapter, we turn to examine some tools which will help us to navigate the trade-offs between the short and long term, and also construct monetary values for certain environmentally scarce resources.

Notes

1. Accessible at www.reportingexchange.com
2. The academic studies in this sub-field have historically referred to corporate environmental and social performance as corporate 'social' performance. CSP therefore refers to the 'E' and 'S' aspects of ESG. The 'G' aspect, governance, is generally studied separately in the academic literature.

References

Bancilhon, C. (2012). *Reporting on Environmental, Social, and Governance Considerations in the Private Equity Sector*. Retrieved from BSR. https://www.bsr.org/en/our-insights/report-view/reporting-on-environmental-social-and-governance-considerations-in-the-priv

Barnett, M. L. (2014). Why Stakeholders Ignore Firm Misconduct: A Cognitive View. *Journal of Management, 40*(3), 676–702.

Bergmann, A., Rotzek, J. N., Wetzel, M., & Guenther, E. (2017). Hang the Low-Hanging Fruit Even Lower – Evidence that Energy Efficiency Matters for Corporate Financial Performance. *Journal of Cleaner Production, 147*, 66–74. https://doi.org/10.1016/j.jclepro.2017.01.074

Borgers, A., Derwall, J., Koedijk, K., & ter Horst, J. (2013). Stakeholder Relations and Stock Returns: On Errors in Investors' Expectations and Learning. *Journal of Empirical Finance, 22*, 159–175. http://www.sciencedirect.com/science/journal/09275398

Bose, S., & Springsteel, A. (2017). The Value and Current Limitations of ESG Data for the Security Selector. *Journal of Environmental Investing, 8*(1), 54–73.

Bradford, T. (2018). *The Energy System: Technology, Economics, Markets and Policy*. Cambridge, MA: MIT Press.

Bronk, R. (2013). Hayek on the Wisdom of Prices: A Reassessment. *Erasmus Journal for Philosophy and Economics, 6*(1), 82–107. http://ejpe.org/archive/

Busch, T., & Friede, G. (2018). The Robustness of the Corporate Social and Financial Performance Relation: A Second-Order Meta-Analysis. *Corporate Social Responsibility and Environmental Management, 25*(4), 583–608. https://doi.org/10.1002/csr.1480

Busch, T., & Lewandowski, S. (2017). Corporate Carbon and Financial Performance: A Meta-Analysis. *Journal of Industrial Ecology*. https://doi.org/10.1111/jiec.12591

Cai, L., & He, C. (2014). Corporate Environmental Responsibility and Equity Prices. *Journal of Business Ethics, 125*(4), 617–635.

Chi, C. G., & Gursoy, D. (2009). Employee Satisfaction, Customer Satisfaction, and Financial Performance: An Empirical Examination. *International Journal of Hospitality Management, 28*(2), 245–253.

Chu, L. Y., & Sappington, D. E. (2013). Motivating Energy Suppliers to Promote Energy Conservation. *Journal of Regulatory Economics, 43*(3), 229–247.

Clark, G. L., Feiner, A., & Viehs, M. (2015). *From the Stockholder to the Stakeholder.* Retrieved from Oxford.

Claver, E., López, M. D., Molina, J. F., & Tarí, J. J. (2007). Environmental Management and Firm Performance: A Case Study. *Journal of Environmental Management, 84*(4), 606–619.

Datamaran. (2018). *Global Insights Report 2018: The Rise of ESG Regulations.* Retrieved from https://www.datamaran.com/wp-content/uploads/2018/10/GIR-2018.pdf

Eccles, R. G., Ioannou, I., & Serafeim, G. (2014). The Impact of Corporate Sustainability on Organizational Processes and Performance. *Management Science, 60*(11), 2835–2857. http://mansci.journal.informs.org/content/by/year

Edmans, A. (2011). Does the Stock Market Fully Value Intangibles? Employee Satisfaction and Equity Prices. *Journal of Financial Economics, 101*(3), 621–640. https://doi.org/10.1016/j.jfineco.2011.03.021

Epstein, M. J., & Roy, M.-J. (2001). Sustainability in Action: Identifying and Measuring the Key Performance Drivers. *Long Range Planning, 34*(5), 585–604.

Esty, D. C., & Cort, T. (2017). Corporate Sustainability Metrics: What Investors Need and Don't Get. *Journal Environmental Investing, 54*(3), 140–154.

Fenton-O'Creevy, M., Nicholson, N., Sloane, E., & Willman, P. (2005). *Traders: Risks, Decisions, and Management in Financial Markets.* Oxford, UK: Oxford University Press.

Flammer, C. (2015). Does Product Market Competition Foster Corporate Social Responsibility? Evidence from Trade Liberalization. *Strategic Management Journal, 36*(10), 1469–1485.

Hawkins, T. R., Singh, B., Majeau-Bettez, G., & Strømman, A. H. (2013). Comparative Environmental Life Cycle Assessment of Conventional and Electric Vehicles. *Journal of Industrial Ecology, 17*(1), 53–64. https://doi.org/10.1111/j.1530-9290.2012.00532.x

Hayek, F. A. V. (1945). The Use of Knowledge in Society. *American Economic Review, 35,* 519–530.

Ho, K. (2009). *Liquidated: An Ethnography of Wall Street.* Durham, NC: Duke University Press.

Hong, H., & Kacperczyk, M. (2009). The Price of Sin: The Effects of Social Norms on Markets. *Journal of Financial Economics, 93*(1), 15–36. https://doi.org/10.1016/j.jfineco.2008.09.001

ICCR. (2019). *Proxy Resolutions and Voting Guide.* Retrieved from https://www.iccr.org/iccrs-2019-proxy-resolutions-and-voting-guide-0

Jiao, Y. (2010). Stakeholder Welfare and Firm Value. *Journal of Banking & Finance, 34*(10), 2549–2561. https://doi.org/10.1016/j.jbankfin.2010.04.013

Jong, P., Paulraj, A., & Blome, C. (2014). The Financial Impact of ISO 14001 Certification: Top-Line, Bottom-Line, or Both? *Journal of Business Ethics,* *119*(1), 131–149. https://doi.org/10.1007/s10551-012-1604-z

Kats, G., Alevantis, L., Berman, A., Mills, E., & Perlman, J. (2003). *The Costs and Financial Benefits of Green Buildings: A Report to California's Sustainable Building Task Force.* Retrieved from https://noharm-uscanada.org/documents/costs-and-financial-benefits-green-buildings-report-california's-sustainable-building-task

Kempf, A., & Osthoff, P. (2007). The Effect of Socially Responsible Investing on Portfolio Performance. *European Financial Management,* *13*(5), 908–922. http://www.blackwellpublishing.com/journal.asp?ref=1354-7798

Kirzner, I. M. (1997). Entrepreneurial Discovery and the Competitive Market Process: An Austrian Approach. *Journal of Economic Literature, 35,* 60–85.

Kitzmueller, M., & Shimshack, J. (2012). Economic Perspectives on Corporate Social Responsibility. *Journal of Economic Literature, 50*(1), 51–84.

Kreander, N., Gray, R. H., Power, D. M., & Sinclair, C. D. (2005). Evaluating the Performance of Ethical and Non-ethical Funds: A Matched Pair Analysis. *Journal of Business Finance and Accounting, 32*(7-8), 1465–1493. http://www.blackwellpublishing.com/journal.asp?ref=0306-686X&site=1

Lin, C.-H., Yang, H.-L., & Liou, D.-Y. (2009). The Impact of Corporate Social Responsibility on Financial Performance: Evidence from Business in Taiwan. *Technology in Society, 31*(1), 56–63.

Lioui, A., & Sharma, Z. (2012). Environmental Corporate Social Responsibility and Financial Performance: Disentangling Direct and Indirect Effects. *Ecological Economics, 78,* 100–111. https://doi.org/10.1016/j.ecolecon.2012.04.004

Lobe, S., & Walkshäusl, C. (2016). Vice Versus Virtue Investing Around the World. *Review of Managerial Science, 10*(2), 303–344.

López-Gamero, M. D., Molina-Azorín, J. F., & Claver-Cortés, E. (2009). The Whole Relationship between Environmental Variables and Firm Performance: Competitive Advantage and Firm Resources as Mediator Variables. *Journal of Environmental Management, 90*(10), 3110–3121. https://doi.org/10.1016/j.jenvman.2009.05.007

Lourenço, I. C., Branco, M. C., Curto, J. D., & Eugénio, T. (2012). How Does the Market Value Corporate Sustainability Performance? *Journal of Business Ethics, 108*(4), 417–428.

Lucas, M. T., & Noordewier, T. G. (2016). Environmental Management Practices and Firm Financial Performance: The Moderating Effect of Industry Pollution-Related Factors. *International Journal of Production Economics, 175,* 24–34. https://doi.org/10.1016/j.ijpe.2016.02.003

Marcus, A. A. (2015). *Innovations in Sustainability.* Cambridge, UK: Cambridge University Press.

McGee, P. (2017, November 8). Electric Cars' Green Image Blackens Beneath the Bonnet. *Financial Times.*

Meinrenken, C. J., & Lackner, K. S. (2015). Fleet View of Electrified Transportation Reveals Smaller Potential to Reduce GHG Emissions. *Applied Energy, 138,* 393–403.

Mollet, J. C., von Arx, U., & Ilic, D. (2013). Strategic Sustainability and Financial Performance: Exploring Abnormal Returns. *Journal of Business Economics, 83*(6), 577–604. https://link.springer.com/journal/volumesAndIssues/11573

Montabon, F., Sroufe, R., & Narasimhan, R. (2007). An Examination of Corporate Reporting, Environmental Management Practices and Firm Performance. *Journal of Operations Management, 25*(5), 998–1014.

Moore, L. L., De Silva, I., & Hartmann, S. (2012). An Investigation into the Financial Return on Corporate Social Responsibility in the Apparel Industry. *Journal of Corporate Citizenship, 45,* 104–122.

Moss, C. B., Livanis, G., & Schmitz, A. (2010). The Effect of Increased Energy Prices on Agriculture: A Differential Supply Approach. *Journal of Agricultural and Applied Economics, 42*(4), 711.

Orlitzky, M., Schmidt, F. L., & Rynes, S. L. (2003). Corporate Social and Financial Performance: A Meta-Analysis. *Organization Studies, 24*(3), 403–441.

Ostrom, E. (2010). Beyond Markets and States: Polycentric Governance of Complex Economic Systems. *American Economic Review, 100*(3), 641–672. http://www.aeaweb.org/aer/

Pellegrini-Masini, G., & Leishman, C. (2011). The Role of Corporate Reputation and Employees' Values in the Uptake of Energy Efficiency in Office Buildings. *Energy Policy, 39*(9), 5409–5419.

Rao, P., & Holt, D. (2005). Do Green Supply Chains Lead to Competitiveness and Economic Performance? *International Journal of Operations & Production Management, 25*(9), 898–916.

Roy, H., & Gitman, L. (2012). *Trends in ESG Integration in Investments.* Retrieved from https://www.bsr.org/reports/BSR_Trends_in_ESG_Integration.pdf

Schmidheiny, S., & Zorraquin, F. J. (1996). *Financing Change: The Financial Community, Eco-Efficiency, and Sustainable Development.* Cambridge, MA: MIT Press.

Schröder, M. (2007). Is There a Difference? The Performance Characteristics of SRI Equity Indices. *Journal of Business Finance & Accounting, 34*(1/2), 331–348. https://doi.org/10.1111/j.1468-5957.2006.00647.x

Serrenho, A. C., Norman, J. B., & Allwood, J. M. (2017). The Impact of Reducing Car Weight on Global Emissions: The Future Fleet in Great Britain. *Philosophical Transactions of the Royal Society A: Mathematical, Physical and Engineering Sciences, 375*(2095), 20160364. https://doi.org/10.1098/rsta.2016.0364

SSEI. (2019). *Database.* Retrieved from http://www.sseinitiative.org/data/

Surowiecki, J. (2004). *The Wisdom of Crowds.* New York, NY: Doubleday.

Surroca, J., Tribó, J. A., & Waddock, S. (2010). Corporate Responsibility and Financial Performance: The Role of Intangible Resources. *Strategic Management Journal, 31*(5), 463–490.

Tang, A. K., Lai, K. h., & Cheng, T. (2012). Environmental Governance of Enterprises and Their Economic Upshot Through Corporate Reputation and Customer Satisfaction. *Business Strategy and the Environment, 21*(6), 401–411.

Transition Pathway Initiative. (2017). *Tesla: Management Quality.* Retrieved from http://www.lse.ac.uk/GranthamInstitute/tpi/company/tesla/

Trudel, R., & Cotte, J. (2009). Does It Pay to Be Good? *MIT Sloan Management Review, 50*(2), 61.

Utz, S., & Wimmer, M. (2014). Are they Any Good at All? A Financial and Ethical Analysis of Socially Responsible Mutual Funds. *Journal of Asset Management, 15*(1), 72–82. https://doi.org/10.1057/jam.2014.8

Wagner, M. (2005). How to Reconcile Environmental and Economic Performance to Improve Corporate Sustainability: Corporate Environmental Strategies in the European Paper Industry. *Journal of Environmental Management, 76*(2), 105–118.

Wagner, M. (2007). Integration of Environmental Management with Other Managerial Functions of the Firm: Empirical Effects on Drivers of Economic Performance. *Long Range Planning, 40*(6), 611–628.

Wagner, M., & Schaltegger, S. (2004). The Effect of Corporate Environmental Strategy Choice and Environmental Performance on Competitiveness and Economic Performance: An Empirical Study of EU Manufacturing. *European Management Journal, 22*(5), 557–572.

WBCSD. (2018a). *Insights from the Reporting Exchange: ESG Reporting Trends.* Retrieved from Geneva: https://www.wbcsd.org/Programs/Redefining-Value/External-Disclosure/The-Reporting-Exchange/Resources/Insights-from-the-Reporting-Exchange-ESG-reporting-trends

WBCSD. (2018b). *Insights from the Reporting Exchange: National, Regional & International Developments.* Retrieved from Geneva: https://www.wbcsd.org/Programs/Redefining-Value/External-Disclosure/The-Reporting-Exchange/Resources/National-regional-and-international-developments

Wong, C. W. Y., Lai, K.-H., Shang, K.-C., Lu, C.-S., & Leung, T. K. P. (2012). Green Operations and the Moderating Role of Environmental Management Capability of Suppliers on Manufacturing Firm Performance. *International Journal of Production Economics, 140*(1), 283–294. https://doi.org/10.1016/j.ijpe.2011.08.031

Zukin, C., & Szeltner, M. (2012). *Talent Report: What Workers Want in 2012.* John J. Heldrich Center for Workforce Development at Rutgers, The State University of New Jersey. Full report available online: http://www.netimpact.org/whatworkerswant

CHAPTER 6

Cost-Benefit Analysis and Discounting

INTRODUCTION

Our review of the relationship between corporate social performance and corporate financial performance in Chap. 5 begs two related questions. First, if the market value of social and environmental performance is not immediately apparent, what weight should we place upon their importance? If an investor believes that a company's efforts to improve biodiversity have negligible impact on short-term financial return, but may have a long-term impact on brand valuation, stakeholder relations, license to operate, and other such intangible factors, then what value should she place on such potential hard-to-quantify benefits? Second, having determined an appropriate weight or value for non-financial benefits, how should she account for the likelihood that such non-financial benefits will only be received in the possibly distant future? This chapter is concerned with potential ways to answer these two related questions.

There are essentially two ways to answer the first question. We can either try to assign some level of financial value to social and environmental performances and then measure success by the imputed financial value of an investment, or we can decide that social and environmental performance standards are non-negotiable requirements of sustainable investing and attempt to evaluate investments on multiple metrics of success. Cost-benefit analysis is a tool that is used to assign monetary values to a range of social and environmental impacts in the context of project assessment. Cost-benefit analysis can therefore provide methods to impute financial

© The Author(s) 2019

S. Bose et al., *The Financial Ecosystem*, Palgrave Studies in Impact Finance, https://doi.org/10.1007/978-3-030-05624-7_6

value to sustainability efforts. When minimum social and environmental performance standards cannot be compromised, then cost-benefit analysis must be supplemented or replaced by multi-criteria analysis or normative judgment.

Once we have imputed a monetary value to sustainability impacts, there remains the question of evaluating intertemporal trade-offs. What value should be placed today on assets that might bring us significant benefits in the distant future, but which are not obviously scarce today? The quantum of each of a long list of ecological services we rely upon but do not explicitly value in monetary terms is surely finite. As such, the value of these ecosystem services will likely rise in future, as their use begins to approach ecological boundaries. All investing decisions have consequences which unfold over time. What method can we utilize to balance the resource requirements of today's *wants* versus future *needs*? Or, in a slightly different vein, do we countenance the satisfaction of today's needs at the cost of future wants? The process of allocating the consumption and saving of wealth (broadly defined) across time is referred to as a problem of intertemporal decision-making. The common analytical tool utilized for intertemporal trade-offs is discounting.

Cost-Benefit Analysis

Cost-benefit analysis (CBA) or benefit-cost analysis is a decision support tool[1] utilized in project assessment. It is a method of ranking alternatives based on the imputed monetary value of flows of costs and benefits attributable to a decision or project. For example, the state of New Mexico utilizes CBA to rank the monetary net benefits of taxpayer-funded prison programs. Based on an evaluation of long-term costs and benefits, the New Mexico Legislative Finance Committee estimates that benefit-cost ratio of providing basic or post-secondary education to incarcerated prisoners far exceeds that of providing treatment programs for domestic violence perpetrators (Pew Charitable Trust & MacArthur Foundation, 2014). In an example of a more macro-level ranking of alternatives, a somewhat controversial prioritization among selected Sustainable Development Goals is justified by a series of back-of-the-envelope CBAs performed by the Copenhagen Consensus Center (Lomborg, 2018).

The modern practice and terminology of cost-benefit analysis was developed by the US Army Corps of Engineers in the 1920s (Persky, 2001), though similar computations can be traced back to at least the

work of pre-Revolutionary French engineers justifying public works and
to the nineteenth century writings of Jules Dupuit (Ekelund Jr. & Hebert,
1999). The Army Corps of Engineers computed the potential value to
affected parties resulting from the costly construction of a public good,
such as a dam or canal. The process of CBA asks the following question:
Are the aggregate benefits for all individuals affected by a project greater
than the aggregate costs? In answering this question, the current practice
of CBA attempts to translate all significant costs and benefits into monetary amounts. Note that it is the sum of individual benefits for a fixed
quantity of the public good that is salient, not the sum quantities demand
by each individual. This is known as the *horizontal sum* of demands for a
public good. Cost-benefit analysis prioritizes those projects which maximize *static efficiency*, that is, it identifies those projects which satisfy the
Kaldor-Hicks compensation criterion. The Kaldor-Hicks criterion requires
that the parties who gain from a project (the 'winners') must gain more
than is lost by the parties who lose (the 'losers'). In principle, if a project
that meets the criterion were to be implemented, the winners could compensate the losers and still have net gains left over (Stavins, 2000). There
is no requirement that the winners actually compensate the losers, merely
that they could do so in principle. The Kaldor-Hicks criterion is a relatively
weak requirement: it merely requires that the sum of gains exceed the sum
of losses without imposing any conditions on the distribution of gains. It
does not require that most affected parties gain from the project—if a few
winners gain a lot and many losers lose a little, then the Kaldor-Hicks
condition may be satisfied. It is here that the Kaldor-Hicks criterion differs
from democratic choice rules: majority voting requires that among affected
constituents, a majority expect net gains from a proposal.

Willingness to Pay

The translation of costs and benefits into monetary values is based on the
concept of *willingness to pay* (WTP). Benefits are the sum of the maximum
amounts that people would be willing to pay for a project outcome, and
costs are the sum of the opportunity costs of the resources required by the
project. It is a feature of many essential goods that the WTP for such
goods is significantly higher than their price. For example, the WTP for
water is generally much higher than the price paid for most households
with available running water. On the other hand, the WTP for luxuries
tends to be closer to their prices.[2]

Value Creation in a Business Context

The two concepts of WTP and opportunity costs in a CBA context originated in the context of social decision-making. They are computed at the *social* level: the WTP is the sum of the WTPs of all affected individuals and the opportunity cost is the cost incurred by everyone, whether or not they are party to an economic transaction. In this sense, the CBA concept of costs and benefits internalizes all externalities.[3] The concepts of WTP and opportunity cost have a natural counterpart in the context of private businesses, which are not necessarily focused on externalities. Brandenburger and Stuart Jr. (1996) consider the case of a business that sells a product to a customer and uses suppliers to manufacture that product. The sale price at which the customer would be indifferent between buying the product and not buying it represents the WTP of the customer. The WTP will depend on inter alia the income of the customer and prices of the substitutes and complements of the product. The opportunity cost of making the product is the sum of opportunity costs of all suppliers. Brandenburger and Stuart note that an exact definition of *value created*[4] by the firm is provided by the difference between WTP and opportunity cost. The distribution of value created (see Fig. 6.1) depends on the price paid by the customer (which determines consumer surplus or the buyer's share) and the price paid by the firm to its suppliers (which determines firm profit and supplier profit).

A clear articulation of the net benefits from a public project can serve to broaden social acceptance among all affected parties. This is one of the key purposes of performing CBAs. In a similar vein, an articulation of the value created by a business venture and the potential distribution of that value across stakeholders can ensure that the ecosystem of customers, employees, and vendors is supportive of corporate investments. An early recognition of the link between social CBAs and the corporate license to operate is made by Wells (1975), who argues that multinational corporations attempting to persuade developing country governments of the social value of their local investments would be well served by articulating return on investment computations using the language and concepts of social CBAs. More recently, Cordes (2017) and Nicholls (2017) compare the practice of CBA with that of social return on investment (SROI), a commonly used method of evaluating the impact of social enterprises that was developed from CBA in the 1990s. The SROI

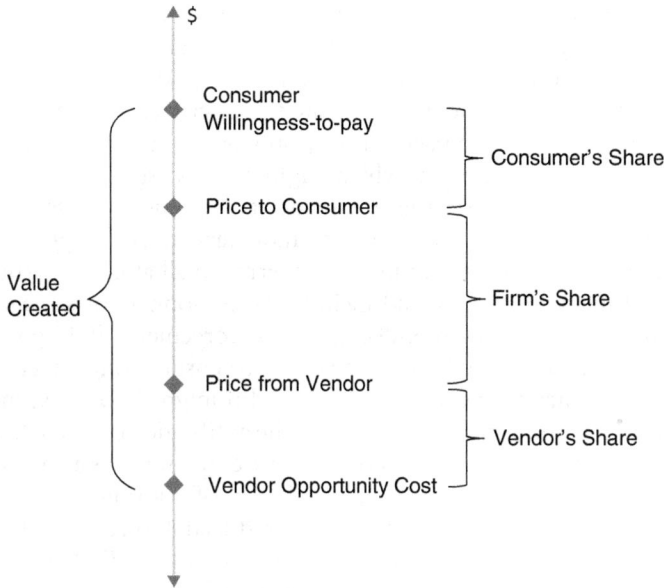

Fig. 6.1 Distribution of value created. (Source: Adapted from Brandenburger and Stuart Jr. (1996))

framework is an attempt to broaden the computation and appeal of CBAs, which were historically limited to government agencies and were generally performed by a limited number of economists. Early CBAs also tended to eschew quantification and monetization of social benefits and costs, a gap that SROI explicitly aims to fill. Because of their common theoretical foundation, there is little conceptual difference between SROI and CBA. There are differences in implementation, but these are more the consequence of context rather than underlying principle (Dufour, 2019).

Antibiotic Resistance: A CBA Example

An example CBA might examine the social, environmental, and financial costs and benefits of a regulatory program to monitor the prescribing of antibiotics by doctors. The purpose of such a program would be to reduce excessive and improper use of antibiotics, which has been linked to an increase in drug-resistant strains of disease-carrying bacteria and a global decline in antibiotic effectiveness (Laxminarayan, 2014). Such a program would have a list of readily enumerated financial costs and benefits, a number of quantifiable impacts with a justifiably broad range of monetary values, as well as some impacts which might be impossible to quantify. The practice of CBA comprises the systematic cataloguing of costs and benefits, translating as much of these into monetary values as possible, and computing the net benefits in monetary terms to all affected parties. The readily enumerated costs would include the personnel costs incurred by the regulatory agency of monitoring and enforcement, the opportunity cost of time spent by medical professionals to ensure compliance, as well as the cost of inconvenience for patients who might have to spend time and money to demonstrate true need for the antibiotic. The benefits of the program might include reduced costs of future treatment as a consequence of lower antibiotic resistance, reduced risk of mortality from future antibiotic-resistant infections, as well as reduced future costs from the diminished need to introduce more virulent antibiotics. Table 6.1 lays out the potential costs and benefits for such a program.

Table 6.1 Potential costs and benefits of a regulatory program to monitor antibiotic prescriptions

Description	Quantitative metric
Costs:	
Salaries of enforcement staff	$
Time spent by medical professionals on compliance activities	Hours
Inconvenience to patients who might have to visit doctors more frequently	Hours, gallons of fuel in travel costs
Benefits:	
Reduced costs of future treatment due to lower antibiotic resistance	$, hours
Reduced risk of mortality from future antibiotic-resistant infections	Lives
Reduced future R&D costs from the diminished need to introduce more virulent antibiotics	$, hours
Reduced quantity of unused antibiotics being disposed in landfills	Milligrams

Source: Authors

Shadow Prices

In reviewing Table 6.1, some costs and benefits are measured in $, while others are measured in time, human lives, and milligrams of antibiotics. The practice of CBA attempts to *monetize* all such metrics by assigning justifiable monetary values to them. The monetary value assigned to each non-dollar metric is called a *shadow price,* in effect an imputed social value of the cost or benefit. The time spent by medical professionals on compliance activities would be *monetized* by multiplying the hours spent by the hourly wage rate of those professionals.[5] To the extent that the hourly wage rate (the shadow price of labor in this case) is set by the labor market for medical professionals, the shadow price is related to and grounded by the bids, offers, and transaction prices in an actual marketplace.

A more difficult monetization problem is posed by the value of lives saved by the reduced mortality from future antibiotic-resistant diseases. CBA utilizes the concept of *value of a statistical life* (VSL) to monetize lives saved. How might one place a monetary value on lives saved? Perhaps thankfully, there is no marketplace whence bids and offers for human lives are readily available. How then might CBA place a shadow price on lives? The practice of CBA has devised techniques to triangulate on the notion of the willingness to pay to save what is called a 'statistical life.' What would one be willing to pay to save one's own life for certain? As the character of Admetus demonstrates in Euripides' play Alcestis, a person may be willing to give up his own parents and his beloved wife for an extra year of life. Surely then, the willingness to pay to save one's own life is next to infinite. The economist's position is that the VSL is meant to represent the value of a 'statistical' life, that is, a random person's life from a population of comparable lives, not one's own life. The notion comes from the recognition that there are situations where we could reduce our risk of death by spending money or time in order to increase safety. When we spend money or time to avoid risking our lives, or accept compensation in order to assume such risks, we implicitly place a monetary value on the increased risk of death. The VSL can be computed by asking individuals how much they would be willing to pay to reduce mortality risk (a method known as *stated preference*) or by observing economic behavior and imputing a willingness to pay for risk reduction (referred to as *revealed preference*).

Computation of VSL

The computation of VSL is inspired by Adam Smith's suggestion that individuals must be induced to work in risky occupations by compensating increases in wages. An individual's VSL is a measure of the WTP for small reductions in mortality risk. For example, a person may be willing to accept a $600 increase in compensation in return for accepting a job that has 1/10,000 higher mortality risk. The VSL in this case would amount to $600/(1/10,000) = $6 million.

The first computation of VSL using this method was presented in Thaler and Rosen (1976). Thaler and Rosen used data from the 1967 Occupation Study of the Society of Actuaries and the 1967 Survey of Economic Opportunity earnings data to estimate the occupational hazard rates for 37 occupations and 900 individuals. Hazard rates varied from 26.7 extra deaths per year per 10,000 jobs for guards to 0.2 extra deaths for linemen and servicemen. Thaler and Rosen concluded that the average person in their sample would be willing to pay at least $8.80 per year in 1967 dollars for an average seat belt that reduces the risk of death from 25×10^{-5} to 20×10^{-5}. Using the logic described above, the implied VSL would be $8.80/(5/100,000) = $176,00 in 1967 dollars.

Revealed Preference Methods

The two categories of imputing WTP, referred to as *non-market valuation* are the revealed preference and stated preference methods.[6] Revealed preference methods of valuation, which include the *hedonic pricing* method, the *travel cost* method, and the *defensive expenditures* method, attempt to infer the value of non-traded attributes from the observed behavior of stakeholders in related markets.

The computation of VSL described in the box above is an example of the application of the hedonic pricing method. This method utilizes the observation that prices for many composite goods and services can be decomposed into separate sub-prices for the constituent parts. For example, a job as a guard may be viewed as a composite service comprising occupation hazards as well as overseeing operations. Similarly, a composite good such as a house can be viewed as a bundle of attributes, which include shelter, living, and storage space, access to jobs and schools, and environmental amenities such as clean air. By utilizing a method similar to the VSL computation above, the willingness to pay for clean air can be gleaned from house price data. The monetary value of the adverse impact of local air pollution can be computed from an estimate of the reduction in home prices associated with increased ambient concentrations of air pollutants. The first such study was performed by Ridker and Henning (1967) using home prices and SO_2 levels for census tracts in metropolitan Saint Louis. Since then, among other studies, the hedonic price method has been used to estimate the willingness to pay to avoid air pollutants and noise disturbances (Le Boennec & Salladarré, 2017), as well as to value amenities as diverse as proximity to wetlands in urban (Frey, Palin, Walsh, & Whitcraft, 2013) and rural areas (Bin & Polasky, 2005) and the presence of solar roofs on homes (Ma, Polyakov, & Pandit, 2016).

The travel cost method of non-market valuation, pioneered by Hotelling (1947), seeks to value environmental amenities where consumption of a market good must be combined with the environmental (non-market) good to facilitate enjoyment of the non-market good. Hotelling conceived this method when asked by the US National Park Service to suggest ways that might be used to value the public benefits of conserved forests. Hotelling's key insight was that visitors to national parks must value their experience of the park at more than the value of the resources they expended to enjoy the park (otherwise, they would not voluntarily expend such resources). Since visitors traveled from near and afar to visit the national parks, the sum of time and money spent by all visitors represented a lower bound on the overall value of the park.

A third method of non-market valuation is referred to as *defensive expenditure* or *averting behavior* or *household production* valuation. The household production model is a form of revealed preference environmental valuation that assumes that consumers can combine a non-market good or bad with a market good to produce a synthetic good that yields well-being. Defensive expenditure or averting models refer to models where consumption of a market good counteracts the effects of a non-market bad. For example, the expenditure of a household on bottled water in the face of perceived risks to their water supply from unconventional shale gas extraction represents a lower bound on the willingness to pay to avoid potentially adverse impacts to drinking water safety (Wrenn, Klaiber, & Jaenicke, 2016). Similarly, the use of particulate-filtering facemasks by Chinese residents on days when air quality drops can be used to estimate a lower bound on the willingness to pay to avoid ambient concentrations of particulate matter (Zhang & Mu, 2018).

Stated Preference Methods

For many economists, the advantage of revealed preference methods of valuation lies in their grounding to actual underlying market transactions. Since economic agents actually expend cash income on or devote non-cash resources to the activities underpinning revealed preference valuations of ecosystem services, one might argue that the resultant monetary willingness-to-pay estimates are not far from observable expenditure. This is a desirable attribute of revealed preference methods. Unfortunately, revealed preference methods can only measure the use value of the ecosystem. In addition to use value, both social and environmental services can have non-use values. It is this type of ecosystem value which revealed preference methods cannot be used to estimate. Non-use values are of three types: *existence value, altruistic value,* and *bequest value.*

Existence value refers to the phenomenon that human beings derive well-being from knowing that many environmental goods exist, even though they may not actually use such goods. For example, when asked, many respondents indicate a willingness to pay to preserve species which they would not actually spend time or money to view in the wild or in captivity. The possibility of existence value implies that there are people who care about the survival of a species even though they may not engage in any market transactions that might reflect that concern. Existence value is a recognition that one can have a kind of platonic love for an ecosystem or an idea without leaving a behavioral trace of one's love. Revealed preference can never discern this type of value, since revealed preference methods require a behavioral trace. Similarly, altruistic value refers to an increase in a person's well-being brought about by an increase in someone else's well-being. Bequest value refers to the desire to pass on a wilderness area or a legacy to the next generation. Even though I might not choose to use that area in any discernible way, I might nevertheless prefer to see it preserved for a future generation. Non-use value is often a material component of the value that people place on sites with unique ecologies, cultural, historic, or religious value.

The only way to elicit estimates of non-use value is to ask people. This can be done through surveys (referred to as *contingent valuation*) or by placing respondents in experimental situations (referred to as *discrete choice experiments*). Contingent valuation surveys ask consumers what they would be willing to pay or accept for a change in an environmental amenity. To be usable as a basis for valid environmental valuations, such surveys must be carefully designed and administered to minimize the likelihood that flippant or false responses might influence the resulting estimates. During the course of the litigation in the aftermath of the Exxon Valdez spill in 1989, a broad consensus was forged on the best practices required of contingent valuation surveys (Arrow et al., 1993). Discrete choice experiments, which developed from methods common in the marketing and psychology literature, construct experimental situations where respondents are asked to choose among alternative experiences involving environmental amenities, with associated attributes and costs (Adamowicz, Louviere, & Williams, 1994). Discrete choice experiments present hypothetical referenda to consumers and then utilize the responses to estimate willingness to pay for related environmental attributes. A recent outline of best practices for both contingent valuation and discrete choice experiments is given in Johnston et al. (2017). An extension of discrete choice methods is the construction of an experimental trading game called the *securities trading of concepts* (STOC), proposed by Dahan, Kim, Lo, Poggio, and Chan (2011). This method induces participants to trade attributes of new products with real or fictitious money, thereby establishing a market-estimated willingness to pay for product attributes (such as ease of use, durability, or size). This method is a combination of prediction markets (see Chap. 12) and discrete choice experiments.[7]

Benefits Transfer

Both revealed and stated preference methods have been utilized extensively to develop shadow prices for a range of ecosystem services in many markets for several decades. Benefits transfer is a practice that attempts to link the shadow prices of related ecosystem services across time and across geographies and thereby reduce the need to re-estimate shadow prices in many situations (Richardson, Loomis, Kroeger, & Casey, 2015). For example, benefit transfer method might utilize an estimate of WTP to avoid nitrogen run-offs computed in 1990 in a European context to estimate a WTP in the United States to avoid nitrogen run-off in 2018. In order to do so, the analyst would adjust the 1990 European shadow price for inflation between 1990 and 2018, and then utilize perhaps a ratio of GDPs per capita between Europe and the United States to adjust the WTP. There exist multiple databases compiled by environmental agencies and industry stakeholders to aid in the process of identifying existing computations of shadow prices.[8] As with any estimation and valuation process that searches for similarities in assets that are widely dispersed in time and distance, many uncertainties and controversies arise (Johnston & Rosenberger, 2010). For example, there is some consensus that site similarity—including similarity of population density, natural resources, and income characteristics of users—is an important determinant of benefits transfer validity and reliability. However, there is no list of guidelines to determine what is similar enough, so cost-benefit analysts are free to use their own judgment. However, these valuation ambiguities are not necessarily greater than those prevalent in the valuation analysis of comparable financial assets. For example, in their research reports, sell-side equity analysts choose peer companies in comparable valuations in a strategic manner, in part to justify optimistically skewed target prices (Franco, Hope, & Larocque, 2015).

In financial valuation, it is routine to utilize comparable market valuation analysis or precedent transactions valuation analysis to construct values of one asset using valuations of comparable assets, even though there might be significant differences in the attributes of the comparable assets.[9] Part of the judgment and expertise in as well as the potential reward from careful valuation arises precisely from the presence of ambiguities. If valuation were straightforward and devoid of controversy, then there would be no reward to careful discernment of the correct underlying value. As we noted in Chap. 1, an investor attempting to value his asset has the option to compare his estimation of the present value of future flows with the amount that another investor might be willing to pay to purchase the asset, which might incorporate the other investor's beliefs about future flows. He is able to infer others' valuations by examining the transaction prices or the bid and ask prices of comparable assets. This ability to compare the contemporaneous assessments of others with our own idiosyncratic forecasts helps to triangulate and anchor valuations of assets. This process is not dissimilar from valuations of ecosystem services using revealed and stated preference methods. As with the construction of shadow prices, comparable market valuation is a combination of precision, judgment, and triangulation. Although the underlying disciplines of the two approaches (environmental economics and financial asset pricing) differ somewhat in principal concerns, there are many similarities in the endeavors to price financial assets and ecosystem benefit flows. As we discussed in Chap. 1, the valuation of stocks and flows are related primarily by the underlying interest rates, sometimes called the capitalization rate in lease valuation. We will turn in the next section to a discussion of the appropriate discount rates used to convert valuations of flows into valuations of assets.

DISCOUNTING

Having determined appropriate shadow prices for the flow of social and environmental benefits, we must consider how to compute their present value. The common method of evaluating trade-offs between the present and the future devised by economists is that of discounting. Discounting is the practice of valuing future flows of benefits at a present *discount*, that is, valuing them less today than we plan to value them in future. This is the natural consequence of an interest rate for investible funds that is greater than zero. A non-zero interest rate implies that savings can earn a rate of return, growing to a nominal value greater than the initially saved sum. Supplies of savings are current offers of real resources available today for use by those with need of funds for investment. Investment demands are bids to use these currently available real resources in mechanisms that promise future benefit rather than current consumption. In theory, the interplay of supply and demand for these funds sets a market interest rate which effectively serves as the price at which flows of benefits today could be converted into flows of benefits in future.[10] The market interest rate represents the relative price of translating wealth in the present into wealth in the future. For investments in projects where the flows of benefits are private, the net present value (NPV) of the project can be computed as a weighted sum of future net benefits where the weights are *discount factors* associated with each future period:

$$NPV = \sum_{t=0}^{\infty} w_t NB_t$$

Where

$$w_t = \frac{1}{\left(1 + interest\ rate\right)^t}\ for\ t = 0,1,2,\ldots$$

It is well known that in any cost-benefit analysis or net present value calculation where the flows of benefits extend into the distant future, the choice of the discount rate is highly influential to the valuation. For example, a number of prominent critiques of the validity of the recommendations of the Stern Review (Stern, 2007) centered on the use of what was then considered an unusually low discount rate (Dasgupta, 2007; Mendelsohn, 2008; Nordhaus, 2007; Weitzman, 2007). What is the appropriate interest rate to discount future cash flows into present value terms? In the context of private cash flows, the interest or discount rate chosen is generally the *weighted average cost of capital (WACC)*, an average of the after tax interest rate on debt and the expected return on equity invested in an enterprise. But what is the appropriate discount rate to use for cash and benefit flows that have a social character? In the context of corporate investments in social responsibility, or impact investments, does it make sense to use a weighted average cost of capital?

The Social Rate of Discount

Hence it is critical to ground the choice of discount rate, perhaps more so than any other assumption, in a cost-benefit analysis. The discount factor that is appropriately used to value social benefit flows is generally different from, and often lower than, the appropriate discount rate in private valuations.

Harberger's Market Rate

An approach to computing a *social opportunity cost of capital (SOC)*, that is congruent to the corporate WACC was suggested by Arnold Harberger[11] and augmented by Lind (1990). As with the WACC, the SOC is computed by evaluating the sources of financing of a public project and obtaining an average of the associated rates of interest. This approach assumes that funds for a public project would potentially displace private investment or private consumption. Also, the SOC approach recognizes that such funds could be partially obtained by borrowing from abroad. The SOC therefore consists of a weighted average of the expected pre-tax return on foregone private investment, the consumption rate of interest and the marginal cost of foreign borrowing. The primary limitation of the SOC is that it is determined by market rates of return. The return on foregone investment, the rate at which current consumption can be financed from future borrowings in the marketplace and the interest rate on foreign borrowings are set by market players who trade in the market for investable funds. Such market rates are descriptive, rather than prescriptive. There are reasons to believe that the market for investable funds would underestimate the value of future consumption and overestimate the value of current consumption. For example, because the market rate of interest is not influenced directly by the choices of future generations, one might expect that it might place too low a weight on their consumption. In addition, to the extent that there are positive externalities from saving embodied in long-lived public goods, individual actors will tend to under-invest in such goods, reducing the supply of funds and increasing the market rate of interest above what is optimal. Third, if the future discount rate is not known with certainty, which is generally the case for rates beyond a few quarters, then performing cost-benefit analysis with discount rates that are lower than expected leads to more robust, less irreversibly erroneous choices.

Ramsey's Prescriptive Formula
An approach conceived by Frank Ramsey (Ramsey, 1928) utilizes a social discount rate (SDR) constructed from society's willingness to trade off present consumption for future consumption. The Ramsey formula recognizes that ultimately, in an infinite horizon model of the economy, the discount factor is society's marginal rate of substitution between consumption in the present and consumption in the future (referred to as the marginal rate of time preference or MRT). This is because, ultimately, the purpose of investment is to facilitate consumption, even though it might be delayed into the infinite future. Similarly, foreign borrowings must ultimately be repaid from foregone future consumption. As such, the Harberger SOC method is a temporary expedient—in the long run, it is the MRT that matters. The MRT is a prescriptive or normative parameter. Ramsey had in mind that society would choose the appropriate value of the MRT according to its ethics. For example, he thought that it was ethically indefensible to use a value other than zero, which would have the consequence that the consumption of future generations would have a different weight than that of the current generation.

A zero MRT does not imply that the social discount rate is zero. With certain limitations on the intertemporal social welfare function, the optimal social discount rate in this infinite horizon model of the economy can be shown to be *SDR = MRT + growth rate × elasticity of MC*. The growth rate is the expected growth rate of future consumption. The elasticity of MC is the elasticity of the marginal utility of consumption. Suppose that the growth rate of future consumption is positive. Then future generations can expect to consume more than the current generation. The model assumes that the marginal utility of consumption declines as consumption increases, that is, there are diminishing returns to additional consumption as consumption increases. If the marginal utility diminishes very steeply, then society would have little incentive to value consumption in future periods when consumption had grown. In that case, there would be a strong incentive to consume more today at the expense of future consumption. Conversely, if growth were expected to be negative, while the marginal utility diminishes steeply, then society would have an incentive to have a negative SDR.

The expected growth rate and the elasticity of the marginal utility of consumption are parameters that can be econometrically estimated. For example, Evans (2005) compiles estimates of the elasticity of MC for 20 OECD countries and finds that the numerical value is close to 1.4. Expected growth rates can be estimated from historical experience, but in the context of discontinuous shifts, it is important to realize that the future can differ sharply from the past. Also, it is important to recognize that in the context of climate change, the consumption growth rate may be significantly lower than the growth rate of GDP per capita due to the need to make investments in adaptation infrastructure (Paul Kelleher & Wagner, 2019). If one were to assume that the future growth rate of consumption would be 1%, and one were to utilize an MRT of zero as suggested by Ramsey, then the social discount rate would amount to SDR = 0% + 1% × 1.4 = 1.4%. Joan Martinez-Alier has articulated an important caveat to this method. He notes that discounting based on the decreasing marginal utility of consumption leads to what he has called the *optimist's paradox*. The expectation of future growth induces us to consume more today, often using up natural resources which are necessary for future well-being. Hence, our present consumption, if it does not preserve natural capital, will actually render us poorer in future (European Commission Environment Directorate-General, 2008).

Declining Discount Rates for Intergenerational Impacts

The formula for the computation of NPV above utilizes the same (constant or time-invariant) interest rate for every period. For intergenerational CBAs, there are good reasons to utilize declining interest rates for periods in the distant future. First, as noted by Cropper, Aydede, and Portney (1992), survey evidence suggests that the individual marginal rates of time preference embedded in respondents' choices about trade-offs in saving lives across time are declining over time. In this study, the annual rate of time preference declines from a high of 3.15% over the first 5 years to a low of 0.04% over the first 100 years. This is an indication that even though the MRT for individuals is significantly higher than zero for near-term investment choices, for intergenerational choices made by individuals, an MRT close to zero is justified. In addition, the actual behavior of savers often involves declining discount rates (Laibson, 1997). Arrow et al. (2014) provide an outline for the logic of using declining discount rates in social, intergenerational CBAs and note that the United Kingdom and France already do so in regulatory CBAs. If individuals use declining discount rates, then it could be argued that they are behaving as if they are trying to account for the optimist's paradox, by assuming that future growth will be low and reducing present consumption.

LIMITATIONS OF THE COST-BENEFIT ANALYSIS APPROACH

There are natural limits to the application of cost-benefit analysis and the related discounting approach. As with most economic analyses, the methods are intended to be applicable for marginal or incremental changes. When faced with discontinuous or irreversible shocks to wealth in any form, the CBA method breaks down.

As we noted earlier, CBA is a route to maximizing static efficiency, not necessarily to achieving sustainability, resilience, or equity, all of which are essential attributes of a desirable ecosystem. CBA attempts to maximize NPV, and in that quest may well neglect other important measures of success. All of us can imagine many negative NPV projects which are nevertheless worth undertaking. Kelman (2000) points out that it would not make sense to perform CBAs to determine whether basic human rights pass an efficiency test. Almost by definition, the value of human dignity is an unquantifiable and non-monetizable concept. The notion that human dignity is non-commensurable with monetary costs and benefits is enshrined in repeated executive directives governing the use of cost-benefit analysis in the context of regulations that govern, inter alia, disability, prison rape, environmental justice in the context of air toxics, health privacy, and age discrimination (Bayefsky, 2014).

A key practical limitation of CBA lies in the expert analytical skills and significant training necessary to utilize it effectively for the measurement of social and environmental impact. While the availability of centralized databases for shadow prices and benefit transfer estimates reduce the cost of recreating benefit evaluations from scratch, the complexity of the underlying computations reduces the broader legitimacy of CBA. As we discussed in Chap. 4, broad legitimacy is maximized if a wide range of diverse stakeholders can be active participants in the process of determining appropriate metrics of impact. From its origins, CBA has developed specialized agencies and expert bureaus performing calculations in a centralized manner. Without widespread education on the meaning and interpretation of CBA concepts, its effectiveness as a tool of persuasion for a range of stakeholders remains limited. Although CBA utilizes the preferences of an aggregation of individuals by evaluating willingness to pay, its menu of choices is usually set in a top-down manner. Sustainability assessment models have been proposed as a viable alternative to cost-benefit analysis. Sustainability assessment models are based on an inter-disciplinary approach that recognizes the need for "accountings" that facilitate more participatory forms of decision-making and accountability. In essence, sustainability accountings keep track of social, environmental, resource, and economic impacts separately and generally eschew the commensurability of these separate categories (Bebbington, Brown, & Frame, 2007). There is also some focus on a participatory determination of impacts at a community level rather than at an expert level. Carolus, Hanley, Olsen, and Pedersen (2018) describe two cases where local stakeholder participation in the earliest stages of CBA can embed local knowledge and legitimacy in the articulation of CBA alternatives, converting CBA into a bottom-up, broadly-embraced tool.

Concluding Remarks

Discounting and the cost-benefit analysis, despite their limitations, allow us to navigate the trade-offs between the short and long term in many routine investment decisions, and also construct monetary values for certain environmentally scarce resources. As we have noted, the choice and use of parameters in these methods are a compromise of precision and judgment. As with all forms of valuation, there is a significant influence of geographic and temporal context. In the next two chapters, we examine the applications of these methods to evaluations of investments in both natural and social capital in a number of specific situations.

Notes

1. For book-length treatments of the practice of cost-benefit analysis and discounting, see Boardman, Greenberg, Vining, and Weimer (2018) or Hanley and Barbier (2009) along with Portney and Weyant (1999).
2. The difference between price and WTP is referred to as *consumer surplus*.

3. An actual CBA may not internalize all externalities if the *standing* of the CBA excludes some affected parties due to jurisdictional limits. The *standing* of a CBA is the list of parties whose costs and benefits are included in the analysis. Since CBAs are meant to support decisions taken by specific decision-making authorities who have jurisdiction over specific populations, a CBA often excludes parties outside the jurisdiction of the decision-making agency. In such case, externalities within the jurisdiction are internalized, while those outside the jurisdiction are not.

4. A concept that is analogous to consumer surplus.

5. This is justified by the assumption that the opportunity cost of time for those professionals amounts to the value of medical services that could have been provided during the time that the professionals worked on compliance. Assuming that the labor market for such professionals is competitively supplied, their wage rate would be equal to the value of their marginal product.

6. For a book-length introduction to non-market valuation methods, see Champ, Boyle, and Brown (2017).

7. We are grateful to Thomas Ball for introducing us to the literature on STOC methods.

8. See WBCSD (2011) and McComb, Lantz, Nash, and Rittmaster (2006) for a guide and a list of benefit transfer study databases.

9. See, for example, Holthausen and Zmijewski (2012) for guidelines on how to perform a comparable valuation analysis of publicly traded companies.

10. In practice, central banks significantly influence the market rate of interest in the short and medium term by setting short-term rates and engaging in market operations, which significantly influence the demand and supply of long-lived financial instruments.

11. See Chapter 10 of Boardman et al. (2018) of the Harberger social opportunity cost of capital (SOC).

REFERENCES

Adamowicz, W., Louviere, J., & Williams, M. (1994). Combining Revealed and Stated Preference Methods for Valuing Environmental Amenities. *Journal of Environmental Economics and Management, 26*(3), 271–292. https://doi.org/10.1006/jeem.1994.1017

Arrow, K. J., Portney, P. R., Sterner, T., Tol, R. S. J., Weitzman, M. L., Cropper, M. L., ... Pizer, W. A. (2014). Should Governments Use a Declining Discount Rate in Project Analysis? *Review of Environmental Economics and Policy, 8*(2), 145–163. https://doi.org/10.1093/reep/reu008

Arrow, K. J., Solow, R., Portney, P. R., Leamer, E. E., Radner, R., & Schuman, H. (1993). Report of the NOAA Panel on Contingent Valuation. *Federal Register, 58*, 4601–4614.

Bayefsky, R. (2014). Dignity as a Value in Agency Cost-Benefit Analysis. *Yale Law Journal, 123*(6), 1732–1782. doi: http://www.yalelawjournal.org/issue

Bebbington, J., Brown, J., & Frame, B. (2007). Accounting Technologies and Sustainability Assessment Models. *Ecological Economics, 61*(2–3), 224–236. http://www.sciencedirect.com/science/journal/09218009

Bin, O., & Polasky, S. (2005). Evidence on the Amenity Value of Wetlands in a Rural Setting. *Journal of Agricultural and Applied Economics, 37*(3), 589–602. http://journals.cambridge.org/action/displayBackIssues?jid=AAE

Boardman, A. E., Greenberg, D. H., Vining, A. R., & Weimer, D. L. (2018). *Cost-Benefit Analysis: Concepts and Practice*. New York, NY: Cambridge University Press.

Brandenburger, A. M., & Stuart, H. W., Jr. (1996). Value-Based Business Strategy. *Journal of Economics and Management Strategy, 5*(1), 5–24. http://onlinelibrary.wiley.com/journal/10.1111/%28ISSN%291530-9134/issues

Carolus, J. F., Hanley, N., Olsen, S. B., & Pedersen, S. M. (2018). A Bottom-Up Approach to Environmental Cost-Benefit Analysis. *Ecological Economics, 152*, 282–295.

Champ, P. A., Boyle, K. J., & Brown, T. C. (Eds.). (2017). *A Primer on Nonmarket Valuation* (Second ed.). New York, NY: Springer Nature.

Cordes, J. J. (2017). Using Cost-Benefit Analysis and Social Return on Investment to Evaluate the Impact of Social Enterprise: Promises, Implementation, and Limitations. *Evaluation & Program Planning, 64*, 98–104. https://doi.org/10.1016/j.evalprogplan.2016.11.008

Cropper, M. L., Aydede, S. K., & Portney, P. R. (1992). Rates of Time Preference for Saving Lives. *American Economic Review, 82*(2), 469–472. http://www.aeaweb.org/aer/

Dahan, E., Kim, A. J., Lo, A. W., Poggio, T., & Chan, N. (2011). Securities Trading of Concepts (STOC). *Journal of Marketing Research, 48*(3), 497–517. https://doi.org/10.1509/jmkr.48.3.497

Dasgupta, P. (2007). Commentary: The Stern Review's Economics of Climate Change. *National Institute Economic Review*, (199), 4–7. http://ner.sagepub.com/content/by/year

Dufour, B. (2019). Social Impact Measurement: What Can Impact Investment Practices and the Policy Evaluation Paradigm Learn from Each Other? *Research in International Business and Finance, 47*, 18–30. https://doi.org/10.1016/j.ribaf.2018.02.003

Ekelund, R. B., Jr., & Hebert, R. F. (1999). *Secret Origins of Modern Microeconomics: Dupuit and the Engineers*. Chicago, IL/London, UK: University of Chicago Press.

European Commission Environment Directorate-General. (2008). In P. Sukhdev (Ed.), *The Economics of Ecosystems & Biodiversity an Interim Report*. Brussels, Belgium: European Union Commission for the Environment.

Evans, D. J. (2005). The Elasticity of Marginal Utility of Consumption: Estimates for 20 OECD Countries. *Fiscal Studies, 26*(2), 197–224. http://onlinelibrary.wiley.com/journal/10.1111/%28ISSN%291475-5890/issues

Franco, G., Hope, O.-K., & Larocque, S. (2015). Analysts' Choice of Peer Companies. *Review of Accounting Studies, 20*(1), 82–109. https://doi.org/10.1007/s11142-014-9294-7

Frey, E. F., Palin, M. B., Walsh, P. J., & Whitcraft, C. R. (2013). Spatial Hedonic Valuation of a Multi-Use Urban Wetland in Southern California. *Agricultural and Resource Economics Review, 42*(2), 387–402. https://www.cambridge.org/core/journals/agricultural-and-resource-economics-review/all-issues

Hanley, N., & Barbier, E. B. (2009). *Pricing Nature: Cost-Benefit Analysis and Environmental Policy.* Cheltenham, UK/Northampton, MA: Elgar.

Holthausen, R. W., & Zmijewski, M. E. (2012). Valuation with Market Multiples: How to Avoid Pitfalls When Identifying and Using Comparable Companies1 Valuation with Market Multiples: How to Avoid Pitfalls When Identifying and Using Comparable Companies. *Journal of Applied Corporate Finance, 24*(3), 26–38. https://doi.org/10.1111/j.1745-6622.2012.00387.x

Hotelling, H. (1947). *Letter to the National Park Service: An Economic Study of the Monetary Evaluation of Recreation in the National Parks.* Washington, DC: US Department of the Interior, National Park Service and Recreational Planning Division.

Johnston, R. J., Boyle, K. J., Adamowicz, W., Bennett, J., Brouwer, R., & Cameron, T. A. (2017). Contemporary Guidance for Stated Preference Studies. *Journal of the Association of Environmental and Resource Economists, 4*(2), 319–405. http://www.journals.uchicago.edu/loi/jaere

Johnston, R. J., & Rosenberger, R. S. (2010). Methods, Trends and Controversies in Contemporary Benefit Transfer. *Journal of Economic Surveys, 24*(3), 479–510. http://onlinelibrary.wiley.com/journal/10.1111/%28ISSN%291467-6419/issues

Kelman, S. (2000). Cost-Benefit Analysis: An Ethical Critique (with Replies). In R. N. Stavins (Ed.), *Economics of the Environment: Selected Readings* (Fourth ed.). New York, NY: Norton & Company.

Laibson, D. (1997). Golden Eggs and Hyperbolic Discounting. *Quarterly Journal of Economics, 112*(2), 443–477. https://academic.oup.com/qje/issue

Laxminarayan, R. (2014). Global Health Threats of the 21st Century: Antibiotic Resistance. *Finance and Development, 51*(4), 19–20. http://www.imf.org/external/pubs/ft/fandd/fda.htm

Le Boennec, R., & Salladarré, F. (2017). The Impact of Air Pollution and Noise on the Real Estate Market. The Case of the 2013 European Green Capital: Nantes, France. *Ecological Economics, 138*, 82–89. https://doi.org/10.1016/j.ecolecon.2017.03.030

Lind, R. C. (1990). Reassessing the Government's Discount Rate Policy in Light of New Theory and Data in a World Economy with a High Degree of Capital Mobility. *Journal of Environmental Economics and Management, 18*(2), S8–S28. http://www.sciencedirect.com/science/journal/00950696

Lomborg, B. (Ed.). (2018). *Prioritizing Development: A Cost Benefit Analysis of the United Nations' Sustainable Development Goals.* Cambridge, UK/New York, NY: Cambridge University Press.

Ma, C., Polyakov, M., & Pandit, R. (2016). Capitalisation of Residential Solar Photovoltaic Systems in Western Australia. *Australian Journal of Agricultural & Resource Economics, 60*(3), 366–385. https://doi.org/10.1111/1467-8489.12126

McComb, G., Lantz, V., Nash, K., & Rittmaster, R. (2006). International Valuation Databases: Overview, Methods and Operational Issues. *Ecological Economics, 60*(2), 461–472. http://www.sciencedirect.com/science/journal/09218009.

Mendelsohn, R. (2008). Symposium: The Economics of Climate Change: The Stern Review and Its Critics: Is the Stern Review an Economic Analysis? *Review of Environmental Economics and Policy, 2*(1), 45–60. https://academic.oup.com/reep/issue

Nicholls, J. (2017). Social Return on Investment—Development and Convergence. *Evaluation and Program Planning, 64,* 127–135. https://doi.org/10.1016/j.evalprogplan.2016.11.011

Nordhaus, W. D. (2007). A Review of the Stern Review on the Economics of Climate Change. *Journal of Economic Literature, 45*(3), 686–702. http://www.aeaweb.org/jel/index.php

Paul Kelleher, J., & Wagner, G. (2019). Ramsey Discounting Calls for Subtracting Climate Damages from Economic Growth Rates. *Applied Economics Letters, 26*(1), 79–82. http://www.tandfonline.com/loi/rael20

Persky, J. (2001). Cost-Benefit Analysis and the Classical Creed. *Journal of Economic Perspectives, 15*(4), 199–208. https://doi.org/10.1257/jep.15.4.199

Pew Charitable Trust & MacArthur Foundation. (2014). *New Mexico's Evidence-based Approach to Better Governance.* Retrieved from https://www.macfound.org/press/grantee-publications/new-mexicos-evidence-based-approach-better-governance/

Portney, P. R., & Weyant, J. P. (Eds.). (1999). *Discounting and Intergenerational Equity.* Washington, DC: Routledge.

Ramsey, F. P. (1928). A Mathematical Theory of Saving. *Economic Journal, 38,* 543–559. http://onlinelibrary.wiley.com/journal/10.1111/%28ISSN%291468-0297/issues

Richardson, L., Loomis, J., Kroeger, T., & Casey, F. (2015). The Role of Benefit Transfer in Ecosystem Service Valuation. *Ecological Economics, 115,* 51–58. https://doi.org/10.1016/j.ecolecon.2014.02.018

Ridker, R. G., & Henning, J. A. (1967). The Determinants of Residential Property Values with Special Reference to Air Pollution. *Review of Economics & Statistics, 49*(2), 246. https://doi.org/10.2307/1928231

Stavins, R. N. (2000). Environmental Economics. In P. Newman (Ed.), *New Palgrave Dictionary of Economics and the Law* (2nd ed.). London, UK: Palgrave Macmillan.

Stern, N. (2007). *The Economics of Climate Change: The Stern Review*. Cambridge, UK: Cambridge UP.

Thaler, R., & Rosen, S. (1976). The Value of Saving a Life: Evidence from the Labor Market. In N. E. Terleckyj (Ed.), *Household Production and Consumption* (pp. 265–302). New York: NBER.

WBCSD. (2011). *Guide to Corporate Ecosystem Valuation: A Framework for Improving Corporate Decision-Making*. Geneva, Switzerland: WBCSD.

Weitzman, M. L. (2007). A Review of the Stern Review on the Economics of Climate Change. *Journal of Economic Literature, 45*(3), 703–724. http://www.aeaweb.org/jel/index.php

Wells, L. T. J. (1975). Social Cost/Benefit Analysis for MNCs. *Harvard Business Review*, March 1975.

Wrenn, D. H., Klaiber, H. A., & Jaenicke, E. C. (2016). Unconventional Shale Gas Development, Risk Perceptions, and Averting Behavior: Evidence from Bottled Water Purchases. *Journal of the Association of Environmental and Resource Economists, 3*(4), 779–817. http://www.journals.uchicago.edu/loi/jaere

Zhang, J., & Mu, Q. (2018). Air Pollution and Defensive Expenditures: Evidence from Particulate-Filtering Facemasks. *Journal of Environmental Economics and Management, 92*, 517–536.

CHAPTER 7

The Monetization of Natural Capital in Corporate Investment

INTRODUCTION

In Chap. 6, we described non-market valuation methods to construct shadow prices that can be used to place monetary values on externalities. We now turn to an examination of the application of such valuation methods in the context of environmental externalities, where these methods have been commonly applied. The next chapter addresses the application of these methods to the valuation of human capital.

In the English language, the use of the words 'natural capital' to mean the productive capacity of land and other 'natural agents' as distinct from machines, tools, and the stock of materials, on the one hand, and from the productive capacity of human labor, on the other hand, dates back to Alvin Johnson's 1909 textbook *Introduction to Economics* (Missemer, 2018). As Missemer points out, Johnson was articulating a new view of nature as a source of productive capacity akin to manufactured and financial 'capital', rather than merely a stock of natural resources which can be extracted for human benefit. The distinction is a subtle one but has profound implications: the concept of 'natural capital' implies an ability to generate growing benefits in the absence of extraction. The neoclassical notion of the marginal productivity of capital and labor had recently been articulated by Johnson's teacher John Bates Clark (Clark, 1899) and Johnson's terminology placed the fecundity of nature in the context of the new capital theory. By 1928, the term

© The Author(s) 2019
S. Bose et al., *The Financial Ecosystem*, Palgrave Studies in Impact Finance, https://doi.org/10.1007/978-3-030-05624-7_7

'natural capital' is considered part of common economic terminology in the United States (Warburton, 1928). Despite the currency of the concept and the term in the 1920s, natural capital was not much discussed in the economics discipline through most of the twentieth century. In 1988, David Pearce resurrected the concept by his definition of natural capital as 'the stock of environmental assets' (Pearce, 1988).

Pearce's groundbreaking article offered up one definition of sustainable development as an economic growth path which maintains a 'constant stock of natural capital'. He outlines a view that natural capital and manufactured capital are substitutable *up to a point*. The issue of substitutability between natural and manufactured capital has been a significant controversy in the context of the monetization of natural capital. This controversy is encapsulated in the debate between the concepts of 'weak' and 'strong' sustainability (Neumayer, 2013). Weak sustainability assumes that natural and other forms of capital (manufactured or human) are substitutable. As we discussed briefly in Chap. 1, one version of the concept of sustainability is the requirement to keep assets as assets and consume only that which represents the periodic flow of benefits. *Weak sustainability* allows the unlimited conversion of one form of capital into another: if your capital asset is an apple tree, then try to eat only the fruit and do not cut down the tree unless you can create a new asset with it. If you must cut down the tree, then use the wood to build another long-lived asset, such as a barn. If you must sell the tree as firewood, then invest the proceeds in a bond or use them to pay for college tuition. As such, weak sustainability merely requires that the total stock of capital (measured in a single commensurable metric such as money) be maintained over time. This is the essence of the Hartwick rule (Hartwick, 1977).

Strong sustainability recognizes the necessity of maintaining the total stock of capital but takes a dim view of unlimited substitutability. It recognizes that some natural assets are unique and irreplaceable by manufactured or human capital. It assumes that certain planetary boundaries cannot be breached (Rockström et al., 2009). Strong sustainability requires both that the proceeds from cutting down trees are reinvested in other forms of capital and that no unique and irreplaceable trees are cut down. Strong sustainability acknowledges that some forms of natural capital are of a different category than manufactured capital as well as exhaustible resources. Natural ecosystems not only provide a flow of benefits, in the way that an oilfield can provide a flow of benefits, but they also have an inherent ability to adapt to changes in the environment and to repair damage from transitory shocks in a way that cannot be expected of simpler stores of wealth. In an exhortation to fellow economists to recognize that natural capital must be treated differently than other forms of capital in models of economic growth, Dasgupta (2008) notes three features that distinguish ecosystems from other forms of capital:

1. Depreciation of natural ecosystems can be irreversible.
2. While some functions of natural ecosystems can be replaced by artificial processes, typically the totality of those functions cannot be served by manufactured or human capital.
3. Ecosystems can collapse abruptly, in time scales that are shorter than required for effective intervention.

The management of ecosystems is increasingly recognized as a complex or 'wicked' problem (DeFries & Nagendra, 2017). DeFries and Nagendra point out that modern techniques of forestry and fisheries management were, until recently, limited to the extraction of maximum sustainable yields of specific commercial products. For example, modern forestry management originating in late eighteenth-century Germany tended to be singularly focused on commercial timber production. Expert awareness of the commercial and subsistence value of a wide range of so-called non-timber forestry products, including outputs as diverse as maple syrup, rattan, palm heart, pine resin, Brazil nut, mushrooms, frankincense, chicle, ginseng, yohimbe, baobab, essential oils, spices, wild teas, herbs, medicines, and personal care items is relatively recent (Shanley, Pierce, Laird, & Guillen, 2001). Modern forestry management's focus on extractible commercial products differs dramatically from indigenous and traditional practices, which tend to see the surrounding local ecosystem as habitat both for humans and other species, as a source of food, building materials, clothing, and medicines, as well as a sacred repository of biodiversity, cultural, and spiritual knowledge. DeFries and Nagendra note that many ecosystem management problems are characterized by multi-dimensionality, complexity, interdependency, non-linearity, uncertainty, unintended consequences, divergence of values, and multiple stakeholders. Valuing this type of 'asset' on the single dimension of money is not likely to be straightforward.

VALUATIONS OF FLOWS OF GOODS AND SERVICES

As we noted in Chap. 1, it is much easier to measure the periodic flows of benefits than a stock of wealth. Moreover, in macro-economic situations with many levels of aggregation, it is simplest to focus only on the benefit flows which are the easiest to value commercially. Even though this type of valuation excludes many important forms of natural capital, country-level valuations of natural capital often do precisely that. For example, Arrow, Dasgupta, Goulder, Mumford, and Oleson (2012) developed a valuation of comprehensive wealth (including manufactured, human, and natural capital) for five countries: the United States, China, Brazil, India, and Venezuela. Natural capital in their definition includes oil and gas[1] and mineral resources, the commercial value of forest timber and land, and a value for non-timber forest benefits (computed by applying a shadow price per hectare to total forest area). In their analysis, the values of non-timber forest benefits range from a low of 3% of measured natural capital in the case of Venezuela to a high of 37% in the case of Brazil. The total value of natural capital that they assign for the five countries in the year 2000 amounts to approximately $22 trillion in 2010 dollars.[2] This represents approximately 14% of the value the authors assign to comprehensive wealth, which totals approximately $132 trillion.[3] These five countries had a combined GDP of $26 trillion in 2011, suggesting that the flow of goods and services represented a 16% annual return on the value of comprehensive wealth of $132 trillion. Because their estimates of comprehensive wealth exclude many types of ecosystem services, the valuation of natural capital seems relatively low. An annual return in excess of 16% appears high in comparison to real returns on assets in those countries in the year 2000. Furthermore, total economic value.

An alternative estimate of the valuation of global natural capital that incorporates a wide range of flows of goods and services is found by reviewing de Groot et al. (2012). de Groot et al. employ a different method of valuing global ecosystems: they list the global area under ten different biomes: open oceans, coral reefs, coastal ecosystems, coastal wetlands, inland wetlands, rivers and lakes, tropical forest, temperate forest, woodlands, and grasslands. de Groot et al. compile 665 estimates of per hectare shadow prices for these biomes from 320 publications to construct their valuation. The shadow prices incorporate the value of 22 different services. These include provisioning services (food, water, raw materials, genetic, medicinal, and ornamental resources), regulating services (air quality, climate mitigation, moderation of disturbance, flood control, waste treatment, erosion prevention, soil fertility maintenance, pollination, and biological control), habitat services (nursery service and genepool protection), as well as cultural services (esthetics, recreation, spiritual experience, and cognitive development). On a per hectare basis, coral reefs and coastal wetlands have by far the highest values, with coral reefs valued at approximately $367,000 per hectare, whereas coastal wetlands are valued at $202,000 per hectare. This compares with $500 per hectare for marine ecosystems, the lowest valued biome on a per hectare basis.[4]

Using the shadow prices of biomes compiled by de Groot et al. (2012), Costanza et al. (2014) estimate that the annual value of ecosystem services amounted to approximately $130 trillion in 2010 dollars in the year 2011. This figure would have to be capitalized into a stock value to generate an estimate of the value of natural capital. An ecosystem flow value of $130 trillion per year, compared to overall GDP of $68 trillion per year, would imply that ecosystem services provide a significant portion of the overall well-being of humans. This relative valuation of ecosystem services would seem to be more in line with anyone who believes, broadly speaking, that natural capital is fundamental and essential to human well-being. The Arrow et al. estimate, on the other hand, would suggest that natural capital comprises a modest fraction of comprehensive wealth. This estimate is an extrapolation of the value of natural capital that is computed by multiplying the impact of marginal changes to ecosystems by a measure of physical quantity. It should not be interpreted as the amount of money that society would accept as compensation for a systemic change that leads to a complete destruction of the natural capital.

VALUATION OF BIODIVERSITY

Unfortunately, it is insufficient to measure only flows of goods and services if one intends to assess sustainability: the analyst has no choice but to face the challenge of measuring the underlying capacity of an asset to generate future flows. As any financial analyst knows, asset valuations are rarely as simple as taking a current flow of benefits and applying a multiple to them. In the situations where that might be the case, there really is no point in investing in analytical skills—there is little ambiguity to potential valuations and therefore little need for the combination of precision and judgment, which makes valuation a decision-relevant piece of information. The good financial analyst does not limit her due diligence to periodic cash flows such as revenue and earnings but also considers many aspects of the system in which a firm operates. It is not enough to consider the dividend yield of a security—it is dividend-paying capacity that matters. A complete examination of dividend-paying capacity includes cyclical factors, competitive position, regulatory considerations, as well as opportunities for reinvestment of corporate profits. For some companies, a robust dividend yield might be a strength—an indication of strong cash flows and efficient but sustainable harvesting of franchise value. For others, a strong dividend yield or excessive share repurchases might signify a paucity of promising opportunities for research and development, an indicator of imminent decline. Which asset valuation model is appropriate is often more important for the accuracy of valuation than how well a model's near term forecasts fit observations. The ecology literature is replete with examples of ecosystems, where rational management to ensure maximum sustainable yields of economically valuable products and services appeared to maintain important species for a while but then subsequently led to collapse. Peterson, Carpenter, and Brock (2003) construct a scenario where managers choose phosphorus input to a lake based on their estimates of whether the lake is eutrophic or oligotrophic.[5] They attempt to maximize the present value of the lake's services consisting of phosphorous sink services and the provision of clear water. Because of uncertain lags between phosphorous input and the apparent onset of murky water, seemingly rational efforts to load the lake with phosphorous when it appears to have clean water can lead to sudden and unplanned eutrophication. In the context of lobster fishing in the Gulf of Maine, Steneck et al. (2011) argue that the overfishing of apex predators such as cod and haddock has led to an overabundance of lobster, a commercially valuable species. The high stocks of lobster have led to dramatic growth in financial revenues, but are associated with a 70% decline in the diversity of species harvested. The reduced marine diversity makes the lobsters of the Gulf of Maine vulnerable to the types of diseases which wiped out the majority of lobsters in Long Island Sound after an anomalous warm summer in 1998. In Chap. 13, we discuss two national ecosystem compensation schemes in China which were successful at increasing a number of direct ecosystem services, such as food production and flood mitigation, but failed to increase habitat for biodiversity.

The complexity of the linkages between different functions of natural capital and related ecosystem services imply that a flows-oriented method will tend to undervalue natural capital (Mace, 2019). Mace argues that it is not enough to select certain easy-to-gather indicators of benefit flows and link these to estimates of the monetary value of associated ecosystem services. In particular, the essential and irreplaceable aspects of natural capital are nature's own capacity to persist, its ability to regrow and reorganize, within limits. This malleability and resilience is a feature that is lacking in manufactured capital as well as in most natural resources such as reserves of fossil fuel or mineral assets. This resilience needs to be valued separately, perhaps as an option or insurance value, because it is likely that resilience will not be manifested in current economically important flows of benefits. For example, green infrastructure such as sand dunes and coastal wetlands may provide no obvious goods and services to a coastal community in the absence of sea level rise or severe storm surges. Mace notes that the valuation of biodiversity is particularly problematic because not only is it directly valued by people and cultures it also plays a critical role in the proper functioning of all natural ecosystems. The resilience of ecosystems is a quality of the fundamental ecological processes that are inextricably linked to the underlying biodiversity. Rockström et al. (2009) point out that of the three planetary boundaries that have already been breached, the one that is furthest from a safe operating space is the rate of biodiversity loss, followed by human interference with the nitrogen cycle and climate change.

Biodiversity in a Sheep Farm
Gary Kleppel, a biology professor at the State University of New York at Albany, who also runs a family sheep farm, describes a singular scourge of sheep farmers: *haemunchus contortus* or the barber pole worm (Kleppel, 2014). This worm attaches to the gut walls of sheep, sucks their blood and causes anemia in the host. The worm's eggs are egested in sheep feces and the emergent larvae can be re-ingested by other sheep. An infestation of barber pole worm can cause the loss of a third of a herd in just a few weeks. A typical industrial farming solution is to apply anthelmintic medications to the whole herd. The medications kill most of the worm population, but a few are immune to the medicine and survive. As a result, the genetic diversity of the worm population in industrial farms has been reduced to those who are immune to many anthelmintics, necessitating a cycle

(*continued*)

(continued)
of new medications followed by new forms of resistance, requiring additional research into new medications. As with the example of antibiotic resistance in Chap. 6, significant internal and external costs result from this resistance.

Unlike industrial sheep farms, small family sheep farms keep chickens alongside the sheep, which are efficient devourers of the worms and their larvae. It is common practice among family sheep farms to let the chickens follow the herds of sheep in rotational pastures and barns to disinfect sheep feces of worms. The proximity of chickens sharply reduces the amount of medication that needs to be administered, increasing the genetic diversity of the worms on the farm and minimizing the proportion of them that are resistant to medication. For additional details on farm management practices that support low medication use, see Kleppel (2014).

Attempting to value the services flowing from this very simple ecosystem would involve valuing the flow of wool, meat, eggs, and chickens. To an analyst or a farmer who understood this symbiosis between sheep and chickens, the worm-reduction services provided by the chickens might be proxied by the reduced cost of developing and administering medication or the reduced likelihood of catastrophic infections. However, in the context of complex and little-understood wild ecosystems, it is unlikely that the valuation analyst or the broader marketplace would know how the whole might be greater than the sum of the parts simply by examining the flows of goods and services.

The valuation of biodiversity is in principle similar to the value placed on diversification in portfolio theory. Just as modern portfolio theory constructs asset pricing by combining the value of periodic returns with that from a lack of correlation, in principle, a complete valuation of ecosystems requires incorporating a valuation of the irreplaceable sources of resilience in natural ecosystems. A cheap form of insurance against catastrophic diseases in crop management is provided by cultivating small amounts of many different species (Weitzman, 2000). Admiraal, Wossink, de Groot, and de Snoo (2013) argue that the key identifiable source of resilience in ecosystems lies in the diversity of ecological functions within the ecosystem and the diversity of species that perform each ecological function. They cite examples of the application of portfolio theory in hay cultivation and fisheries management.

Ecosystem Valuation in the New York Bight: The Use of Triangulation

The New York Bight is a 16,000 square mile coastal ecosystem stretching from Montauk, New York, to Cape May, New Jersey. The area includes both marine and estuarine habitats. Many products of the New York Bight are of significant economic, cultural, and recreational value to the 22 million people who live nearby. The Bight provides extractive, direct-use resources, such as fish, shellfish, and waterfowl, as well as non-extractive observable wildlife such as whales and migratory birds. While the market value of the flows of goods and services such as marine commodities and the revenue from related economic activity are easily quantified, less tangible benefits such as intricate ecological functions, esthetic and cultural value are difficult to incorporate in a monetary valuation. Nevertheless, an analytical approach that uses multiple valuation methods to triangulate can delineate the parameters of prudent financial investment in ecosystem preservation (Alcaraz et al., 2019).

Alcaraz et al. (2019) perform three different approaches to valuation: they extrapolate from the values of stocks of the shortfin mako shark (an apex predator), the river herring (a forage fish), and the revenue of the broader ecotourism industry dependent on the Bight. They utilize contingent valuation studies to estimate values of the mako shark, an ecological production function to estimate values of the river herring and market prices to estimate ecotourism revenue. Each approach integrates ecological and financial indicators in a model that compares a baseline scenario to an alternative that would, through conservation policy, improve ecosystem health.

CORPORATE VALUATIONS OF UNDERLYING
ECOSYSTEM SERVICES

To what extent has an understanding of the value of ecosystem services and biodiversity affected investment decision-making by corporations or the broader financial ecosystem? There are a number of efforts to incorporate valuation of ecosystem services into public policy and private decision-making. The United Nations Millennium Ecosystem Assessment was launched in 2001 to evaluate the impact of humans on global ecosystems (Millennium Ecosystem Assessment, 2005). In 2007, as a result of a proposal by the environment ministers of the G8+5, a study of the growing cost of biodiversity loss and ecosystem degradation entitled The Economics of Ecosystems and Biodiversity (TEEB) was launched (European Commission Environment Directorate-General, 2008). The UN System of Environmental Economic Accounting (UNSEEA) is a framework to incorporate an accounting of ecosystem service values into national income accounts. The World Bank is a lead partner in Wealth Accounting and the Valuation of Ecosystem Services (WAVES), an initiative "that aims to promote sustainable development by ensuring that natural resources are mainstreamed in development planning and national accounts".

There is increasing recognition amongst corporations that the value of underlying ecosystem services needs to be considered in investment decisions. The World Resources Institute (WRI) and WBCSD have spearheaded efforts to make ecosystem review and valuation methods and tools easily accessible to corporate managers not trained in cost-benefit analysis and non-market valuation methods (WBCSD, 2011, 2012; World Resources Institute, 2015). WRI notes that the impacts and dependencies of corporate activity on ecosystems creates numerous risks and opportunities in most sectors. The beverage industry depends on ample and cheap sources of freshwater. The agricultural sector depends on erosion and flood control, natural pollination and pest control. Tourism depends on the recreational value of coral reefs, while the insurance sector depends on their coastal protection services to limit flood damage claims. WRI and WBCSD assist companies with their efforts to identify, measure, and value the natural capital impacts and dependencies of their operations and supply chains. Table 7.1 lists potential risks and opportunities faced by businesses as a result of ecosystem degradation. WBCSD (2012) showcases the review process of specific ecosystem impacts and dependencies at five large corporations: Akzo Nobel, BC Hydro, Mondi, Rio Tinto, and Syngenta.

Table 7.1   Sample corporate risks and opportunities arising from ecosystem degradation

Risks	Opportunities
Market and product	
Customers switching to competitors who are perceived to have a smaller ecosystem impact	Implementing and communicating sustainable procurement choices or reducing product lifecycle impacts
Operational	
Higher costs of raw materials or freshwater and increased incidence of flooding	Increased eco-efficiency investments or green infrastructure in corporate facilities
Regulatory	
New regulations or community opposition	Multi-stakeholder initiatives to identify shared value investing opportunities in ecosystem protection
Financing	
Lenders incorporating ecosystems review into environmental due diligence	Responsible investors increasing portfolio allocations to companies that restore degraded ecosystems or potential monetization opportunities in new environment-related markets

Source: Adapted from WBCSD (2012)

The Natural Capital Coalition, a multi-stakeholder alliance of approximately 300 organizations, hosted by the Institute of Chartered Accountants in England and Wales (ICAEW), launched the Natural Capital Protocol, a voluntary framework to identify and measure the business impacts on and dependencies upon the natural environment (Natural Capital Coalition, 2016). The Natural Capital Protocol Toolkit, developed by WBCSD, is a repository of publicly available free and paid digital tools that aid in the process of identifying and evaluating ecosystem implications of corporate activity. Examples include Coastal Capital, a WRI guidebook listing valuation studies of coastal ecosystems in the Caribbean, and TESSA, a Toolkit for Ecosystem Service Site-based Assessment developed by the Royal Society for the Protection of Birds and partners. Two key tools for corporate ecosystem valuations are inVEST (Integrated Valuation of Ecosystem Services and Tradeoffs), a software program designed by the Stanford Natural Capital Project to aid in evaluating the social and environmental impacts of land-use changes (Tallis & Polasky, 2009) and Aqueduct, a water risk analyzer developed by WRI (2013). Other efforts to document and assess corporate ecosystem valuation and biodiversity measurement tools include Lammerant (2018), Natural Capital Committee (2017), and Waage and Kester (2015).

As we noted in Chap. 4, Kering Corporation has been a pioneer in maintaining an environmental profit & loss account (EP&L), which tracks the external costs of pollution that result from the company's activities. In 2011, Puma, a sports apparel maker acquired by Kering, issued its first EP&L. Puma worked with TruCost and PWC to carry out the underlying analysis. Kering subsequently enhanced the methodology and incorporated all its luxury brands into the latest available 2017 EP&L. The current methodology computes the physical and monetary value of air pollution, GHG emissions, land-use changes, waste generation, water consumption, and water pollution, much as would be done in a social cost-benefit analysis. These impacts are computed for five tiers of activity: Tier 0 represents the company's direct operations (its stores, warehouses, and offices), Tier 1 represents operations of its product assembly processes, Tier 2 represents the impact of manufacturing processes, Tier 3 represents raw material processing, and Tier 4 represents raw material production. These tier divisions do not quite correspond neatly with the Scope 1, 2, and 3 boundary distinctions recognized by the GHG Protocol Corporate Standard. Scope 1 emissions are direct emissions from owned or controlled sources. Scope 2 emissions are the result of indirect emissions from the generation of purchased energy. Scope 3 emissions refer to all other emissions in the supply chain and in the use of products and services (downstream emissions). The Kering typology excludes downstream emissions. Hence, Kering's impact should equal Scope 1, 2, and 3 minus downstream impacts. In order to construct estimates of upstream impacts, the EP&L methodology utilizes a proprietary version of an environmentally extended input-output (EE-IO) model. EE-IO models take country-level economic input-output models which track the monetary value of inputs and outputs of all sectors and combine these with coefficients of environmental impact per dollar of output in each sector. One example of an open-source EE-IO model maintained by Carnegie-Mellon University is available at www.eiolca.net.

For 2017, Kering reports an EP&L of €482 million. This is the imputed monetary value of environmental damages caused by the production and sale of Kering's products. This amount is approximately 4.3% of Kering's 2017 revenue of €11 billion. If Kering's EP&L is accurate, then we would have grounds for some optimism. The EP&L implies that if Kering could increase prices per unit by just enough such that revenue increased by 4.3% and divert the extra revenue to offsetting its environmental impacts, then we could be sure that Kering was imposing no net external damages on the environment. It is not clear that Kering could increase its prices per unit without losing revenue; this would depend on the price elasticity of demand for its products. Nevertheless, if the overall environmental impact of all of Kering's activities is really just 4.3% of its total revenue, and other corporations have comparable levels of impact, then the challenge of internalizing externalities or compensating external stakeholders for corporate environmental damage is perhaps difficult but surmountable.

As the underlying EE-IO model is proprietary, it is not possible to publicly audit or verify Kering's EP&L.[6] Unlike some sustainability reports, which are assured by a third party, Kering's EP&L does not appear to be assured or verified. As with many non-market valuations focused on periodic flows of benefits, Kering's EP&L does appear to exclude certain costs of ecosystem degradation. In particular, there is no explicit cost for biodiversity, though it is possible that some cost is included in the shadow price used for land-use change. Despite these limitations, Kering's EP&L has established the company as a pioneer in the transparency of its supply chain environmental impact. There are just a handful of companies that publish EP&L reports, including Novo Nordisk and Philips. Novo Nordisk's detailed methodology has been published by the Danish government (Danish Environmental Protection Agency, 2014).

Climate Reporting Frameworks

The EP&L methodology is a laudable innovation that has the potential to dramatically improve estimates of the values of natural capital. The compilation of an EP&L is costly, and it is unlikely that a large number of corporations would adopt the innovation without regulatory pressure. As we discussed in Chap. 4, ESG reporting frameworks, such as the GRI, have been widely adopted by many corporations. Here, we describe a few reporting frameworks specifically focused on natural capital and climate.

CDP

The CDP (formerly known as the Carbon Disclosure Project) is a UK-based non-profit organization created in 2000 upon the initiative of a coalition of 35 institutional investors interested in using corporate carbon emissions data in their security selection process. CDP sends questionnaires to the largest publicly traded companies regarding their Scope 1, 2, and 3 emissions, and then compiles responses in a database that is available to the public and subscribers.[7] It is the repository of the longest-running time series of corporate climate disclosures. It has attempted to collect carbon emissions data on all Financial Times Global 500 firms since 2002 and all S&P 500 firms since 2006 (Kim, 2018). As of March 2019, the CDP's investor membership now comprises more than 500 institutional investors with nearly $100 trillion in assets under management. This level of investor representation makes it highly likely that companies receiving questionnaires would respond. Because the bulk of the disclosures are responses to a common questionnaire, there is a high level of consistency across responses. As such, CDP data is widely used in academic studies of the relationship between environmental disclosure and financial performance. Since 2003, corporate emissions transparency has improved as a result of CDP reporting. Transparency has significantly increased for Scope 1 and 2 emissions, but that is less the case with Scope 3 emissions (Matisoff, Noonan, & O'Brien, 2013). There is some evidence that corporate disclosures of carbon emissions in CDP surveys are more accurate and detailed than those in corporate sustainability reports. In particular, Depoers, Jeanjean, and Jérôme (2016) note that disclosure to the CDP is in response to structured questions from specific stakeholders, namely, institutional investors, whereas disclosures in corporate sustainability reports are in the form of discretionary and open-ended communications targeted to a broad range of relatively diffuse stakeholders. Depoers et al. hypothesize that corporate management will selectively report more favorable measures of carbon emissions in sustainability reports than they are able to in the CDP disclosures. Depoers et al. find that, for a sample of French firms disclosing emissions in both sustainability reports and to the CDP, their mean and median emissions reported in sustainability reports were statistically significantly lower than those reported to CDP. The sustainability report median was approximately 76% of the CDP-reported median. This finding sharply increases the value of the CDP information relative to other disclosures.

CDSB

The Climate Disclosure Standards Board (CDSB) is also a UK-based non-profit organization founded at the World Economic Forum in 2007. It has published a framework and a set of principles that aim to help businesses report environmental and natural capital information with the same level of rigor that is customary for financial information and to encourage the reporting of consistent climate information that will help investors make decisions about strategy, investment performance, and future prospects (CDSB, 2018). CDSB has an explicit goal of constructing reporting principles based on other widely adopted standards and frameworks such as GRI and CDP. CDSB has laid out seven principles for reporting environmental information, including a commitment to relevance, materiality, consistency, comparability, and an effort to be forward-looking. To this end, it is collaborating with CDP, XBRL International, and Fujitsu to develop a climate change reporting taxonomy to facilitate consistency of reporting concepts across scales and geographies. This initiative has the potential to eliminate some of the inconsistencies reported by Depoers et al. In addition, CDSB has worked with the TCFD (see below) to launch a hub of information and tools related to climate disclosure.

TCFD

The Financial Stability Board (FSB) is a group of finance ministries and central banks from G20 countries established after the 2009 G20 summit in London. The FSB is hosted and funded by the Bank of International Settlements (BIS) in Switzerland. The FSB's Taskforce for Climate-related Financial Disclosure (TCFD) is the most recent initiative in the context of corporate natural capital disclosure. The TCFD, formed in December 2015, is composed of 31 members selected by the FSB to broadly represent users and preparers of climate disclosures. The TCFD was a response to a call by Mark Carney, Chairman of the FSB, "to develop climate-related disclosures that 'could promote more informed investment, credit, and insurance underwriting decisions' and, in turn, 'would enable stakeholders to understand better the concentrations of carbon-related assets in the financial sector and the financial system's exposures to climate-related risks" (TCFD, 2017). As outlined in the quote, the TCFD embodies an effort to report on both impacts and dependencies on the environment. The aim of the TCFD is to make climate disclosures more actionable for investment banks, lenders, and insurance underwriters. In this sense, its target audience includes a broader array of players within the financial ecosystem.

The TCFD is an initiative more directly linked to the financial sector than previous such endeavors. It is chaired by Michael Bloomberg, founder of the Bloomberg information service. Its secretariat consists of Mary Shapiro, formerly chair of the US SEC, and two Bloomberg employees. Almost all the members of the taskforce are from for-profit reporting corporations, financial institutions, insurance companies, and key accounting or ratings providers in the financial ecosystem. Other than a single member from the PRI, there appears to be little representation from civil society on the Task Force. Nevertheless, according to the TCFD website, as of February 2019, more than 580 organizations support the TCFD. The majority of these are corporations, but nearly 70 comprise trade associations in the financial sector, business interest groups, and government bodies, including the governments of the UK, France, Belgium, Sweden, and Canada. The European Commission's Technical Expert Group on Sustainable Finance, established in July 2018 to assist the Commission in the implementation of proposed regulation on climate benchmarks, utilizes the TCFD definitions of climate-related physical and transition risk (EU Technical Expert Group, 2019). Although the TCFD recommendations remain a voluntary framework with no jurisdictional authority, their association with the FSB gives them legitimacy within the financial sector because finance ministries and central banks can apply significant pressure and moral suasion to the financial ecosystem even in the absence of regulation. The TCFD Knowledge Hub, accessible at tcfdhub.org, is an extensive repository of a diverse range of materials that aid investors and corporations with the preparation and interpretation of climate-related disclosures. Since the publication of its final report in 2017, the TCFD has worked to encourage adoption of its disclosure recommendations by issuers and users.

Concluding Remarks

We have noted above the challenge of incorporating a proper valuation of the benefits of biodiversity and of critical functions of resilience within ecosystems into investment decision-making. A subtler understanding of nature, which recognizes its periodic flows of benefits as well as the deep parameters of its inherent malleability, taxes the analytical frameworks we have available for valuation. Inadequate valuation is inextricably linked with misaligned incentives.

Within a large corporation dependent on many ecosystems throughout the world, it is likely that an ecosystem services review of the kind recommended by WRI, WBCSD, or the Natural Capital Coalition will help identify key vulnerabilities in those ecosystems which facilitate economic activity and profit generation. Just as universal owners (see Chap. 3) face some internalization of externalities due to their sheer size, so many large corporations dependent on healthy ecosystems can be expected to make choices that preserve those ecosystems both for their future profit as well as for a broader range of stakeholders. In the case of the CDP, institutional investors have been remarkably successful at creating a widespread culture of reporting on carbon emissions, with very little assistance from regulations. The relative complexity of the quantification of the drivers of natural resilience and biodiversity is somewhat greater than in the case of carbon emissions. Nevertheless, it is possible that a concerted engagement between institutional, especially universal asset owners, large corporations experienced in ecosystems service reviews and conservation-focused civil society can create new pressures and new incentives in the form of conservation-related financial instruments that begin to internalize some of the external costs of reduced resilience. We discuss some of these nascent instruments in Chap. 13.

Echoing a theme that we discussed in Chap. 6, there is a trade-off between complexity of valuation and widespread legitimacy. For example, the EP&L is a promising technique founded upon cost-benefit analysis and economic input-output analysis that has the potential to reveal the shortest path to eco-efficiency. However, it is most likely to be widely embraced if its underlying assumptions are simple, transparent, and open to discussion, perhaps with a mechanism for participatory input. Ultimately, the legitimacy of the appeal to natural capital comes from human actors, often those whose livelihoods are closest to subsistence on natural ecosystems. The products and services of natural capital have been referred to as the "GDP of the poor" (Sukhdev, 2009). The monetary valuation of natural capital is thus closely linked to human dignity and the valuation of human capabilities. Hence, we turn in the next chapter to an examination of the link between human capital and good stakeholder relations.

NOTES

1. Arrow et al. (2012) do not compute a value for coal resources.
2. Arrow et al. (2012) compute a value of $17.9 trillion for natural capital in 2000$ for these five countries. Using the change in the US GDP deflator between 2000 and 2010, this would amount to $22 trillion in 2010$.
3. Based on Table 2 of Arrow et al. (2012).
4. Values have been converted to 2010$ using the US GDP deflator.
5. A eutrophic lake has high nutrient input, high plant content, and murky water and is likely to have algal blooms. An oligotrophic lake has low nutrient input, low levels of plant production, and relatively clear water.
6. Earlier versions of Kering's EP&L provided greater detail on the range of shadow prices utilized for monetization. As of May 2019, the Kering methodology page www.kering.com/en/sustainability/ep-l/methodology/ displays an error.
7. A respondent may choose to respond confidentially, in which case, its emissions data is not available to the public.

REFERENCES

Admiraal, J. F., Wossink, A., de Groot, W. T., & de Snoo, G. R. (2013). More than Total Economic Value: How to Combine Economic Valuation of Biodiversity with Ecological Resilience. *Ecological Economics, 89*(0), 115–122. https://doi.org/10.1016/j.ecolecon.2013.02.009

Alcaraz, M., Carfagno, E., Guillen, M. J., Higgins, G., Ingram, A., Kestenbaum, A., … Visokey, B. (2019). *Advancing Marine Conservation in New York Waters through Ecological Valuation. Mimeo.* New York, NY: Columbia University.

Arrow, K. J., Dasgupta, P., Goulder, L. H., Mumford, K. J., & Oleson, K. (2012). Sustainability and the Measurement of Wealth. *Environment and Development Economics, 17*(3), 317–353. http://journals.cambridge.org/action/displayBackIssues?jid=EDE

CDSB. (2018). *CDSB Framework for Reporting Environmental Information, Natural Capital and Associated Business Impacts.* Retrieved from cdsb.net/framework

Clark, J. B. (1899). *The Distribution of Wealth: A Theory of Wages, Interest and Profits.* New York, NY: Macmillan.

Costanza, R., de Groot, R., Sutton, P., van der Ploeg, S., Anderson, S. J., Kubiszewski, I., … Turner, R. K. (2014). Changes in the Global Value of Ecosystem Services. *Global Environmental Change-Human and Policy Dimensions, 26*, 152–158. https://doi.org/10.1016/j.gloenvcha.2014.04.002

Danish Environmental Protection Agency. (2014). *Methodology Report for Novo Nordisk's Environmental Profit & Loss Account.* Retrieved from https://www2.mst.dk/Udgiv/publications/2014/02/978-87-93178-03-8.pdf

Dasgupta, P. (2008). *Nature in Economics. Environmental and Resource Economics, 39*(1), 1–7. https://link.springer.com/journal/volumesAndIssues/10640

de Groot, R., Brander, L., van der Ploeg, S., Costanza, R., Bernard, F., Braat, L., … van Beukering, P. (2012). Global Estimates of the Value of Ecosystems and their Services in Monetary Units. *Ecosystem Services, 1*(1), 50–61. https://doi.org/10.1016/j.ecoser.2012.07.005

DeFries, R., & Nagendra, H. (2017). Ecosystem Management as a Wicked Problem. *Science, 356*(6335), 265. https://doi.org/10.1126/science.aal1950

Depoers, F., Jeanjean, T., & Jérôme, T. (2016). Voluntary Disclosure of Greenhouse Gas Emissions: Contrasting the Carbon Disclosure Project and Corporate Reports. *Journal of Business Ethics, 134*(3), 445–461. https://doi.org/10.1007/s10551-014-2432-0

EU Technical Expert Group on Sustainable Finance. (2019, June 18). *Financing a Sustainable European Economy: Report on Benchmarks.* Retrieved from https://ec.europa.eu/info/sites/info/files/business_economy_euro/banking_and_finance/documents/190618-sustainable-finance-teg-report-climate-benchmarks-and-disclosures_en.pdf

European Commission Environment Directorate-General. (2008). The Economics of Ecosystems & Biodiversity an Interim Report. In P. Sukhdev (Ed.). Brussels, Belgium: European Union Commission for the Environment.

Hartwick, J. M. (1977). Intergenerational Equity and the Investing of Rents from Exhaustible Resources. *American Economic Review, 67*(5), 972–974. http://www.aeaweb.org/aer/

Kim, J. (2018). *A Multi-Step Model of Boundary Spanning and Absorptive Capacity: The Differential Impact of Board and Top Management Team Experience on the Development of Sustainability-Related Capabilities*. (79), ProQuest Information & Learning. Retrieved from https://ezproxy.cul.columbia.edu/login?qurl=https%3a%2f%2fsearch.ebscohost.com%2flogin.aspx%3fdirect%3dtrue%26db%3dpsyh%26AN%3d2018-30342-154%26site%3dehost-live%26scope%3dsite. Available from EBSCOhost psyh database.

Kleppel, G. (2014). *The Emergent Agriculture: Farming, Sustainability and the Return of the Local Economy*. Gabriola Island, BC: New Society Publishers.

Lammerant, J. (2018). *Assessment of Biodiversity Accounting Approaches for Businesses and Financial Institutions*. Retrieved from https://ec.europa.eu/environment/biodiversity/business/news-and-events/news/news-106_en.htm

Mace, G. M. (2019). The Ecology of Natural Capital Accounting. *Oxford Review of Economic Policy, 35*(1), 54–67. https://academic.oup.com/oxrep/issue

Matisoff, D. C., Noonan, D. S., & O'Brien, J. J. (2013). Convergence in Environmental Reporting: Assessing the Carbon Disclosure Project. Business Strategy and the Environment (John Wiley & Sons, Inc), *22*(5), 285–305. https://doi.org/10.1002/bse.1741

Millennium Ecosystem Assessment, M. (2005). *Ecosystems and Human Well-Being*. Washington, DC: Island Press.

Missemer, A. (2018). Natural Capital as an Economic Concept, History and Contemporary Issues. *Ecological Economics, 143*, 90–96. https://doi.org/10.1016/j.ecolecon.2017.07.011

Natural Capital Coalition. (2016). *Natural Capital Protocol*. Retrieved from www.naturalcapitalcoalition.org/protocol

Natural Capital Committee. (2017). *How to Do It: A Natural Capital Workbook*. Retrieved from https://assets.publishing.service.gov.uk/government/uploads/system/uploads/attachment_data/file/608852/ncc-natural-capital-workbook.pdf

Neumayer, E. (2013). *Weak Versus Strong Sustainability*. Cheltenham, UK: Edward Elgar.

Pearce, D. (1988). Economics, Equity and Sustainable Development. *Futures: The Journal of Policy, Planning and Futures Studies, 20*, 598–605. https://doi.org/10.1016/0016-3287(88)90002-X

Peterson, G. D., Carpenter, S. R., & Brock, W. A. (2003). Uncertainty and the Management of Multistate Ecosystems: An Apparently Rational Route to Collapse. *Ecology, 84*(6), 1403–1411.

Rockström, J., Steffen, W., Noone, K., Persson, Å., Chapin Iii, F. S., Lambin, E. F., ... Foley, J. A. (2009). A Safe Operating Space for Humanity. *Nature, 461*, 472. https://doi.org/10.1038/461472a

Shanley, P., Pierce, A. R., Laird, S. A., & Guillen, A. (2001). *Tapping the Green Market: Management and Certification of Non-timber Forest Products.* London, UK: Earthscan.

Steneck, R. S., Hughes, T. P., Cinner, J. E., Adger, W. N., Arnold, S. N., Berkes, F., ... Worm, B. (2011). Creation of a Gilded Trap by the High Economic Value of the Maine Lobster Fishery. *Conservation Biology, 25*(5), 904–912.

Sukhdev, P. (2009). Costing the Earth. *Nature, 462*(7271), 277.

Tallis, H., & Polasky, S. (2009). Mapping and Valuing Ecosystem Services as an Approach for Conservation and Natural-Resource Management. *Annals of the New York Academy of Sciences, 1162*(1), 265–283. https://doi.org/10.1111/j.1749-6632.2009.04152.x

TCFD. (2017). *Final Report: Recommendations of the Task Force on Climate-related Financial Disclosures.* Retrieved from https://www.fsb-tcfd.org/wp-content/uploads/2017/06/FINAL-TCFD-Report-062817.pdf

Waage, S., & Kester, C. (2015). *Making the Invisible Visible: Analytical Tools for Assessing Business Impacts & Dependencies Upon Ecosystem Services.* Retrieved from https://www.bsr.org/en/our-insights/reportview/making-the-invisible-visible-analytical-tools-for-assessing-business-impact

Warburton, C. (1928). Economic Terminology: Factors of Production and Distributive Shares. *American Economic Review, 18*(1), 65–74.

WBCSD. (2011). *Guide to Corporate Ecosystem Valuation: A Framework for Improving Corporate Decision-Making.* Geneva, Switzerland: WBCSD.

WBCSD. (2012). *The Corporate Ecosystem Services Review: Guidelines for Identifying Business Risks and Opportunities Arising from Ecosystem Change.* Geneva, Switzerland: WBCSD.

Weitzman, M. L. (2000). Economic Profitability Versus Ecological Entropy. *Quarterly Journal of Economics, 115*(1), 237–263. https://academic.oup.com/qje/issue

World Resources Institute. (2015). *Revaluing Ecosystems: Pathways for Scaling Up the Inclusion of Ecosystem Value in Decision-Making.* Retrieved from https://www.wri.org/publication/revaluing-ecosystems

WRI. (2013). *Aqueduct: Measuring and Mapping Water Risk.* Retrieved from https://www.wri.org/our-work/project/aqueduct

CHAPTER 8

Human Capital and the Returns to Stakeholder Relations

In Chap. 7, we underlined the need to move beyond the simplistic evaluation of stocks and flows in the context of the valuation of natural capital, given nature's inherent thicket of interlinkages and the complex sources of its resilience. A nuanced perspective on nature which recognizes its flows of benefits while also respecting the deep parameters of its visceral connection to humans taxes the analytical frameworks we have for valuation. The limits of the analytical valuation approach loom even larger when we attempt to value the importance of what has been referred to as human capital. Acknowledging the importance of human cognition, attention, engagement, ingenuity, dignity, and a host of other attributes to the sustainable creation of value necessarily leads to a complex understanding of that factor of production glibly called labor.

Human Capital: From Cost to Asset

The theme of human capital management and financial returns to stakeholder relations is a clichéd trope in sustainable finance that in earlier times would have been said to reflect the obvious. A standard company report claims "our people are our greatest asset". So much is evident. Every aspect of value creation in a company depends on people. Management strategy consultants have argued that human capital supply-demand imbalances are likely to prevent significant value-creating opportunities from being pursued in a number of major economies by 2030 (Strack, Baier, Marchingo,

© The Author(s) 2019   181
S. Bose et al., *The Financial Ecosystem*, Palgrave Studies in Impact
Finance, https://doi.org/10.1007/978-3-030-05624-7_8

& Sharda, 2014). Finance has struggled somewhat with this idea, even though it is standard in the world of business and in economics. The value of human labor has been routinely a component of wealth calculations perhaps from time immemorial. The first national-scale accounting of wealth in western Europe was the Domesday Book prepared upon the orders of William I, the new conqueror of England in the eleventh century which was then a fertile agricultural land producing significant surpluses (Jones, 2018). The Domesday Book is an inventory of income, tax assessments, and the wealth of each shire in the country. The wealth consisted of pastures, meadows, woods, fish ponds, plows, mills, and six types of available labor, including slaves and tenant laborers[1] (McDonald & Snooks, 1985). William Petty's seventeenth-century balance sheet of England's wealth attributed £25 million of a total wealth of £40 million to labor (Slack, 2004). Petty called "the daily labour of the people...the father and seed of wealth".

The evolution of finance has haltingly and belatedly come to terms with the obvious, even though the dismal science did arrive there first, starting with Adam Smith, whose reputation as a free market theorist belies his advocacy of adequate wages for all. In an analysis of the posthumous recharacterization of Adam Smith's writings, the economic historian Emma Rothschild shows that his writings on commercial freedom were emphasized while his support for political freedom for the laboring poor was conveniently forgotten in England in order to distance his legacy from the revolutionary fervor in France. Rothschild quotes Smith thus: "No society can surely be flourishing and happy, of which the far greater part of the members are poor and miserable. It is but equity, besides, that they who feed, clothe and lodge the whole body of the people, should have such a share of the produce of their own labour as to be themselves tolerably well fed, clothed and lodged" (Rothschild, 2001). Rothschild points out that during his lifetime, Smith was known as a friend of the poor and always argued that high wages were the "necessary *effect* and *cause* of the greatest public prosperity" (emphasis added).

Furthermore, Smith's analysis of the drivers of differential compensation in the range of occupations remains the foundation of the modern theory of the returns to human capital investment. The value in the heterogeneity of human skills and attributes became apparent during the industrialization observed by Smith. He noted that skills and acquired training could be thought of as productive as a machine. This view of human capital separates the human being from his abilities. Subsequent economists were careful to emphasize this separation to address the moral difficulties of valuing the human being versus the monetization of his training. In Chap. 6, we noted the artifice in the definition of a value of a statistical life, which is not meant to signify the value of an individual life, but rather a statistical average willingness to pay. John Stuart Mill wrote (quoted in Folloni and Vittadini (2010)): "The human being himself I do not class as wealth. He is the purpose for which wealth exists. But his acquired capacities, which exist only as a means, and have been called into existence by labour, fall rightly, as it seems to me, within that designation". Folloni and Vittadini show that Alfred Marshall maintained a similar distinction, arguing that it was impossible to value Yellowstone Park, unless we accepted a range of values that were several 100% apart. He argued that we might compute a lower limit on the value of public parks and humans, but seldom an upper limit.

Folloni and Vitadini outline two methods of valuing human capital for the economy as a whole that were standard approaches before the mid-twentieth century. The first, known as the *retrospective method,* is a computation of the accumulated rearing cost of children, most clearly articulated by Ernst Engel in 1883. Engel estimated that children in different German social classes had different annual costs of maintenance and he assumed that the investment cost of humans was equal to the cumulative cost of rearing them to adulthood. The second method, more commonly used today and first developed in the actuarial literature by William Farr in 1853, is known as the *prospective method.* Farr, whose goal was to determine the tax-paying capacity of individuals, computed the value of an individual's human capital at each age as the present actuarial value of his expected annual earnings (taking into account his mortality) after deducting personal living expenses. This method computes the value of human capital as equal to the present value of future labor income streams. Farr's method, enhanced to include variation in demographic and educational characteristics as well as estimations of the non-pecuniary benefits of human capital (Oreopoulos & Salvanes, 2011) is now the standard method of valuing human capital stock, for example, in Hamilton and Hepburn's analysis cited in Chap. 1 (Hamilton & Hepburn, 2014). Both methods have drawbacks. The retrospective method obviously assumes that the cost of training is equivalent to its future value and ignores the opportunities that individuals might exploit due to their training. The prospective method is most closely related to the standard method of valuing physical capital. However, in the case of human capital, which can be used both for enhancing the utility of leisure as well as for earnings, the assumption that differences in wages are equivalent to differences in productivity both in market and non-market sectors is problematic.

Modern human capital theory, articulated by adherents of the Chicago School emphasized the investments that an individual might make in her own training so as to reap its future rewards in the form of higher wages and greater choice of occupation (Becker, 1962; Mincer, 1958; Schultz, 1959). This shift in protagonist from the state to the individual further underscores the separation of the human and her attributes, sidestepping the moral difficulties of valuing human capital as if that were the same as humans. By highlighting the individual's right to choose to invest in herself, human capital theory facilitates a monetary estimate of skills and training that is a measure of the wealth owned by the trainee who becomes the decision-maker, rather than the state (which was the case with Petty's valuation). Becker also argued that corporate expenditure on employee training should be viewed as investments in human capital, rather than as a periodic expense, precipitating the shift in perspective from labor as a cost to human capital as an asset in a corporate context. Becker's insight rested on the premise that part of the value of the training flowed to the employer, while part of it flowed to the trainee, so that training was an investment for the individual and the employer.

Human Capital and Worker Rights

As we showed in Chap. 3, the corporation was always intended to serve the interests of society at large, often embodied in the form of a state which both needed to generate revenue for its operations and to provide for the common weal so as to avert mutiny and revolution. The symbiosis of state and corporation began with the willingness of the state, represented by monarchies and mercantile elites, to provide protections and privileges for companies in return for contributions to the state treasury. In more recent times, in Victorian Britain, the privileges of the corporate form ceased to be the preserve of quasi-public enterprises implicitly and explicitly regulated in the public interest, giving way to newly formed private companies over which the state claimed no right or duty of control (Taylor, 2006).

Nevertheless, government, regulators, and civil society, including labor unions and religious groups, worked to establish labor standards alongside the development of the corporate form. There has been a profound transformation over centuries from varied and hierarchical rights characterized by caste and occupation to an acceptance of equal and universal human rights. The route has been circuitous, with the concept of 'human rights' having been articulated only very recently (Moyn, 2014). The hierarchy of trades reflected in feudal and caste systems (for example, in the Domesday Book categories of labor), the abolition of the transatlantic slave trade and subsequent abolition of slavery, and the growing inclusion of women in the workforce, can be linked to the widespread adoption of norms reflecting some measure of the notion of equal treatment of people. Concurrently, there has been significant progress in standards for the protection of the health and safety of workers, limitations on hours, and special requirements for vulnerable communities such as children, and an expectation that wages and benefits are sufficient to meet basic needs. That progress occurred as a consequence of diverse social struggles in a number of countries around the world, and was articulated globally through international organizations in the twentieth century in the wake of the two world wars.

The end of the nineteenth century saw appalling conditions for labor in the industrialized world. Working days were often 12–16 hours, wages were maintained at starvation level, women and children were routinely exploited and workers often braved bullets to strike. For example, a watershed moment in American labor relations occurred on April 20, 1914, when members of the Colorado National Guard and security guards employed by the Colorado Fuel & Iron Company (owned and managed by John D. Rockefeller Jr.) armed with at least two machine guns and Springfield rifles, attacked a tent colony of 1200 striking miners and their wives and children. The ensuing battle, which led to the deaths of 21 strikers, including women and children, came to be known as the Ludlow Massacre. The site of the battle is now a National Historic Landmark (Simmons, Simmons, Haecker, & Siebert, 2008). The massacre drew widespread public sympathy for miners and forced Rockefeller to dramatically change labor management practices throughout the family empire and engage in a novel public relations effort to improve his own reputation.

The International Labor Organization

The International Labor Organization (ILO) was formed as result of Part XIII of the 1919 Treaty of Versailles, partly to meet the demands of civil society to ameliorate working conditions and partly to drain working class sympathies for the Soviet model. The Treaty gave the ILO authority to bypass national governments who were signatories and to work directly with labor ministries to implement its mission to establish everywhere humane conditions of labor and to institute and implement a system of international labor legislation (Wallin, 1969). The ILO has been called the first international organization focused on 'welfare internationalism,' that is, the idea that multilateral organizations should cater to the material welfare of individuals or the global common weal, rather than solve conflicts between governments (Steffek & Holthaus, 2018). After the formation of the United Nations, the ILO became its first specialized agency. Unique among UN organizations, the ILO is composed of a tripartite representative structure that includes employer and worker bodies alongside governments. The ILO was also tasked with the "collection and distribution of information on all subjects relating to the international adjustment of conditions of industrial life and labor" (Thomas, 1996). The 1944 Declaration at the ILO conference in Philadelphia dedicates the organization to a lofty set of principles and goals that remain to be fulfilled almost everywhere.

> The Conference reaffirms the fundamental principles on which the Organization is based and, in particular, that:
>
> (a) labour is not a commodity;
> (b) freedom of expression and of association are essential to sustained progress;
> (c) poverty anywhere constitutes a danger to prosperity everywhere;
> (d) the war against want requires to be carried on with unrelenting vigour within each nation, and by continuous and concerted international effort in which the representatives of workers and employers, enjoying equal status with those of governments, join with them in free discussion and democratic decision with a view to the promotion of the common welfare. (ILO, 2019)

The Declaration goes on to dedicate the ILO to advance full employment, raise standards of living, facilitate job satisfaction, ensure minimum living wages, and recognize the right of collective bargaining.

The Universal Declaration of Human Rights

An additional civil society initiative that complicates our discussions of the valuation of human capital is the 1948 Universal Declaration of Human Rights. The foundational role of the United Nations in establishing a Universal Declaration of Human Rights in 1948 both reflected and hastened the advancing concern with the global common weal in the wake of the devastation wreaked by World War II. When adopted, there were only eight abstentions, and not one nation in opposition other than from the Soviet bloc, plus Saudi Arabia and South Africa. Although the Declaration is not a treaty, the intent was to provide an expression of fundamental values shared by members of the international community, which has since had a significant impact on international law and national legislation around human rights. The preamble begins: "Whereas recognition of the inherent dignity and of the equal and inalienable rights of all members of the human family is the foundation of freedom, justice and peace in the world." Several articles in the Declaration relate directly to the recognition of human rights in the workplace. The extraordinary vision and resolve of the drafters produced a document that, for the first time, articulated the rights and freedoms to which every human being is equally and inalienably entitled. Now available in more than 360 languages, the Declaration is the most translated document in the world—"a testament to its global nature and reach. It provides a foundation for a just and decent future for all, and has given people everywhere a powerful tool in the fight against oppression, impunity and affronts to human dignity."

The profile of the UN Declaration has ebbed and flowed with Cold War politics. Nevertheless, the international civil society efforts to advance the economic, social, and human rights in the form of the ILO and the Universal Declaration demonstrate a globally robust stakeholder legitimacy for the cause of a fair share of output for workers. In Chap. 1, we noted that the scale and power of corporations dwarfs the resources available to the governments of most countries to regulate the societal impact of corporate activity. The apparent impotence of most governments in the face of the global power of the largest corporations limits the credibility of any effort at sustainable development that does not include the corporate sector as a driving force. While the civil society initiatives have laudable goals, they cannot be achieved today without the application of intense pressure upon corporations. The record of corporate achievements on human rights is better than it was during the time of the Ludlow Massacre, but there is much to improve (see the CHRB example later in the chapter). Responsible investors can be a critically important funnel through which to channel civil society pressures that aim to increase productivity and propagate prosperity to all.

The Collevecchio Declaration
In 2003, a group of more than 100 civil society organizations endorsed the Collevecchio Declaration (named after the town where it was signed), a statement on the role of the financial sector in promoting sustainable development. The Declaration states: Financial Institutions (FIs) such as banks and asset managers can and must play a role in advancing environmental and social sustainability. This declaration calls on FIs to embrace six main principles which reflect civil society's expectations of the role and responsibilities of the financial services sector in fostering sustainability.

1. Commitment to sustainability—fully integrating environmental, social, and economic factors.
2. Commitment to 'do no harm'—preventing detrimental environmental and social impacts.
3. Commitment to responsibility—paying for their full share of social and environmental risks.
4. Commitment to accountability—enabling stakeholders to have an influential voice.
5. Commitment to transparency—robust, regular disclosures, and responsiveness to requests.
6. Commitment to sustainable markets—actively supporting public policy which facilitates full-cost accounting.

As corporations and financial markets have expanded in scale and scope, their roles have come to be recognized as equally important as those of state actors in the achievement of the UN Sustainable Development Goals (SDGs). More recently, the decline in formal employment by large stable employers and a shift toward globally outsourced supply chains, migrant workforces, and the advent of the 'gig' economy has further complicated the work of all stakeholders in their efforts to advance even the most basic standards of a humane work environment. A promising development in this process is the recognition by some investors of the centrality of human capital and stakeholder relations to the sustainable creation of investor value, especially in high skill, high value-added sectors. Investors have allied with non-governmental organizations (NGOs) and public bodies which have long called for companies to identify the metrics of importance to human capital management arguing that civil society demands that companies be accountable for their impact not just on their immediate workforce, but the communities they operate within. A complete understanding of this link transforms investor perceptions of labor as a cost into human capital as an asset, much as Smith saw high wages as the "necessary effect and cause of the greatest public prosperity".

CalPERS Integration of Human Capital in Its Investment Beliefs
In 2013, the California Public Employees Retirement System (CalPERS) recognized the integral role of human capital in corporate value creation by adopting the following as one of its ten Investment Beliefs:

Long term value creation requires the effective management of three forms of capital: financial, physical and human.

Sub-beliefs:

Governance is the primary tool to align interests between CalPERS and managers of its capital, including investee companies and external managers.

Strong governance, along with effective management of environmental and human capital factors, increases the likelihood that companies will outperform over the long-term and manage risk effectively.

CalPERS may engage investee companies and external managers on their governance and sustainability issues, including:

Governance practices, including but not limited to alignment of interests;

Risk management practices;

Human capital practices, including but not limited to, fair labor practices, health and safety,

responsible contracting and diversity;

Environmental practices, including but not limited to climate change and natural resource availability. (CalPERS, 2013)

The Relationship to Financial Returns

There is significant evidence that the quality of human capital management and stakeholder relations has a beneficial impact on financial returns for investors.

Human Capital Management

A recent meta-study of the research literature examined 92 empirical studies of the relationship between human capital policies and financial outcomes such as return on equity, return on investment, and profit margins. The majority of studies (73%) found positive correlations between human capital management and financial performance, while just one study found a negative correlation (Bernstein & Beeferman, 2015). In total, 26% of the studies found mixed or no correlation. The studies originated in multiple countries and industrial sectors, and were conducted over three decades. Bernstein and Beeferman focus on a range of workplace management practices as well as employer training. While the studies do not demonstrate causality from these practices to performance, the robust association indicates that a review of an investee company's human resources practices is material to the goals of investors. The authors point out that many of the studies are conducted from the perspective of corporate managers, so they utilize metrics of human capital management which are not generally disclosed to investors.

A class of study examined by Bernstein and Beeferman investigated the impact of what is referred to as high-performance work practices: comprehensive and standardized employee recruitment and selection procedures, incentive compensation and performance management systems, and extensive employee involvement and training. Mark Huselid conducted an early study of these practices which led to a sub-genre of such analyses (Huselid, 1995). Huselid examined 968 publicly traded US firms and found positive correlations between high-performance work practices and both Tobin's Q and return on capital employed. An alternative specification of human capital performance is provided by external rankings of employee satisfaction at large firms (Edmans, 2011). Edmans constructed annually rebalanced, value-weighted portfolios of the "100 Best Companies to Work for in America", as published annually by Fortune magazine. He found that an investment strategy that invested in these portfolios over a 25-year period demonstrated an annual outperformance of 3.5% relative to the risk-adjusted benchmark.[2]

Stakeholder Relations

Consistent with the economic theory of human capital outlined above, some scholars of corporate finance have viewed stakeholder welfare-enhancing activities by corporations as investments in value-creating intangibles such as reputation and human capital (Zingales, 2000). Yawen Jiao constructed a measure of corporate stakeholder welfare using ratings computed by Kinder, Lydenberg & Domini (KLD),[3] an independent social choice investment advisory firm (Jiao, 2010). Stakeholders consisted of employees, customers, communities, and the environment. For 822 firms in the S&P 500 and the Domini Social 400, Jiao found that an increase in the stakeholder welfare score led to an economically significant increase in Tobin's Q, after controlling for return on assets, sales growth, and R&D intensity. In a subsequent similar study, Borgers, Derwall, Koedijk, and ter Horst (2013) note that their measure of stakeholder welfare was positively associated with long-term risk-adjusted returns between 1992 and 2004. They note that the strength of relationship diminished considerably between 2004 and 2009. Borgers et al. attribute the subsequent weaker relationship to the increased attention to the importance of stakeholder welfare by activist institutional investors which likely eliminated the mispricing attributable to under-disclosed stakeholder welfare measures. Another study that combines publicly available data from multiple independent signals of stakeholder relations performance is by Coleman (2011). Coleman compiles data for S&P 500 firms in 1998–2003 from the US Environmental Protection Agency's listings of Federal penalties levied on corporations for environmental non-compliance, unsafe workplace citations by the Occupational Health & Safety Administration, SEC civil lawsuits against corporations related to financial reporting, and Consumer Product Safety Commission recalls. He uses the four variables to construct a measure of counterparty risk faced by stakeholders who might transact with the corporation (as customer, vendor, employee, or community). Coleman finds that Environmental Protection Agency (EPA) penalties and product recalls are associated with lower profit margins and lower shareholder returns, indicating that the welfare of the consumer and community stakeholders have a positive relationship to shareholder return.

INVESTOR DEMANDS FOR HUMAN CAPITAL DISCLOSURE

Investors have begun to consider the impact of human capital management on corporate performance. The ILO reports that occupational accidents or work-related diseases cause more than 2.8 million deaths annually. In addition, there are some 374 million non-fatal work-related injuries and illnesses each year. The economic burden of poor occupational safety and health practices is estimated at 3.94% of GDP each year (Hämäläinen, Takala, & Kiat, 2017). An appreciation of human capital management as a potential risk is beginning to extend beyond issues of health and safety, to include issues such as diversity and inclusion.

The Human Capital Management Coalition (HCMC) was formed by institutional investors following the collapse of a building named Rana Plaza housing five garment manufacturers in Dhaka, Bangladesh. On April 24, 2013, the eight-storey commercial building collapsed following structural failure, killing 1134 and injuring approximately 2500. The majority of the dead and injured were making garments on contract for major multinational companies. The Rana Plaza incident is considered the deadliest ever accident in the garment industry globally. The building's owner, Sohel Rana, ignored warnings to avoid using the building after cracks in the structure appeared the previous day. Garment workers were ordered to report to work as usual, and the structural collapse occurred at 8:57 am after diesel generators had to be started on the top floor due to a power cut. The accident demonstrated that the multinational companies outsourcing manufacture to these facilities were not effectively monitoring working conditions.

The HCMC was formed during the Council of Institutional Investors (CII) bi-annual meeting in July 2013 at which an investor response to Rana Plaza was discussed. Of particular concern were reports that Walmart, the largest retailer in the world, was unaware that its garments had been manufactured at Rana Plaza. According to the *New York Times*, a Canadian supplier for Walmart had used a factory on the fifth floor of the building to make jeans for Walmart a year before the collapse, though Walmart denied having any production in the building at the time of the collapse (Greenhouse, 2014). Concurrently, an investor group led by the Interfaith Center on Corporate Responsibility (ICCR) released an Investor Statement signed by over 200 organizations calling on global brands to pledge to implement the internationally recognized core labor standards set by the ILO as well as to implement four specific recommendations:

join the legally binding Accord on Fire and Building Safety signed by trade
unions, brands and retailers with NGOs as witness signatories;

commit to strengthening local trade unions and ensuring a living wage for
all workers including through their engagement with the Bangladesh
government;

publicly disclose all their suppliers including those from Bangladesh;

ensure that appropriate grievance mechanisms and effective remedies,
including compensation, are in place for affected workers and families.
(ICCR, 2013)

The Gap Talent Dashboard

In 2014, Gap increased its minimum wage for US employees to $9
per hour in 2014 and $10 per hour in 2015, affecting 65,000 of
their 90,000 employees and also developed a Talent Dashboard,
their first effort to provide their board with an integrated overview
of workforce issues such as turnover, employee engagement, external hiring and internal promotions, employee positions and tenure,
productivity, and diversity. They later introduced a productivity measure and report that in 2014 they saw a 10% increase in job applications, which they regarded as significant as previous measures to
boost the number of applicants had been unsuccessful. The company
also discussed with investors new programs for particular demo-
graphics, including the long-term unemployed to help them prepare
for job interviews, and 'at risk' individuals. It also set up a Talent
Council to foster communication between executives and retail
employees, and a cross-functional team of senior staff to develop
integrated reporting at the company in future. Their work became
the focus of a Washington Post article about the experience of
increasing its minimum wage where Senior Vice President Dan
Henkle reported that a double digit increase in applications for jobs
led them to believe there would be an improvement in the quality of
Gap's talent pool (McGregor, 2014).

In 2017, the HCMC petitioned the SEC to require issuers to disclose
information about their human capital management policies, practices,
and performance (Miller, 2017). In response, the SEC's Investor Advisory
Group commented "In contrast to the financial markets' view of human

capital as a source of value, the SEC's historical approach to the workforce has been to view human capital as a cost. The Commission's disclosure frameworks—both quantitative and qualitative—have not kept pace with the shift towards human capital management as a primary source of value. Valuation of firms with few hard assets based on public SEC-mandated disclosure alone is increasingly difficult. Currently available information is not consistent, verified, or comparable across companies. Yet human capital management metrics such as those outlined below are a routine part of financial due diligence in mergers and acquisitions transactions." The SEC Investor Advisory Committee (IAC) concluded that "Institutional and retail investors have a pronounced interest in clear and comparable information about how firms approach human capital management. High quality human capital management practices correlate with lower employee turnover, higher productivity, and better corporate financial performance producing a considerable and sustained alpha over time. Yet current accounting standards discourage and obscure workforce investment by reflecting it only as an expense not distinguished from other inputs. Investing in research and development, by contrast, is identified by a separate line item in the income statement" (SEC Investor Advisory Committee, 2019). Despite the recommendations of the committee, statements by William Hinman, Director of the SEC's Division of Corporate Finance, suggest that it is unlikely that the SEC will mandate specific human capital disclosures in the near future (Maiden, 2019).

Diversity

There is a growing interest in diversity within corporate leadership groups which is increasingly referenced in investor statements, and also in national codes of practice. In 2019, California required its locally headquartered publicly listed companies to have at least one female board member by 2020. Other jurisdictions such as Spain, France, and Norway have more stringent requirements on gender diversity (Creary, McDonnell, Ghai, & Scruggs, 2019). In South Africa, corporations are required to report their scores on performance on Broad-Based Black Economic Empowerment, which comprised metrics including the proportion of Black and female directors and managers. Strategy management consultants have reported a positive relationship between gender and ethnic diversity and financial performance. According to Mckinsey & Company, out of over 1000 companies in 12 countries, those with the most diverse leadership—in the top quartile for gender—were 21% more likely to earn above average profits, while those in the top quartile for ethnic/cultural diversity were 33% more likely to outperform. Companies in the bottom tier of leadership diversity (both gender and ethnicity) were 29% less likely to achieve above average profitability (Hunt, Prince, Dixon-Fyl, & Yee, 2018). The academic studies on diversity in general have ambiguous conclusions. A meta-analysis of 140 studies finds that female board representation is positively related to accounting returns. The relationship between female board representation and market performance is neutral overall, but the relationship is positive in countries with greater gender parity and negative in countries with low gender parity (Post & Byron, 2015). Some scholars have argued that measures of board diversity are correlated with lower firm idiosyncratic risk (Bernile, Bhagwat, & Yonker, 2018), while others have suggested that this relationship is spurious (Sila, Gonzalez, & Hagendorff, 2016). It appears that diversity matters, but focusing on a single dimension such as gender is insufficient. Rather, the benefits of analytic diversity are likely to stem from a combination of gender, ethnicity, cultural and occupational backgrounds, and age. This is likely to parallel our review of broad social legitimacy in the context of sustainability accounting initiatives in Chap. 4 and social network analysis in Chap. 9.

A number of institutional investors have pressed companies to increase certain dimensions of board diversity. CalPERS identified diversity and inclusion as one of several cross-cutting themes in its review of academic evidence in the Sustainable Investment Research Initiative as having the potential to positively impact both risk management and returns. CalPERS' rationale for the focus on diversity and inclusion is premised on two goals: (a) to avoid the 'group think' which was identified by the IMF as a key contributor to the 2008 financial crisis, and (b) to access an array of talent that can offer the range of skills, insight, and experience which complex global businesses demand. Vanguard, the largest institutional investor of passively managed funds, states that it is focused on diversity in the board composition of its investee companies: "Our primary interest is to ensure that the individuals who represent the interests of all shareholders are independent, capable and appropriately experienced. We also believe that diversity of thought, background and experience, as well as of personal characteristics (such as gender, race, and age) meaningfully contributes to a board's ability to serve as effective, engaged stewards of shareholders' interests." The report goes on to describe examples of companies (whose names were withheld) where Vanguard had focused on improving board quality through enhanced diversity, commenting "we intend to push for additional board diversity so that boards can better unlock the benefits of having a wide range of perspectives" (Vanguard, 2018).

THE ROLE OF NGOs IN CIVIL REGULATION

Civil society groups have long recognized the outsized impact of corporate activity on stakeholders. The range of issues they address have increased as companies in turn have become more significant in the wider economy. One view is that NGOs have an emerging role in civil society to instigate the regulation of emerging impacts of corporate behavior, putting stakeholders into a critical role alongside and sometimes preceding investors and regulators (Hutton, MacDougall, & Zadek, 2001). The three main contributions that NGOs can make:

1. Enhance welfare—when acting as civil regulators, NGO campaigns can be an effective method of achieving welfare-enhancing social and/or environmental goals. Davis, Lukomnik, and Pitt-Watson (2006) argue that "In a civil society, political parties, an independent judiciary, a free press, impartial law and civic bodies are the core sustainers of democracy. Parallel institutions of a civil economy can be understood as engaged shareowners, independent monitors, credible standards and civil-society organizations participating in the marketplace."
2. Enhance investment analysis—by enhancing information flows on corporate performance in social, ethical, and environmental issues that may be material to share price, NGOs can improve investment analysis (plus as they lobby for new rules, may also provide insight into future regulatory trends).
3. Enhance market trust—Waygood (2013) quotes Korten (1995): "an economic system can remain viable only so long as society has mechanisms to counter the abuses of either state or market power". Waygood's preferred system is democratic pluralism, which combines "the forces of the market, government and civil society"—a vital part of the system.

Waygood argues that the next important step is for players in the financial ecosystem to ally with NGOs in formal partnerships, such as WWF and Insight teaming up on sustainable homes and Aviva on the Natural Finance

Initiative. It remains to be seen whether such formal partnerships lead to concerted action or risk the co-option and dilution of civil society goals given the potential imbalance in power between large global corporations and civil society organizations. Nevertheless, Waygood's articulation of the need for a combination of diverse actors in the regulatory enterprise is undoubtedly correct.

The growing role of civil society in articulating stakeholder interests, above and beyond the legal purpose of the company is to be seen in both common law and civil law governance regimes.

The need to find balance between managing financial, human, and natural capital has led to a growing convergence between shareholder primacy and stakeholder models of the firm. Common law markets increasingly provide examples of companies demonstrating their view that value creation for investors requires attention to the needs and expectations of stakeholders. Conversely, in civil law markets companies articulate a need to provide risk-adjusted returns to investors in order to maintain their access to capital at an acceptable cost. Both demonstrate the recognition that a shared value approach rather than a shareholder primacy focus can drive sustainability more effectively, not least because it routinizes a focus on long-term inclusive prosperity. This convergence has driven the growing call for standards and metrics around human capital and stakeholder relations (as explored in Chap. 4), regulatory initiatives that foster protection of human capital, and consumer and community initiatives such as the fair trade movement.

Falling Short on the Corporate Human Rights Benchmark

Despite the growing attention from investors, civil society and regulators, the issues and performance metrics in human capital management remain poorly defined, with best practices often falling short of minimum standards. A sobering example is the results compiled by the Corporate Human Rights Benchmark (CHRB), a multi-stakeholder initiative started in 2013 to rate the human rights performance of major global corporations in a subset of industries. The initiative is chaired by Steve Waygood, Head of Responsible Investment for Aviva, a multinational insurance company headquartered in London and draws on expertise from six other organizations: a Dutch association of responsible investors, a Dutch pension fund, a Nordic private bank, a human rights NGO, a think tank, and a London-based charity. CHRB utilized the UN Guiding Principles on Business and Human Rights, developed by John Ruggie, to evaluate the level of implementation of the 'corporate responsibility to respect human rights' (UN Human Rights, 2011). This is interpreted to mean the implementation of human rights due diligence, including the assessment of actual and potential human rights risks, acting upon the apparent risks, tracking the effectiveness of actions taken to address human rights impacts, and disclosing how a company addresses risks and impacts.

The CHRB provided its first ranking in 2018 assessing the extent to which 101 major global companies reflected the Principle guidance in their public reporting. The results make for grim reading. The Chair commented in the report on the project, "The overall picture is deeply concerning: most companies score poorly on the Benchmark, indicating weak implementation of the UN Guiding Principles on Business and Human Rights. This raises questions for investors and consumers as to whether these companies are serious about ending harm to people in their pursuit of profit" (Corporate Human Rights Benchmark, 2018). The report focused on three main sectors where human rights are seriously impacted: agricultural products, apparel manufacturing, and extraction.

The Preamble to the ILO constitution includes a reference to the need for a 'living wage' and 'the protection of children' (ILO, 2019). The UN Global Compact calls for businesses to eliminate all forms of forced and compulsory labor and the effective abolition of child labor (UNGC, 2019). The UN Guiding Principles cite the minimum standards set by the ILO and also articulate the corporate responsibility to support human rights defenders—those who report serious allegations which deserve a response from the company (UN Human Rights, 2011). None of the companies assessed reported commitments on a living wage, and in the apparel manufacturing sector, half of the companies did not report measures to ensure that no child labor was employed across their supply chain. Only 3% of the companies assessed reported that they were able to respond positively to allegations of human rights abuse. According to the report, the Brazilian mining conglomerate Vale S.A. scored highly on its human rights record. The company was subsequently removed from the list after the Brumhadino dam disaster in January 2019. The potential for improved access to capital for corporate human rights leaders is highlighted in the CHRB report, citing the example of Danone, the French food company. In 2018, Danone issued a €300 million social bond, the first from a corporate issuer since the social bond principles were promulgated by the International Capital Market Association in June 2017. The bond has a seven-year maturity and carries a 1% coupon (Owen, 2018). Proceeds will be allocated to projects promoting positive social impact on Danone's stakeholders, including suppliers, local communities, people with specific nutritional needs and funds for enhanced health coverage and an extended maternity, parental leave, and postnatal care policy for Danone's employees.

Concluding Remarks

The advent of human capital management as a due diligence matter for investors has shifted the paradigm from labor as a cost to human capital as an asset—a transformation initiated by Gary Becker's economic theory of human capital. There is a growing recognition that stakeholder relations are also a source of shared value—but this is somewhat held back by a lack of clarity around standards and reporting. The broad coalition of multi-stakeholder initiatives pressing for wider non-financial disclosures described in Chap. 4 is a manifestation of alliances between investors and other stakeholders to improve disclosures. The story of human capital and stakeholder relations is at the heart of defining corporate purpose. Now investors have caught on.

That consideration for investors is now growing to encompass not only companies' direct employment of labor, but to their global supply chains. There are some contradictory trends. The role of trade unions, a nineteenth-century representation of protection for human capital has waned in many markets, and in their wake government, regulators, consumers, and other stakeholders have attempted to extend the reach of worker protections, reflecting growing societal expectations that labor rights be respected and protected in all jurisdictions. The resulting impact is uneven and contested. Arguably, investors have been late to the debate. Nevertheless, the growing evidence of the economic impact of good human capital management and returns to stakeholder relations has given the financial ecosystem a self-interested concern with improvement, whilst the retreat of state and trade unions has left civil society with a new focus on the providers of finance as a new source of influence in advancing human welfare. The extent to which this is remunerative for investors, or reflects their privileged position as the arbiters of a global system lacking public enforcement, is a matter of debate. The shift toward concerns for sustainability in finance has placed sharp focus on the legitimacy and purpose of investors in relation to their impact upon, and their reliance on, human and other forms of capital discussed in earlier chapters.

This is a new dynamic, and it has the economic motivation that could drive a different kind of change. Investors are starting to realize that sustainable returns are driven by corporate prowess in managing human capital and stakeholder relations. Civil society groups have rightly called for so long for people to be valued, but there is a new appreciation in finance that human capital is an asset, to be protected and to be invested in. The partnership between civil society and corporations has the potential to make real progress on the global ambition to promote broad-based human well-being. One must be cautious because there is no immediate coincidence of interest, but there is a possibility of aligning the financial ecosystem with the goals of sustainable development because ultimately, dispersed ownership of large global corporations implies that the interests of citizen investors overlap with those of civil society.

Notes

1. Labor resources consisted of slaves, villeins, bordars, cottars, coscets, and coliberts.
2. More precisely, the strategy earned a four-factor alpha of 3.5%, after accounting for the four Carhart risk factors: market beta, size, value, and momentum (Carhart, 1997).
3. KLD has since been acquired by MSCI.

References

Becker, G. S. (1962). Investment in Human Capital: A Theoretical Analysis. *Journal of Political Economy, 70*(5), 9–49.

Bernile, G., Bhagwat, V., & Yonker, S. (2018). Board Diversity, Firm Risk, and Corporate Policies. *Journal of Financial Economics, 127*(3), 588–612.

Bernstein, A., & Beeferman, L. (2015). *The Materiality of Human Capital to Corporate Financial Performance*. Retrieved from https://lwp.law.harvard. edu/files/lwp/files/final_human_capital_materiality_april_23_2015.pdf

Borgers, A., Derwall, J., Koedijk, K., & ter Horst, J. (2013). Stakeholder Relations and Stock Returns: On Errors in Investors' Expectations and Learning. *Journal of Empirical Finance, 22*, 159–175. http://www.sciencedirect.com/science/journal/09275398

CalPERS. (2013). *Investment Beliefs*. Retrieved from https://www.calpers.ca. gov/page/about/organization/calpers-story/our-mission-vision

Carhart, M. M. (1997). On Persistence in Mutual Fund Performance. *Journal of Finance, 52*(1), 57–82. http://onlinelibrary.wiley.com/journal/10.1111/%2 8ISSN%291540-6261/issues

Coleman, L. (2011). Losses from Failure of Stakeholder Sensitive Processes: Financial Consequences for Large US Companies from Breakdowns in Product, Environmental, and Accounting Standards. *Journal of Business Ethics, 98*(2), 247–258. https://doi.org/10.1007/s10551-010-0544-8

Corporate Human Rights Benchmark. (2018). Key Findings: Apparel, Agricultural Products and Extractives Companies. Retrieved from https://www.corporate-benchmark.org/sites/default/files/documents/CHRBKeyFindings2018.pdf

Creary, S. J., McDonnell, M.-H., Ghai, S., & Scruggs, J. (2019). When and Why Diversity Improves Your Board's Performance. *Harvard Business Review Digital Articles*, 2–6. Retrieved from   https://hbr.org/2019/03/when-and-why-diversity-improves-your-boards-performance

Davis, S., Lukomnik, J., & Pitt-Watson, D. (2006). *The New Capitalists: How Citizen Investors Are Reshaping the Corporate Agenda*. Boston, MA: Harvard Business School Press.

Edmans, A. (2011). Does the Stock Market Fully Value Intangibles? Employee Satisfaction and Equity Prices. *Journal of Financial Economics, 101*(3), 621–640. https://doi.org/10.1016/j.jfineco.2011.03.021

Folloni, G., & Vittadini, G. (2010). Human Capital Measurement: A Survey. *Journal of Economic Surveys, 24*(2), 248–279. http://onlinelibrary.wiley.com/journal/10.1111/%28ISSN%291467-6419/issues

Greenhouse, S. (2014, March 29). 3 Retailers Give to Aid Bangladesh Workers. *New York Times*, p. b5L.

Hämäläinen, P., Takala, J., & Kiat, T. B. (2017). *Global Estimates of Occupational Accidents and Work-related Illnesses 2017*. Ministry of Social Affairs and Health, Finland Retrieved from http://www.icohweb.org/site/images/news/pdf/ Report%20Global%20Estimates%20of%20Occupational%20Accidents%20 and%20Work-related%20Illnesses%202017%20rev1.pdf

Hamilton, K., & Hepburn, C. (2014). Wealth. *Oxford Review of Economic Policy, 30*(1), 1–20. http://oxrep.oxfordjournals.org/content/by/year

Hunt, V., Prince, S., Dixon-Fyl, S., & Yee, L. (2018). *Delivering Through Diversity*. Retrieved from https://www.mckinsey.com/~/media/mckinsey/business%20 functions/organization/our%20insights/delivering%20through%20diversity/ delivering-through-diversity_full-report.ashx

Huselid, M. A. (1995). The Impact of Human Resource Management Practices on Turnover, Productivity, and Corporate Financial Performance. *Academy of Management Journal, 38*(3), 635–672. https://doi.org/10.2307/256741

Hutton, W., MacDougall, A., & Zadek, S. (2001). Session 3—Topics in Business Ethics—Corporate Stakeholding, Ethical Investment, Social Accounting. *The Ethics of Good Business: A Young Fabian Conference, 32*, 107–117.

ICCR. (2013). *Investor Statement on Bangladesh*. Retrieved from https://www.iccr.org/investor-statement-bangladesh

ILO. (2019). *ILO Constitution: Annex*. Retrieved from http://www.ilo.org/dyn/normlex/en/f?p=1000:62:130021412171665::NO:62:P62_LIST_ENTRIE_ID:2453907:NO#A1

Jiao, Y. (2010). Stakeholder Welfare and Firm Value. *Journal of Banking & Finance, 34*(10), 2549–2561. https://doi.org/10.1016/j.jbankfin.2010.04.013

Jones, M. J. (2018). Domesday Book: An Early Fiscal, Accounting Narrative? *The British Accounting Review, 50*(3), 275–290. https://doi.org/10.1016/j.bar.2017.10.002

Korten, D. C. (1995). *When Corporations Rule the World*. West Hartford, CT: Kumarian Press.

Maiden, B. (2019). SEC Official Cautions on New ESG Disclosure Rules. *Corporate Secretary*.

McDonald, J., & Snooks, G. D. (1985). Statistical Analysis of Domesday Book (1086). *Journal of the Royal Statistical Society. Series A (General), 148*(2), 147–160. https://doi.org/10.2307/2981946

McGregor, J. (2014, October 13). At Gap, Selling a Place to Work, Not Just Khakis. *Washington Post*. Retrieved from https://www.washingtonpost.com/news/on-leadership/wp/2014/10/13/at-gap-selling-a-place-to-work-not-just-khakis/

Miller, M. (2017, July 6). *Petition to SEC*. HCMC. Retrieved from https://www.sec.gov/rules/petitions/2017/petn4-711.pdf

Mincer, J. (1958). Investment in Human Capital and Personal Income Distribution. *Journal of Political Economy, 66*, 281–302. https://doi.org/10.1086/258055

Moyn, S. (2014). *Human Rights and the Uses of History*. London, UK: Verso.

Oreopoulos, P., & Salvanes, K. G. (2011). Priceless: The Nonpecuniary Benefits of Schooling. *Journal of Economic Perspectives, 25*(1), 159–184. http://www.aeaweb.org/jep/

Owen, N. (2018). Danone Joins Social Club and Achieves Tight Pricing. *GlobalCapital, 125*–125. Retrieved from https://www.globalcapital.com/article/b17fvcgdmc8h8m/danone-joins-social-club-and-achieves-tight-pricing

Post, C., & Byron, K. (2015). Women on Boards and Firm Financial Performance: A Meta-Analysis. *Academy of Management Journal, 58*(5), 1546–1571. https://doi.org/10.5465/amj.2013.0319

Rothschild, E. (2001). *Economic Sentiments: Adam Smith, Condorcet and the Enlightenment*. Cambridge, MA: Harvard University Press.

Schultz, T. W. (1959). Investment in Man. *An Economist's View, 33*, 109–117.

SEC Investor Advisory Committee. (2019). *Recommendation of the Investor Advisory Committee Human Capital Management Disclosure*. Retrieved from https://www.sec.gov/spotlight/investor-advisory-committee-2012/human-capital-disclosure-recommendation.pdf

Sila, V., Gonzalez, A., & Hagendorff, J. (2016). Women on Board: Does Boardroom Gender Diversity Affect Firm Risk? *Journal of Corporate Finance, 36*, 26–53. https://doi.org/10.1016/j.jcorpfin.2015.10.003

Simmons, R. L., Simmons, T. H., Haecker, C., & Siebert, E. M. (2008). *National Historic Landmark Nomination: Ludlow Tent Colony.* National Park Service Retrieved from https://www.nps.gov/archeology/months/ NP_NHL_Nomination_Ludlow.pdf

Slack, P. (2004). Measuring the National Wealth in Seventeenth-Century England. *Economic History Review, 57*(4), 607–635. http://www.wiley.com/bw/journal.asp?ref=0013-0117&site=1

Steffek, J., & Holthaus, L. (2018). The Social-Democratic Roots of Global Governance: Welfare Internationalism from the 19th Century to the United Nations. *European Journal of International Relations, 24*(1), 106–129. https://doi.org/10.1177/1354066117703176

Strack, R., Baier, J., Marchingo, M., & Sharda, S. (2014). *The Global Workforce Crisis: $10 Trillion at Risk.* Retrieved from https://www.bcg.com/en-us/ publications/2014/people-organization-human-resources-global-workforce-crisis.aspx

Taylor, J. (2006). *Creating Capitalism: Joint Stock Enterprise in British Politics and Culture.* Woodbridge, UK: Boydell Press.

Thomas, A. (1996). The International Labour Organisation. Its Origins, Development and Future. *International Labour Review, 135*(3/4), 261.

UN Human Rights. (2011). *Guiding Principles on Business and Human Rights.* Retrieved from https://www.ohchr.org/Documents/Publications/ GuidingPrinciplesBusinessHR_EN.pdf

UNGC. (2019). *The Ten Principles of the UN Global Compact.* Retrieved from https://www.unglobalcompact.org/what-is-gc/mission/principles

Vanguard. (2018). *Investment Stewardship Annual Report.* Retrieved from https://about.vanguard.com/investment-stewardship/perspectives-and-commentary/2018_investment_stewardship_annual_report.pdf

Wallin, M. (1969). Labour Administration: Origins and Development. *International Labour Review, 100*(1), 51.

Waygood, S. (2013). Financial Institutions and Non-Governmental Organizations: An Advocacy Partnership for Sustainable Capital Markets? *Journal of Applied Corporate Finance, 25*(3), 68–75. https://doi.org/10.1111/jacf.12031

Zingales, L. (2000). Search of New Foundations. *Journal of Finance, 55*(4), 1623–1653. http://onlinelibrary.wiley.com/journal/10.1111/%28I SSN%291540-6261/issues

CHAPTER 9

Capital Structure and Social Capital: Diverse Forms of Investment

INTRODUCTION

In the last two chapters, we focused on the dependencies of corporate activity on the healthy functioning of natural and human capital. Having understood the seamless and multivalent connections between a sustainable natural environment, engaged and healthy employees, and the maintenance of corporate productivity, the notion that the corporation should be run solely on behalf of its shareholders seems a blinkered approach. It is clear that natural and human capital are just as important as manufactured capital beyond the short term. In an accounting sense, we might place these three types of capital on the asset side of the balance sheet.[1] What then about the liability side of the balance sheet? How do we finance natural and human capital?

Let us first examine how manufactured capital is financed: by equity, debt, liabilities, and other types of financial capital. The practice of finance recognizes that there are many different types of providers of financial capital, both on- and off-balance sheet. Financial capital available to an enterprise comes with many different requirements: maturity, risk of principal loss, liquidity, volatility, counterparty risk, need for collateral, participation in earnings growth, and minimum environmental, social, and governance (ESG) thresholds. The capital structure of an enterprise denotes its choice of a particular set of financial capital types from an almost infinite and malleable variety of potential types. The choice of capital structure is in part driven by the nature of the assets of the firm.

© The Author(s) 2019
S. Bose et al., *The Financial Ecosystem*, Palgrave Studies in Impact Finance, https://doi.org/10.1007/978-3-030-05624-7_9

For example, assets whose market value or periodic cash flows are volatile are less likely to be financed by debt. Assets whose value is hard to discern without highly specialized knowledge (such as art and antiques) or those intricately linked with high levels of personal trust are more likely to be financed by narrowly held equity. Assets whose owners want to extract maximum monetary value in a short time might employ high-powered incentive structures such as those prevailing in private equity investment firms. If capital markets are deep, that is, there is adequate supply in each category of financial capital, then an enterprise with a complex expected cash flow profile might be expected to have a complex capital structure. Once we recognize that there are other forms of capital on the asset side of the balance sheet (natural and human capital), then we should expect that there are financiers of those other forms of capital whose requirements for maturity, risk, ESG requirements, and so on will need to be addressed. Our understanding of the sources of finance for an enterprise needs to be broadened to match our recognition that natural and human capital are critical assets for the generation of value.

In a widely cited paper, Porter and Kramer (2006) argue that "the mutual dependence of corporations and society implies that both business decisions and social policies must follow the principle of shared value…that is, choices must benefit both sides". In a continuing discussion of this theme after the global financial crisis, Porter and Kramer (2011) argue that in order to regain broader societal legitimacy, businesses must move away from focusing only on generating profits to spearheading economic activity which benefits a wide range of stakeholders. They refer to the strategy of generating value for stakeholders as 'shared value creation'. They cite a number of "companies known for their hard-nosed approach to business—such as GE, Google, IBM, Intel, Johnson & Johnson, Nestle, Unilever and Wal-Mart" as having initiated efforts to create shared value. In Porter and Kramer's view, 'value' is economic and social benefits relative to cost, rather merely 'doing good'. This presumably means that shared value creation must undergo a cost-benefit analysis test (see Chap. 6). In principle, incorporating such a shared value creation assessment criterion into corporate investment choices has the potential to recognize and steward the essential contribution of human and natural capital into shareholder value. We examine in detail two related cases.

Dow Chemical: Creating Shared Value with Natural Capital?

In 2011, The Dow Chemical Company announced a 5-year $10 million partnership with The Nature Conservancy "to advance the incorporation of value of nature into business, and to take action to protect the earth's natural systems and the services they provide people, for the benefit of business and society" (Asquith, 2011). The partnership intended to disseminate its lessons broadly, with peer-reviewed published results to help other companies integrate the value of conservation into business decision-making. We describe a peer-reviewed case study below.

In the context of industrial site remediation, different restoration choices can have different implications for ecosystem service flows, monetary capital, and operating costs. An intriguing teaching case study, selected by the Agricultural and Applied Economics Association (AAEA) Case Study Committee for presentation at the 2018 AAEA annual meeting and subsequently peer-reviewed, presents an example where Dow and the City of Midland, Michigan, appear to coordinate their restoration choices for two adjacent decommissioned industrial sites in a manner that is beneficial to town residents, the local ecosystem, and Dow's shareholders (Guertin, Polzin, Rogers, & Witt, 2019). The authors note that Dow Chemical "has a stated goal to apply a 'business-decision process that values nature' and to deliver $1 billion in 'value through projects that are good for business and good for ecosystems'". The City of Midland aims to connect and maintain open spaces and is responsible for ensuring that its expenditures are cost-effective and serve the interests of Midland residents. The case study lays out three alternative plans for the restoration of the two sites, along with associated impacts on ecosystem services and monetary costs. The first site, owned by Dow Chemical, consists of 23 acres including an ash pond containing 90,000 cubic yards of waste ash from a former coal-fired power plant. The adjacent site, owned by the City, is a 14.5 acre abandoned concrete facility (known as the 4D facility). Both sites are on the banks of the Tittabawassee River, which runs through downtown Midland. The three restoration options, which were developed by a project team including Dow employees, scientists from The Nature Conservancy, as well as collaborators from AECOM and EcoMetrix Solutions Group, consist of:

(a) capping the Dow ash pond site (leaving the ash in situ and covering it with synthetic material, soil, and grass, and committing to long-term monitoring of the groundwater to prevent future leaks)

(b) ecological restoration of the Dow ash pond site (excavating the ash and restoring the site to native forest, prairie, and wetland)

(c) ecological restoration of both the Dow ash pond site and the City 4D facility (with connecting trails and overlooks between the two sites).

For the Dow site, the ecological restoration (alternative b) had $1.6 million lower installation cost and $44,000 lower annual operating costs than alternative (a) For the City-owned site, the ecological restoration alternative would cost $1.1 million more in installation cost than a traditional restoration alternative. However, the ecological alternative had approximately $2500 in lower annual operating costs (see Table 4 in Guertin, Polzin, et al. (2019)). The team used a specialized modeling tool called the Ecosystem Services Identification and Information Tool (ESII Tool) jointly created by Dow, TNC, and EcoMetrix to estimate the type and amount of ecosystem services expected under the alternative plans (ESIITool, 2019). The tool generates estimates of changes in water provisioning, air, and water quality control, climate regulation, erosion prevention, and other services resulting from land use changes in temperate inland zones. In a related paper Guertin, Halsey, Polzin, Rogers, and Witt (2019) note that the capping would lead to a reduction in many ecosystem services relative to the baseline of the unremediated sites. Therefore, it would be better from an ecosystems perspective to perform the ecological restoration, ideally on both sites. For Dow Chemical, this was the easy choice since its installation and operation costs would be lower for the ecological alternative. The challenge, of course, lay in persuading the City that it was cost-effective to pay the extra cost of the ecological restoration for its property. Guertin, Halsey, et al. (2019) note that there would be many community benefits to the ecological restoration, including restoration of riverfront across from downtown Midland, an extensive network of open space connected by trails, recreational space, and potential reductions in flood insurance rates due to the flood control properties of ecological restoration. Fortunately, for the City of Midland, it appears that Momentum Midland, a local non-profit supported by local foundations and corporations including Dow, donated $2.2 million to help restore the 4D site (Hoag, 2017).[2] This case study appears to present an example of a situation where corporate initiative, coordination of plans, and targeted allocation of corporate social responsibility resources leads to joint benefits for corporate shareholders, a local community, and local ecosystems. Perhaps this is exactly what Porter and Kramer have in mind when they state: "When a well-run business applies its vast resources, expertise, and management talent to problems that it understands and in which it has a stake, it can have a greater impact on social good than any other institution or philanthropic organization".

However, the larger historical context is revealing and important to note. The Dow Chemical Company was founded in 1897 and is headquartered in Midland. The company has an infamous history of manufacturing toxic and hazardous chemicals such as napalm and Agent Orange in the 1950s and 1960s. Since 2001, Dow Chemical has owned Union Carbide, a company made infamous by the 1984 Bhopal gas disaster which caused 3787 deaths. In 2008, Dow Chemical reached an agreement with the U.S. EPA and the Michigan Department of Environmental Quality to remove 50,000 cubic yards of dioxin-contaminated sediment from the Tittabawassee River near Midland (Barringer, 2007). Given the history of Dow's long tenure and chemical manufacturing activities in Midland, one might simply view the case study as an example of a polluting corporation dispensing some resources to clean up its image in its hometown as an afterthought. This type of remedial action barely qualifies as shared value creation. Full recognition of the value of natural capital near its own headquarters would have involved an articulated strategy and *ex ante* investments to prevent dioxin contamination in the first place. Nevertheless, the collaboration between Dow and The Nature Conservancy does demonstrate the possibilities arising from a genuine exchange of localized and specialized knowledge between a powerful corporation with 'vast resources, expertise and management talent' and a highly regarded non-profit focused on the conservation and management of ecosystems. The ESII Tool is an important output of the collaboration, which makes it feasible for non-biologists to estimate the impact of land use changes on a set of ecosystem services. Furthermore, this type of collaboration encourages a shift in the manner in which it is acceptable to articulate the meaning of value creation in a large corporate investment appraisal context.

SHARED VALUE WITH HUMAN CAPITAL:
PRIVATE EQUITY AND EDUCATION

Equal access to education is widely acknowledged to generate broadly shared social benefits. For this reason, education is often a highly subsidized activity in most countries. In addition to direct government funds for schools and universities, many governments provide significant subsidies for student loans and tax incentives and exemptions for students, schools, universities, employers, and lenders. Society is thus a significant provider of off-balance sheet capital to and a key ultimate beneficiary of the enterprise of education. In this sense, society, as represented by the state, is an investor in the human capital of the country. In principle, taxes collected from the future earnings of graduates trained through societal subsidies represent the return of capital invested by the state. In its deployment of the subsidies, the state relies upon various types of public, for-profit, and non-profit organizations to manage the delivery of education.

As we have already noted in Chap. 3, the separation between investor and management (or ownership and control) gives rise to the central problem of agency theory: how to align incentives. The state would benefit if its subsidies led to higher lifetime earnings for graduates, broadening, and deepening the tax base. Unfortunately, the government cannot (yet) formulate subsidy and incentive schemes that depend on the lifetime earnings of graduates since this would require withholding payments over decades. The quality of higher education across providers is not immediately apparent to prospective students or the government, partly because the outcome of education depends both on the effectiveness of teaching and the student's effort in acquiring skills.

In the United States, for-profit higher education experienced dramatic growth in recent decades, growing from 0.2% in 1970 to 9.1% of total enrolment in 2009 (Deming, Goldin, & Katz, 2012). In 2009, for-profit colleges had a disproportionately higher share of enrolment by female students and by traditionally underserved students, specifically students older than 25 and underserved racial minorities. Although the average for-profit institution at the time enrolled approximately 600 students and was thus smaller in size than the average non-profit institution, the largest for-profit firms were major, profitable publicly traded corporations, with several enrolling more than 50,000 students each (Bennett, Lucchesi, & Vedder, 2010). The for-profit institutions received 74% of their revenue from government grants and loans, with the largest corporations receiving more than 80% of their revenue in government funds. In 2010, the US Senate

Health, Education, Labor, and Pensions Committee began an oversight investigation of the for-profit sector, reviewing the dramatic increase in students and the associated increase in government grants and concessionary loans. The resulting Senate report found that incentives of for-profit colleges owned by publicly traded corporations and private equity funds were particularly misaligned with those of students: "Federal law and regulations currently do not align the incentives of for-profit colleges so that the colleges succeed financially when students succeed" (United States Senate, 2012). The report noted that in 2009, taxpayers contributed more than $30 billion in funds to the revenue of the sector, yet more than half of the students who enrolled discontinued their studies without a certificate or diploma within a median of 4 months. Three-year cohort default rates in 2008 on student loans, which are provided by the government, for for-profit colleges amounted to 25%, while those of public institutions were 11% and those of private non-profits were 8% (Deming et al., 2012). After a series of regulatory actions to address some of the findings of the Senate report, many of the largest corporations experienced sharp declines in enrolment and revenue, layoffs, as well as revocation of licenses. A number of listed companies went bankrupt, were delisted or were downsized and acquired by private equity firms.

Eaton, Howell, and Yannelis (2018) examine the role of high-powered profit-maximizing incentives in the context of private equity managed higher education. Private equity managers have especially high-powered incentives to maximize profits because they receive a significant portion of those profits in the form of management incentive fees. It is thus likely that private equity managers would have stronger incentives to increase revenue than to ensure long-term quality. For example, the Senate report cited above notes that for-profit colleges employed 10 times as many college recruiters than career support staff to help students find jobs. In a subsidized industry with outcomes becoming known after many years, it is easier to intensify management focus on capturing government aid at the expense of student outcomes. Using a novel database of 88 private equity deals and 994 schools with private equity ownership, Eaton et al. find that private equity buyouts of existing colleges not only lead to higher enrollment and profits, but also to lower education inputs, higher tuition, higher per-student debt, lower graduation rates, lower student loan repayment rates, and lower earnings among graduates. Using a set of tests examining the impact of regulatory events and thresholds, Eaton et al. find that private equity-owned schools are better able to capture government aid.

Our examination of the role of for-profit colleges in higher education in the United States underscores the critical importance of aligning incentives when corporate management depends heavily on societal capital to generate investor returns. Understanding that in an education context, private equity managers of colleges are effectively administering public funds for broader public benefit allows us to view their role in new light. The correct model now becomes that of a trustee, acting on behalf of the state, to advance a broad societal goal, while also earning a fair return on capital and resources deployed. Such a view would change the appropriate control structure for the outsourcing of education to private equity. For example, it would suggest that private equity managers have a fiduciary duty to the educational goals of society as a whole, in addition to those to their LPs.

Horizon Mismatch Example: Employee Pensions and Private Equity
The usual capital structure of a company gives priority to unsecured creditors before shareholders. This means that in a liquidation of the company, unsecured creditors must be repaid before any of the assets can be used to return shareholder capital. This is generally what would happen in bankruptcy. Pension obligations are considered unsecured liabilities and as such, there is an expectation that they would be discharged before shareholders could receive any value from the company's assets. However, this order of priority does not apply if the company appears to be a going concern and is not apparently facing liquidation. In the case of companies owned and controlled by private equity firms, it is possible and relatively common for a company to pay dividends to the shareholders or management fees to the private equity firm while deferring contributions to employee pension plans. So long as the company continues to operate and pay pension claims as they fall due, and other creditors allow it, the company may declare dividends or pay the private equity firm for services rendered.

What if the company pays out dividends or pays advisory fees to the private equity manager, withholds pension contributions, and then subsequently declares bankruptcy? Suppose that in bankruptcy, there are not enough assets left over to pay the pension obligations. Would the bankruptcy court ask the shareholders to return their dividends or the private equity firm to return their fees so that pension

---

(*continued*)

(continued)

obligations can be fulfilled? The court would only do so if these payments had been made within one year of the bankruptcy filing. If the dividend had been paid two years before the filing, then the presumption is that the dividend was proper, and not an attempt to fraudulently convey assets away from other creditors such as pension beneficiaries.

The Washington Post describes examples of some investments owned by Sun Capital, a private equity firm, where significant dividends and fees were paid by the portfolio companies to Sun Capital two years before bankruptcy (Whoriskey, 2018). Marsh, a midwestern grocery chain founded in 1931, was bought by Sun Capital in 2006 for $325 million. Marsh faced financial difficulties as a result of the 2008 recession, management turnover and narrow margins from intense competition. Sun Capital was able to sell off Marsh's stores for a total of $348 million over a number of years. Whoriskey notes that some of this money went back to Sun Capital while some of it stayed in Marsh. Eventually, in 2017, Sun Capital put Marsh into bankruptcy. Whoriskey (2018) notes that Sun Capital's limited partners lost approximately $500,000 of their investment in Marsh between 2006 and 2017. The article notes that Sun Capital itself made money on the deal, because it collected annual management fees amounting $1 million per year, as well as undisclosed fees on the sale of Marsh assets. It is quite likely that the Marsh investment, including fees earned, was profitable for Sun Capital. Nevertheless, when the company entered bankruptcy, it left unpaid more than $80 million in debts to workers' severance and pensions. Similarly, the article notes that in the case of two other investments owned by Sun Capital, significant dividends were paid to Sun Capital two years before bankruptcy, while in bankruptcy, significant pension obligations remained unpaid.

The example in the box above suggest that private equity managers, even though they are owners and controllers of a fund's portfolio company, are not necessarily the residual risk takers. In the case of Marsh, the grocery store employees took the residual risk—it was their pension that effectively subsidized dividends to shareholders. It was partly by deferring contributions to the employee pension plans that Marsh was able to pay

Sun Capital two years before the bankruptcy. In this type of capital structure, the human capital, in the shoes of the grocery store employees funded payments to providers of financial capital who were both owners and controllers.

THE DIFFUSE BENEFITS AND COSTS OF CORPORATE SUSTAINABILITY

As we have noted in Chaps. 5 and 8, corporate sustainability programs produce a variety of outcomes ranging from the tangible to the intangible, and the environmentally to socially focused. Each of these outcomes affects company financial performance differently and achieves various results. There are intermediate drivers of corporate financial success arising from sustainable practices, such as competitive advantage, reputation development, and the growth of mutually beneficial partnerships (Mollet, von Arx, & Ilic, 2013). Also, frequently noted are benefits related to enhanced customer or employee satisfaction and overall firm reputation (Wagner & Schaltegger, 2004). These types of benefits can be linked to investments in stakeholder relations, which is a form of social capital for the company. It has been argued that the most significant economic benefit to firms that incorporate the value of ecosystem services into investment choices for fossil fuel and chemical companies (such as Dow Chemical above) likely stems from brand value, research and development, competitive differentiation, and employee satisfaction, with direct benefits arising from a more responsibly maintained ecosystem representing a far smaller and perhaps negative contribution (Gonenc & Scholtens, 2017; Lioui & Sharma, 2012). Of course, such a view may reflect what can feasibly be revealed in the short timeframe of project assessment and it is possible that the direct benefit of ecosystem services will eventually account for a more prominent if not the primary long-term consideration. The diffuse nature of benefits from sustainability initiatives implies that the legal and financial boundaries of the firm cannot limit our assessment of beneficial impact. Asking whether investors benefit from sustainability initiatives in the short horizon is necessarily an incomplete approach.

Conversely, the example of the for-profit higher education sector demonstrates the ease with which a single stakeholder can appropriate the capital of others in the short term in the presence of the inevitable misaligned incentives. An implication of our analysis of the legal personhood of the corporation in Chap. 3 is the difficulty of punishing the legal person that mediates relationships between 'owners' and other stakeholders. As the British Lord Chancellor Edward Thurlow (1731–1806) famously asked "Did you ever expect a corporation to have a conscience when it has not a body to be kicked, nor a soul to be damned?" Diffuse costs and benefits and legal personhood impose constraints on the capital structure of an enterprise that can lead to irreconcilable trade-offs between the efficiency of matching asset characteristics to capital sources and the difficulty of punishing specific stakeholders of the firm without hurting others (Iacobucci & Triantis, 2006).

Social Network Analysis: A Test of the Diversity of Capital

Social network analysis (SNA) is a technique of describing the salient characteristics of a particular social structure (or topology) using *graph theory*. It seeks to add precision to common ways of describing attributes of social groupings. For example, social network analysis constructs measures of the density of interactions between two randomly selected individuals in a social grouping or measures the percentage of individuals who are directly connected with more than a given percentage of all individuals in the network. Social network analysis became a standard tool of sociologists sometime after the publication of the results of studies of human interactions by Jacob Moreno, who drew diagrams to describe the social relations he could discern among groups such as schoolchildren (Moreno, 1934). A social network is composed of *vertices* or *nodes* connected by *links* or *edges*. The vertices, also called *actors* by sociologists, might be individuals or organizations. The links might represent relationships, for example, friendships or board membership or an ownership relationship between a company and its subsidiary. A key insight of sociologists is that the attributes of networks cannot be deduced by aggregating the attributes of the nodes: the network must be studied directly.

Many networks are characterized by three common phenomena: short global path lengths, high local clustering, and skewed degree distributions (Watts, 2004).

Short Global Path Length: This refers to the characteristic that in many networks, the number of nodes that must be traversed to travel between any random pair of nodes is usually relatively small. The nodes which are most likely to be traversed are referred to as broker nodes. For example, in the famous 'small world experiment' of Stanley Milgram, it took an average of approximately six *brokers* for a random person in Omaha, Nebraska to connect to a person in Boston, Massachusetts. The concept of 'small world' or short global path length is articulated in the popular notion that there are just six degrees of separation between most individuals in the world.

High Local Clustering: This is a measure of local structural cohesion of the network. If there is a high density of connections between nodes, then they are said to be clustered. Typically, networks display local clustering, with many 'structural holes', that is, parts of the network where nodes are sparse. Local clusters are also called cliques.

Kogut and Walker (2001) used SNA to describe German firms and their ownership ties between 1993 and 1997. They show that the network of firms exhibited short global path lengths and high local clustering and that firms that acted as social *brokers* were disproportionately likely to be involved in merger activity.

Skewed Degree Distributions: This refers to the phenomenon that the majority of nodes are linked to just a few other nodes, while a small number of nodes are linked to a very large number of nodes. Hence the median number of links per node is low relative to the maximum number of links per node. This feature suggests that a few nodes, those that are connected to many other nodes, are really important. It turns out, however, that the really important nodes are those that are referred to as bridges, and they tend to have just a few connections. What makes bridges important is that they connect nodes that would otherwise have a very long social distance between them. The nodes that are connected to many other nodes are not terribly important, because they can usually be replaced by other nearby nodes who are connected to the same neighbors. A celebrated example of a bridge node is Paul Revere in the social networks of revolutionary America (Han, 2009). Bridge nodes are said to have a high *betweenness* score. Betweenness of a node is a measure of the likelihood that any given journey between two random nodes has to pass through that node.

BRIDGES AND ARBITRAGE

These three characteristics of networks result in social structures comprising many groups of densely connected individuals, where the groups are bridged by a few key *brokers*. These bridges or brokers are the intersections between different social cliques. The notion of social capital refers to the potential of bridges to connect disparate worlds and spur collective action or benefit from arbitrage between groups (Burt, 2005). Burt points out that it is not the volume of contacts that one might have on LinkedIn that matters, but the number of brokers (and the distance to them) to whom one is linked.

The concept of a bridge or broker is similar to the concept of an arbitrageur in financial markets (Shleifer & Vishny, 1997) or an entrepreneur in an Austrian economics sense (Kirzner, 1997). An arbitrageur must bridge disparate markets or world-views to construct a vision of similarity between different assets and formulate a hypothesis of convergence in the valuations of such different assets. In order to discover opportunity, an arbitrageur cannot surround himself with like-minded individuals. By definition, *ex ante*, an arbitrageur must see things which others do not see. Eventually, in the fullness of time, the arbitrageur may be proved a visionary or a crank, but in the present, the arbitrageur places a high value on sourcing information from a diversity of perspectives.

A key advantage of social network analysis is that it has the potential to reveal underlying similarities and differences between groups of actors, and identify bridges, perhaps telling us something about the value of social capital that actors in the network can marshal. Social network analysis has been used to reveal underlying diversity and similarity within the interlocking network of global sustainability accounting initiatives (Thistlethwaite & Paterson, 2016). Thistlethwaite and Paterson examine nine sustainability accounting initiatives (such as Global Reporting Initiative [GRI], Climate Disclosure Project [CDP], International Integrated Reporting Council [IIRC], and Sustainability Accounting Standards Board [SASB]) and trace the relationships between them and over time by tracking the individuals who are members of their boards and the organizations which employ the board members. There is significant overlap between people, organizations, and initiatives, making the network an affiliation network. Thistlethwaite and Paterson also collect biographical data on the board members, such as training, occupation, and citizenship and compute the betweenness scores of the individual board members. They use the social network analysis to examine the diversity of sustainability accounting initiatives. They note that the earliest initiatives (GRI and the Coalition for Environmentally Responsible Economies [CERES]) were non-governmental organization (NGO)-initiated to pressure corporations to disclose their social and environmental performance. The NGO-led ESG initiatives then spawned carbon-centric initiatives which were needed given the relatively specialized knowledge necessary for carbon accounting. Eventually, the need to engage investors (rather than just corporations) led to a dominance of accounting backgrounds among the actors in most recent initiatives because financial accountants are trained to reduce the information asymmetry between investors and corporations. The advent of pressure to disclose ESG information, though initiated by civil society, became the preserve of accountants, whom Thistlethwaite and Paterson refer to as 'epistemic arbitrageurs'.

Thistlethwaite and Paterson's social network analysis suggests that the actors on the boards of sustainability initiatives have remarkably narrow origins, compared to the initial conception of GRI as an UN-supported initiative and the current broad legitimacy of the UN SDGs. They show that the citizenship of 62% of the network of board members of these nine sustainability accounting initiatives is either from the United States or the United Kingdom. This Anglo-American dominance and under-representation of continental Europe, Latin America, non-Anglophone Asia and most of Africa hardly suggests broad legitimacy across comparative corporate governance systems, not to mention broader cultural, racial, and geo-political divides. Thistlethwaite and Paterson also show that there are weak links within the network to environmental NGOs and international organizations, but the deepest links (in the sense of dense interconnections) are all to the largest accounting firms and their professional and trade associations. This dominance by a single profession carries all the risks of monocultures that a study of ecosystems suggests (Chap. 5). This monoculture is particularly troubling considering the argument made by John Coffee, a law professor focused on corporate governance, examining the scale of corporate fraud in the Anglo-American markets between 2000 and 2003. Writing before the 2007–2008 financial crisis, Coffee notes that the relative absence of large scale corporate frauds in continental Europe can be attributed to the differential roles of professional gatekeepers—accountants, attorneys, securities analysts, and rating agencies (Coffee Jr., 2006).

Clearly, the networks of sustainability accounting initiatives need an army of Paul Reveres, bridges and entrepreneurs who can form links between disparate worlds. An irreplaceable characteristic of social capital is that it does not rely only on one metric of success such as monetary willingness to pay, carbon-intensity or even an index of job satisfaction among employees. Social capital, relying as it does on the visions of bridges, necessarily values success measured in multiple currencies or metrics. While bridges are critical, they are valuable precisely because there is heterogeneity within the network. There is little value to a bridge that connects two geographically separate but culturally similar worlds. The effort to connect analytically diverse marketplaces is perhaps one of the most important contributions that a sustainable finance practitioner can bring in the effort to achieve sustainability. We describe briefly four areas where this type of social bridging is integral to the process of curating different sources of capital.

Our description of social capital here relies on the value of bridges in network analysis. Other conceptions of social capital exist in parallel to this idea. A related but different notion of social capital is described by Robert Putnam in a much-cited article entitled '*Bowling Alone*' (Putnam, 1995). Putnam, in his earlier study of the effectiveness of sub-national governments in different regions of Italy, finds that the norms and networks of civic engagement, as expressed in the vibrancy of civil society organizations, powerfully affect the performance of representative government. Putnam argues that sub-national jurisdictions with better schools, faster economic development, lower crime, and more effective local government require civic engagement such as voter turnout, newspaper readership, and even membership in choral societies and football clubs. In his article, Putnam argues that there was a sharp decline in civic participation in the United States and that this decline threatens the quality of democracy and the quality of life. The title of his article alludes to Putnam's observation that between 1980 and 1993 the total number of bowlers in America increased by 10%, while league bowling decreased by 40%. Putnam states that "'social capital' refers to features of social organization such as networks, norms, and social trust that facilitate coordination and cooperation for mutual benefit". This idea of social capital refers to the norms of generalized reciprocity, the emergence of trust in social networks and polycentric attempts at collective action that are a feature of civic engagement. This view of social capital is related but more general than the concept of bridges in social networks that we have used above. The concept of bridges or brokers as social capital focuses on the actors that aggregate information from diverse sub-communities. It takes as a given the presence of heterogeneity and fragmentation in society, and seeks links that can nevertheless facilitate coalitions between disparate stakeholders in the broader ecosystem.

Curating Capital Sources

Public-Private Partnerships

As we noted in Chap. 3, the first corporations can be viewed as public-private partnerships. The scale and power of the corporation today can threaten and disrupt the traditional models of governance. In such a world, it is perhaps no wonder that existing governance infrastructure, particularly systems that assume the public sector is the primary actor responsible for making and enforcing appropriate rules, can be outdated and blunt. Public-private partnerships, broadly conceived and carefully constructed so that they do not become devices to privatize profits and socialize losses, have the potential to curate different sources of capital in some applications. We examine these further in Chaps. 11, 12, 13, and 14 in the context of social impact bonds, green banks, environmental impact bonds, and the split of funding between basic and applied research.

Securitization and Municipal Finance

In the United States and a few other jurisdictions, there exists a deep and vibrant market for the issuance of debt securities by sub-national jurisdictions of various sizes. This marketplace allows direct connections between polycentric providers of local public goods and a diffuse network of beneficiaries and capital providers. Securitization facilitates lower costs of capital by aggregating small, idiosyncratic risks into diversified ones. We examine securitization and the municipal finance market in Chap. 12 in the context of decentralized approaches to portfolio construction.

Cooperative Movement: The cooperative movement recognizes that participatory monitoring and control by employees and customers can sharply improve outcomes within the relatively closed cultures of corporations. We examine these concepts in Chap. 15.

CONCLUDING REMARKS

Recognizing that many sustainable development challenges require careful curation of a diverse array of stakeholder capitals, it becomes critical for the sustainable finance practitioner to appreciate the diversity, malleability, and complementarity of capital sources. This requires an open-minded study of the strengths and weaknesses of different types of capital source, including narrowly and widely distributed equity, mezzanine and convertible debt, subordinated, senior and secured debt, guarantees, public endorsements from non-governmental organizations, community legitimacy, and widespread adoption across inter alia cultural, racial, economic, gender, and geo-political divides. So long as the words capital and investor connote financial capital and financial investor, any investor-centric approach to sustainable finance is likely to signal a narrow outlook lacking societal legitimacy. Just as nature's resilience embodies the capacity to turn waste into nutrients, that is, lead into gold in the context of ecosystems, so hitherto unrecognized value is to be found in discarded forms of capital (such as natural or human) which are not often counted in standard finance. A key concept that is a source of comparative advantage for financial practitioners is their ability to be 'epistemic arbitrageurs'. It is routine in the context of the 'alchemy of finance' that finance professionals strive to generate outsize returns from a vision of convergence between previously unconnected worlds combined with efforts to proselytize such a vision to the broader marketplace.

As we near the conclusion of the analytical foundations' section of the book and look forward to examining applications of sustainable finance, it is perhaps important to remember the following caveat from a teacher of sociology: "not everything that can be counted counts, and not everything that counts can be counted".[3] This antimetabole reminds us that the frameworks for sustainability accounting (Chap. 4), the literature on the links between sustainability investments and observed financial performance (Chap. 5), and the project assessment techniques of cost-benefit analysis and inter-temporal discounting (Chap. 6), represent neither a subset nor a superset of every skill and knowledge we must marshall for a holistic examination of the drivers of sustainability. This means that the sustainable finance analyst must be adept at three practices all at once: quantitative analysis wherever it can meaningfully measure risk-adjusted return, qualitative judgment wherever numerical metrics cannot accurately represent risk and return, and the intuition to recognize where each or both of these two practices apply. We turn now to an analysis of the methods for portfolio construction available to the saver and insurance provider, the household and the asset owner who is concerned with sustainability of all forms of capital, where these three practices must all play a role.

NOTES

1. Note that the word 'capital' has many shades of meaning even in a narrow finance context. Economists commonly use physical, natural, and human 'capital' to denote assets. In a double-entry book-keeping sense, the word 'capital' has an inherent ambiguity: it denotes physical capital such as property, plant and equipment, or intangible capital such as patents and trademarks both of which constitute assets. However, the word also denotes the sources of financing for such assets, as in 'shareholder capital'.
2. The website of Momentum Midland lists eight organizations under 'Funding Support', including The Dow Chemical Company, Dow Corning Corporation, The Herbert H. and Grace A. Dow Foundation, Chemical Bank and four other foundations. The website also lists 31 members on its advisory council, including 7 members who list Dow Chemical or Dow Corning as affiliations (Momentum Midland, 2019).
3. Although this quote is often attributed to Albert Einstein, the evidence suggests that it was coined by Cameron (1963).

REFERENCES

Asquith, C. (2011). Dow Chemical and the Nature Conservancy Team Up to Ask, What Is Nature Worth? *Solutions: For a Sustainable & Desirable Future, 2*, 20–21.

Barringer, F. (2007, 7/18/2007). Michigan: Dioxin Deal. *New York Times.* Retrieved from https://www.nytimes.com/2007/07/18/us/18brfs-dioxin.html

Bennett, D. L., Lucchesi, A. R., & Vedder, R. K. (2010). *For-Profit Higher Education: Growth, Innovation and Regulation.* Retrieved from https://files.eric.ed.gov/fulltext/ED536282.pdf

Burt, R. S. (2005). *Brokerage and Closure: An Introduction to Social Capital.* Oxford, UK: Oxford University Press USA – OSO.

Cameron, W. B. (1963). *Informal Sociology: A Casual Introduction to Sociological Thinking.* New York, NY: Random House.

Coffee, J. C., Jr. (Ed.). (2006). *Gatekeepers: The Professions and Corporate Governance.* New York, NY: Oxford University Press.

Deming, D. J., Goldin, C., & Katz, L. F. (2012). The For-Profit Postsecondary School Sector: Nimble Critters or Agile Predators? *Journal of Economic Perspectives, 26*(1), 139–164. https://doi.org/10.1257/jep.26.1.139

Eaton, C., Howell, S., & Yannelis, C. (2018). *When Investor Incentives and Consumer Interests Diverge: Private Equity in Higher Education* (National Bureau of Economic Research, Inc., NBER Working Papers: 24976). Retrieved from http://www.nber.org/papers/w24976.pdf

ESIITool. (2019). *ESII The Tool That Helps You Make Better Decisions. Better for Your Organization and Better for Nature.* Retrieved from https://www.esiitool.com/

Gonenc, H., & Scholtens, B. (2017). Environmental and Financial Performance of Fossil Fuel Firms: A Closer Inspection of their Interaction. *Ecological Economics, 132,* 307–328. https://doi.org/10.1016/j.ecolecon.2016.10.004

Guertin, F., Halsey, K., Polzin, T., Rogers, M., & Witt, B. (2019). From Ash Pond to Riverside Wetlands: Making the Business Case for Engineered Natural Technologies. *Science of the Total Environment, 651,* 419–426. https://doi.org/10.1016/j.scitotenv.2018.09.035

Guertin, F., Polzin, T., Rogers, M., & Witt, B. (2019). Incorporating Co-Benefits and Environmental Data into Corporate Decision-Making. *American Journal of Agricultural Economics, 101*(2), 615–623. https://doi.org/10.1093/ajae/aay095

Han, S.-K. (2009). The Other Ride of Paul Revere: The Brokerage Role in the Making of the American Revolution. *Mobilization: An International Quarterly, 14*(2), 143–162.

Hoag, A. (2017). Midland gets $4.7 million in gifts for work on Tridge, downtown property. *MLive.* Retrieved from https://www.mlive.com/news/saginaw/2017/02/midland_gets_47_million_in_gif.html

Iacobucci, E. M., & Triantis, G. (2006). Economic and Legal Boundaries of Firms. *American Law & Economics Association Papers,* 39), 1–39),47.

Kirzner, I. M. (1997). Entrepreneurial Discovery and the Competitive Market Process: An Austrian Approach. *Journal of Economic Literature, 35,* 60–85.

Kogut, B., & Walker, G. (2001). The Small World of Germany and the Durability of National Networks. *American Sociological Review, 66*(3), 317–335. https://doi.org/10.2307/3088882

Lioui, A., & Sharma, Z. (2012). Environmental Corporate Social Responsibility and Financial Performance: Disentangling Direct and Indirect Effects. *Ecological Economics, 78,* 100–111. https://doi.org/10.1016/j.ecolecon.2012.04.004

Mollet, J. C., von Arx, U., & Ilic, D. (2013). Strategic Sustainability and Financial Performance: Exploring Abnormal Returns. *Journal of Business Economics, 83*(6), 577–604. https://link.springer.com/journal/volumesAndIssues/11573

Momentum Midland. (2019). *Our Team.* Retrieved from http://www.momentum-midland.org/our-team

Moreno, J. L. (1934). In H. H. Jennings (Ed.), *Who Shall Survive? A New Approach to the Problem of Human Interrelations.* Washington, DC: Nervous and mental disease publishing co.

Porter, M. E., & Kramer, M. R. (2006). Strategy & Society: The Link Between Competitive Advantage and Corporate Social Responsibility. *Harvard Business Review, 84*(12), 78–92.

Porter, M. E., & Kramer, M. R. (2011). Creating Shared Value. *Harvard Business Review, 89*(1/2), 62–77.

Putnam, R. D. (1995). Bowling Alone: America's Declining Social Capital. *Journal of Democracy, 6*, 65–78. https://doi.org/10.1353/jod.1995.0002

Shleifer, A., & Vishny, R. W. (1997). The Limits of Arbitrage. *Journal of Finance, 52*(1), 35–55. http://onlinelibrary.wiley.com/journal/10.1111/%28I SSN%291540-6261/issues

Thistlethwaite, J., & Paterson, M. (2016). Private Governance and Accounting for Sustainability Networks. *Environment and Planning C: Government & Policy, 34*(7), 1197–1221. http://epc.sagepub.com/content/by/year

United States Senate. (2012). *For Profit Higher Education: The Failure to Safeguard the Federal Investment and Ensure Student Success*. Washington, DC. Retrieved from https://www.help.senate.gov/imo/media/for_profit_report/PartI-PartIII-SelectedAppendixes.pdf

Wagner, M., & Schaltegger, S. (2004). The Effect of Corporate Environmental Strategy Choice and Environmental Performance on Competitiveness and Economic Performance: An Empirical Study of EU Manufacturing. *European Management Journal, 22*(5), 557–572.

Watts, D. J. (2004). The "New" Science of Networks. *Annual Review of Sociology, 30*, 243–270.

Whoriskey, P. (2018, December 29). Bankruptcy Aids Firms in Shedding Their Pension Debts. *Washington Post*. Retrieved from https://www.washingtonpost.com/business/economy/as-a-grocery-chain-isdismantled-investors-recover-their-money-worker-pensions-are-short-millions/2018/12/28/ea22e398-0a0e-11e9-85b6-41c0fe0c5b8f_story.html

CHAPTER 10

Sustainable Investing and Asset Allocation at Global Scale

There are few savers in the global financial ecosystem who save without pressing future needs. Typically, savers are not seeking returns in order to finance indulgences, but for specific future purposes, such as retirement needs, educational or wedding expenses, the purchase of capital goods such as a cow, bicycle, car, or house, or as insurance against possible future calamities. Savers, when they convert monetary savings into investments, invest with an underlying concern for expected returns that they need or hope for. They have considerations of when they will need to convert those returns into cash and what leeway they might have if the returns are not realized. They have a variety of risk tolerances: what intermediate swings in value they can tolerate, what permanent loss of capital would be catastrophic, how much longer they might postpone the achievement of their goals if necessary. The broadening swathe of the population who are investors implies that the purpose of finance extends far beyond wealth preservation and enhancement for the privileged few.[1] Institutional asset owners such as pension funds, sovereign wealth funds, endowments, mutual funds, and insurance funds who allocate the savings of the citizen investor amounted to approximately $120 trillion of the estimated $420 trillion in total financial capital in 2016 (Willis Towers Watson, 2017).

Financial sustainability in the ecosystem means facilitating the fulfillment of the shared future needs and wants of the wider population of savers. Acknowledging the broad social dimension of this capital stewardship role of the financial ecosystem collapses the traditional paradigm

© The Author(s) 2019
S. Bose et al., *The Financial Ecosystem*, Palgrave Studies in Impact
Finance, https://doi.org/10.1007/978-3-030-05624-7_10

which puts shareholders and stakeholders into separate categories. Shareholdings, and other forms of investment, derive from the savings of stakeholders as employees and citizens with savings or as tax payers who both support the banking system and sovereign wealth funds. Hence, even those markets which consider shareholder primacy to be their model, are ultimately serving stakeholders, who have not just financial interests, but other goals that include widespread prosperity, social cohesion, and environmental integrity (Charkham & Simpson, 1999).

MODERN PORTFOLIO THEORY

The analytical framework utilized by investment managers to structure the allocation of the savings of asset owners into asset classes and securities has come to be known as modern portfolio theory. The problem of determining how best to invest in order to meet the financial goals of the saver is called the portfolio choice problem.

Mean-Variance Optimization

One specific way of formulating the portfolio choice problem for an investor, known as modern portfolio theory, originated in the now seminal article entitled 'Portfolio Selection' by Harry Markowitz (Markowitz, 1952). A similar analysis of the problem as the one in Markowitz's paper was contemporaneously presented by Andrew Roy (Roy, 1952). Markowitz was concerned with articulating a mathematical formulation that justified the ancient and widespread preference for diversification in investment behavior. He notes that any investment rule that seeks to maximize the present value of returns cannot possibly explain the observed diversification, since such a rule would necessarily guide an investor to select a single security in which to invest—the security that offered the highest expected return. Therefore, in order to explain the common investor behavior of diversification, Markowitz incorporates a measure of risk into the formulation of the investor's problem: that of the expected variance of the portfolio return.

Previous authors had somewhat cavalierly assumed that diversification and the law of large numbers would ensure that the actual portfolio return would be close to the expected portfolio return, obviating a need to consider the variance of the portfolio return. They assumed that diversification would essentially eliminate risk. Markowitz's key insight was to show that the covariance between securities in the portfolio would make it impossible to diversify away all the risk. So long as there was some positive covariance between portfolio securities, there would remain some non-diversifiable risk (Rubinstein, 2002). By diversifying, an investor, who seeks to achieve a given portfolio return, could reduce the variance of portfolio return, but could not eliminate it because many securities in the portfolio had positive covariance. This insight should focus the investor's attention on a security's contribution to portfolio variance, rather than on its own variance: the former is salient even in a diversified portfolio, but the latter is irrelevant. Markowitz (and Roy's) approach, which came to be known as mean-variance optimization, suggests that the investor should restrict her choices to a set of *efficient* portfolios: a portfolio is considered efficient if none other gives either (i) a higher expected return and the same variance of return or (ii) a lower variance of return and the same expected return. Mean-variance optimization is a normative theory: it is an exhortation to investors to choose securities in a particular way, assuming that they define return as financial return and risk as variance of portfolio return.

Factor Models

In order to be implemented, mean-variance optimization requires an unusually large number of numerical inputs. For n securities, the investor must estimate $(n^2 - n)/2$ covariances for the optimization in addition estimates of security returns and variances. For example, a procedure that analyzes 200 potential securities as candidates for inclusion in the portfolio requires estimates of 200 future returns, 200 variances of return, and 19,900 covariances between the returns of the individual securities. This is generally unreasonable, so the standard practice is to impose *ex ante* conditions on the structure of covariances by assuming that the securities tend to co-move according to their relationships to just a few so-called factors (Fabozzi, Gupta, & Markowitz, 2002). For example, the market model or market factor model assumes that securities all tend to move together somewhat with the overall stock market index (Sharpe, 1963). In more elaborate models, the magnitude of stock co-movement and interdependence is affected by fundamental factors such as industry membership or valuation multiples, macroeconomic factors such as the term structure of interest rates, and statistical factors extracted from a data mining process (Connor, 1995). Connor's review of the historical experience for 779 large market capitalization US stocks between 1985 and 1993 suggests that these factors explain approximately 45% of portfolio returns.

The Capital Asset Pricing Model

The Capital Asset Pricing Model (CAPM) is a theory that is related, but different from the prescriptive recommendation of mean-variance optimization. The CAPM describes a capital market in which all investors are assumed to independently select the Markowitz-efficient portfolios that meet their risk tolerance preferences. Assuming they do so, the CAPM computes the characteristics of the resulting equilibrium, when supply equals demand in the capital market (Lintner, 1969; Sharpe, 1964). The assumptions of the CAPM hypothesis include

   (i) all investors have identical expectations about security returns, variance, and covariances,
  (ii) there is a risk-free asset, which is borrowed or lent at identical rates,
 (iii) all investors are risk-averse Markowitz mean-variance optimizers with a common investment horizon,
  (iv) the only source of risk comes from the investment portfolio,
   (v) and there are no non-traded assets and markets are perfect (each investor is a price-taker who does not believe he can influence price, there are no transaction costs and no costs of acquiring information).

While these assumptions are clearly unrealistic, for some theorists, unrealistic assumptions are not a reason to jettison a hypothesis: the validity of a hypothesis is determined by tests of the similarity between reality and the theory's predictions.[2] The CAPM predicts that in equilibrium, each investor's chosen portfolio of risky assets has the same composition as all other investors' portfolios. Moreover, this portfolio consists of the market portfolio, which is the aggregate of all portfolios. The market portfolio is mean-variance efficient for all investors and any other portfolio of risky assets is inferior. In equilibrium, investors do not receive any risk premium (called alpha) to hold diversifiable, idiosyncratic, issuer-related risk. Rather, CAPM investors price each security in the market so that its expected return is linearly related to its contribution to market risk. The sensitivity of its expected return to its market risk contribution is called its beta.

Investment managers understand that neither the assumptions, nor the implications of CAPM are realistic. Nevertheless, managers routinely use the attributes of the theory to describe in relatively precise terms certain aspects of investment behavior. A key implication of the CAPM theory is that most investors ought to hold the market portfolio, since idiosyncratic risks are uncompensated in a world where it is easy to diversify away from them. They also use the theory to construct a method of decomposing realized returns into idiosyncratic and market risk (alpha and beta), facilitating performance attribution (Rosenberg, 1981). The CAPM theory provides a method to compute the expected return on a security *ex ante* based on just the expected return on the market portfolio and the sensitivity of the security's return to the market return, its beta. *Ex post*, this expected return can be compared to realized return and the difference can be decomposed into that part which is attributable to the market return being different from the expected market return (called the return attributable to market risk, or the beta return) and the residual (called the return attributable to idiosyncratic risk, or the alpha return). Given the CAPM assumptions, the *ex ante* alpha return is equal to zero. Any non-zero alpha return that is realized *ex post* arises from departures from the restrictive assumptions of the CAPM theory.[3] This performance attribution method privileges passive investing in a broad index of stocks, requiring that deviations from the passive index be justified by the potential to generate excess risk-adjusted return due to asymmetric information or institutional constraints that limit investment in some types of securities. Passive investing, under CAPM, came to mean investing in a chosen broad index, while active investing came to mean discretionary deviations (in security selection and timing) from a broad index that is chosen *ex ante* as a benchmark. In this construct, alpha is a measure of the return to active management, while beta is the return from passive investing.

Arbitrage Pricing Theory (APT)

An extension of the CAPM that relaxes some assumptions and exploits factor models (see above) is the Arbitrage Pricing Theory (APT) proposed by Ross (1976). APT generalizes the sources of non-diversifiable risk to include factors other than the risk of the market portfolio. For example, the APT would allow computation of risk premiums for investing in particularly risky industries or in small-capitalization companies (generally considered riskier than large-capitalization companies), or for investing in high growth companies, in addition to the market risk premium that characterizes the CAPM theory. Post-APT, the concept of beta as a risk premium for investing in non-diversifiable market risk became more general:

the investor can now be said to be earning different betas for investing in different kinds of systematic risk. Alpha, in the context of APT, refers to the residual return from the active selection of securities and possibly market timing that is not attributable to the systematic factors considered in the particular set of factors included in the chosen APT model. For a detailed review of types of factors and their empirical risk premia for United States and European equities and bonds, see Koedijk, Slager, and Stork (2016).

The implementation of APT in investment management opens up the possibility that in principle, the APT could be extended to incorporate a broader array of systemic risks, such as those posed by depletions of natural capital, or degradation in stakeholder relations or a paucity of social legitimacy, though there has been little theoretical work in this direction.

Portfolio Theory Versus Practice

For the normative recommendations of mean-variance optimization to be effective in minimizing risk, a number of key assumptions and modifications to the procedure are essential. It is well known that the procedure is not robust to small perturbations in the assumptions of return, variance, and covariance, causing the procedure to recommend excessive re-balancing as the efficient portfolio changes erratically over time. Hence, analysts might use ad hoc requirements on the magnitude of portfolio re-balancing to minimize trading and transaction costs (Fisher, 1975). Additional practical issues interpreting assumptions and estimating inputs for the implementation of MPT are described in Brealey (1990) and Wilford (2012).

Covariance as the Tip of an Iceberg

The mean-variance optimization framework is premised on the simplistic notion that the variance of portfolio return is a good way to measure risk. This premise is appropriate only in very limited circumstances (Szegö, 2002).[4] The variance of portfolio return is hardly the only plausible measure of risk: Markowitz himself favored semi-variance in practical applications and Szegö outlines others (such as expected regret, expected shortfall, and conditional value at risk) which are robust to a broader class of probability distributions and are sufficiently easy to compute. Unfortunately, modern portfolio theory has yet to be modified to incorporate a broader range of risk measures and metrics of co-movement.

Furthermore, it is likely that in the context of long-horizon consequences of investing, the appropriate probability distributions are numerically indeterminate. The covariance (and variance) of two random variables can be calculated if the characteristics of the joint probability distribution of the variables are known. Its computation requires knowing, with certainty, the numerical mean of the distribution, as well as the numerical probabilities associated with the range of possible values. In assuming that the investor knows or can estimate the joint probability distribution of the returns of his portfolio, advocates of modern portfolio theory are in the venerable company of generations of economic and finance theorists who choose to depend on this crucial assumption. For tractable mathematical guidance in portfolio construction, the assumption that probability distributions for all salient outcomes can be compared numerically is essential. Situations where numerical comparison is not possible are referred to in economics as "uncertainty". Lucas writes that "In cases of uncertainty, economic reasoning will be of no value" (Lucas, 1977). Not all economic theorists were so quick to stand on this convenient crutch. The distinction between measurable risk and unmeasurable uncertainty originates with Frank Knight: uncertainty is defined as a risk that is not insurable. Knight viewed risk as "a quantity susceptible of measurement" and described uncertainty as "unmeasurable" and "non-quantitative" (Knight, 1921). John Maynard Keynes, in *A Treatise on Probability*, states "that there are some pairs of probabilities between the members of which *no* comparison of magnitude is possible" (Keynes, 1921). Subsequently, Keynes calls this concept "uncertainty" and attributes the desire to hold cash balances (liquidity preference) to uncertainty regarding future interest rates and to our lack of confidence in numerical estimates of the probability of different future consequences of our choices: "our desire to hold money as a store of wealth is a barometer of the degree of our distrust of our own calculations and conventions concerning the future" (Keynes, 1937). In a bibliometric study, Geoffrey Hodgson demonstrates the decline in the use of the concept of Knight-Keynes uncertainty in mainstream economics. Using electronic archives of economics journals, he shows that the frequency of appearance of this concept has fallen rapidly from the 1950s. He argues that the decrease in the use of the uncertainty concept is related to the increasing mathematical formalization of economics which necessarily eschews the unmeasurable (Hodgson, 2011).

Amongst investment practitioners, the recognition of uncertainty does not necessarily lead to higher liquidity preference. For investors with long-horizon liabilities, it may be rational to earn a liquidity premium because near-term liabilities are small (relative to capital) or partially discretionary. David Swensen, the manager of the Yale University endowment since 1985, articulated an investment approach which expanded the notion of diversification to include illiquid asset classes such as emerging markets equities, high-yield debt and private equity investments (Swensen, 2000). As we noted in Chap. 1, J.M. Keynes also served as manager of a college endowment, advocating investments in the new asset class of equities (including significant allocations to emerging markets of the time). The Swensen approach, also called the Yale model or the endowment model, determines optimal fixed allocations to liquid and illiquid asset classes based on expectations of long-run returns, variances, and covariances. Intermediate re-balancing is expected to aid long-term performance by re-deploying capital away from temporarily high-performing asset classes into temporarily low-performing asset classes. This approach can work during time periods when there is some degree of long-run mean reversion in asset class returns and covariances.

The ideas underlying MPT could in principle illuminate portfolio choice among a broad range of assets. The analysis has been extended to include human capital and could be applied, with significant modifications, to other forms of capital. However, for MPT to serve as a useful analytical framework for natural and social capital, its conception of the measurement of risk would have to become significantly more sophisticated. Portfolio variance, the basic measure of risk in MPT is applicable to a rather narrow subset of numerically measurable probability distributions. Numerically measurable probability distributions are themselves useless in describing situations of uncertainty which characterize many long-term consequences of investment choice. As we saw in Chaps. 7, 8, and 9, the risks embedded in the management of natural, human, and social capital are of a different category from financial capital. Recognizing that risk is a multi-dimensional concept, with many quantifiable, unquantifiable, and unknown attributes makes the characterization of risk on the single dimension of portfolio variance seem either exceedingly brave or exceedingly ignorant. Covariance does measure a modicum of risk, but it seems unlikely that it could measure much more than a small proportion of it when we consider alternative forms of capital.

Broadening Conceptions of Non-diversifiable Risk

We noted that an implication of the CAPM theory was that the mean-variance optimizing investor would choose the market portfolio as his primary risky asset. Generalizations such as the APT incorporate other forms of non-diversifiable risk such as industry, liquidity, or style risk. APT constructs a narrative framework for the investor insofar as it allows him to make a judgment that his expected returns might come from such-and-such factor, and after the passage of time, it allows him to determine whether realized returns came from that factor or from something else. For example, APT-inspired empirical studies might compute the portion of historical returns in portfolios attributable to investing in small-capitalization stocks. The investor might extrapolate that by overweighting small-capitalization stocks relative to the market portfolio,[5] he should expect to earn a higher return than the market portfolio. If he subsequently does not earn the expected higher return, he can check to see whether his portfolio holdings diverged from the small-capitalization benchmark (in which case his underperformance was due to his security selection) or whether it did not diverge and the underperformance is instead due to a reduction or elimination of the risk premium paid to small-capitalization stocks.

The reduction or elimination of risk factors is a central implication of the efficient markets hypothesis (EMH). The EMH was first articulated by Jules Regnault, a nineteenth-century French stockbroker whose work subsequently influenced Louis Bachelier (Jovanovic & Le Gall, 2001). As conceived in early versions, the EMH predicts that asset prices in a perfectly competitive market incorporate all available information, are essentially unpredictable and follow a "random walk", making it difficult or impossible to earn persistent risk premiums. Regnault constructed the random walk model to show that short-term speculation inevitably leads to ruin. The EMH has had mixed empirical success, with many examples of predictability for different assets. The theory has evolved to allow for transient risk premiums identified and earned by acquirers and processors of information who speculate and dissipate those premia through their trading activity (Grossman & Stiglitz, 1976). Subsequent enhancements of the hypothesis take into account transactions costs, the availability and cost of leverage and the potential dissipation of risk premia due to the misalignment of interests between investor and investment manager. A detailed history of the theoretical and empirical development of EMH is constructed in Ang, Goetzmann, and Schaefer (2011).

Performance attribution with the correct set of factors can be an incredibly revealing exercise for many complex and opaque investment strategies. For example, convertible debt securities are hybrid instruments that are characterized by equity risk, credit risk, interest rate risk as well as optionality. The appropriate factors that drive returns are those which individually explain a significant portion of the returns to assuming each of these risks. The period 1999–2006 was one when convertible arbitrage hedge funds generally performed very well relative to the overall stock market and were able to sharply increase assets under management from asset growth and investment performance. Mark Anson shows that during this time period, the systematic factors that drove the return in this sector were: Russell 1000 index returns (a proxy for broad equity performance), 10-year US treasury bonds (a proxy for returns to long-duration, low-credit risk securities), high-yield bond returns (a proxy for returns to low-rated fixed-income securities), the level of the VIX (a measure of short-term implied volatility and a proxy for option valuations), and recent past returns in the convertible arbitrage sector (Anson, 2008). Anson's analysis demonstrates that convertible arbitrage hedge fund outperformance was caused not by their security selection, but by their systematic factors. Indeed, their returns to security selection (termed alpha) were collectively negative, partially offsetting the wind in their sails from systematic factors largely outside their control (termed beta).

The Feedback Loop Between Portfolio Choice and the Ecosystem

A key aspect of consideration for the largest asset owners is the interdependence of factor risk premia and portfolio allocation choices. As an equilibrium construct, the philosophy underlying MPT should envisage that the returns earned from assuming systematic risk will be dissipated in accordance with the EMH. However, in routinized processes of investment choice, the factor risk premia are taken to be exogenous, estimated from historical returns, instead of being considered both an output of and an input to the investment choice process. Few practitioners or researchers consider the feedback loop between investment choices and the environmental, social, and economic system (J. Hawley & Lukomnik, 2018). In Chap. 2 we noted that the plasticity and adaptability of financial intermediaries suggest that there are few deep parameters (in the sense of Lucas (1976)) in the financial ecosystem. If the largest asset owners consciously or unconsciously allocate significant capital to assuming systematic risks, then the consequent low-risk premia for such risks will lead to misallocation of real resources as economic agents in the real economy underprice such risks. This is true of universal owners (J. P. Hawley & Williams, 2000). It is also true if there is herd behavior by smaller asset owners. During times like the global financial crisis, the confluence of systematic risks which can threaten the survival of the financial ecosystem is revealed, potentially creating an epiphanal transformation of systematic risks into systemic risks. An acknowledgment of the range of systemic risks and the interdependence between investor choice and systemic risk suggests a need to radically revise investment management practices beyond those arising out of MPT (Christian, 2011). In particular, the largest investors, given their inability to generate significant performance from alpha, must consider how to reduce systemic risks so that their beta returns are not eliminated by periodic crises. Universal owners are thus compelled to act not just by allocating financial capital, but also by engaging with companies, intermediaries, and regulators to reduce systemic risk wherever feasible. Lydenberg discusses the limitations of MPT and argues that asset owners must go beyond their portfolio financial allocations and consider the portfolio-level and systemic-level environmental, social, and governance impacts (Lydenberg, 2016). In assessing the adequacy of modern portfolio theory, one is tempted to abuse a Shakespearean quote thus: "There are more things in heaven and earth, MPT, than are dreamt of in your philosophy".

Asset Allocation

The Salience of Liabilities and Incentive Alignment

As we noted earlier, the typical saver has specific financial goals. For the asset owners working on behalf of savers, these financial goals can be thought of as liabilities, as they rise to the level of obligation. Examples include pension funds with a defined benefit structure, education and health savings plans with clear future disbursements, and sovereign wealth funds whose periodic returns are utilized for national welfare. Ultimately, the financial objectives of these investors support human welfare, including retirement provision in old age, health care, education, housing, and insurance. This implies that there is a confluence between the social purpose of such investments and the financial objectives meant to provide for these aspects of human welfare.

In a globally complex and interdependent economy, the process of deploying these savings to provide for the streams of income needed for social purposes puts a premium upon aligning interest throughout the investment chain to ensure that horizon, risk, fees, and return ambitions do not undermine the integrity and efficiency of the financial ecosystem. In Chap. 1, we refer to this challenge as the first incarnation of the principal-agent problem. The second incarnation (that of aligning the interest of shareholder and corporate management) is well understood in the context of the separation of ownership and control and the consequent potential for rent-seeking behavior in the corporate form. The same logic applied to investor governance would provide a new framework for a sustainable financial ecosystem, one that deploys savings in support of beneficiaries' ultimate needs rather than intermediary efforts to maximize profits in the context of misaligned incentives.

Without Anson's performance attribution, one would have been forgiven for assuming that convertible arbitrage managers were highly intelligent alpha generators. Performance attribution with the appropriate systematic factors is an indispensable legacy of the APT that has the promise to facilitate the discrimination between the lucky and the smart. After the global financial crisis of 2007–2008 when most asset classes declined sharply, many observers argued that diversification across asset classes was far lower than had been assumed. A key source of regret from large asset owners was the observation that highly incented active investment managers such as hedge funds and private equity funds were not able to outperform the market portfolio of liquid stocks and bonds. In the aftermath of the crisis, the largest asset owner at the time, the Norwegian Government Pension Fund, instituted an evaluation of the performance of active investing strategies in its own portfolio (Ang, Goetzmann, & Schaefer, 2009). Ang et al. performed a factor-based performance attribution for the returns of the Norwegian fund between 1998 and 2008. They found that active management of the equity portfolio had provided a tiny portion of overall return outperformance. Active fixed-income management had provided no discernible outperformance. The proportion of total fund variance attributable to active management was less than 1% for equities, and less than 3% for bonds. Furthermore, more than 70% of the returns to active management were attributable to systematic factors (that is beta) rather than to security selection and timing (or alpha). This implies that active investment managers, who had high-powered incentives to generate returns were barely adding alpha to the fund's performance. Since their incentive contracts were not linked to the appropriate systematic factors (and in some cases they were not linked to any benchmark), their fees rewarded them for returns attributable to systematic factors (beta) rather than their own choices (alpha).

For a diversified portfolio, the allocation choice across asset classes is a significant driver of return variance (Brinson, Hood, & Beebower, 1986). One of the most direct and widely used applications of mean-variance optimization is top-down allocation across asset classes (Fabozzi et al., 2002). In the wake of the crisis and the recognition that many factors within each asset class were correlated with factors in other asset classes, academics and practitioners have proposed analysis of common factors across asset classes which drive sharp increases in correlations across strategies during crises. For example, Asl and Etula (2012) construct a model of multi-asset class allocation that utilizes a range of factors including equity market risk, inflation and interest rate risk, risk in short-term credit conditions, risk in market-wide liquidity conditions, systematic exchange rate risk, and risks specific to emerging markets. A subsequent review of the Norwegian Fund's performance recommends a new dynamic model of capital allocation to asset classes and delegation to investment managers that accounts for the opportunity cost of funds and encourages allocations to active managers only when expected returns are likely to exceed such costs (Ang, Brandt, & Denison, 2014).

The Largest Asset Allocators

The overwhelming flow of investment funds is derived from investors with long-term objectives. The world's largest asset allocators (Table 10.1), such as the Government Pension Investment Fund of Japan, the Norwegian Pension Fund, the China Investment Corporation, the South Korean National Pension, the All Pensions Group in the Netherlands, and the California Public Employees Retirement System are examples of asset owners with intergenerational liabilities. According to a survey of global asset owners, the largest 100 such funds allocate $19 trillion of the $120 trillion invested on behalf of the citizen investor (Willis Towers Watson, 2018).

Even for the largest asset owners, their size relative to the financial power of the largest banks is somewhat limited. We noted in Chap. 2 that the notional derivatives exposure of a single large, but not the largest bank in the world amounted to $57 trillion. The largest financial intermediaries

Table 10.1 The 15 largest asset owners

Rank	Asset owner	Country	Assets (in billions)		Type
1	Government pension investment	Japan	$	1443.6	Pension fund
2	Government pension fund	Norway	$	1063.5	Pension fund
3	China investment corporation	China	$	900.0	Sovereign wealth fund
4	Abu Dhabi investment authority	UAE	$	828.0	Sovereign wealth fund
5	National Pension	South Korea	$	582.9	Pension fund
6	APG	Netherlands	$	564.5	Pension fund
7	Federal Retirement Thrift	USA	$	531.5	Pension fund
8	Kuwait investment authority	Kuwait	$	524.0	Sovereign wealth fund
9	SAMA foreign holdings	Saudi Arabia	$	514.0	Sovereign wealth fund
10	HKMA investment portfolio	Hong Kong	$	456.6	Sovereign wealth fund
11	SAFE investment company	China	$	441.0	Sovereign wealth fund
12	GIC private limited	Singapore	$	359.0	Sovereign wealth fund
13	National Social Security	China	$	341.4	Pension fund
14	CalPERS	USA	$	336.7	Pension fund
15	Qatar investment authority	Qatar	$	335.0	Sovereign wealth fund

Source: Adapted from Willis Towers Watson (2018)

have the size and scale necessary for significant market power. The power of an asset owner as a single actor in this ecosystem is limited, but can be enhanced through collective action. The largest 100 asset owners globally are primarily publicly owned institutions. The Willis Towers Watson report comments that "Asset owners are too important to fail in their mission … They have little choice but to take their financial and social responsibilities seriously, to lead from the front and not to shrink away from the big issues".

Overall asset allocation for this group of global owners is in three categories: public equities at 46%, fixed income at 27%, and alternatives at 25%, with the remainder in cash. Each of these asset classes presents different opportunities for sustainability driven by investors, demanding a multifaceted strategy across the total portfolio. The view that sustainable investing could involve selecting positive impact securities and selling negative impact securities and generating 'ESG alpha' from such security selection, while valuable, is challenging to implement for the largest asset owners given their scale. For investors of such scale and longevity, there is nowhere to run to. Their investment returns reflect the global economic outlook given their exposure to global equity risk. They have a strong interest in the stability of the capital markets in order to protect their assets. Consequently, universal owners cannot easily exit markets or investments. As they have nowhere to hide from systemic risk, they need to address it. Among the 20 largest asset owners in the world, a number of the global pension funds (such as the Government Pension Investment Fund [GPIF] of Japan, Norges Bank Investment Management, APG, Stichting Pensioenfonds Zorg en Welzijn [known as PFZW, formerly PGGM], California Public Employees Retirement System [CalPERS] and Canada Pension Plan) are cited as leaders in sustainable investment. They have crafted asset allocation to reflect their liabilities and have developed strategies within asset classes which aim to address both portfolio wide and systemic risk. Several of these global asset owners have established investment parameters which exclude certain companies or sectors based on their sustainability impact. For APG, this includes companies manufacturing anti-personnel weapons, such as cluster bombs. For CalPERS, this includes tobacco, assault weapons for personal use, and companies that derive a majority of their revenue from thermal coal or present egregious violations of human rights.

Defined Benefit Funds

The pension funds among the largest asset owners generally have defined benefit obligations to their beneficiaries. This pension promise to replace a level of income in working life introduces expectations, and demands on portfolio returns that need to be managed with great care. If the realized investment returns are not sufficient to pay the pension promise, the employers or the state will be required to increase contributions into the fund. Pension funds are designed for sustainability due to their intergenerational obligations. The trustees who govern the pension funds have fiduciary duties of prudence, loyalty, and care which must be exercised without favor to any particular cohort of beneficiaries. Hence, pensioners drawing their retirement savings have an interest in near-term steady cash flows, and future beneficiaries have an equal claim to cash flows that may not be drawn upon for many decades hence.

Pension funds also demonstrate another feature of sustainability, which is the circular flow of funds—deploying these to investments that generate returns, providing capital to the economy, and then harvesting these returns through the life cycle of the beneficiaries' entitlements. When there are significant leakages from this flow of funds (Ambachtsheer, Fuller, & Hindocha, 2013), pension contributions have to increase to make up the maintenance of living standards.

Pension fund investors face fixed and growing liabilities, as life expectancy increases and medical costs grow along with the needs of the elderly. The asset allocation choice to cover liabilities as and when they fall due has been affected by two secular trends. The first is demographic and the second is financial.

Life expectancy has grown faster than retirement ages have risen. The result is a longer period of retirement as a proportion of working life which is the time during which savings are accumulated. This factor has also had an impact on provision of public pensions. When a federal social security fund was proposed by Theodore Roosevelt in the 1912 presidential campaign, the life expectancy of men was just 51, so a typical working man would have a very short duration in retirement. This would have meant that the payments expected from social security would have been needed for a short period of time, relative to a lifetime of savings contributions. By the end of the twentieth century, in a welcome development for human welfare, life expectancy for the working man had grown to 15 years beyond retirement, and close to 20 years for women. A further demographic shift relates to birth rates, whereby the ratio of working to retired persons in the economy has narrowed, to the point where major economies are facing a bulge in the retiree population and shrinkage of the working population whose contributions to retirement provision via taxes make up a significant proportion of the financing. The potential impact is seen in economies as divergent as China, Japan, Germany, and the United States.

Alongside these two demographic shifts that affect asset allocation has been a fall in returns from the major asset classes investors have relied upon to generate the returns that pay pensions and other liabilities: stocks and bonds. For most asset owners, the decline in interest rates since the 1980s has forced asset allocation to take on greater market risk and/or increase contributions to offset return shortfalls.

Sovereign Wealth Funds

Sovereign wealth funds have varied objectives, intended to support the welfare goals established by their government at national or regional level. Examples include the Norwegian Pension Fund, which invests the revenues from oil production and diversifies these into an investment portfolio to generate returns for the population of Norway. The Chinese, Australian, and Singaporean government's sovereign wealth funds are likewise intended to offer a savings vehicle for surplus funds to be invested for protection against future economic distress. The Kuwaiti Sovereign Wealth fund has similarly long-term intentions for national protection which were called upon after the invasion of the country during the Gulf War and oil production was hit hard by the conflict. The sovereign wealth fund kept the country solvent whilst it rebuilt its economy and restored revenues from oil. For Saudi Arabia, its sovereign wealth fund is accumulating assets which the government intends will provide the capital to transition the economy from oil to a more broadly diversified.

Defined Contribution Funds

Unlike defined benefit funds, defined contribution (DC) funds do not guarantee a fixed payout upon retirement in the United States. Defined contribution fund sponsors invest the contributions of each individual employee, and allow the employee to withdraw the returns attributable to those contributions upon retirement. DC funds are structured into individual risk bearing accounts and are not pooled with others. DC funds offer a level of investment choice to the individual investor, mediated by the plan options provided by the plan sponsor. DC fund participants tend to have a greater allocation to public equities than institutional investors. Their allocation is also more pro-cyclical and more sensitive to macroeconomic conditions: DC fund participants drastically reduce exposure to equities during recessions (Sialm, Starks, & Zhang, 2015). Some studies find that individual investment choice is irrationally influenced by mutual fund name changes (Cooper, Gulen, & Rau, 2005). Upon examining a large sample of US discount brokerage investors, Bailey, Kumar and Ng find that these behaviorally biased investors typically make poor decisions about fund style and expenses, trading frequency, and timing, resulting in poor performance (Bailey, Kumar, & Ng, 2011). There is evidence to suggest that DC participants do not diversify their investments appropriately and the freedom to choose how retirement funds are invested can leave workers worse off (Ahmed, Barber, & Odean, 2018). Ahmed et al. perform a calibrated simulation showing that the allocation choice in DC funds can lead to lower utility and greater risk of income shortfalls relative to private accounts without choice. However, there is also evidence suggesting that individual investors in the aggregate react in a rational and forward-looking way to leading indicators of market cycles. One study finds that fund investors alter the riskiness of their portfolios in response to shifting economic conditions, increasing risk as the economy is expected to improve and reducing risk in anticipation of economic downturns (Chalmers, Kaul, & Phillips, 2013).

The individual approach to investment choice in DC funds limits the possibilities for collective action to pressure investment managers to limit fees. One study of DC funds, based on data from 3,500,401(k) plans with $120 billion in assets, suggests that fees and investment menu restrictions in an average plan lead to annual costs of 0.78% in excess of index funds (Ayres & Curtis, 2015). Those fees compound to reduce the retirement value of the DC fund. In a hypothetical example to illustrate the cumulative impact of compounded investment costs, Davis, Lukomnik, and

Pitt-Watson (2016) outline the savings behavior of three sisters, one who lives in the United States, one who lives in the United Kingdom, and one who lives in the Netherlands. Due to differences in the annual investment expenses paid by the different sisters, it is likely that the sisters in the United States and United Kingdom will need to save 50% more than the one in the Netherlands for the same annual payout during retirement. Another analysis concludes that between 1990 and 2012 in the United States, defined benefit plans outperformed defined contribution plans by 0.7% per year. This differential remains even after controlling for size and asset allocation, suggesting that the likely explanation is higher fees in defined contribution accounts (Munnell, Aubry, & Crawford, 2015). John Bogle, after a long career in setting up the fee-minimizing mutual financial intermediary Vanguard, railed against the US investment management industry for a range of practices which drove up costs for the smallest investors (Bogle, 2016). DC plan sponsors have recently focused on reducing plan fees. An annual industry survey prepared by the Callan Institute notes that for the third consecutive year, fee reviews have been the top cited action by plan sponsors to enhance their fiduciary compliance (Callan Institute, 2019).

A further concern with DC funds is the limited transparency of holdings and the restricted ability of fund participants to affect manager choices on proxy voting and engagement with portfolio companies. The investor may have very limited information about the issuers that comprise fund holdings. The growing concern with sustainability across society has opened up an opportunity for managers to offer a glimpse into their portfolios. Investment managers are also under pressure to be held accountable for their choices when they allocate clients' capital. New groups have formed in recent years, which send emails to fund managers calling on them to vote in support of sustainability proposals at companies. These requests do not have legal force. There is nothing in the governance structure of a DC fund investment contract which puts intermediaries into dialogue with their clients, other than via marketing departments. This has led to some investment managers facing petitions from civil society groups, calling upon them to play an active role in ensuring that the customers' funds are deployed with sustainability in mind. For example, a group of campaigners has accused BlackRock, the largest asset manager, of lagging behind other major investors in its support of climate-related shareholder resolutions (Thompson, 2019). The situation has been complicated as investment managers have become listed companies themselves, giving them an interest in serving their own shareholders. Investment managers are increasingly articulating their approach to sustainability through statements, CEO vision pronouncements and signing on to initiatives that articulate good practices, such as the Principles for Responsible Investment (PRI) and the Task Force on Climate-related Financial Disclosures (TCFD). Some financial institutions have gone so far as to establish a stakeholder council, or consultative body, to respond to criticism and also improve the company's understanding of societal expectations around their role as intermediaries. For example, Wells Fargo has launched a stakeholder advisory council to look at ways of "serving the financial needs of underserved communities, diversity and social inclusion, and environmental sustainability" (Kilroy, 2017). The council's launch follows the settlement by Wells Fargo of claims that it set up deposit and credit card accounts for clients without their permission.

There are other examples of DC fund design which offer greater accountability and alignment with participant interests. The Australian model of industry funds provides for a governing body with equal representation from employers and trade union representatives (Volpato & Scheerlinck, 2015). Likewise, the Taft-Hartley funds in the United States were designed with a similar structure. The governance structure which most closely aligns with beneficiaries' interests on systemic risks would in turn foster a setting in which sustainability can be expressed through asset allocation. There are investment managers who have specifically targeted the growing interest in sustainability by institutional asset owners and retail investors. At the aggregate level, the pressure from institutional investors appears to cause improvements in environmental and social metrics in portfolios. In a study of 3277 non-US firms from 41 countries over the 2004–2013 period, Dyck et al. find that greater institutional ownership is associated with higher firm-level environmental and social scores and argue that the relationship is causal (Dyck, Lins, Roth, & Wagner, 2019).

THE VALUE OF SYSTEMIC ENGAGEMENT

In his treatise entitled *Exit, Voice and Loyalty*, Albert Hirschman constructs a framework to analyze situations where consumers of a service can respond to degradation in quality in two ways: they can stop buying the service (*exit*) or choose to alert the service provider and try to induce change (*voice*) (Hirschman, 1970). Exit is generally associated with market relations, where there is less opportunity and incentive for constructive dialogue and reduced likelihood of repeated interaction. Voice is generally a feature of modern political systems, which require a robust mechanism for the airing of citizen dissatisfaction. Hirschman builds on Karl Polanyi's argument that the modern market economy and the modern political state function as complementary systems to regulate human relations after industrialization (Polanyi, 1944). Hirschman argues that in situations where customers are loyal, their intimate and accumulated knowledge can render their voice highly effective in inducing productive change. To the extent that a universal owner has few viable exit options, its communications with investment managers and corporate management can significantly improve efficiencies and reduce agency costs. In the Hirschman framework, effective communication requires more than the threat of exit from a market transaction. In the financial ecosystem, this means that possibility for effecting value-enhancing change at portfolio companies may be as important as the covariance of expected return on their stocks. In addition, the decline of the state's regulatory power in the face of the largest corporations forces the universal owner to engage in collective action to induce regulatory efforts.

A number of the largest asset owners have been deeply involved in increasing portfolio allocations to sustainable investing strategies and to pressing for change at investee companies. The largest asset owner, the Japanese Government Pension Investment Fund has enshrined the consideration of ESG factors into its investment principles and expects to allocate 10% of its Japanese equity holdings to ESG assets and is a signatory of the PRI (Takeo & Shigeki, 2017). The Norwegian Parliament has legislated a set of guidelines for the sovereign wealth fund. The guidelines require that the fund should not be invested in companies that contribute to violations of fundamental ethical norms, manufacture certain types of weapon, base their operations on coal, or produce tobacco (Council on Ethics for the Government Pension Fund Global, 2017). The New York State Comptroller Thomas DiNapoli has pledged to double the New York State Common Retirement Fund's sustainable investments to $20 billion over the next decade. This would represent approximately 10% of its current assets under management. In addition, DiNapoli will establish a "watch list" of investment managers not focused on the fund's ESG policy (Butera, 2019).

The Universal Owner Strategy at CalPERS

As a result of the 2007–2008 global financial crisis, CalPERS funded status dropped from above 100% to just over 60%. This crisis led to a number of new initiatives to improve the funded status, recognize systemic risks, and develop strategies to reduce them. The focus was on both portfolio-level and system-wide efforts.

The fund adopted a set of ten investment beliefs in 2013 which articulated the basis upon which to construct its approach to asset allocation, including a liability-driven asset structure, a long investment horizon, congruency with wider stakeholder views, and a multifaceted view of risk.

Portfolio Efforts: The fund reduced its expected annual future returns to 7%, increasing the expected current contributions from members. This, along with the California Governor's revision to pension benefits implies that there is an expectation that in 30 years, the plan will be fully funded, assuming that the 7% target return is met.

The fund has increased its allocation to private equity and is developing a best practices reporting framework for private equity fees earned by general partners (GPs), through its membership in the trade association Institutional Limited Partners Association (ILPA). The ILPA Transparency Initiative, launched in 2015 is an effort to address shared reporting and compliance challenges by establishing common standards for fee and expense reporting as well as compliance disclosures among investors and fund managers. The initiative highlighted the expenses, differing time horizons, and opacity of many standard practices in the private equity management industry. CalPERS is exploring the establishment of new vehicles, using examples used by other asset owners doing the same in Canada and Australia. The goal is to achieve alignment of interest through the restructuring of fees, extending time horizons and requiring that managers incorporate and report on CalPERS Principles. This restructuring is expected to allow CalPERS to gain scalable exposure to the private equity asset class with improved insight and accountability.

Systemic Efforts: CalPERS has a long history of engaging in collective action on behalf of the citizen investor (see Chap. 2 for Climate Action 100+ and Chap. 8 for the Human Capital Management Coalition, two such initiatives that CalPERS supported). The plan has routinely established new organizations to represent investors, engaging with policy makers on financial market regulation, working with international bodies such as the World Bank and OECD to develop international standards that could be rolling out in emerging markets, and constructed a total fund sustainable investment strategy.

Concluding Remarks

The CalPERS example illustrates a particular way in which sustainable asset allocation can move beyond mean-variance optimization and asset allocation using a limited set of quantitatively measurable risks. It is clear that selecting securities to invest in is a tiny portion of the asset owner's work. Modern portfolio theory has facilitated essential aspects of this work, most notably in articulating a clear framework for performance attribution and for counseling against active investment management in the context of near efficient markets. It has also provided an important method for determining the optimal way to delegated investment management. Other aspects of MPT, particularly its very limited portrayal of the nature of risk and the tendency to forget the interdependence of portfolio choice and systemic outcomes, have been rather unhelpful.

Investors are beginning to explore new forms of allocation and contracting in order to ensure the alignment of interest between their long-term goals and the shorter horizon self-interest of financial intermediaries. Such measures range from establishing contracts that allow asset owners to retain control over proxy votes cast by public equity managers, to the establishment of bespoke investment vehicles in private markets to bringing alignment on horizon, fees and values with the asset owner. Investor networks such as PRI and the International Corporate Governance Network have developed guides for their members that establish model contracts between asset owners and investment managers in a bid to align interest, without which sustainability can only be realized intermittently and to the extent that market opportunity drives decisions. These initiatives underline the need for asset owners to collectively exercise voice, which Hirschman showed to be far more effective than exit in repeated interactions. In the next chapter, we address the even more difficult challenge of maintaining feedback loops when investment decisions are far more decentralized.

Notes

1. See Chapter 1 of Davis, Lukomnik, and Pitt-Watson (2006) for an account of the transition between 1970 and 2004 from primary ownership of the world's largest corporations by wealthy individuals to the dominance of institutionalized investment vehicles that pool the savings of the citizen investor.
2. In a famous articulation of this view, Milton Friedman argues that a theory that assumes that leaves consciously change their placement and orientation on a tree to maximize exposure to sunlight might be a good theory if its

implications fit empirical reality, even though few would agree to ascribe consciousness to leaves (Friedman, 1953). Friedman's methodological positivism has been criticized by other economists (Caldwell, 1982). See also Wilson (2012) and Gould and Lewontin (2006).

3. For an example of performance attribution in this vein, see Perold (2004).
4. Szegö notes that the Markowitz model is applicable only to the case of elliptic distributions, like normal or t-distributions with finite variances, but not to symmetric distributions with fat tails or to asymmetric distributions.
5. And either underweighting, eschewing, or shorting large-capitalization stocks.

References

Ahmed, J., Barber, B. M., & Odean, T. (2018). Made Poorer by Choice: Worker Outcomes in Social Security Vs. Private Retirement Accounts. *Journal of Banking & Finance*, *92*, 311–322. https://doi.org/10.1016/j.jbankfin.2016.08.003

Ambachtsheer, J., Fuller, R., & Hindocha, D. (2013). Behaving Like An Owner: Plugging Investment Chain Leakages. *Rotman International Journal of Pension Management*, *6*(2), 18–27. https://doi.org/10.3138/ripjm.6.2.18

Ang, A., Brandt, M. W., & Denison, D. F. (2014). *Review of the Active Management of the Norwegian Government Pension Fund Global*. Retrieved from https://www0.gsb.columbia.edu/faculty/aang/papers/AngBrandtDenison.pdf

Ang, A., Goetzmann, W. N., & Schaefer, S. M. (2009). *Evaluation of Active Management of the Norwegian Government Pension Fund – Global*. Retrieved from https://www0.gsb.columbia.edu/faculty/aang/papers/report%20Norway.pdf

Ang, A., Goetzmann, W. N., & Schaefer, S. M. (2011). *The Efficient Market Theory and Evidence: Implications for Active Investment Management*. Boston, MA: Now.

Anson, M. (2008). The Beta Continuum: From Classic Beta to Bulk Beta. *Journal of Portfolio Management*, *34*(2), 53–64. http://www.iijournals.com/loi/jpm

Asl, F. M., & Etula, E. (2012). Advancing Strategic Asset Allocation in a Multi-Factor World. *Journal of Portfolio Management*, *39*(1), 59–66. http://www.iijournals.com/loi/jpm

Ayres, I. A. N., & Curtis, Q. (2015). Beyond Diversification: The Pervasive Problem of Excessive Fees and "Dominated Funds" in 401(K) Plans. *The Yale Law Journal*, *124*(5), 1476–1552.

Bailey, W., Kumar, A., & Ng, D. (2011). Behavioral Biases of Mutual Fund Investors. *Journal of Financial Economics*, *102*(1), 1–27. https://doi.org/10.1016/j.jfineco.2011.05.002

Bogle, J. C. (2016). Putting Investors First: Guest Editorial. *Journal of Portfolio Management, 42*(2), 9–13. http://www.iijournals.com/loi/jpm

Brealey, R. A. (1990). Portfolio Theory Versus Portfolio Practice. *Journal of Portfolio Management, 16*(4), 6–10. http://www.iijournals.com/loi/jpm

Brinson, G. P., Hood, L. R., & Beebower, G. L. (1986). Determinants of Portfolio Performance. *Financial Analysts Journal, 42*, 39–44. https://doi.org/10.2469/faj.v42.n4.39

Butera, C. (2019, June 10). *New York Comptroller Aims to Double Pension Plan's ESG Funding.* Chief Investment Officer. Retrieved from https://www.ai-cio.com/news/new-york-comptroller-aims-doublepension-plans-esg-funding/

Caldwell, B. J. (1982). *Beyond Positivism: Economic Methodology in the Twentieth Century.* Boston, MA: Allen & Unwin.

Callan Institute. (2019). *Defined Contribution Trends.* Retrieved from https://www.callan.com/wp-content/uploads/2019/04/Callan-DC-Trends-Survey-2019.pdf

Chalmers, J., Kaul, A., & Phillips, B. (2013). The Wisdom of Crowds: Mutual Fund Investors' Aggregate Asset Allocation Decisions. *Journal of Banking and Finance, 37*(9), 3318–3333. http://www.sciencedirect.com/science/journal/03784266

Charkham, J., & Simpson, A. (1999). *Fair Shares: The Future of Shareholder Power and Responsibility.* New York, NY: Oxford University Press.

Christian, L. (2011). *A New Foundation for Portfolio Management.* Retrieved from https://rsfsocialfinance.org/wp-content/uploads/downloads/2011/10/A-New-Foundation-for-Portfolio-Management.pdf

Connor, G. (1995). The Three Types of Factor Models: A Comparison of Their Explanatory Power. *Financial Analysts Journal, 51*(3), 42. https://doi.org/10.2469/faj.v51.n3.1904

Cooper, M. J., Gulen, H., & Rau, P. R. (2005). Changing Names with Style: Mutual Fund Name Changes and Their Effects on Fund Flows. *Journal of Finance, 60*(6), 2825–2858. https://doi.org/10.1111/j.1540-6261.2005.00818.x

Council on Ethics for the Government Pension Fund Global. (2017). *Guidelines for Observation and Exclusion of Companies from the Government Pension Fund Global.* Retrieved from https://etikkradet.no/files/2017/04/Etikkraadet_Guidelines-_eng_2017_web.pdf

Davis, S., Lukomnik, J., & Pitt-Watson, D. (2006). *The New Capitalists: How Citizen Investors Are Reshaping the Corporate Agenda.* Boston, MA: Harvard Business School Press.

Davis, S., Lukomnik, J., & Pitt-Watson, D. (2016). *What They Do with Your Money: How the Financial System Fails Us and How to Fix It.* New Haven, CT: Yale University Press.

Dyck, A., Lins, K. V., Roth, L., & Wagner, H. F. (2019). Do Institutional Investors Drive Corporate Social Responsibility? International Evidence. *Journal of Financial Economics, 131*(3), 693–714. https://doi.org/10.1016/j.jfineco.2018.08.013

Fabozzi, F. J., Gupta, F., & Markowitz, H. M. (2002). The Legacy of Modern Portfolio Theory. *Journal of Investing, 11*(3), 7. https://doi.org/10.3905/joi.2002.319510

Fisher, L. (1975). Using Modern Portfolio Theory to Maintain an Efficiently Diversified Portfolio. *Financial Analysts Journal, 31*(3), 73–85. https://doi.org/10.2469/faj.v31.n3.73

Friedman, M. (1953). The Methodology of Positive Economics. In M. Friedman (Ed.), *Essays in Positive Economics* (pp. 3–43). Chicago, IL: University of Chicago Press.

Gould, S. J., & Lewontin, R. C. (2006). The Spandrels of San Marco and the Panglossian Paradigm: A Critique of the Adaptationist Programme. In E. Sober (Ed.), *Conceptual Issues in Evolutionary Biology*. Cambridge, MA: MIT Press.

Grossman, S. J., & Stiglitz, J. E. (1976). Information and Competitive Price Systems. *American Economic Review, 66*(2), 246–253. http://www.aeaweb.org/aer/

Hawley, J., & Lukomnik, J. (2018). The Long and Short of It: Are We Asking the Right Questions? Modern Portfolio Theory and Time Horizons. *Seattle University Law Review, 41*(2), 449–474.

Hawley, J. P., & Williams, A. T. (2000). *The Rise of Fiduciary Capitalism: How Institutional Investors Can Make Corporate America more Democratic.* Philadelphia, PA: University of Pennsylvania Press.

Hirschman, A. O. (1970). *Exit, Voice, and Loyalty: Responses to Decline in Firms, Organizations, and States.* Cambridge, MA: Harvard University Press.

Hodgson, G. M. (2011). The Eclipse of the Uncertainty Concept in Mainstream Economics. *Journal of Economic Issues, 45*(1), 159–175. http://www.tandfonline.com/loi/mjei20

Jovanovic, F., & Le Gall, P. (2001). Does God Practice a Random Walk? The 'Financial Physics' of a Nineteenth-Century Forerunner, Jules Regnault. *European Journal of the History of Economic Thought, 8*(3), 332–362. http://www.tandfonline.com/loi/rejh20

Keynes, J. M. (1921). *A Treatise on Probability*. London, UK: Macmillan & Co.

Keynes, J. M. (1937). General Theory of Employment. *Reply to Symposium, 51*, 209–223.

Kilroy, M. (2017, December 21). Wells Fargo Forms Stakeholder Advisory Council, Names CalSTRS' Anne Sheehan to Group. *Pensions & Investments*. Retrieved from https://www.pionline.com/article/20171221/ONLINE/171229968/wells-fargo-forms-stakeholder-advisory-council-names-calstrs-anne-sheehan-to-group

Knight, F. (1921). *Risk, Uncertainty and Profit*. Chicago, IL: University of Chicago Press.

Koedijk, K. G., Slager, A. M. H., & Stork, P. A. (2016). Investing in Systematic Factor Premiums. *European Financial Management, 22*(2), 193–234. http://onlinelibrary.wiley.com/journal/10.1111/%28ISSN%291468-036X/issues

Lintner, J. (1969). The Valuation of Risk Assets and the Selection of Risky Investments in Stock Portfolios and Capital Budgets: A Reply. *Review of Economics and Statistics, 51*(2), 222–224. http://www.mitpressjournals.org/loi/rest

Lucas, R. E. (1976). Econometric Policy Evaluation: A Critique. *Carnegie-Rochester Conference Series on Public Policy, 1*, 19–46. https://doi.org/10.1016/S0167-2231(76)80003-6

Lucas, R. E. (1977). Understanding Business Cycles. *Carnegie-Rochester Conference Series on Public Policy, 5*, 7–29.

Lydenberg, S. (2016). Integrating Systemic Risk into Modern Portfolio Theory and Practice. *Journal of Applied Corporate Finance, 28*(2), 56–61. https://doi.org/10.1111/jacf.12175

Markowitz, H. (1952). Portfolio Selection. *Journal of Finance, 7*(1), 77–91. https://doi.org/10.2307/2975974

Munnell, A. H., Aubry, J.-P., & Crawford, C. (2015). *Investment Returns: Defined Benefit vs. Defined Contribution Plans.* Retrieved from https://crr.bc.edu/wp-content/uploads/2015/12/IB_15-211.pdf

Perold, A. F. (2004). The Capital Asset Pricing Model. *Journal of Economic Perspectives, 18*(3), 3–24. http://www.aeaweb.org/jep/

Polanyi, K. (1944). *The Great Transformation.* New York, NY: Farrar & Rinehart.

Rosenberg, B. (1981). The Capital Asset Pricing Model and the Market Model. *Journal of Portfolio Management, 7*(2), 5–16. https://doi.org/10.3905/jpm.1981.408793

Ross, S. A. (1976). The Arbitrage Theory of Capital Asset Pricing. *Journal of Economic Theory, 13*(3), 341–360. http://www.sciencedirect.com/science/journal/00220531

Roy, A. D. (1952). Safety First and the Holding of Assets. *Econometrica, 20*, 431–449.

Rubinstein, M. (2002). Markowitz's "Portfolio Selection": A Fifty-Year Retrospective. *Journal of Finance, 57*(3), 1041–1045. https://doi.org/10.1111/1540-6261.00453

Sharpe, W. F. (1963). A Simplified Model for Portfolio Analysis. *Management Science, 9*(2), 277–293. https://doi.org/10.1287/mnsc.9.2.277

Sharpe, W. F. (1964). Capital Asset Prices; a Theory of Market Equilibrium under Conditions of Risk. *Journal of Finance, 19*, 425–442.

Sialm, C., Starks, L., & Zhang, H. (2015). Defined Contribution Pension Plans: Mutual Fund Asset Allocation Changes. *American Economic Review, 105*(5), 432–436. http://www.aeaweb.org/aer/

Swensen, D. F. (2000). *Pioneering Portfolio Management: An Unconventional Approach to Institutional Investment.* New York, NY: Free Press.

Szegö, G. (2002). Measures of Risk. *Journal of Banking & Finance, 26*(7), 1253–1272. https://doi.org/10.1016/S0378-4266(02)00262-5

Takeo, Y., & Shigeki, N. (2017). *Biggest Pension Fund Craves More After Foray into ESG Assets.* New York, NY: Bloomberg.

Thompson, J. (2019, January 13). Larry Fink Urged to Make BlackRock Tougher on Climate Change. *Financial Times.*

Volpato, K., & Scheerlinck, E. (2015). AIST Superannuation Governance: Paper Examining International and Australian Governance Trends. *Journal of Business Systems, Governance & Ethics, 10*(3), 75–96.

Willis Towers Watson. (2017). *The Asset Owner of Tomorrow: Business Model Changes for the Great Acceleration.* Retrieved from London: https://www.thinkingaheadinstitute.org/-/media/Pdf/TAI/Research-Ideas/theasset-owner-of-tomorrow.pdf

Willis Towers Watson. (2018). *The Thinking Ahead Institute's Asset Owner 100: The Most Influential Capital on the Planet.* Retrieved from London: https://www.thinkingaheadinstitute.org/en/Library/Public/Research-and-Ideas/2018/10/AO_100_2018_research_paper

Wilford, D. S. (2012). True Markowitz or Assumptions We Break and Why It Matters. *Review of Financial Economics, 21*(3), 93–101. https://doi.org/10.1016/j.rfe.2012.06.003

Wilson, D. S. (2012). A Tale of Two Classics. *New Scientist Archive, 213*(2857), 30–31. https://doi.org/10.1016/S0262-4079(12)60754-4

CHAPTER 11

Impact Investing

After the global financial crisis in 2007–2008, the pursuit of financial profit alone is viewed by many as unsustainable and detrimental to long-term societal interest. In Chap. 1, we outlined four underlying drivers of sustainable finance: the advent of the citizen investor and the intergenerational transfer of investment decision-making power, the relative impotence of jurisdictionally constrained regulatory agencies in the face of globalized corporate power, widespread concern with planetary boundaries, and the search for an ethical grounding and a socially beneficial purpose for financial activity. Together, these drivers militate toward a role for investing activity that marries financial objectives with environmental and social goals.

In Chap. 4, we outlined the decision-theoretic logic of expanding the set of performance metrics beyond financial return in the context of the principal-agent problem. Chapters 5, 6, 7, 8 and 9 outlined the concurrent financial benefits of advancing a range of non-financial metrics of performance, such as environmental management and harmonious stakeholder relations. Chapter 10 examines the portfolio allocation methods available to an investor concerned with mitigating adverse impacts on social and natural ecosystems while ensuring a sustainable financial return. An earlier book in Palgrave Studies in Impact Finance series provides a book-length academic treatment of the field of impact investing with an in-depth focus on the instruments, mechanisms, and actors in the field (Spiess-Knafl & Scheck, 2017).

© The Author(s) 2019   253
S. Bose et al., *The Financial Ecosystem*, Palgrave Studies in Impact Finance, https://doi.org/10.1007/978-3-030-05624-7_11

The stated aspiration of the impact investing community is to go beyond the mitigation of the adverse impacts of economic activity and to make a virtue of investing in businesses that demonstrably improve society. Understandably, stated in such general terms, the notion of impact investing has broad appeal. There appears to be steady and inexorable growth in Google searches for the term 'impact investing'. The concept of impact investing arises from a recognition that some investing activity might require a non-financial goal as the primary objective, with financial returns acting as a secondary but important objective. This view of the primary goal of investment as social benefit is especially prevalent among younger generations. According to a 2018 survey of over 10,000 millennials from 36 countries, 43% and 39% of respondents, respectively, identified 'generate jobs' and 'improve society' as the top two priorities for businesses, compared to only 25% who view 'profit generation' as the main business purpose (Deloitte, 2018). If these views are maintained as the respondents' age, then perhaps it will be commonplace to expect that investors will shun the single-minded pursuit of financial return and instead embrace a model of blended value creation. Impact investing, which is a novel, but popular label for certain investment strategies, offers promise to be just such a model.

Impact Investing Defined

The Global Impact Investing Network (GIIN) defines impact investments as *"investments made with the intention to generate positive, measurable social and environmental impact alongside a financial return"* (Global Impact Investing Network, 2017). GIIN's definition places primary importance on intention: it assumes that traditional investing activity can deliver social value, but it is the *intention* to generate social and environmental impact that characterizes an 'impact investment'. Of the four core characteristics of impact investing enumerated by GIIN, intentionality is first. The other three core characteristics listed by GIIN are the use of impact data in investment design, the management of impact performance, and contributions to the growth of impact investing (Global Impact Investing Network, 2019a). The OECD, in its definition of social impact investing, also lists investor intent as a key characteristic of impact investing (OECD, 2019).

Understandably, there are debates about the precise boundary of impact investing. GIIN's emphasis on 'intention' results in a somewhat inchoate concept. Intention is not a measurable or objectively verifiable attribute of behavior. The presence or absence of intention cannot be falsified by anyone other than the investor. An investor can claim *ex ante* good intentions, but as the saying goes: the road to hell is paved with them. Conversely, an investor may have unannounced good intentions which may not be discerned by an objective third party. In principle, the focus on 'intention' implies that any investor who believes she invests for beneficial and measurable non-financial impact is an impact investor. For instance, an activist hedge fund manager who invests in a publicly listed company as a self-declared way to exert influence on the company's environmental practices could call himself an impact investor so long as he made efforts to measure his non-financial impact. On the other hand, a profit-seeking investor who had no intention of benefitting society but who nevertheless makes an investment into a company that develops life-saving medicines with obvious social benefits would not be classified as an impact investor, by the GIIN definition. Under the 'intentionality' test, investments from governments on behalf of the common good can theoretically be characterized as investing for impact, but government investments in health, education, or infrastructure are not generally characterized as impact investments in the literature or in databases which claim to catalog impact investments. Despite the value placed on 'intention' by GIIN and some observers of the impact investing community, it cannot be a defining characteristic of the concept. Alternative formulations of the characteristics of impact investing make no mention of intentionality (see below).

In principle, the GIIN definition places social and environmental impact at the same level of importance as financial return. This is perhaps the more salient aspect of the definition. Investing with the acknowledgment that non-financial objectives are at least as important as financial return could be the defining attribute. A pioneering book on impact investing, one of whose authors was central to the coining of the term, states that "impact investing recognizes that investments can pursue financial returns while also intentionally addressing social and environmental challenges" (Bugg-Levine & Emerson, 2011). By this criterion, impact investing is indistinguishable from socially responsible investing (SRI) or faith-based investing which excludes investments with negative social or environmental impact, and is willing to accept a return penalty for such exclusions, if necessary. As we noted in Chap. 10, sustainable asset allocation that includes socially responsible investing, best-in-class environmental, social, and governance (ESG) security selection, active engagement, targeted sector allocations, and principled exclusions are essential components of a strategy that seeks to generate sustainable return on the financial, human, and natural capital that is the legacy of all humanity. Bugg-Levine and Emerson state that for the framers of the term 'impact investing', the terms "socially responsible investing and ethical investing seemed burdened with moral obligation or personal, normative judgement and a history of negative screening that focused on what type of firms to avoid". It is implausible that an objectively defined 'impact investing' should exclude the intentionality that grows out of moral obligation and include other forms of intentionality that presumably stem from amoral obligations, whatever those might be. How could intentionality, which is an interior, unverifiable feeling, be anything other than 'personal, normative judgement'?

The Global Sustainable Investment Alliance (GSIA) defines impact investing in a more pragmatic way:

> Impact Investing: Targeted investments aimed at solving social or environmental problems. Impact investing includes community investing, where capital is specifically directed to traditionally underserved individuals or communities, or financing that is provided to businesses with a clear social or environmental purpose. (Global Sustainable Investment Alliance, 2019)

GSIA's focuses on community-based investing and on investments in enterprises with a clear social or environmental purpose are also common characteristics of impact investments, though they are not listed as one of GIIN's four core characteristics. The Global Steering Group for Impact Investment, a successor group to the Social Impact Investment Taskforce established under the UK's presidency of the G8, also employs a more inclusive definition. It states that "real impact is measurable, ... drives change at scale ... and adds up for everyone" (Global Steering Group for Impact Investment, 2019). As Spiess-Knafl and Scheck point out, "to date, a coherent and undisputed definition of the term 'impact investing' is still missing" (Spiess-Knafl & Scheck, 2017).

Although its boundaries are somewhat blurry, impact investing exists as a separate category, with surveys and databases of specific populations that enumerate the approximate global scale of the activity. GIIN's research team compiled a database of the impact investors from GIIN's surveys and its own membership, supplemented by other impact investing networks worldwide, such as the New Ventures Network, Mission Investors Exchange and the Indian Impact Investors Council. According to GIIN estimates, there are 1340 known impact-investing organizations around the world, and they together manage approximately $502 billion in total assets (Global Impact Investing Network, 2019b). Albeit small compared to the size of the equity market (at least \$70 trillion as of 2016), the impact investing sector is vibrant. It has been growing fast and may experience even faster growth in the future. There are predictions for the sector to reach up to \$1 trillion in managed assets by 2020 (Freireich & Fulton, 2009; O'Donohoe, Leijonhufvud, Saltuk, Bugg-levine, & Brandenburg, 2010). Clearly, the estimate of \$502 billion excludes broader sustainable investing strategies such as ESG integration and screening which together amount to approximately \$30 trillion (Global Sustainable Investment Alliance, 2019).

EVOLUTION OF IMPACT INVESTING

Investing is an ancient concept, which involves putting in time, effort, and capital to an endeavor that can yield a future return. Investing with the intent to achieve non-financial goals such as military or political gain, social harmony, or even world domination has occurred through time immemorial. The notion that a merchant must pursue a responsible and harmonious relationship with nature and society is embedded in Confucian principles dating back to the fifth-century BC (Wang & Juslin, 2009). A disciple of Confucius, Xun Zi (316–237 BC), in explaining one the principles, writes: "So the Dao in which business interest comes first will not work and is not the right Dao, social righteousness has to come before business interest and that is Dao."[1] Our review of the history of the corporate form revealed that societal purpose was inextricably linked to financial return in the advent of the earliest joint-stock companies (Chap. 3). Bugg-Levine and Emerson note that the centrality of community welfare goals in investment activity is discernible among the Quakers in the seventeenth-century England and the later Shaker congregations in Colonial America (Bugg-Levine & Emerson, 2011). Perhaps the activity of investing is somewhat like that of eating, which might be said to involve the ingestion of caloric content while fulfilling other goals, such as satisfying tastes, discovering new flavors and recipes, making friends, reducing environmental impact, and a myriad other goals. The notion that investing has the only or even the primary purpose of securing financial return may be too narrow a definition, just as the statement that eating is primarily ingesting calories would be a woefully incomplete description.

Development Finance for the Private Sector: A Progenitor of Impact Investing

Modern forms of investment for social impact began with the establishment of development finance institutions such as the Commonwealth Development Corporation (CDC) in the United Kingdom in 1948 and the World Bank's International Finance Corporation (IFC) in 1956 (O'Donohoe et al., 2010). Funded by national governments and donations, CDC and IFC invest in developing countries by supplying anchor funding to impact projects which if successful would attract subsequent private capital in order to further scale. This type of initial public investment seeks to provide a positive informational spillover that only a first mover that is willing to substitute some financial reward for social benefit can generate.[2]

For example, the IFC, along with a number of private and public partners, funded the Lighting Africa project which develops and promotes off-grid solar lighting products (Lighting Africa, 2019). The project started with pilots in Kenya and Ghana in 2009 and provided affordable lighting to more than 32 million people in Africa, where 600 million people are not connected to the electricity grid and who are mostly relying on kerosene lamps and candles for lighting (Lighting Africa, 2019). Kerosene lights are of low quality and can cause health and environmental hazards. The Lighting Africa project provides solar products to consumers through microloans from microfinance institutions and crowd-sourcing platforms. At the same time, there are obvious social and environmental benefits with affordable access to electricity and the use of cleaner energy. The demonstrated success of the Lighting Africa project (Castalia Strategic Advisors, 2014) perhaps provided an impetus to subsequent private ventures focused on pay-as-you-go financing for off-grid lighting and appliances in East Africa such as M-KOPA, Off-Grid Electric, Azuri Technologies, and Mobisol.

We outline how the term impact investing evolved from the blending of social and environmental objectives along with financial returns. As shown in Table 11.1, impact investment is placed in the middle of an investment spectrum that spans the two extremes of philanthropy and traditional investments.[3] Philanthropic organizations primarily distribute grants and seek to maximize social impact without any regard to financial

Table 11.1 Investment spectrum

Social value →			Blended	← Financial value		
Philanthropy	Social investment	Program-related investment	**Impact investment**	ESG investment	Socially responsible investment	Traditional investment
Pure philanthropic grant-making without expectation of financial return	Investment that generates social impact as well as some financial return	Investment that generates social impact and expects at least a return of the principal	**Investment in companies whose primary goal is to deliver social and environmental benefits, whilst also delivering a competitive financial return**	Investment in companies that track environmental, social, and governance performance metrics	Investment that excludes socially and environmental questionable companies	Investment that aims to maximize financial returns only

Source: Adapted from the Advantage Ventures Analysis (2011) and the European Venture Philanthropy Association (EVPA, 2016). https://evpa.eu.com/about-us/what-is-venture-philanthropy

return, while traditional investments pursue maximum profit irrespective of impact. These two opposite approaches persist as separate categories of economic activity.

In the 1960s and 1970s, the middle of the spectrum started to emerge. Driven by concerns regarding the Vietnam War, some traditional investors started to seek social value alignment by avoiding investments in socially and environmentally problematic companies, such as tobacco companies, alcohol companies, weapons manufacturers, companies that employ child labor, and companies from 'rogue nations'. While still profit-driven, these investments that screen for negative social and environmental impacts were later termed socially responsible investments (SRIs). Vietnam War protestors also demanded that university endowments divest themselves of defense contractors, and the investment trend encouraged greater corporate social responsibility (CSR).[4] Later, sustainable (or ESG) investing evolved from socially responsible investing (see Chap. 4).

Concurrently, philanthropic organizations such as the Ford and Rockefeller Foundations considered options to make their grant-making more impactful and last longer. They pioneered social investment in the form of low-interest loans as alternatives to the dispensing of grants, for example, to finance affordable housing projects. While still aiming for social impact, the repaid loans and accrued interest also replenished the funding pool and allowed the foundations to be more sustainable. Almost 50 years ago, the Ford

Foundation pioneered the first program-related investments (PRIs). A PRI is intended to have beneficial social impact, but incorporate an expectation of the return of principal, at a minimum. PRIs are typically strategies employed by charitable foundations in the United States where the Internal Revenue Code requires that foundations disburse a minimum of 5% of their funds each year. Under the Code, PRIs are treated as grants and as such can be counted toward the foundations' mandatory giving requirement even though there is an expectation that the funds will eventually be returned.

The concept of impact investing appeared in the 2000s, out of the confluence of development finance, program-related investing and social enterprise (discussed in Chap. 15), and sustainable investing (Trelstad, 2016). The term 'impact investing' was coined in 2007, when the Rockefeller Foundation held a meeting of selected investors at its Bellagio Center in Italy to discuss the ways in which social and environmental performance of an investment can be better combined with its financial return (Jackson, 2012). The participants were the early investors who were already involved in community development finance, microfinance institutions, and investments in green technology. While investing for blended value is not a new concept, there was a shared view among the participants that the existing resources were insufficient to addressing persistent poverty, social inequality, and environmental degradation. In the face of declining overseas aid and domestic social spending from developed countries, private capital had to be mobilized in order to scale businesses that create social and environmental benefits (Freireich & Fulton, 2009).

Concessionary Versus Non-concessionary Impact Investment

It is clear from how impact investing evolved that it had two antecedents: one from philanthropy and the other from responsible investment, which meet in the middle. What follows is then two types of impact investment: one that sacrifices some financial return for greater impact and another that aims to produce social impact whilst also delivering a minimum market return. The philanthropy origins of social enterprise and PRI pioneered by foundations are concessionary investments in that the investors are willing to take below-market financial returns for social gains, while the traditional investment root with SRI and ESG investments would demand at least a market rate of return. The majority of investors are oriented toward financial returns and view impact and financial returns as trade-offs. A 2018 GIIN survey of 229 impact investors with a combined investment of $33.5 billion in 2017 reported that 64% of the surveyed investors expect a market rate of return on their investments, 20% expect below but close to market return, and 16% expect below-market return and mainly capital preservation. Over 90% of the investors also reported that they either met or outperformed their expectations (Global Impact Investing Network, 2018).

The Impact Investing Ecosystem

Ever since the term 'impact investing' was disseminated to a broader audience after the Rockefeller Foundation meeting in Italy, numerous stakeholders adopted the term, which is also used interchangeably with social impact investing and social finance. The stakeholders can be divided into four categories: asset owners (e.g. high-net-worth individuals [HNWI]) who own capital, asset managers (e.g. fund managers) who deploy capital, service providers (e.g. banks, consulting companies, and standard-setting organizations), and perhaps most importantly users of capital (e.g. small businesses) (Jackson, 2013b). Figure 11.1 illustrates the impact-investing ecosystem and how various stakeholders interact with each other.

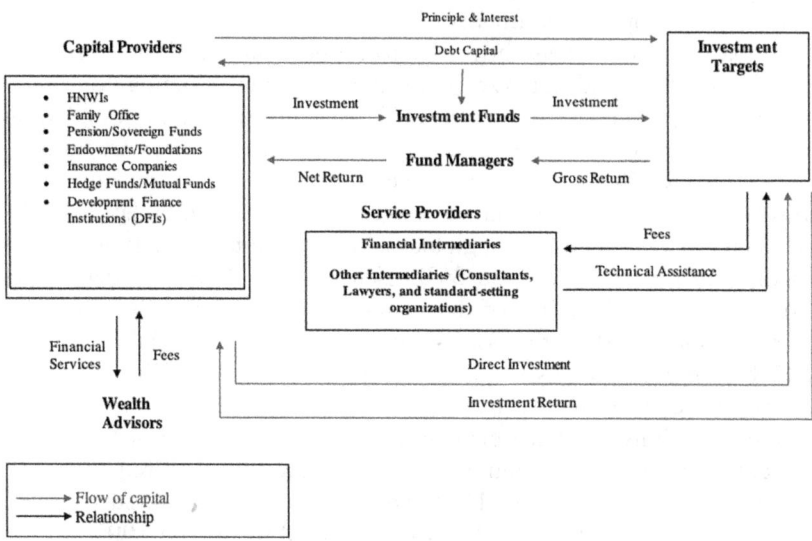

Fig. 11.1 The impact investment ecosystem. (Source: Adapted from World Economic Forum Investors Industries and Deloitte Touche Tohmatsu (2013))

Asset Owners and Impact Investment Funds

Among the many providers of impact capital, the major ones are high-net-worth individuals (HNWI), family offices, and foundations. Similar to venture capital investors (see Chap. 14), impact investors (at least the non-concessionary ones) are expected to have a higher risk tolerance appropriate for investing in small- and early-stage enterprises. Such investments are more suitable for rich individuals and family offices, who answer to fewer stakeholders and are more flexible in exercising investment discretion. Mainstream institutional investors such as pension funds and insurance companies may be repelled by the small deal size, the high cost of due diligence per dollar of investment, and the subjectively valued social impacts of these investments. As a consequence of their fiduciary duty to beneficiaries, institutional investors may find it difficult to venture beyond non-concessionary investments that sacrifice financial return for social and environmental gain.

HNWI and family offices have been the leading capital providers to impact funds. Generational loss of wealth is a major concern for high-networth individuals and their families, and impact investment is seen as a way to increase family cohesion and legacy and is particularly popular with younger family members. It is estimated that one in five family offices own some type of impact investments.[5]

Impact investing is also attractive to foundations which may prefer to fund new ideas and catalyze innovation without assuming long-term financial responsibility. In this sense, impact investment by foundations could be a process similar to venture capitalists investing in start-up businesses (Berry, 2016), sometimes referred to as 'venture philanthropy'. Instead of offering grants, foundations can operate as a 'foundation bank', which make investments through loans, loan guarantees, equity, and fixed-income instruments (Salamon & Burckart, 2014). Most foundations do not spend more than 10% of their endowments on impact investments. For example, in 2017, the Ford Foundation committed $1 billion of its $12 billion endowments to mission-related investments. This is because many impact investments are classified as mission-related (serving the foundation's mission while generating market return) and hence cannot be counted toward the foundation's mandatory giving requirements, unlike concessionary PRIs. There are notable exceptions, such as the F.B. Heron Foundation, which decided in 2012 to commit 100% of their assets to impact investments (Heron, 2018). The Nathan Cummings

Foundation made the same announcement earlier in 2018 to also commit all of their assets which total close to $0.5 billion to investments that help reduce social inequality and mitigate climate change (The Nathan Cummings Foundation, 2018). TONIIC, which is a network of investors focused on deepening their commitment to impact investing, publishes a survey of investors who have chosen to commit 100% of their portfolios to impact assets (TONIIC, 2018).

Although development finance institutions are not significant impact investors in scale of assets invested, they are an essential player in catalyzing innovations (see earlier box on development finance). For example, the World Bank and the International Finance Facility for Immunization developed a vaccine bond, which use the proceeds of a bond issuance to retail investors to provide developing countries with immediate funds for vaccine deployment, with funds being repaid when aid donors deliver on their pledges of future support (Jack, 2008). Development finance institutions usually prefer to provide anchor funding that can be catalytic. For example, the Inter-American Development Bank invested in New Ventures Mexico, which in turn consults with small and medium-sized enterprises (SMEs) whose goal is to generate positive social and environmental outcomes in their local communities. The African Development Bank contributed $100 million in anchor funding to Credit Suisse's $500 million Agvance Africa Fund that invests in the agribusiness in Africa (African Development Bank Group, 2012).

Sovereign wealth funds manage significant assets and generally focus on national development goals. Although many do incorporate ESG criteria, most of their investments are not driven by impact. There are rare examples, such as the sovereign funds of Abu Dhabi and Malaysia for whom alleviating social problems is a stated goal. However, one may argue that by intentionally focusing on national development capacity, sovereign wealth funds can be viewed as impact investors in a broader sense.[6]

University endowments are not significant impact investors. However, given the pressure from students and alumni pushing for sustainable investment and divestment from a range of investments, some universities with large endowments are increasingly concerned with socially responsible investing.

While PGGM, Zurich Insurance, Prudential, and Nuveen are institutional investors in affordable housing, microfinance, and community banks, the contribution to impact investing from mainstream investors such as pension funds, insurance companies, and other liability-constrained investors remains limited. Given their fiduciary responsibility, mainstream investors are more likely to invest in impact funds which can generate market or above market returns.

Most of the major impact investors are based in Europe and the United States. Although the majority of assets are deployed in the developing countries, a full 81% of investors are headquartered in the United States, Canada, Western Europe, and Oceania (Global Impact Investing Network, 2018). This difference in location between the majority of investors and investees implies a significant gap in knowledge, outlook, language, social traditions, and cultural perspective between the two most important stakeholders in the impact-investing ecosystem. One explanation for the lack of investors from developing countries is regulatory constraint. For example, in China, foundations set up as non-profit organizations are prohibited from investing in for-profit businesses. Despite the rise in the number of billionaires from emerging markets, developing country high-net-worth investors have been slow to adopt this relatively new investment concept. In a survey conducted by the Asian Development Bank (2011), investors identified lack of information regarding impact on investment opportunities, lack of access, and lack of diversity in financial instruments as obstacles to increased volume in impact investing.

Service Providers

Aside from asset providers and fund managers, other entities are involved in the impact-investing ecosystem. Large banks and financial institutions are building up teams to either develop new investment products or research ways to incorporate investing with impact, investee enterprises are working on innovative approaches to collect operational and impact data in order to accurately measure social returns, and academia is beginning to conduct more rigorous evaluations of social benefits derived from impact investments (Dichter, Adams, & Ebrahim, 2016).

There are additional intermediaries, such as consulting firms, lawyers, and standard-setting organizations which are working with foundations, fund managers, and individual investors to facilitate their visions in impact investing. They are also building platforms, developing action plans, and designing evaluation tools to encourage and guide new entrants. International forums and inter-governmental organizations, such as the World Economic Forum and the UN's Sustainable Development Goals (SDGs) are also helping to raise public awareness and the profile of impact investing.

Lastly, partnerships combining the strengths of government, philanthropy, and corporations may have the potential to yield the most social benefit (Buffett & Eimicke, 2018). Governments around the world are working with private investors in developing innovative financial instruments and exploring investment vehicles that can achieve social impact neither can achieve alone. Of course, the role of government in allocating capital for impact goes beyond just public and private partnership. As we previously pointed out, one can argue that most investments by governments qualify as impact investing under the intentionality definition.

Investee Companies

According to GIIN's latest impact investor survey, the majority of investors (54%) focus on both environmental and social impact, 40% focus exclusively on social impact, and only 6% target environmental impact alone (Global Impact Investing Network, 2018). The United States and Canada receive the most investments as a single region, followed by Latin America and the Caribbean, and sub-Saharan Africa. Approximately 54% of the assets under management by impact investors were deployed in developing countries.

As shown in Fig. 11.2, the sectors receiving the highest levels of funding were food and agriculture, microfinance and other financial services,

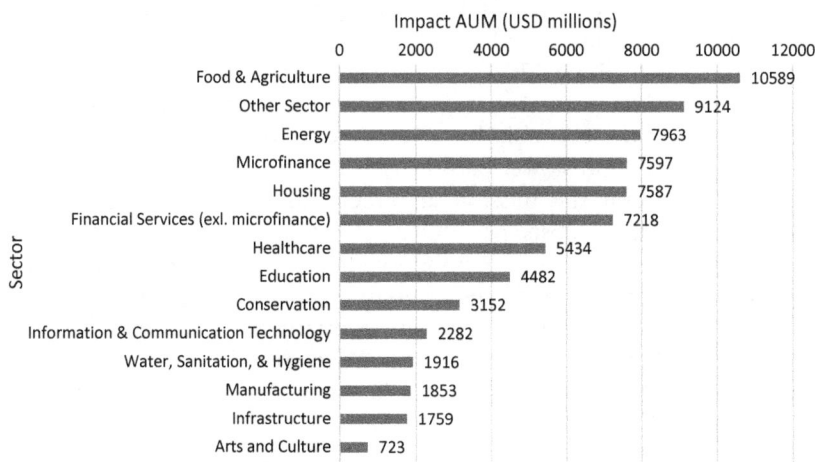

Fig. 11.2 Impact asset allocation by sector. (Source: Adapted from the GIIN Annual Impact Investor Survey (2018))

housing, and energy. Developed countries receive more funding in the housing and the energy sectors. In developing countries, a significant population are still facing food shortages and remain underserved by large banks, so they receive more impact funding in the agriculture and food sector, followed by microfinance. Impact investing in emerging markets began with microfinance institutions providing small loans to women and farmers, to whom it is very difficult to obtain credit from traditional banks. Large commercial banks typically do not serve rural areas and require collateral which cash-poor farmers find difficult to provide. More recently, impact funds have begun to invest in the agribusiness and fair-trade sectors to help improve the livelihoods of farmers in poorer countries.

INVESTMENT INSTRUMENTS

Impact investing is an investing approach across all asset classes, including cash and cash equivalents, fixed income, real estate, infrastructure, public equity, and investment funds (Emerson & Smalling, 2015). For instance, there are certificates of deposit, savings accounts, and money market accounts offered by community banks that only lend to organizations targeting social and environmental outcomes. While the majority of instruments utilized in impact investing are similar to those employed in traditional investing, the particular challenges of impact enterprises and the aspiration to embed impact management into the investing process calls for new kinds of financial instruments. For example, Armeni and Ferreyra de Bone (2017) note that relative to traditional investments in early-stage enterprises, impact investors face the challenges of higher perceived credit risk, lower expected returns, longer investment horizons, riskier and slower path to viable scale, limited exit opportunities that maintain the mission alignment of impact enterprises, and higher transactions costs per dollar of invested capital. Armeni and Ferreyra de Bone describe a number of alternative transaction structures in debt, equity, closed-end funds, and grant-making employed in impact investments in Latin America. GIIN maintains a repository of reports and articles that discuss existing and new financing structures used by impact investors to invest in early-stage companies focused on social and environmental impact.[7]

Fixed Income: Green Bonds, Social Impact Bonds, and Revenue-Based Loans

Impact investments that can result in steady cash flows can include the issuance of long and short-term bonds by governments and corporations with proceeds going into projects and businesses that benefit the environment and society. For example, with a three-year maturity and an interest rate tied to the U.S. treasury rates, the International Finance Corporation (IFC) issued a green bond to finance projects that help lower emissions in developing countries. Green bonds are discussed in greater detail in Chap. 14.

There are also non-traditional bond structures, such as the *social impact bond*. Social impact bonds have a number of names: pay for performance bonds, success bonds, or social benefit bonds. Despite being labeled a bond, a social impact bond is not a fixed-income instrument, as its return is contingent on delivering social outcomes. Social impact bonds are designed primarily for private investors, and allow them to fund a social intervention which, if successful, triggers a financial payment from the government funded through cost savings induced by the success. However, if the intervention turns out to be unsuccessful, investors would lose their principal and periodic return. When the provision of social programs is costly and risky in delivering desired outcomes, governments are in principle able to design a social impact bond which transfers the risks associated with an experimental implementation to private investors, and only have to commit financial resources in paying the investors if the project becomes successful.

Traditionally, these bonds are intended for social outcomes such as education and reducing recidivism, and are aimed to leverage private capital with dwindling government budgets and philanthropic contributions. A fairly recent phenomenon, the first social impact bond was designed to fund a rehabilitation program for prisoners in the United Kingdom in 2010 and raised £5 million (Disley, Rubin, Scraggs, Burrowes, & Culley, 2011). The program worked with 2000 prisoners who had short-term sentences and provided them with mental health, housing, and employment support for a 12-month period and reduced recidivism by 9%, higher than the target of 7.5% (Anders & Dorsett, 2017). As a result, the investors were paid a 3% annual return on top of their principal out of the savings from reduced incarceration rates. Since 2010, the 32 social impact bonds have been issued in the UK, with 10 in the United States and 19 in 14 other countries, with a total market value of $514 million (Floyd, 2017).

In recent years, social impact bonds have been adopted in Australia, Canada, the United Kingdom, and the United States. However, the complexity of the bonds' structure can make evaluation and formulation controversial (Jackson, 2013b). We discuss environmental impact bonds—a variant of social impact bond for financing conservation in Chap. 13.

Examples of *revenue-based loans* are described by Armeni and Ferreyra de Bone (2017). These loan instruments require the investee enterprise to make periodic payments which are indexed to revenue, cash flow, or other financial indicators until a fixed multiple of the original investment has been repaid. These instruments often incorporate flexible payment schedules, including significant initial periods when no periodic payments are due as well as relatively long grace periods. They eschew a fixed maturity, allowing repayment until the predetermined multiple is returned. The *demand dividend* structure (Santa Clara University, 2013) limits payment to a proportion of free cash flow (25–50%) so that enough cash flow remains in the enterprise for reinvestment. Demand dividend loans facilitate seasonal variation in repayments, which are a critical innovation in agricultural enterprises. In the context of agricultural microloans in Bangladesh, a randomized control trial (RCT) demonstrated that seasonality-aware repayment schedules perform just as well as standard repayment schedules in maintaining borrower discipline and low default rates (Shonchoy, 2014).

Real Asset Investments

As explained further in Chap. 14, the financing of real assets is far easier than the financing of expenses incurred by early-stage enterprises. Real asset financing in the impact-investing context nevertheless requires a focus on achieving market rate returns while ensuring impact in challenging cash flow situations that depend significantly on policy initiatives. A number of municipal bond funds in the United States target investments in real assets that constitute local public goods, including affordable housing, green infrastructure, waste management, and sustainable transportation. Real estate impact investments in developed countries are dominated by affordable housing projects, encouraged for example in the United States by the Low-Income Housing Tax Credit which has an annual budget to issue tax credits to new construction and rehabilitation of rental houses targeting low-income households. Private equity funds are financing affordable housing in developing countries. For instance, the Vital

Capital Fund which is predominantly focused on impact investing in Africa has committed $92 million in building 40,000 affordable housing units as well as community facilities and providing services such as clean water, education, sanitation, and power in Angola, while aiming for a 20% financial return on its investments (Vital Capital Fund, 2015). Renewable energy and sustainable infrastructure are also areas that attract a high level of participation from impact investors.

Private Equity/Venture Capital Investment Funds

Due to the typically small size of impact investee enterprises, large institutional investors usually avoid direct investments. They instead prefer to allocate assets into private investment funds as limited partners, which then place capital into enterprises that target low-income populations and/or environmental protection. As most of these funds are open only to accredited investors meeting threshold net worth requirements, detailed information about such funds can be hard to access for non-accredited investors and members of the public. ImpactAssets and ImpactBase maintain publicly available databases of private impact investing funds that meet their criteria. ImpactBase lists 426 funds in its database[8] with average target assets under management (AUMs) ranging from $42 million for fixed-income funds to $175 million for real assets funds. In April 2019, ImpactAssets lists ten funds with AUM greater than $250 million that are also signatories of the UN PRI: Bamboo Capital Partners, Calvert Impact Capital, Creation Investments Capital, DBL Partners, Developing World Markets, MicroVest Capital Management, Mirova Natural Capital, North Sky Capital, The Lyme Timber Company, and Turner Impact Capital. These funds list clean-tech, affordable housing, natural resources and conservation, and nutrition, health, and wellness as primary focus areas for investee enterprises. The primary SDGs listed by the funds are 1 No Poverty, 7 Affordable and Clean Energy, 8 Decent Work & Economic Growth, 10 Reduce Inequality, 13 Climate Action, and 15 Life on Land.

Other Asset Classes

For retail investors, financial and social objectives can be jointly achieved by investing in impact-related mutual funds and ESG-focused ETFs (exchange-traded funds). For example, the Columbia Threadneedle Social Bond Fund, an open-ended mutual fund invests in school infrastructure in districts where a third of students live below the poverty line, a proportion which is 1.5x the US average. The fund manager collaborates with Sustainalytics, an impact measurement consultancy, to publish an annual assessment of the social and environmental impact of its bond portfolio. New fintech companies such as Swell Investing and Change Finance aim to make impact investing accessible to the broader public and the citizen investor. Swell Investing is an online trading platform that allows retail investors to invest as little as $50 in their portfolio of companies, which operate in social and environmental related business sectors such as green technology, clean water, zero waste, renewable energy, disease eradication, and healthy living (Swell, 2019). Change Finance has developed impact focused ETFs that exclude non-ESG companies which small investors can trade on the stock exchange.

Given the limited number of publicly traded companies that are 'intentionally' seeking social impact, the social stock exchange (SSE) founded in 2013 in London allows investors to trade the stocks of about 50 companies that meet the SSE criteria to be admitted as a social impact enterprise. Through a partnership with NEX, a UK-based regulated electronic trading exchange, the SSE functions similar to a traditional stock exchange. There are analogous exchanges elsewhere in the world including the Impact Exchange in Singapore, the SASIX in South Africa, and the Social Venture Connexion in Canada, which facilitates private share placement and crowdfunding for impact-driven companies.

There is some criticism that investments in publicly traded equities do not involve 'intentionality' insofar as the investee enterprises do not generally have the stated goal of beneficial social outcomes. Given the lack of verifiability of intention and the ease with which insincere intentions can be articulated, perhaps impact investing should not be defined by statements, but rather by actual efforts to measure and manage impact.

CHALLENGES AND PROGRESS

While the blended value approach places impact investing at the intersection of capitalism and philanthropy, this integration is perhaps also its biggest criticism—whether impact investing can effectively serve two masters. The conventional wisdom is that a capitalist market economy works best when government and charity focus on public goods and social welfare, and let the private sector care about efficiency and profit.

Additionality Test

Brest and Born (2013) posit that an impact investment would only have impact if it increases either the quantity or quality of the social outcome beyond what can be achieved with a socially neutral investor. It would seem that a perfectly sound investment opportunity is just likely to attract traditional investors, who are as likely to deliver as much social impact (albeit unintended) as impact investors, so what an impact investor pursuing market returns can add to an investee in a large and competitive market is not very clear. Unless of course, impact investors are allowed to make a financial concession in exchange for social impact—paradigmatic of program-related investments by foundations. In this sense, value alignment is much easier to achieve than value creation without making financial concessions, yet the former is more consistent with ESG or socially responsible investment strategies that are not strictly impact investing. Conversely, in situations where traditional capital may not be available to support a nascent enterprise with high risk of success, impact investing would pass the 'additionality' test in creating positive value. From this perspective, if there is only limited capital for impact, it should be directed toward projects that would otherwise find no investors.

According to this logic, impact investing in public markets would only be genuinely different from traditional investing if they are financially concessionary, where traditional investments will not go. One may still argue that an investor may achieve better results by pursuing social and financial returns simultaneously if there are unexploited synergies between the two goals. For example, it is perceivable that by committing to socially responsible corporate behavior, a firm is able to improve its branding and employee loyalty, which in turn leads to lower employee turnover and higher productivity. Alternatively, firms that are dedicated to social goals may attract longer term shareholders and avoid the short-termism that plagues public companies, which in turn promotes sustainable profit (Robb & Sattell, 2016). However, if there are added financial benefits from CSR behaviors and targeting social impact, profit-maximizing firms are just as likely to exploit them in large and competitive markets.

Academic research has been scarce on documenting added value from non-concessionary impact investments (Clarkin & Cangioni, 2016). Rigorous empirical studies by economists are limited given the lack of data that can help them draw conclusions beyond the result outlined in

Chap. 5 that socially responsible investments do not perform significantly different from regular investments (Kreander, Gray, Power, & Sinclair, 2005; Lobe & Walkshäusl, 2016; Robb & Sattell, 2016; Schröder, 2007).

Impact Evaluation

While impact investing has received a lot of attention in investment circles, in news publications, and among world leaders, a persistent problem holding it back is the lack of a widely accepted framework to measure impact. If creating impact is truly the objective, perhaps it is more important to assess the value created for the investees rather than worry about the potential lack of additionality induced by an investor. If we were to convince more investors into making concessionary investments for impact (because non-concessionary investments have not yet passed the additionality test), we would need more data, on whether the investments have truly benefited the society or the environment and by how much. An impact evaluation will ensure our expectations are met and our finite resources are not being misplaced, particularly when the poor and marginalized are the target population. Without sufficient impact data (most impact funds are new, and few have data longer than a few years) or a standardized framework to document progress and establish track record, institutional investors, for example, would find it hard to justify increased participation to a wider group of stakeholders.

In this regard, progress has been made in recent years. Researchers and practitioners are working to improve the impact measurement system. More public data has been made available, and numerous social and environmental metrics have been adopted by the impact investing community. For example, established by GIIN, the Rockefeller Foundation, the B Lab, and Acumen, the Impact Reporting and Investment Standards (IRIS, 2018) has standardized metrics in the social and environmental dimensions which investors can use to track their impact performance (also see Chap. 4). Similar to the Morningstar and Standard and Poor's ratings systems, the Global Impact Investing Rating System (GIIRS), driven by the U.S. based non-profit B Lab designed a system of a common set of metrics to independently measure and rate companies and funds in performance areas of workers, governance, community, and the environment (also see Chap. 4). Other impact assessment tools such as Pulse, developed by Acumen Fund and Social Return on Investing (SROI), focuses on the monetization of social impact. In addition, due to the variety of impact investment situations, individual investors are charting their own course in coming up with proprietary metrics and measurement tools.[9] Despite these efforts, a large divergence in approach and rigor exists among the self-evaluations of impact investors, and additional efforts are needed to reconcile the standardized and the decentralized systems going forward.

More importantly, an assessment of impact would require separating outcome from output. Output is the product or service produced by an investee company, and outcome is the effect the output has on the environment or society. The standard metrics publicly provided by IRIS and GIIRS typically measure investment outputs, such as the number of schools built and the number of mosquito nets distributed, but not outcomes such as increase in enrolment and reduction in malaria cases. GIIN reports that over 95% of impact investors claim that they measure and report social and environmental impacts (Global Impact Investing Network, 2018). However, a closer look at these reports would reveal that most metrics used are for output—dollars invested, number of jobs created, and number of people served, all of which are basic financial and operational indicators necessary but not sufficient. In fact, the focus on output can at times be problematic, such as when microfinance institutions report on the amount of loans outstanding, which may be an indicator of indebtedness and correlate negatively with impact.

On the other hand, indicators related to outcome—types of job, income, and gender make-up of the beneficiary, and in-school performance of students and their graduation rates—constitute data which may be more difficult to collect and isolate. As a result, we cannot easily reach conclusions as to whether impact investments are reaching the intended audience and are having the intended long-term effect. Consider a school building project aimed at boosting school enrolment in a poor region. Even when we observed an increase in school enrolment, we are not sure that simultaneous government policies or funding initiatives might have not contributed to the uptick. We also have to consider whether enrolments at the new school are merely being transferred from existing schools, in which case the intended social impact would have been diluted. In addition, the building and maintenance of the new school may reduce the resources that can otherwise go to public schools, or serve to whisk away the best students—all countervailing impacts that need to be considered and netted out, especially when they can be more systemic than the intervention itself. As Jackson (2013a) pointed out, "the process of achieving meaningful social impact in poor communities is complex, nuanced, dynamic and, in fact, often uncertain". Therefore, to ascertain any cause and effect relationships in a conclusive manner, evaluation methods similar to those used in social science research such as randomized control experiments with the help of counterfactual groups would have to be utilized. If impact investors truly believe that their own interventions are overwhelmingly positive, then it would be unethical of them to carry out randomized control trials where a counterfactual group was denied the positive intervention.

Lessons can be learned from microfinance institutions, such as the Consultative Group to Assist the Poor, housed at the World Bank, which collects extensive outcome data and conducts randomized evaluations of their microfinance projects. Other approaches may include participatory methods that aim at evaluating outcomes for the wellbeing of individuals and the incorporation of what is called the theory of change, borrowed from the field of program evaluation. The theory of change will specify a model with underlying logic, causal links, assumptions, influences, and the expected outcomes of a project. Through the collection of performance data, this model can then be tested against the actual experienced process and results (Rogers, 2008).[10]

To persuade more investors to join the impact space and justify an increase in capital, it is important to evaluate if there are sufficient plausible investment opportunities in each sector.[11] Otherwise, a surge in capital may serve to create a bubble. The current market lacks information to signal capital to places where it is most needed. New investors are slow to enter the market because of a dearth in knowledge, guidelines, and performance benchmarks. On the other hand, given the high expectation for future growth, new entrants may overestimate the market potential. Microfinance institutions faced similar challenges, and it is another reason for developing standardized impact metrics so that the progress of the sector can be objectively documented.

Estimating financial return can be a challenging but familiar exercise. Predicting social and environmental outcomes and then attaching values to them would be much harder. Impact investors would need to treat impact measurement as performance measurement as well as essential management practices of a business, not merely for marketing or branding purposes. The Impact Management Project, launched by Bridges Impact as a network of standard-setting organizations has facilitated and coordinated an effort to measure impact by outcomes, which addressed for the first time several of the evaluation issues that have been identified thus far.

The IFC has launched the Operating Principles for Impact Management, a set of minimum thresholds for managing investment funds with the intent to contribute to measurable positive social or environmental impact, alongside financial returns (Mirchandani, 2019).

Other challenges remain. The absence of a uniform definition and clear boundaries are creating confusions that permeate the impact investment ecosystem, making it harder to attract new capital, to standardize assessment, and fan prejudice against the size and profitability of impact investments. Not to mention that impact evaluation if done right is often very costly.

Many of the dilemmas impact investing faced today, which we have discussed, can be traced back to its two diametrically opposed origins—one from investors seeking to do less bad and then more good, and the other from philanthropists seeking to expand their toolkit beyond grants (or improve from a negative 100% return on investments). Are concessionary investors wasting our resources trying to chase financial return, or are non-concessionary investors creating any additional social value by aligning their goals with social impact? Both theory and data seem to be against the latter (Brest, Gilson, & Wolfson, 2018). But if non-concessionary investors are left out and we also exclude ESG and program-related investments in employing the most restrictive definition of impact investing, then the space is filled with only concessionary investments, perhaps a much narrower and less appealing concept to traditional capital. At the same time, pure philanthropists reject the idea that profit-driven businesses should be given the same recognition in promoting social equality or environmental sustainability (Bugg-Levine & Emerson, 2011).

Lastly, the small size of the narrowest definitions of impact investing creates two important limitations. The first is obvious: the small amounts of capital available in the impact investing space are miniscule relative to the scale of the investment needs of the UN SDGs. The second is more subtle. It is not just investment dollars that increase when the scale of the market increases: it is also the number and diversity of stakeholders. The popularity of an investment category that limits participation can never be sustainable because its legitimacy cannot be felt by broad swathes of people. For example, our review of cost-benefit analysis in Chap. 6 demonstrated its value as an expert analytical tool. However, we noted that its ability to persuade stakeholders is limited by its lack of participatory foundations. Considering the role of the financial ecosystem, it is clear that all investments, intentional or unintentional, additional or not additional, have impact, for good or ill. Considering the three essential roles of the financial ecosystem described in Chap. 1 and taking a broader perspective, perhaps making a fine distinction based on articulated intentionality, or provable and direct causal links between investment and outcome is splitting hairs. If the definition of impact investing is inclusive enough to encompass a diverse range of investing approaches and consequently a larger population of stakeholders, then the expert pronouncement on intentionality or additionality becomes less important as a source of legitimacy. Voluntary widespread adoption by a broad swathe of responsible investors can become the evidence of intentionality and additionality on its own.

THE WAY FORWARD

Impact investors are usually expected to invest during the early stages of a social venture, with higher risks and a long horizon for profitability. As such, impact investments frequently serve as seed funding. Maintaining social change is often complex and subject to larger scale social and political factors outside the control of investors. Many impact funds are new and do not have long track records. Despite their fast growth, impact investing is still in its infancy and is facing difficulties in attracting mainstream capital. However, as the market matures with more data and accepted standards, there is cause to be optimistic about its future potential.

Impact investing has come a long way from traditional finance in eschewing the single bottom line approach and channeling much needed capital into social projects that will go unfunded by traditional capital. However, even with transformative possibilities of impact investing, it still largely follows an investor-primacy model, one that focuses on investors doing well while also doing good. For impact investors, the ultimate goal is to catalyze change, whether about transitioning to a more sustainable economy or giving more opportunities to the poor. However, our existing institutions have evolved to maintain the status quo, including a financial incentive system and organizational structure which prevent new players from easily disrupting the incumbent elite. In addition, the gap between the geographic locations of impact investors and investees can engender neo-colonialist attitudes, a long-standing feature of development finance in the global south. For example, land grabs by renewable energy projects often cause irreparable harm to local communities, who are supposed to be beneficiaries of such projects.

Spiess-Knafl and Scheck highlight another essential aspect of impact investing. They note that impact investing has gained prominence because developmental problems are increasingly complex (Spiess-Knafl & Scheck, 2017). The solutions require collaborations between multiple stakeholders. The one-dimensional drive for market efficiency is unlikely to solve complex social problems like poverty, child mortality, hunger, lack of health care and education, and access to clean air and clean water, which are still plaguing a large part of the world. For the impact-investing marketplace to attain persistent and widespread legitimacy, its focus has to shift from the investor to a broader range of stakeholders, parallel to our analysis in Chap. 4. In this sense, perhaps the lack of additionality is a cause to celebrate the relative insignificance of the investor and to elevate the investee so that she is on par with the investor. This is difficult and perhaps impossible, given the sheer asymmetry in power and wealth between the best-known impact investors and most investees (Giridharadas, 2018), but perhaps it is worth striving for. As Sir Ronald Cohen (2013), who chairs the Social Impact Investment Taskforce once commented, we need a *"profound cultural change in the way we deal with society's problems"*, on the part of every stakeholder including governments, philanthropy, private business, and individuals. Many of his recommendations for such as change to take place are geared toward government leadership—in building the ecosystem and the market for impact investing, removing legal obstacles, and becoming a large buyer of social outcomes such as through social impact bonds (Social Impact Investment Taskforce, 2014). Perhaps it is time to move away from an investor-primacy model and transition to a participatory stakeholder approach to capitalism (Armeni & Whelan, 2018). Such an approach is one in which communities are involved in co-designing, managing, and owning impact projects, as pioneered by Transform Finance, an impact investor network which aims to ensure that impact projects produce more value than they extract, and that risks and rewards are balanced among all stakeholders (Transform Finance, 2018).

Environmental and social challenges are increasingly difficult for the public sector to address alone. Declining budgets due to debt and fiscal austerity are plaguing governments in developed and developing countries alike. Limited resource restricts the scope and the scale by which philanthropic organizations can solve social issues. Most global assets reside with the private sector. Impact investing, which we reviewed in this chapter is one way to bring together diverse stakeholders to address global challenges including climate change and social inequality, but we need to be open-minded and bold in seeking new partnerships, new solutions, and new ideas.

Notes

1. Author translation of the principle 君子爱财、取之有道, as collected in the volume Zeng Guang Xian Wen (增广贤文), a compilation of idioms by scholars from the Ming and Qing Dynasties.
2. For model of information externalities and the spillover value of an initial investment, see Caplin and Leahy (1998).
3. Traditional investing in the present sense which aims exclusively at monetary returns on the purchase of a good or an asset is rather a recent development—essentially a move away from what was historically the point of investing. We are now going back to a more balanced approach, with increasing number of investors instead of focusing on single line returns start to embrace social and environmental impacts with their investments in a double (or triple) bottom line model. Triple bottom line was a term that John Elkington claimed to have coined in 1994 (Elkington, 2018). Instead of focusing solely on the profit and loss accounts, the triple bottom line is a sustainability framework to also evaluate companies based on the social impact of their products and services, as well as the environmental impact of their business model and production processes.
4. As part of the trend, more and more international brands paid attention to the working conditions of their employees, and promoted EHS (environment, health, and safety) awareness in their supply chain companies. Organizations such as the World Business Council for Sustainable Development (WBCSD) and the Business for Social Responsibility (BSR) that provide networking and sustainability consulting services boast hundreds of members comprised of some of the largest brands in the world (Business for Social Responsibility, 2019; World Business Council for Sustainable Development, 2019). CSR companies may even decide to allocate part of their revenue to charity and use more renewable energy, measures that are not traditionally tied to short-term profitability.
5. According to The Global Family Office Report 2017 by UBS & Campden Wealth (2017), 20% of the family offices worldwide are engaged in impact investing.
6. It is unclear whether GIIN's estimate of 1340 impact investors include any sovereign wealth funds.
7. Available at https://thegiin.org/repository-of-alternative-financing-structures-for-early-stage-impact-investing
8. Data is as of August 2017.
9. Refer to Flynn, Young, and Barnett (2015) for a more comprehensive list of impact assessment tools.

10. See Jackson (2013a) for details on how to build a theory of change evaluation model.

11. For example, Hiromichi Mizuno, who oversees Japan's Government Pension Investment Fund, cites "the lack of mainstream impact investing products" as a hurdle to allocating significant institutional assets to this strategy (Kapadia, 2019).

REFERENCES

African Development Bank Group. (2012). *AfDB Sponsors Fund of Funds for Agribusiness in Africa – Board Approves Equity Investment of USD 100 Million in Agvance Africa* [Press release]. Retrieved from https://www.afdb.org/en/news-and-events/afdb-sponsors-fund-of-funds-for-agribusiness-in-africa-board-approves-equity-investment-of-usd-100-million-in-agvance-africa-9267/

Anders, J., & Dorsett, R. (2017). *Peterborough Social Impact Bond: Final Report on Cohort 2 Analysis.* London, UK: NIESR.

Armeni, A., & Ferreyra de Bone, M. (2017). *Innovations in Financing Structures for Impact Enterprises: Spotlight on Latin America.* Retrieved from https://publications.iadb.org/en/innovations-financing-structures-impact-enterprises-spotlight-latin-america

Armeni, A., & Whelan, T. (2018). How Investors Can Drive the Shift from Shareholder Primacy to Stakeholder Capitalism. *Impact Alpha.*

Asian Development Bank. (2011). *Impact Investors in Asia: Characteristics and Preferences for Investing in Social Enterprises in Asia and the Pacific.* Mandaluyong City, Philippines: Asian Development Bank.

Berry, J. M. (2016). Negative Returns: The Impact of Impact Investing on Empowerment and Advocacy. *PS: Political Science & Politics, 49*(3), 437.

Brest, P., & Born, K. (2013). Unpacking the Impact in Impact Investing. *Stanford Social Innovation Review, 14*, 33.

Brest, P., Gilson, R. J., & Wolfson, M. A. (2018). *How Investors Can (and Can't) Create Social Value* (ECGI Working Paper No. 394).

Buffett, H. W., & Eimicke, W. B. (2018). *Social Value Investing: A Management Framework for Effective Partnerships.* New York, NY: Columbia University Press.

Bugg-Levine, A., & Emerson, J. (2011). *Impact Investing: Transforming How We Make Money While Making a Difference* (1st ed.). San Francisco, CA: Jossey-Bass.

Business for Social Responsibility. (2019). *Our Mission.* Retrieved from https://www.bsr.org/en/about

Caplin, A., & Leahy, J. (1998). Miracle on Sixth Avenue: Information Externalities and Search. *Economic Journal, 108*(446), 60–74. https://doi.org/10.1111/1468-0297.00273

Castalia Strategic Advisors. (2014). *Evaluation of Lighting Africa Program: Final Report*. Retrieved from https://www.thegef.org/sites/default/files/project_documents/2950-521198Lighting%2520Africa%2520-%2520External%2520Terminal%2520Evaluation.pdf

Clarkin, J. E., & Cangioni, C. L. (2016). Impact Investing: A Primer and Review of the Literature. *Entrepreneurship Research Journal, 6*(2), 173.

Cohen, R. (2013). *G8 – Launch of the Taskforce on Social Impact Investment*. Retrieved from http://www.huffingtonpost.co.uk/sir-ronald-cohen/g8-launch-social-impact-taskforce_b_3452877.html

Deloitte. (2018). *2018 Deloitte Millennial Survey*. Retrieved from https://www2.deloitte.com/content/dam/Deloitte/global/Documents/About-Deloitte/gx-2018-millennial-survey-report.pdf

Dichter, S., Adams, T., & Ebrahim, A. (Producer). (2016). The Power of Lean Data. *Stanford Social Innovation Review*. Retrieved from https://ssir.org/articles/entry/the_power_of_lean_data

Disley, E., et al. (2011). *Lessons Learned from the Planning and Early Implementation of the Social Impact Bond at HMP Peterborough*. RAND Europe, Research Series 5/11. UK Ministry of Justice.

Elkington, J. (2018, June 6). 25 Years Ago I Coined the Phrase "Triple Bottom Line." Here's Why It's Time to Rethink It. *Harvard Business Review*, 2–5. Retrieved from https://hbr.org/2018/06/25-years-ago-i-coined-the-phrase-triple-bottom-line-heres-why-im-giving-up-on-it

Emerson, J., & Smalling, L. (2015). *Construction of an Impact Portfolio: Total Portfolio Management for Multiple Returns*. Retrieved from https://www.impactassets.org/files/Issuebrief_No.15.pdf

Floyd, D. (2017). *Social Impact Bonds: An Overview of the Global Market for Commissioners and Policymakers*. Retrieved from http://socialspider.com/wp-content/uploads/2017/04/SS_SocialImpactReport_4.0.pdf

Flynn, J., Young, J., & Barnett, C. (2015). *Impact Investments: A Literature Review* (CDI Paper).

Freireich, J., & Fulton, K. (2009). *Investing for Social and Environmental Impact*. GIIN Monitor Institute.

Giridharadas, A. (2018). *Winners Take All: The Elite Charade of Changing the World*. New York, NY: Alfred Knopf.

Global Impact Investing Network. (2017). *What You Need to Know About Impact Investing*. Retrieved from https://thegiin.org/impact-investing/need-to-know/#what-is-impact-investing

Global Impact Investing Network. (2018). *Annual Impact Investor Survey 2018*.

Global Impact Investing Network. (2019a). *Core Characteristics of Impact Investing*. Retrieved from https://thegiin.org/characteristics

Global Impact Investing Network. (2019b). *Sizing the Impact Investing Market*. Retrieved from https://thegiin.org/research/publication/impinv-market-size

Global Steering Group for Impact Investment. (2019). *Driving Real Impact*. Retrieved from https://gsgii.org/about-us/

Global Sustainable Investment Alliance. (2019). *Global Sustainable Investment Review*. Retrieved from http://www.gsi-alliance.org/wp-content/uploads/2019/06/GSIR_Review2018F.pdf

Heron. (2018). *Conscious Portfolio Construction*. Retrieved from https://www.heron.org/conscious-portfolio-construction-1

IRIS. (2018). *IRIS Metrics | IRIS*. Retrieved from https://iris.thegiin.org/metrics

Jack, A. (2008, March 23). Vaccine Bond in Strong Demand. *Financial Times*.

Jackson, E. T. (2012). *Accelerating Impact: Achievements, Challenges and What's Next in Building the Impact Investing Industry*. New York, NY: The Rockefeller Foundation.

Jackson, E. T. (2013a). Interrogating the Theory of Change: Evaluating Impact Investing Where it Matters Most. *Journal of Sustainable Finance & Investment, 3*(2), 110.

Jackson, E. T. (2013b). Evaluating Social Impact Bonds: Questions, Challenges, Innovations, and Possibilities in Measuring Outcomes in Impact Investing. *Community Development, 44*(5), 616.

Kapadia, R. (2019). How the World's Largest Pension Manager Is Trying to Make ESG Investing More Popular. *Barron's*. Retrieved from https://www.barrons.com/articles/pension-manager-esg-impact-investing-51555020782

Kreander, N., Gray, R. H., Power, D. M., & Sinclair, C. D. (2005). Evaluating the Performance of Ethical and Non-ethical Funds: A Matched Pair Analysis. *Journal of Business Finance & Accounting, 32*(7–8), 1493.

Lighting Africa. (2019). *Our Impact*. Retrieved from https://www.lightingafrica.org/about/our-impact/

Lobe, S., & Walkshäusl, C. (2016). Vice Versus Virtue Investing Around the World. *Review of Managerial Science, 10*(2), 344.

Mirchandani, B. (2019). What You Need to Know About the IFC's Operating Principles for Impact Management. *Forbes*.

O'Donohoe, N., Leijonhufvud, C., Saltuk, Y., Bugg-levine, A., & Brandenburg, M. (2010). *Impact Investments: An Emerging Asset Class* (J. P. Morgan, Ed). New York, NY: Rockefeller Foundation/GIIN.

OECD. (2019). *Social Impact Investment 2019. The Impact Imperative for Sustainable Development*. Paris: OECD Publishing. Retrieved from https://doi.org/10.1787/9789264311299-en

Robb, R., & Sattell, M. (2016). Socially Responsible/Impact Investing: Theoretical and Empirical Issues. *Capitalism and Society, 11*(2), Article 2. Retrieved from https://papers.ssrn.com/sol3/papers.cfm?abstract_id=2886082

Rogers, P. J. (2008). Using Programme Theory to Evaluate Complicated and Complex Aspects of Interventions. *Evaluation, 14*(1), 48.

Salamon, L. M., & Burckart, W. (2014). Foundations as 'Philanthropic Banks'. In L. M. Salamon (Ed.), *New Frontiers of Philanthropy. A Guide to the New Tools and Actors Reshaping Global Philanthropy and Social Investing* (pp. 165–208). Oxford, UK: Oxford University Press.

Santa Clara University. (2013). *Demand Dividend: Creating Reliable Returns in Impact Investing.*

Schröder, M. (2007). Is There a Difference? The Performance Characteristics of SRI Equity Indices. *Journal of Business Finance & Accounting, 34*(1–2), 348.

Shonchoy, A. S. (2014). Concluding Remarks. In A. S. Shonchoy (Ed.), *Seasonality and Microcredit: The Case of Northern Bangladesh* (pp. 105–107). Tokyo: Springer Japan.

Social Impact Investment Taskforce. (2014). *Impact Investment: The Invisible Heart of Markets: Harnessing the Power of Entrepreneurship, Innovation and Capital for Public Good.*

Spiess-Knafl, W., & Scheck, B. (2017). *Impact Investing: Instruments, Mechanisms and Actors.* New York, NY: Palgrave Macmillan.

Swell. (2019). *Swell's Portfolio.* Retrieved from https://www.swellinvesting.com/homepage

The Nathan Cummings Foundation. (2018). *NCF Commits to 100 Percent.* Retrieved from https://nathancummings.org/ncf-commits-to-100-percent/

TONIIC. (2018). *T100: Insights from the Frontier of Impact Investing 2018.* Retrieved from San Francisco, CA: https://thegiin.org/impact-investing/need-to-know/#what-is-impact-investing

Transform Finance. (2018). *Transformative Finance Principles.* Retrieved from http://transformfinance.org

Trelstad, B. (2016). Impact Investing: A Brief History. *Capitalism and Society, 11*(2), Article 4. Retrieved from https://papers.ssrn.com/sol3/papers.cfm?abstract_id=2886088

UBS & Campden Wealth. (2017). *The Global Family Office Report 2017.* Retrieved from https://www.ubs.com/global/en/wealth-management/uhnw/global-family-office/global-family-office-report-2017.html

Vital Capital Fund. (2015). *Kora Housing.* Retrieved from https://vital-capital.com/kora-housing/

Wang, L., & Juslin, H. (2009). The Impact of Chinese Culture on Corporate Social Responsibility: The Harmony Approach. *Journal of Business Ethics, 88*(3), 433–451. https://doi.org/10.1007/s10551-009-0306-7

World Business Council for Sustainable Development. (2019). *Our Members.* Retrieved from https://www.wbcsd.org/Overview/Our-members

CHAPTER 12

Decentralized Finance

Our review of the varieties of investor in Chap. 9 highlighted the need to blend different types of investor to address the financing needs of any particular sustainability challenge. In Chaps. 10 and 11, we have outlined the potentially beneficial role of investors in allocating capital at a macro and micro scale. In Chap. 10, we described the top-down portfolio choice decisions of large asset owners. In Chap. 11, we focused on bottom-up direct impact investing. Here we focus on a middle layer. How can communities finance local public goods that call for capital both from small local investors and larger regional sources of capital? What promising institutions exist to scale up savings flows between investors and issuers without having to go through a highly centralized global or national financial ecosystem? Is it feasible to form communities of different types of investor extending beyond geographical boundaries in the same way that the largest asset owners engage in collective action to magnify their voice in negotiations with the largest financial intermediaries and global corporations? Can these alliances operate as conduits for financing and feedback between small responsible investors and issuers? We attempt to answer these questions by reviewing examples of self-organizing behavior by smaller issuers and investors and asking what aspects of these examples are promising ingredients of a sustainable financial ecosystem at the regional scale.

© The Author(s) 2019
S. Bose et al., *The Financial Ecosystem*, Palgrave Studies in Impact Finance, https://doi.org/10.1007/978-3-030-05624-7_12

The Value of Decentralized Decision-Making

In Chap. 5, we briefly discussed the value of decentralized feedback loops and the potential that a set of inter-connected and related markets with prices can provide. Viewed in a systems context, a price system that responds to changes in relative scarcity represents the most important technology in the financial ecosystem to relieve dispersed scarcities not obvious or important to a centralized decision-maker. Here we delve a little deeper into this idea, keeping in mind that the price system is neither as far-reaching nor as information-laden as we would like it to be. Recall also the point made by Elinor Ostrom that blunt and ineffective regulation by a centralized state crowds out decentralized monitoring activities by individual users of public goods (E. Ostrom, 2010). If a centralized regulator claims to address systemic risks, small investors will be lulled into a false sense of safety and financial intermediaries will eliminate costly due diligence because they can justifiably blame the regulator when the crisis erupts. The precious social value of decentralized monitoring will remain unrealized.

In Chap. 3, we noted that voluntary corporate governance standards in the United States in the nineteenth century appeared to have been sufficiently high that there was an explosion of corporate financing between 1790 and 1860 despite the absence of any central regulation preventing managerial malfeasance (Wright & Sylla, 2011). Throughout the nineteenth century, the market for municipal bonds grew steadily in the United States and was instrumental in financing capital-intensive urban water provision infrastructure as the country grew and urbanized (Cutler & Miller, 2006). This municipal finance market, which is the largest and most varied in the world, developed for a century without the assistance of a centralized regulator or even any rating agency to provide consistent assessments of the credit risk of issuers (Platz, 2011).

The notion that it is the regulator's responsibility to minimize systemic risks while the investor can focus on her own portfolio's return and variance is obviously a fantasy. In Chap. 10, we described the extra-financial collective action efforts of the largest asset owners to address systemic risks in the face of an absent global regulator and an impotent national one. Our recognition of the interdependence of investor choice and systemic risk suggests that we can view the financial ecosystem as a common-pool resource (CPR) as described by E. Ostrom (2010). Ostrom points out that carefully designed experimental studies demonstrate that isolated, anonymous individuals overharvest from common-pool resources. Allowing participants in the experiments to communicate with each other tends to reduce overharvesting, contrary to game-theoretical predictions.[1] If investors remain vigilant about systemic risks and incorporate these into their due diligence, they can potentially steer their own portfolio away from such risks. If they talk to others, they may induce others to emulate their portfolio choices. If there are enough investors with like-minded assessments of systemic risks, capital for destabilizing activities will dry up.

This is the analogue in the investing ecosystem of the waggle dance of honeybees. Swarms of honeybees choose one out of many potential nesting sites discovered and reported by scouts through a process of decentralized but collective decision-making. When a colony needs to find a site for a new hive, about 5% of the bees act as scouts and search for candidate locations. The scouts return to the swarm and perform a waggle dance with some probability if they find a good candidate. The length of the dance conveys the quality of the site. The dance recruits other scouts to independently verify the quality of the candidate. When a quorum of scouts form at a specific site, all scouts return to the swarm to alert the colony. Within a few days, all scouts point to the same high-quality site. No single bee compares all sites (Visscher & Camazine, 1999). The swarm arrives at its decision through a self-organizing process that involves recruitment and quorum sensing (Golman, Hagmann, & Miller, 2015). This process of collective decision-making through *recruitment* and *quorum sensing* is prevalent among ants and even bacteria (Atkinson & Williams, 2009).

We note that the tepid relationship between corporate social performance and corporate financial performance (see Chap. 5), somewhat counterintuitively, can aid collective action. If investors could expect to monetize their non-financial due diligence in the short run, they would have less incentive to engage in collective action efforts. If the scout bees who discovered a good hive site could feasibly enjoy the benefits of the site at the expense of the rest of the swarm, they would have little incentive to alert the colony about the good site they discovered! It is only if environmental, social, and governance (ESG) performance does not reward handsomely in the short term, that investors have an incentive to persuade others about the salience of their concerns. This effort at persuasion should be a two-way street: it alerts other investors to the systemic concerns of one investor and separately seeks validation from heterogeneous and independent risk assessment.

Polycentric Finance

Elinor Ostrom cites early work on *polycentric* governance structures as the inspiration for her research on the decentralized management of CPRs. The term polycentrism was coined by Vincent Ostrom, Charles Tiebout, and Robert Warren in an analysis of metropolitan government in the United States (V. Ostrom, Tiebout, & Warren, 1961). V. Ostrom et al. decried the prevalent view at the time that assumed that the multiplicity of political units in a metropolitan area was a pathological phenomenon. The conventional view asserted that "there were too many governments and not enough government". The usual prescription for this supposed problem was to recommend reorganization into larger governmental units, leading to a gargantuan central metropolitan authority. In contrast, V. Ostrom et al. preferred to study the potential value of many centers of decision-making that are formally independent of each other forming a system they termed 'polycentric'. They argued that metropolitan governments existed to provide local public goods, whose impact is associated with a particular 'public'. Some public goods might affect the whole nation, while others might affect a neighborhood. Parks can be provided by small townships, but air pollution control is generally provided at the state or higher level. In a globalized world where the technological costs of transactions between parties far removed geographically are relatively low, the 'public' in some cases might constitute members who are geographically dispersed but hold a common purpose.

For example, retirees who are beneficiaries of a pension fund in California may live in California, Connecticut, Costa Rica, or China. Though geographically dispersed, they all have an interest in capital stewardship efforts that attempt to do no harm in all those jurisdictions. V. Ostrom et al. argue that within a metropolitan area, the intersections and divergences of the needs and capabilities of different publics will determine the appropriate level of polycentry. This means that scale should be endogenous: when an attribute of a public good is measurable or has close proxies which are measurable, then its provision can be scaled up, and the appropriate provider can be a single gargantuan government agency. When the attributes are not measurable, then local conduits of non-pecuniary representation, such as town councils and dialogue are essential because small communities present low monitoring costs. Diverse public preferences, competition between town councils, combined with the process of some inhabitants voting with their feet, would lead to a sorting of inhabitants with different preferences regarding the quality and quantity of local public goods.[2] Competition by different town councils in the provision of local public goods, combined with the possibility of exit, is a form of recruitment and quorum sensing that facilitates experimentation and resilience. Even in the context of a global pollutant such as carbon, regulation at the polycentric scale has been far more effective at inducing abatement than at global scale (Cole, 2011).

What lessons can we draw from a recognition of the polycentric management of CPRs that might help us to realize the value of decentralized monitoring in the financial ecosystem? CPR management by communities whose scale lies between the gargantuan state or corporation and the self-interested individual facilitates experimentation at non-threatening scales, followed by learning and cross-influence. Elinor Ostrom argues that "humans have a more complex motivational structure and more capability to solve social dilemmas than posited in earlier rational-choice theory. Designing institutions to force (or nudge) entirely self-interested individuals to achieve better outcomes has been the major goal posited by policy analysts...We need to ask how diverse polycentric institutions help or hinder the innovativeness, learning, adapting, trustworthiness, levels of cooperation of participants, and the achievement of more effective, equitable, and sustainable outcomes at multiple scales" (E. Ostrom, 2010). What are the attributes that bring this about? Ostrom lists six essential features of situations that encourage cooperation between individuals and avert the tragedy of the commons in CPR management:

1. Communication between the full set of participants is feasible.
2. Reputations of participants are known.
3. The marginal per capita return (MPCR) is high.[3]
4. Entry and exit are feasible at low cost.
5. Longer time horizon of participants.
6. Agreed-upon sanctioning capabilities.[4]

In the financial ecosystem, polycentric communities formed to test new approaches and learn from them might adopt some or all of these essential features. For example, some key goals of one type of decentralized finance based on blockchain is to allow transactions between the full set of participants, make reputations publicly available at no cost, reduce the entry and exit costs of transactors, and employ smart contracts to provide low-cost monitoring and sanctioning (see below). This means discriminating between those measurable attributes of public goods which can be feasibly regulated by a central agency and those incommensurable attributes which are best left to a Tiebout sorting process.

DIVERGENCE IS A SIGNAL OF DECENTRALIZATION

Different investors have different views on what the most pressing systemic risk might be, such as incentive alignment, social cohesion, diversity, or climate risk. There is no single global regulation that would be desirable to all or even the majority of investors. It is well known that different ESG ratings providers have differing emphases. The rank correlations of issuers ranked by six different ratings providers is low, even after accounting for stated differences in approach among the raters (Chatterji, Durand, Levine, & Touboul, 2016). This is usually seen as problematic. There is much hand-wringing that divergent ratings imply that corporate social responsibility is not commensurable. Chatterji et al. caution that "these results call into question the validity of social ratings, which impact managerial actions around the world [and] guide trillions of dollars of investment". Understanding the nature and value of polycentric management implies that divergent social ratings actually increase the resilience of the financial ecosystem. If it were possible for a single rater to measure the concept of social responsibility, then it is unlikely that the 'trillions of dollars' of capital allocated according to that single rating would advance the social responsibility of the financial ecosystem. Just as polycentric governance recognizes that there are multiple 'publics' for different public goods, so there are diverse 'socials' for different corporate social responsibilities. The idea that a handful of raters could measure the impact on these diverse 'societies' is a quixotic fantasy. In Chaps. 5 and 9, we discussed the analytical monocultures and relative homogeneity of backgrounds that beset many approaches to risk assessment in the financial ecosystem. In Chap. 10, we noted the influence of modern portfolio theory which is overly concerned with very limited measures of risk and is founded on the principle that most investors have symmetric expectations about the future.

Mainstream investment managers may be worried about ratings divergence because their analytical frameworks are less capable of dealing with ambiguity. Nevertheless, as Keynes noted, the long-term value investor is necessarily *ex ante* contrarian—significant outperformance can only come from being very different from the average investor (see Chap. 1).

Divergent ratings provide a method for differential recruitment. If each divergent rating could be linked to capital allocated according to its ratings philosophy, then we would have a method of quorum sensing that signaled the most popular assessments of non-financial risk.

Integrating the divergence of expectations is a critical element of the role of the financial ecosystem. This generally means integrating both measurable ratings and unmeasurable judgment into the security selection process. Amar Bhidé analyzes the role of centralized, mechanistic banks and the backward-looking statistical models of credit risk used by rating agencies to assess mortgage-backed securities in precipitating the global financial crisis. He writes that unlike "with old-fashioned municipal or corporate bonds,... with multi-level asset-backed securities, however, contact with the final borrower was impossible; rating agencies, and issuers, had to rely on statistical models rather than case-by-case judgments" (Bhidé, 2010). The removal of judgment from credit decisions that Bhidé fingers is a consequence of key violations of Ostrom's list of features above. Communications between investors and the ultimate borrowers are not feasible: each security might have hundreds of thousands of underlying mortgages. Reputations of borrowers are known through imperfect quantitative measures—the judgment from face-to-face interactions has been completely eliminated in the modern mortgage banking market. The MPCR is low. Exit is costly for investors because the asset-backed securities do not trade in liquid markets. Key participants in the community had very short time horizons. Specifically, the banks packaging the securities typically earned commissions on structuring the transaction but did not hold on to them as long-term investors. There appeared to be no internal sanctioning mechanisms for banks for saddling clients with securities of dubious value or for ratings agencies for misrating securities.

THE CURATION OF CAPITAL

In Chap. 9, we noted that many sustainable development challenges require careful curation of a diverse array of stakeholder capitals. This requires an open-minded study of the strengths and weaknesses of different types of capital source, including both community legitimacy and even impersonal asset-backed securities. Given Bhidé's critique of mechanistic centralization and the absence of human judgment in the packaging of assets in securitization, does securitization provide any value in a sustainable financial ecosystem? If the mortgage-backed securities market failed to meet the majority of Ostrom's prerequisites for cooperation, why should we consider this asset class as a potential tool in sustainable finance? The answer lies in the diversity of situations and actors that finance must serve. It would be hubris to rule out any particular instrument or to prescribe a specific blanket solution. Just as polycentric governance refuses to pre-judge the appropriate scale of metropolitan government to supply a particular local public good, polycentric finance cannot be prejudiced against any particular instrument. The essence of financial decision-making is that effective solutions are designed in a decentralized way, tailored to the particulars of cash flow expectations, maturity, volatility, and other sources of both financial and systemic risk.

One dimension to which they should not be tailored is geography. Some critics of securitization are occasionally nostalgic about 'old-fashioned banking' which involves the banker lending to borrowers he knows. This quaint concept sounds pleasing, and harkens to the period before Polanyi's great transformation when economic and social relations were embedded in the same networks (Polanyi, 1944). The logic of this position evaporates when we realize that the merging of social and economic networks within a small geographic area when power is unequally distributed can be quite limiting for the borrower. Moreover, if the local bankers were to lend only to those whom they know, they would end up with a geographically concentrated portfolio. Asset-backed securitization is useful insofar as it allows investor capital to transcend the barriers of geography. The consequent geographical diversification can sharply reduce the cost of capital so long as the problems of adverse selection and moral hazard do not rear their ugly heads.

The Benefits of Securitization

The risk of a loan can be decomposed into a portion that is related to measurable factors, and a portion that requires judgment. An originator of loans, if he is to exercise judgment needs to know the borrowers and as a result, geographic proximity to the borrowers is helpful. However, if the use of proceeds of the loan is for an easily measurable asset, then there will generally be other lenders, in other geographies, who will be comfortable taking on the asset risk. Securitization allows an originating bank to offload its most measurable risks to other investors with a lower expected return on capital. Securitization provides the bank with low cost, fixed maturity funding that relieves the need to hold liquid, low yield assets to meet withdrawal requests (Loutskina, 2011). Offloading the easiest-to-value risks frees up more capital for the bank to allocate to the more illiquid, more difficult to value, less measurable risks.

Suppose that a bank has lent to thousands of mortgage borrowers. The ease of measurement arises from the statistical average of values across the thousands of homes. The present value of future cash flows from the mortgages depends on both the credit risk of the borrower as well as the value of the underlying collateral (the houses). Credit risk of a borrower is harder to measure than the value of a home, because if necessary, the home could be sold to recover the loan. The borrower cannot be sold, and cannot be forced to work hard to repay the loan. The statistical averages across thousands of borrowers will have significantly greater variance than those across homes. It is in this sense that physical capital is generally easier to value (and finance) than human capital. Consequently, the interest rate for mortgages, whose primary risk is the value of the underlying collateral, is generally far lower than the interest rate on lending directly to an individual borrower. Securitization facilitates credit expansion by allowing bank capital to be used to fund the portion of credit risk that is hard to transfer to the less informed.

Securitization provides a positive feedback loop that can be problematic. Since lenders' assessments of the appropriate loan size are influenced by house prices from recently concluded transactions, increasing house prices increase willingness to lend, which in turn increase house prices (Wachter, 2018). In order for this feedback loop to be cut, it is crucial that originators maintain the stringency of underwriting standards, so that the asset prices do not enter a credit-induced bubble. When originators do not have special knowledge of the borrowers (as is the case in the United States where a significant portion of lending is by non-bank lenders who have no other relationship to their borrowers) and where there are high fees to be earned from concluding a transaction, there is little incentive in the system for maintaining credit quality. In that case, the recruitment and quorum sensing features of the system are destabilizing: they induce the swarm to follow the wrong signals because scouts receive a high commission for each site they are able to sell to the swarm.

Green Banks

Financing for clean energy and energy efficiency infrastructure at the consumer level is more difficult than financing renewable energy investments by utility-scale electricity generators. In Chap. 14, we discuss financing for large-scale deployments of renewable energy assets. In this chapter in the context of decentralized finance, we discuss the special problems of financing consumer-level investments necessary to reduce energy consumption. The challenge of decentralized finance arises because the cost of vetting small investments for viability and return potential is high, relative to the size of the investment. A key task of financial intermediation is to screen investments for their viability. Screening typically requires a fixed amount of time per investment. Hence, screening costs rise linearly with the number of investments, not the monetary value of investments. When investments are sufficiently similar or standardized, there may be some economies of scale in screening.

An additional difficulty arises in the context of residential energy efficiency investments due to the significant variation in cost-benefit ratios across end-users (Allcott & Greenstone, 2012). Energy efficiency investments produce both private and public benefits, although some of these benefits are reduced by subsequent increases in energy consumption due to what is termed the rebound effect.[5] For example, Figus, Turner, McGregor, and Katris (2017) consider the economy-wide effects of supporting increases in energy efficiency in residential energy use in the United Kingdom. They find that the increase in GDP triggered by increased energy efficiency delivers greater household incomes than the immediate private benefits of efficiency improvement. In the United States, energy efficiency benefits vary significantly across regions, which make it important to tailor financing incentives by region (Callaway, Fowlie, & McCormick, 2018). Many end-users for whom private energy efficiency benefits are significant have no need for publicly subsidized incentives. Conversely, those for whom the value of energy efficiency savings is high as a proportion of household income, that is, low-income households, are also those most likely to have poor access to credit to finance energy efficiency improvements (Gillingham & Palmer, 2014). The variation across end-users implies that nationwide financing guidelines will lead to misallocation of capital.

How can we then utilize securitization to help finance investments in environment-friendly assets, differentiating by end-user and without inducing the bubbles that arose in the context of mortgages? Green banks provide an example of the beneficial curation of different types of capital to finance clean energy assets. A green bank is public, quasi-public, or non-profit entity intended to accelerate the deployment of clean energy using limited public capital to attract private capital investment in clean energy projects. Much as the process of securitization can help to bring low-cost capital to fund assets with easily measurable risks, green banks aim to leverage scarce public capital by attracting private investment to fund the easiest-to-value renewable energy assets. It is expected that such private capital will require a cost of capital that is lower than could be achieved if individual borrowers attempted to fund such assets with their own credit capacity. If successful, a green bank can make clean energy more affordable and accessible to low-income consumers. Figure 12.1 shows a simplified flow chart of initial capital flows funded by a green bank.

A green bank receives funding from taxpayers to finance clean energy assets. Among the taxpayers, there is some variation in the desire for clean energy assets and the capacity to pay for them. Some taxpayers are more willing and able to fund clean energy assets than others. Others may be agnostic about the value of environmental impact but may nevertheless be interested in funding long-lived, easily valued assets with stable return characteristics. A capital curation mechanism such as a green bank allows those who have a greater preference for clean energy assets to become private investors funding such assets, in addition to providing indirect funding as taxpayers. If the investors are domiciled in other jurisdictions but want to invest for geographical diversification, then this will be their only method of funding such assets.

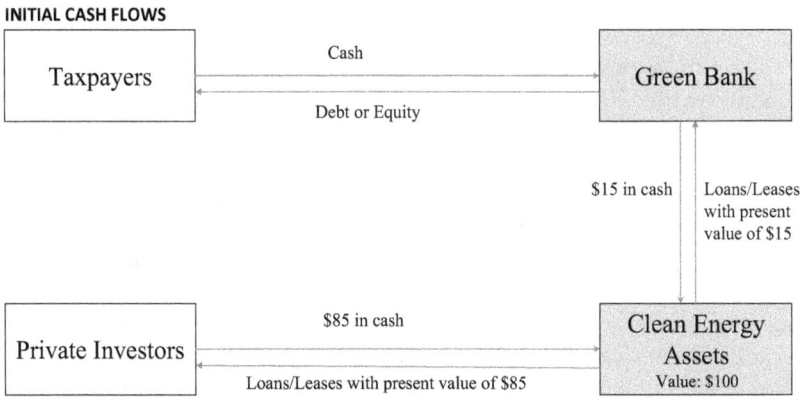

INITIAL CASH FLOWS

Fig. 12.1   Green bank initial capital flow. (Source: Adapted from Probst (2014))

Green banks utilize the following financing tools to leverage public funds:

1. *Direct Investment*: private investors may contribute capital to the green bank directly, in the form of preferred equity and subordinated or senior debt.
2. *Co-Investment: private investors are more likely to co-invest with the green bank due to the* implicit public endorsement that the green bank's involvement provides.
3. *Credit Enhancement*: a green bank may provide loan loss reserves for local and community banks who lend directly to household borrowers to purchase clean energy assets. Since the loan reserve is typically a small fraction of the total lending, this tool leverages public capital many times over.
4. *Warehousing*: green banks extend lines of credit to local banks to aggregate standardized energy efficiency or renewable energy loans before packaging for sale or securitization.
5. *Securitization*: green banks initiate pioneering securitizations of renewable energy and energy efficiency assets because the novel nature of the underlying cash flows and the absence of a statistical record implies that most lenders are not initially adept at structuring such assets.
6. *Capacity Building*: a green bank may help develop the expertise and software necessary to structure loans and securities whose underlying value depend on the energy savings induced by investments in renewable assets and energy efficiency improvements.

The Connecticut Green Bank, the first green bank in the United States, was formed in 2011. Established by the state legislature by statute, the bank's stated objective is to achieve cleaner, less expensive, and more reliable sources of energy while creating jobs and supporting local economic development (Connecticut Green Bank, 2019). The bank receives annual financial support from electricity users in the state in the form of a $0.001 per kilowatt-hour surcharge, which amounts to approximately $7–10 per household per year, or about $27 million per year. Due to its ability to tap private capital to leverage its public funding, it has been able to deploy over $1.3 billion in clean energy investments between 2011 and 2018 with this modest level of public funding. Projects recorded through 2016 show that for every $1 of public funds committed by the bank, an additional $6 in private investment was deployed. The Connecticut Green Bank helped to pioneer the Commercial Property Assessed Clean Energy (C-PACE) financing program, a public-private initiative to accelerate energy efficiency improvements.[6] The C-PACE program allows building owners to finance efficiency improvements with a loan that is repaid as part of subsequent property tax payments. As the loan is secured by a lien on the property, and because default rates on property taxes are extremely low, private lenders provide low interest loans for such energy efficiency improvements (Leonard, 2014). In the box below, we examine an example of an unusual securitization of solar energy credits by the Connecticut Green Bank.

A Securitization of Residential Solar Energy Credits

The Connecticut Green Bank concluded a novel securitization of $39 million in Solar Home Renewable Energy Credits (SHRECs) in April 2019 (Kang, 2019). The securitization monetized the SHRECs generated through its Residential Solar Investment Program (RSIP). The RSIP provides incentives to homeowners to install solar energy infrastructure. In return for the incentives, the bank receives the renewable energy credits generated. Renewable energy credits are tradable credits that represent one megawatt-hour of electricity generated from a renewable energy source. Connecticut utilities are required to purchase SHRECs to comply with state and regional clean energy goals (such as Renewable Portfolio Standards and the Regional Greenhouse Gas Initiative). Previous securitizations had packaged the value of energy from residential solar power installations, or related tax credits. The SHREC transaction was the first time that a securitization occurred where the only asset being securitized are renewable energy credits.

The sale was composed of two tranches of SHRECs produced by 105 megawatts of 14,000 residential solar photovoltaic (PV) systems. The Bank has employed a local contractor to monitor the level of renewable energy produced by every residential solar installation. When energy output drops below what can be expected due to weather variation and seasonality, the Bank alerts the homeowner to resolve the issue. The homeowner has an incentive to correct the issue quickly because he receives value from the electricity generated. This arrangement ensures that SHRECs that securitization envisages are actually generated over the life of the security.

The SHRECs will be aggregated by the bank and sold in annual tranches to Connecticut's two investor-owned utilities at a predetermined price over 15 years. The securitization allows the Bank to receive funds upfront in lieu of future payments from the two utilities for the purchase of the SHRECs (KBRA, 2019).

Securitization of renewable energy assets provides an example of a very direct link between capital provision and environmental impact. Because securitization strips out just the asset that an investor is interested in financing, it allows a very clean signal of investor interest and borrower demand. Green banks are instrumental in curating different kinds of investor into a package that meets the specific needs of diverse end-users investing in energy efficiency infrastructure. Since most green banks are focused on particular areas (states in the United States and relatively small countries elsewhere), they are more likely to evaluate accurately the local environmental benefits of clean energy investments. The SHREC example embodies a very close monitoring of value generation by the issuing bank at a local level. In addition, the widespread scrutiny that a quasi-public entity such as a green bank receives makes it unlikely that outsized transaction fees or commissions would become a feature of such securitizations. The green investment bank in the United Kingdom, which was founded in 2012 but later privatized in 2018, has been criticized for shifting its focus away from the United Kingdom to international projects (Turvill, 2019). In 2016, the British Parliament's Environmental Audit Committee urged ministers not to support the proposed privatization if the bank's stated objectives were not protected by its new private owner (Materials Recycling World, 2016).

Securitization of specific environmental assets institutes a form of recruitment and quorum sensing in the financial ecosystem. If green banks are able to amass a sufficient scale of a specific environmental asset to package it such that statistical averages become meaningful, then they are able to attract investors who are willing to assume measurable, easy-to-value risks. If investors believe that the returns from the securitization are justified, then it becomes feasible for the green bank to recycle the capital into additional securitizations. Assuming that the green bank monitors the assets (as in the SHREC example), then the high level of capital allocated to the environmental asset will support monitoring activities.

Thematic Investing

What about situations where it is difficult to separate a specific asset from the rest of the enterprise? In the SHREC example, investors could choose to invest in just the residential renewable energy credits. In most environmental or social investment opportunities, it is not possible to link the flow of capital with a specific impact in this manner. The difficulties of proving direct impact when there are many confounding factors imply that we cannot be sure that investors will factor in the less direct, less measurable environmental and social impact into their assessment of risk and return. Fortunately, in the context of listed equities, investors appear to reduce the cost of capital for firms with an environmental impact. In general, greater public disclosures about the financial risks of an investment reduce the cost of capital (Botosan, 2006; Easley & O'Hara, 2004). A number of studies find that voluntary disclosure of overall ESG sustainability performance also has a significant negative influence on the cost of equity (Dhaliwal, Li, Tsang, & Yang, 2011; El Ghoul, Guedhami, Kwok, & Mishra, 2011; Ng & Rezaee, 2015; Sharfman & Fernando, 2008).

Information flow can reduce the cost of capital for borrowers. The difficulty is that information is multi-dimensional and hard to process. An investor interested in funding a specific type of impact will have to read through reams of information before she understands whether a particular investment has the impact she desires. This makes it much harder to target capital toward specific impacts in a single security. One way in which investors can direct capital to broader aggregations of impact is through thematic investing. In a very broad sense, selecting securities with greater performance on a range of sustainability metrics is a form of thematic investing. What makes thematic investing valuable from a decentralized perspective is the varieties of themes that might be selected by different investors, especially if those selections can be made cheaply and by a wide array of investors. This requires diverse ratings of issuers on a range of idiosyncratically defined sustainability metrics that are made available to the investing ecosystem at negligible cost.

Our review of the social network analysis of sustainability accounting initiatives in Chap. 9 suggested that there are an Anglo-American dominance and an under-representation of continental Europe, Latin America, non-Anglophone Asia, and most of Africa in the assessment of non-financial metrics of listed equities. This is problematic because such narrow origins reduce the legitimacy and local suitability of centralized efforts at measuring sustainability performance of listed issuers. Many of the listed issuers are global corporations with operations in many regions. Since perspectives on sustainability are likely to vary across regions, it is essential to air local measurements of sustainability performance. The Inter-American Development Bank (IDB), which is focused on financing development projects in Latin America and the Caribbean, has pioneered the sustainability performance assessment of large publicly traded multinational corporations with a significant presence in the region from a regional, rather than a global, perspective (see below).

Combining ESG and Sustainable Development in IndexAmericas[7]
In 2016, the IDB initiated a method of quantifying the environmental, social, and governance as well as the sustainable development performance of listed issuers with a significant presence in the Latin America and Caribbean region. The method evaluates 6000 issuers on 157 key performance indicators (Galeano, 2018; IDB, 2019). In contrast to the approaches employed by other ratings providers, IDB incorporates its assessment of the alignment between the bank's own sustainable development objectives in the region and the policies and activities of listed issuers. The top 100 issuers amongst the assessed companies, diversified across industry sector, are announced annually. A selection from the top 100 issuers are presented with awards by *Latin Trade*, an industry magazine.

The IDB has fostered local efforts to develop similar sustainability assessments evaluated from the country level within the region. In 2018, IDB and Bolsas y Mercados Argentina (BYMA), the Argentine stock exchange entity, launched a sustainability index for Argentine listed issuers.

IDB is owned by 48 countries, including 26 borrowing countries from the region and 22 non-borrowing countries from outside the region. The borrowing countries collectively have slightly more than 50% of the voting power on the IDB board. The IDB is the largest multilateral source of financing for the region. IndexAmericas is therefore an endorsement by a locally owned and locally involved actor whose mission is focused on regional sustainable development, rather than solely on the interests of lending countries or on profit maximization.

The IndexAmericas list of issuers represents a portfolio of companies that could comprise a thematic investment for capital allocated to sustainable development in the region. Since the list is publicly available and prepared by a local endorser, other investors could in principle incorporate the endorsements in their own investing strategy. This type of information processing for local sustainable development is a valuable form of recruitment for the investing ecosystem.

Thematic investment outside the domain of sustainable investing is common. Thematic investing refers to constructing a portfolio of investments significantly different from the market portfolio, designed to capture returns through exposure to long-term structural trends in the economy. Thematic investing could involve selecting a portfolio of securities associated with the growth of organics, or renewable energy, or artificial intelligence and robotics. An investor could pick a handful of themes that she believes are likely to proliferate, leading to growth in the associated portfolios. Thematic investment necessarily eschews investing in the status quo, because the portfolio construction differs from the market portfolio by design. Because thematic investing requires an idiosyncratic narrative which has the potential to be far more engaging to individual investors than passive investing, it has become popular with financial advisors looking for ways to increase client engagement with their portfolios (Cherney, 2016). Ellevest, an investment advisor and online investing platform with a focus on investing in women offers thematic impact portfolios focused on gender-lens investing. Many studies have demonstrated that educating women and girls has catalyzed economic growth. Fully leveraging the talents of women by addressing gender wage gaps, eliminating discrimination and violence, and incorporating gender diversity in the investment analysis and portfolio construction process has the potential to unlock new sources of return (Quinlan & VanderBrug, 2017). Thematic investing, unlike passive investing, embodies the features of recruitment and quorum sensing. Exchange-traded funds (ETFs) designed to mimic thematic investing portfolios have proliferated in recent years.

The challenge for thematic investing is to ensure that thematic portfolio construction is cheap, widely available, and influenced by a wide range of perspectives. To the extent that thematic portfolios carry high expenses, their construction can become the excuse that justifies high investment fees. When thematic portfolios are constructed in a black-box manner, then it requires a credulous investor to buy into the notion that a few experts possess greater wisdom than the crowd, a principle decidedly at odds with decentralized finance. To the extent that they are constructed by diverse communities and are widely available at negligible cost, they represent potential signals of widespread investor interest. Not only do they indicate diverse investor interest in new ideas, they may also signal trends that companies and marketers should note.

How can builders of thematic portfolios tap the wisdom of crowds? Is there a way to utilize collaborative ecosystems in the investing world in the manner that open source coding efforts leverage the wisdom of a wide variety of individuals, with self-organization and self-monitoring as suggested by Ostrom? A collaborative question-and-answer search platform like Quora is able to provide specific responses to specific questions from diverse individuals that are nevertheless valuable to other observers. Is it feasible to tap crowdsourced investment ideas that are both valuable and not designed to manipulate? This requires accessing the opinions of a wide variety of individuals on listed issuers, with maximum transparency on the motives of idea-generators. Two initiatives appear to attempt to do just that. One is JUST Capital, a non-profit that annually surveys Americans "to identify the issues that matter most in defining just business behavior today" (JUST Capital, 2019). It then ranks issuers on categories such as good jobs, fair pay and strong benefits, employee education, support for local communities, customer privacy, and environmental impact. The JUST rankings are announced annually, having been published since 2016.

An intriguing business model that attempts to aggregate the wisdom of the crowd is Motif Investing. In 2012, Motif created an investing website that let users buy a portfolio of 30 stocks that comprise a thematic investment portfolio, such as one focused on social media or mobile internet. At the time, thematic investment ETFs offered similar functionality, but Motif charged a relatively low $9.99 to a user investing in a thematic portfolio of 30 stocks, with no ongoing management fees, whereas ETFs generally charged ongoing expenses (Robehmed, 2012). What is intriguing about Motif's model is the ability for anyone to build their own thematic portfolios and make them available to other Motif users. This cuts down the time and expense of creating new portfolios and significantly diversifies the perspectives and philosophies that go into portfolio construction. In the first 5 months after Motif launched this functionality, 15,000 customer portfolios were created, double the number of open-end US mutual funds at the time (Vasan, 2013). Motif virtually eliminates the barriers to portfolio construction and facilitates tracking of the performance of a diverse arrays of themes. While the approach provides recruitment, quorum sensing is more difficult, because far greater funds are invested outside the platform than in the platform.

An important function of polycentric governance that remains missing from thematic investing is the ability to communicate without necessarily transacting. As we noted in Chap. 4, investing for the planet means incorporating the voices of the billions of people who do not have the liquid funds to invest but are nevertheless affected by the actions of global corporations. Polycentric governance places a premium on the feedback loop available through political forums in small townships where the nature of the local public good is neither standardized nor easily scalable. Ideally, thematic investors and others would be able to communicate not only their chosen portfolios, but also their preliminary ideas, their working drafts of portfolios, their tentative theories of the future. This airing of the analytical process could facilitate social learning linked to the discipline of investing. The ESG-related actions of issuers are evaluated in different ways by different sustainable investors.

In addition, thoughtful investors are capable of being persuaded to change their views when faced with reasoned analysis. The possibilities from the exercise of disputation are the very bedrock of adversarial legal systems around the world. A number of alumni from the sustainability management program at Columbia University have begun a startup venture named Sustain Investing Co., which aims to facilitate friendly discussion about specific ESG actions by listed issuers and translate the resulting insights into a participatory investment portfolio.[8] Sustain is a community-driven investment fund open to anyone with an interest in sustainable investing (Sustain Investing Co, 2019). Members' conversational history is viewable to the entire community. Crucially, members are asked to upvote or downvote the continual actions of issuers, along with a request for thoughtful commentary, leading to a reasoned assessment on a history of corporate actions. Unlike centralized ESG rating agencies, Sustain Investing offers a grassroots-led, decentralized governance aware platform to aggregate the wisdom of crowds into action-sensitive ratings of companies.

THE POTENTIAL AND PITFALLS OF BLOCKCHAIN

Ostrom's six preconditions for the emergence of cooperation suggest a number of aspects of a sustainable financial ecosystem. First, it is necessary to reduce the costs of matching and transacting between investors and issuers. Second, it would be good if the complete reputations of market participants could be costlessly advertised. Third, it is important to reduce the cost of entry for small issuers and investors. Finally, low-cost monitoring and sanctioning within the marketplace (for example, with easy reputational updates) would constrain bad behavior. Blockchain, or distributed ledger systems (DLT), promise that many of these features could be incorporated at low cost in new transaction architectures.

Blockchain Functionality

A blockchain is a consecutively ordered collection of data sets (called blocks) where each block lists multiple transactions, labeled TX1 through TXn (see Fig. 12.2). Each block also contains the hash value[9] of the preceding block (called the 'parent'), a timestamp and a nonce, which is an arbitrary random number (that can be used just once) issued in an authentication protocol to verify the hash value.

The blockchain is extended by new blocks and therefore represents a complete ledger of the transaction history. This set of elements preserves the integrity of the entire blockchain through to the first block (known as the 'genesis block'). Copies of the entire blockchain are maintained by decentralized nodes on a network. Each addition to the blockchain must be verified by a majority of nodes. If the nodes agree by a consensus mechanism on the validity of transactions in a new block and on the validity of the block itself, the block can be added to the chain (Nofer, Gomber, Hinz, & Schiereck, 2017). The basic ideas for blockchain are conceived by Haber and Stornetta in their proposal for computationally practical procedures for time-stamping digital documents so that it is infeasible for a user to back-

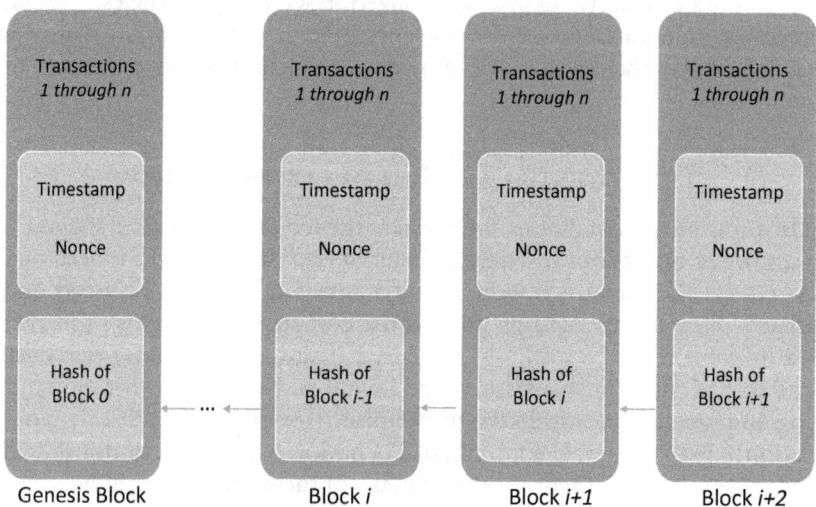

Fig. 12.2 Example blockchain. (Source: Adapted from Zheng, Xie, Dai, Chen, & Wang (2017))

date or forward-date her document, even with the collusion of a time-stamping service (Haber & Stornetta, 1991).

Readers familiar with old-fashioned double-entry bookkeeping ledgers can visualize the blockchain as a continually updated ledger account, with all transactions recorded since inception, without loss of historic information caused by the periodic carrying over of cumulative balances into new ledger books. One can visualize the distributed ledger aspect by imagining a coterie of Franciscan friars checking the validity of each new block of transactions and simultaneously entering the new block into their ledger copies only after agreeing that the new block is valid. The previous blocks are never erased or modified when new blocks are added.

The blockchain makes it possible for a decentralized network of nodes to agree, at regular intervals, about the true state of shared data. This shared data can encapsulate the cumulative effect of many types of online transactions, including payments and exchanges of non-physical assets, in the absence of a privileged central intermediary. The resulting digital marketplace may allow increased competition due to lower barriers to entry. It may lower privacy risk by distributing identity information to multiple nodes in cryptographic form instead of leaving it at the whim of a single intermediary. Finally, DLT could allow participants to make joint investments in shared infrastructure without assigning market power to the platform operator (Catalini & Gans, 2016). For example, if family members choose to share their precious photos over a social networking platform, those photos would disappear if the platform were to delete the family's accounts. In a DLT system, a manipulator would need to persuade the majority of nodes to delete those accounts, a considerably more difficult task.

The organic diffusion process embedded in Bitcoin, perhaps the most famous application of blockchain, employs high-powered incentives similar to the venture capital model to reward early adopters of the Bitcoin platform (Catalini & Gans, 2016). Thankfully, many thoughtful observers have already questioned the social value of high-powered incentives (Admati, 2017). It is unlikely that incentive structures such as those embedded in Bitcoin mining will provide much value to a sustainable financial ecosystem. Blockchain networks can differ sharply from the Bitcoin model in terms of consensus mechanism, identity anonymity, protocol efficiency and electricity consumption, immutability, ownership and management, and transaction approval process (Casino, Dasaklis, & Patsakis, 2019). There is, however, a trade-off between the speed of transaction approval and the immutability of the blockchain. Networks that require less computational checks for validity also increase the risk of collusion attacks that could successfully change the record.

Applications to Sustainable Finance

Three potential applications to sustainable finance are immediately obvious and frequently discussed: prediction markets, distributed corporate governance, and trade finance.

Prediction Markets Prediction markets are the classic decentralized device designed to aggregate the wisdom of crowds. In a prediction market, agents can speculate on the outcome of future events, such as who might win an election. Those who are correct in their forecast, win money, and those who are incorrect lose money. Typically the winners win the amount lost by the losers, less transaction costs. Players face a negative sum game, but the predicted probabilities before the resolution of uncertainty provide a useful signal to society at large. The benefit of the prediction market arises from the avoidance of the misallocation of capital which might result from incorrect forecasts. Auger is a DLT-based platform for prediction markets that operates without any intermediary, thus minimizing the cost of operation (Peterson, Krug, Zoltu, Williams, & Alexander, 2018). The cost-minimization has the potential to maximize the societal benefit-cost ratio of improved forecasts.

Corporate Governance Many major financial intermediaries have begun to invest in blockchain and DLT, and stock exchanges have proposed using the technology for trading and tracking of the ownership of corporate equities (Yermack, 2015). Nofer et al. state that when the US investment bank Bear Stearns was acquired by JPMorgan Chase in 2008, the number of shares offered to the acquirer was larger than the shares outstanding in the books of Bear Stearns (Nofer et al., 2017). Yermack lays out a number of implications of using blockchain to track share ownership for managers, institutional investors, small shareholders, auditors, and civil society. For example, transparent and real-time ownership records might prevent an activist investor from buying shares in one market to influence management, while simultaneously selling shares short in a different exchange to nullify his economic interest in the company. In our example of Sustain Invest described above, community members could choose to display their share ownership in a consensually verified manner to increase the import of their statements and votes. DLT-based corporate ownership has the potential to marry economic interests and shareholder engagement and facilitate distributed governance that is difficult to imagine given the current system.

Trade Finance Trade finance is the general term for banking services aimed at mitigating credit risk for exporters and importers. Most exporters and importers are small- and medium-sized enterprises (Colgan, 2019) who face significant obstacles and costs in the existing antiquated system of letters of credit that govern payments based on milestones in the delivery process. ING Bank and HSBC have initiated a live trade finance platform using blockchain for food and agriculture firm Cargill. The shared platform allows parties in the supply chain to view inventory records and effect payments in real time (Lee, 2018). Wang et al. propose a blockchain-based system of inventory and receivables financing for small and medium enterprises that can reduce costs and also facilitate a seamless system of lending and repayment using smart contracts (Wang, Lin, & Luo, 2019).

The Limits of Blockchain

Despite its promise for the decentralization of finance, there are significant limits to the application and integrity of blockchain technology, caused by the excessive need for computing power, the threat of illicit cryptanalysis by quantum computers and perhaps most importantly, the limits of standardization and measurability in human affairs. In order to verify that each new block is valid, nodes must perform CPU-intensive cryptographic computations. The continual verification of a lengthening history imposes absurd requirements on computation power (Budish, 2018). The structure of validating transactions in the Bitcoin blockchain is akin to nearly everybody simultaneously counting their gross and net wealth every time they purchase a coffee. While computers are much faster at computation than humans, the design seems flawed in a human world where history becomes vanishingly unimportant and the present looms large. The architecture of blockchain is designed to make us remember everything. This is a machine that Herbert Simon, with his recognition of cognitive limits, would have gladly smashed.

Hawlitschek et al. argue that the conceptualization of trust differs substantially between the contexts of blockchain and the sharing economy. They state that while blockchain technology can partially replace the need for trusted platform providers, blockchain systems without external sources of trust are barely transferable to sharing economy interactions (Hawlitschek, Notheisen, & Teubner, 2018). It is also well known that current blockchain architectures can be decoded with quantum computers. When blockchain was first conceived, quantum computers were a distant fantasy, but now they appear increasingly feasible (Fedorov, Fedorov, Kiktenko, & Lvovsky, 2018).

CONCLUDING REMARKS

The limitations of blockchain for the ultimate realization of a sustainable decentralized financial ecosystem provide hope that the indeterminacy and spontaneity of human intuition and judgment will continue to shape our shared quest for a sustainable future. Decentralized decision-making can significantly enhance the resilience of the circular flow of savings in the ecosystem. New models of polycentric and distributed governance, including some incorporating blockchain, can facilitate a virtuous feedback loop between stakeholders and the coupled natural and human system. In the next chapter, we turn to a review of new financing methods designed to sustainably manage natural capital infrastructure.

NOTES

1. So long as participants are rational, self-interested, and they interact repeatedly a finite number of times, game theory predicts that would overharvest the CPR.
2. This process is now referred to as a *Tiebout process*.
3. This means that the value of each individual contribution to the social good is high. This is more likely to be the case when there are fewer participants.
4. Internal sanctions chosen by the participants tend to increase cooperation and monitoring. External sanctions imposed by a central regulator, on the other hand, tend to crowd out internal monitoring.
5. The rebound effect is an example of the Jevons paradox. Investments in energy efficiency reduce the marginal cost of using energy, thereby inducing subsequent increases in the consumption of the outputs of energy use, such as hot water or internal ambient temperature. This leads to increases in energy consumption, though the increases only partially offset the initial reduction in energy use resulting from energy efficiency investments.

6. For an outline of a range of public-private initiatives for renewable energy and energy efficiency such as guarantee structures, on-bill programs and property-assessed clean energy (PACE) programs in addition to green banks, see Probst (2014).
7. As a matter of disclosure, one of the authors of the present volume (Bose) has worked as Principal Investigator of sponsored research related to IndexAmericas conducted at Columbia University and funded by IDB.
8. As a matter of disclosure, two of the authors of the present volume (Bose & Guo) teach in Columbia's Sustainability Management program.
9. The hash value is an output of a cryptographic hash function which takes the previous block as an input. A hash function converts an input of letters and numbers into an encrypted output of a fixed length.

REFERENCES

Admati, A. R. (2017). A Skeptical View of Financialized Corporate Governance. *Journal of Economic Perspectives, 31*(3), 131–150. https://doi.org/10.1257/jep.31.3.131

Allcott, H., & Greenstone, M. (2012). Is There an Energy Efficiency Gap? *Journal of Economic Perspectives, 26*(1), 3–28. http://www.aeaweb.org/jep/

Atkinson, S., & Williams, P. (2009). Quorum Sensing and Social Networking in the Microbial World. *Journal of the Royal Society, Interface, 6*(40), 959–978. https://doi.org/10.1098/rsif.2009.0203

Bhidé, A. (2010). *A Call for Judgment: Sensible Finance for a Dynamic Economy.* New York, NY: Oxford University Press.

Botosan, C. A. (2006). Disclosure and the Cost of Capital: What Do We Know? *Accounting & Business Research (Wolters Kluwer UK), 36*, 31–40. https://doi.org/10.1080/00014788.2006.9730042

Budish, E. (2018). *The Economic Limits of Bitcoin and the Blockchain* (NBER Working Papers: 24717). National Bureau of Economic Research, Inc. Retrieved from http://www.nber.org/papers/w24717.pdf

Callaway, D. S., Fowlie, M., & McCormick, G. (2018). Location, Location, Location: The Variable Value of Renewable Energy and Demand-Side Efficiency Resources. *Journal of the Association of Environmental and Resource Economists, 5*(1), 39–75. http://www.journals.uchicago.edu/loi/jaere

Casino, F., Dasaklis, T. K., & Patsakis, C. (2019). A Systematic Literature Review of Blockchain-Based Applications: Current Status, Classification and Open Issues. *Telematics and Informatics, 36*, 55–81. https://doi.org/10.1016/j.tele.2018.11.006

Catalini, C., & Gans, J. S. (2016). *Some Simple Economics of the Blockchain* (NBER Working Papers: 22952). National Bureau of Economic Research, Inc. Retrieved from http://www.nber.org/papers/w22952.pdf

Chatterji, A. K., Durand, R., Levine, D. I., & Touboul, S. (2016). Do Ratings of Firms Converge? Implications for Managers, Investors and Strategy Researchers. *Strategic Management Journal, 37*(8), 1597–1614. https://doi.org/10.1002/smj.2407

Cherney, N. (2016). Investing in Change: What Advisors Need to Know About Thematic Investing. *Investment Advisor, 36*(11), 30–34.

Cole, D. H. (2011). From Global to Polycentric Climate Governance. *Climate Law, 2*(3), 395–413.

Colgan, C. (2019). How Community and Midsize Banks Fuel America's Export Economy. *ABA Banking Journal, 111*(3), 22–24.

Connecticut Green Bank. (2019). *About Us.* Retrieved from https://www.ctgreenbank.com/about-us-2017/

Cutler, D., & Miller, G. (2006). Water, Water Everywhere: Municipal Finance and Water Supply in American Cities. In E. L. Glaeser & C. Goldin (Eds.), *Corruption and Reform: Lessons from America's Economic History* (A National Bureau of Economic Research Conference Report) (pp. 153–183). Chicago, IL/London, UK: University of Chicago Press.

Dhaliwal, D. S., Li, O. Z., Tsang, A., & Yang, Y. G. (2011). Voluntary Nonfinancial Disclosure and the Cost of Equity Capital: The Initiation of Corporate Social Responsibility Reporting. *Accounting Review, 86*(1), 59–100. https://doi.org/10.2308/accr.00000005

Easley, D., & O'Hara, M. (2004). Information and the Cost of Capital. *Journal of Finance (Wiley-Blackwell), 59*(4), 1553–1583. https://doi.org/10.1111/j.1540-6261.2004.00672.x

El Ghoul, S., Guedhami, O., Kwok, C. C. Y., & Mishra, D. R. (2011). Does Corporate Social Responsibility Affect the Cost of Capital? *Journal of Banking and Finance, 35*(9), 2388–2406. http://www.sciencedirect.com/science/journal/03784266

Fedorov, A. K., Fedorov, A. K., Kiktenko, E. O., & Lvovsky, A. I. (2018). Quantum Computers Put Blockchain Security at Risk. *Nature (London), 563* (7729), 465–467. https://doi.org/10.1038/d41586-018-07449-z

Figus, G., Turner, K., McGregor, P., & Katris, A. (2017). Making the Case for Supporting Broad Energy Efficiency Programmes: Impacts on Household Incomes and Other Economic Benefits. *Energy Policy, 111*, 157–165.

Galeano, V. (2018). INDEX Americas Sustainability Award 2018. *Latin Trade (English), 26*(1), 33–38.

Gillingham, K., & Palmer, K. (2014). Bridging the Energy Efficiency Gap: Policy Insights from Economic Theory and Empirical Evidence. *Review of Environmental Economics and Policy, 8*(1), 18–38. https://academic.oup.com/reep/issue

Golman, R., Hagmann, D., & Miller, J. H. (2015). Polya's Bees: A Model of Decentralized Decision-Making. *Science Advances, 1*(8). https://doi.org/10.1126/sciadv.1500253

Haber, S., & Stornetta, W. S. (1991). How to Time-Stamp a Digital Document. *Journal of Cryptology, 3*(2), 99–111. https://doi.org/10.1007/BF00196791

Hawlitschek, F., Notheisen, B., & Teubner, T. (2018). The Limits of Trust-Free Systems: A Literature Review on Blockchain Technology and Trust in the Sharing Economy. *Electronic Commerce Research and Applications, 29,* 50–63. https://doi.org/10.1016/j.elerap.2018.03.005

IDB. (2019). *Index Americas Methodology.* Retrieved from https://indexamericas.iadb.org/en/Methodology

JUST Capital. (2019). *Polling the American People.* Retrieved from https://just-capital.com/polling/

Kang, J. (2019). Green Bank Markets "SHREC" Solar ABS Deal. *Global Capital,* n.p.

KBRA. (2019). SHREC ABS 1 LLC: SHREC Collateralized Notes, Series 2019–1. Retrieved from https://www.krollbondratings.com/show_report/16842

Lee, P. (2018). Trade Finance on Blockchain Moves to Full Production. *Euromoney, 49*(590), 16–16.

Leonard, W. A. (2014). Clean Is the New Green: Clean Energy Finance and Deployment Through Green Banks. *Yale Law & Policy Review, 33*(1), 197–229.

Loutskina, E. (2011). The Role of Securitization in Bank Liquidity and Funding Management. *Journal of Financial Economics, 100*(3), 663–684. https://doi.org/10.1016/j.jfineco.2011.02.005

Materials Recycling World. (2016). MPs Call for Halt to Sale of Green Investment Bank. *Materials Recycling World, 205,* 6–6.

Ng, A. C., & Rezaee, Z. (2015). Business Sustainability Performance and Cost of Equity Capital. *Journal of Corporate Finance, 34,* 128–149. http://www.sciencedirect.com/science/journal/09291199

Nofer, M., Gomber, P., Hinz, O., & Schiereck, D. (2017). Blockchain. *Business & Information Systems Engineering, 59*(3), 183–187. https://doi.org/10.1007/s12599-017-0467-3

Ostrom, E. (2010). Beyond Markets and States: Polycentric Governance of Complex Economic Systems. *American Economic Review, 100*(3), 641–672. http://www.aeaweb.org/aer/

Ostrom, V., Tiebout, C. M., & Warren, R. (1961). The Organization of Government in Metropolitan Areas: A Theoretical Inquiry. *American Political Science Review, 55*(4), 831–842.

Peterson, J., Krug, J., Zoltu, M., Williams, A. K., & Alexander, S. (2018). *Augur: A Decentralized Oracle and Prediction Market Platform.* Retrieved from https://github.com/AugurProject/whitepaper/blob/master/english/whitepaper.pdf

Platz, D. (2011). Tapping Capital for Water: The History in the United States and Implications for Asia. *Environment and Urbanization ASIA, 2*(1), 29–44. https://doi.org/10.1177/097542531000200104

Polanyi, K. (1944). *The Great Transformation.* New York, NY: Farrar & Rinehart.

Probst, C. (2014). *Private Sector Financing and Public-Private Partnerships for Financing Clean Energy.* Retrieved from http://spm.ei.columbia.edu/files/2014/09/SPM_Probst_FinancingCleanEnergy.pdf

Quinlan, J., & VanderBrug, J. (2017). *Gender Lens Investing: Uncovering Opportunities for Growth, Returns, and Impact.* Hoboken, NJ: Wiley.

Robehmed, N. (2012). Motif Investing: Money Grows on Ideas. *Forbes.com*, p. 21.

Sharfman, M. P., & Fernando, C. S. (2008). Environmental Risk Management and the Cost of Capital. *Strategic Management Journal, 29*(6), 569–592. https://doi.org/10.1002/smj.678

Sustain Investing Co. (2019). *Sustain: Know What You Own.* Retrieved from https://www.sustaininvesting.com/

Turvill, W. (2019). Cable Furious at Green Bank 'Sell-Out Scandal'. *Mail on Sunday*, p. 94.

Vasan, P. (2013). The Rise of DIY Investment Funds. (Cover Story). *Money Management Executive, 21*(33), 1–6.

Visscher, P. K., & Camazine, S. (1999). Collective Decisions and Cognition in Bees. *Nature, 397*(6718), 400–400.

Wachter, S. M. (2018). Credit Risk Transfer, Informed Markets, and Securitization. *FRBNY Economic Policy Review, 24*, 117–137.

Wang, R., Lin, Z., & Luo, H. (2019). Blockchain, Bank Credit and SME Financing. *Quality & Quantity, 53*(3), 1127–1140. https://doi.org/10.1007/s11135-018-0806-6

Wright, R. E., & Sylla, R. (2011). Corporate Governance and Stockholder/Stakeholder Activism in the United States, 1790–1860: New Data and Perspectives. In J. Koppell (Ed.), *Origins of Shareholder Advocacy.* New York, NY: Palgrave Macmillan.

Yermack, D. (2015). *Corporate Governance and Blockchains* (NBER Working Papers: 21802). National Bureau of Economic Research, Inc. Retrieved from http://www.nber.org/papers/w21802.pdf

Zheng, Z., Xie, S., Dai, H., Chen, X., & Wang, H. (2017, June 25–30). *An Overview of Blockchain Technology: Architecture, Consensus, and Future Trends.* Paper presented at the 2017 IEEE International Congress on Big Data (Big Data Congress).

CHAPTER 13

Conservation Finance and Payment for Ecosystem Services

Introduction

Viewed holistically, natural ecosystems comprising the vast diversity of biomes that continue to evolve on the earth are the sine qua non of sustainable human well-being. Ecosystems include marine, coastal, inland water, forest, dryland, island, mountain, polar, cultivated, and urban lands. These biomes and their interaction with humans are the indispensable sources of well-being on earth. Of the earth's ice-free land, 78% consist of biomes with significant human habitation or land use (Ellis & Ramankutty, 2008). It is possible to delineate the direct benefits that flow from these biomes to human society as a whole and attempt to value them using the techniques of environmental valuation described in Chaps. 6 and 7. This is also part of the research agenda of the United Nations Millennium Ecosystem Assessment (Millennium Ecosystem Assessment, 2005) and efforts to value natural capital and ecosystem services. As we note in Chap. 2, a commonly cited attempt to value global ecosystem services in monetary terms (Costanza et al., 2014) estimates that they are valued at approximately $130 trillion annually.

Ecosystem services include *provisioning* services such as food and water, *regulating* services such as the regulation of floods and droughts, *supporting* services such as soil formation and nutrient cycling, and *cultural* services such as recreational and spiritual value. Some of these services have immediate economic benefits and are relatively easily valued through revealed preference methods (see Chap. 6). Others are inherently resistant

© The Author(s) 2019
S. Bose et al., *The Financial Ecosystem*, Palgrave Studies in Impact Finance, https://doi.org/10.1007/978-3-030-05624-7_13

to the notion of temporal and material value. Direct monetary estimates of *use* value can be computed from the market values of the products of hunting, logging, and fishing. Conversely, the use values attributable to biodiversity in controlling agricultural pests and of wetlands and forests in providing a wide range of ecosystem services and recreational values are often ignored and difficult to value (Ando & Shah, 2016). Furthermore, *existence* values can only be surmised through contingent valuation methods, a procedure that is less grounded by market transactions.

As we saw in Chap. 6, the *public good* nature of many ecosystems implies that it is the *horizontal sum* of individual demands that matters for societal valuation. The societal value of an output of the ecosystem for any particular individual might be small, indeed too small to induce any market transaction or visible effort on the part of that individual. However, in aggregate, the (horizontal) sum of these individual values is significant, and indeed the sum of values of all individuals over all outputs of the ecosystem must be highly material (since a properly functioning ecosystem is essential to well-being).

For any individual actor, the private value of preserving the ecosystem is smaller than the private effort required to maintain it, a phenomenon commonly referred to as 'the tragedy of the commons'. This 'tragedy' is isomorphic to Mancur Olson's point that the individual incentives for collective action are not generally aligned with aggregate social benefit but rather with the difference between individual per capita benefits and individual per capita costs (Olson, 1971). For example, if individual fishermen, aiming to maximize their own catch, are oblivious to the negative impact that overfishing can have on the ecosystem, then their self-interested behavior will lead the fish stock falling below the critical level needed for regeneration—a consequence that is detrimental to everyone's long-term interest. The same logic can apply to hunting and logging, and when these activities are not carefully managed, individual actors who derive direct use values from killing animals and harvesting trees can drive these species to extinction.

According to the dominant scholarly world-view of the mid-twentieth century, the optimal method of escaping the 'tragedy' or the collective action problem consisted of either hierarchical regulation by a centralized state of individual self-seeking behavior, or the privatization of commonly owned resources by a single profit-maximizing owner (Ostrom, 2010). Such regulation or privatization was considered the only way to eliminate the negative externalities of habitat and species loss which accompanied resource extraction or land-use change. Elinor Ostrom, along with kindred thinkers, displaced this rather simplistic view of the types of socio-economic systems that optimally provide public goods. Ostrom referred to ecosystem services as *common property resources (CPRs)*. CPRs differ from *public* goods, which are defined as those goods whose consumption is *non-rival* in that the usage of the good by one person does not diminish its availability for another person. Consumption of CPRs is *subtractible* or *rival* in that use by one individual subtracts the availability for others. For example, urbanization shrinks natural spaces, intense water consumption exhausts groundwater reserves and slows river flow, and agriculture converts habitat to farming fields. CPRs differ from private goods (such as food and clothing) in that their benefits are generally *non-excludable*: it is difficult or expensive to limit the benefits of the CPR to specific individuals. Knowledge and the defense of a community are examples of public goods, while lakes and marine ecosystems are examples of CPRs. Ostrom notes that scholars and policymakers around the world, overly influenced by Garrett Hardin's "portrayal of the users of a common-pool resource being trapped in an inexorable tragedy of overuse and destruction", assumed that CPRs were effectively owned unmanaged and rushed to assign private property rights to them. However, research by Ostrom and others demonstrate that many CPRs are effectively conserved and managed by a polycentric set of interacting governance structures, some of which are self-organized by CPR users out of a shared understanding of common costs and benefits as well as the value of diversity of interventions.

What is the optimal scale of conservation activities? One estimate is that $300–400 billion is needed annually to finance conservation and restoration of ecosystems, but currently only $52 billion is being allocated to these efforts (Huwyler, Käppeli, Serafimova, Swanson, & Tobin, 2014). If the value of ecosystem services is indeed $130 trillion annually, then $300–400 billion is likely to be an underestimate since it represents just 0.3% of the overall flow of services. There are very few, if any, assets where the maintenance costs represent just 0.3% of the overall cash flows. This suggests that for the ecosystem as a whole, conservation expenditure is likely to generate a high return. Of course, due to the presence of externalities, it is likely that such high returns to conservation will not be manifested in private investments. Nevertheless, a range of public and private conservation finance instruments which we outline below attempt, with moderate success, to encourage conservation behavior.

CONSERVATION FINANCE DEFINED

Conservation finance is a form of financial structuring aiming to realign incentives so as to increase the pay-off to preservation relative to consumption. By providing monetary incentives for societal conservation at localized scales, it has the potential to encourage differentiated conservation behavior adapted to polycentric situations where command-and-control regulation or outright privatization is inappropriate or ineffective. It involves the use of a range of financial mechanisms in funding the conservation and restoration of ecosystems, and can place supra-national, national, and sub-national governments, charitable organizations or private investors in the role of funder or capital provider. Often, the ecosystems most in need of preservation and management and at greatest risk of degradation are those whose inhabitants have low disposable monetary income to devote to conservation. It is these ecosystems that are likely to generate little short-term cash flow and pose a high degree of long-term risk. As such, private sector capital has been a relatively minor funder of ecosystems and natural capital. Charitable organizations and national governments, through grants, donations, and government budget allocations have been the leaders in funding natural conservation.

PUBLIC CAPITAL

Modern archeological studies have demonstrated that humans have actively manipulated forest ecologies for at least 45,000 years (Roberts, Hunt, Arroyo-Kalin, Evans, & Boivin, 2017). Humans populated extensive and long-lasting settlements in the tropical forests in Borneo and Melanesia 45,000 years ago and in South Asia 36,000 years ago. It is therefore unlikely that the 'tragedy of the commons' was inexorable or even widespread throughout most of human history in the context of forest management. Perhaps the oldest form of societal-induced conservation consisted of sylvanic cultures that placed a high sacred value on forests, animistic conceptions of mountains, rivers, animals, and grandiose tall trees. Yi (2012) describes the institutionalization into state rituals of the cultural and environmental significance of trees in Korea, Mongolia, and northeastern China in the twelfth century. The contemporaneous Ahom rulers of northeastern India venerated key tree species in royal ceremonies, acknowledging the dependence of their sylvan-cultural economy on forest ecosystems (Bhattacharjee, 2017). The Magna Carta and its twin document, the Charter of the Forest, guaranteed the rights of commoners to draw their sustenance from the forest at a time when it was the primary source of most goods and services and when monarchic overreach in the centuries after the Norman Conquest threatened to starve peasants by limiting access to royalty (Linebaugh, 2008).

In modern times, in Anglo-American jurisdictions, which lack a significant history of common property ownership, the state purchase of land, financed through fees and taxation, has become a method of achieving societal conservation. The Boston Common, a city park established in 1634, is considered the oldest example in the English-speaking world where people are taxed in order to support a public space that provides both public and private benefits (Levitt, 2005). Yosemite National Park was first designated as a state park in 1864 in California, and Yellowstone was the first national park designated in 1872. Today, there are 60 national parks and over 10,000 state parks that are protected by the U.S. government, and even more land is temporarily protected by the federally funded Conservation Reserve Program. Elsewhere in the world, the Bogd Khan Uul National Park was established in 1778 by the Mongolian government, although the area was chartered by the Chinese Ming Dynasty in the sixteenth century for its sacredness and beauty and kept off limits to extractive activities (McFarland, 2017).

Debt-for-Nature Swap

While government revenue has traditionally been a very important source of revenue for conservation, many protected land areas lack sufficient financial resources to be effective after creation, especially in less developed countries, where government financial capacity can be limited. To ameliorate this problem, Thomas Lovejoy, formerly the Vice President of the World Wildlife Fund (WWF) conceived a financial mechanism—the debt-for-nature swap—in 1984 that instead of converting debt claims to equity ownership, would extinguish the debt in exchange for a financial commitment from the debtor government to fund conservation projects through a local environmental agency. The debt-for-nature swaps were only made possible as many of the less developed countries that were saddled with external debts were also the ones without the necessary capital to manage some of the world's most vulnerable natural areas. The WWF pioneered the idea with other environmental organizations in negotiating debt-for-nature swap programs with countries such as Bolivia, Costa Rica, Ecuador, the Philippines, Madagascar, Poland, and Zambia in its early phase (Asiedu-Akrofi, 1991).

The Bolivian government became the first country to participate in a debt-to-nature swap, in 1987. Conservation International, an environmental non-governmental organization (NGO) based in the United States purchased $650,000 of Bolivian debt for a heavily discounted price of $100,000 and swapped it with the Bolivian government for the shares of a local environmental company that the government set up to preserve 1.6 million hectares of grasslands and forest in the Beni River Region. In theory, a debt-for-nature swap is meant to benefit all parties. The debtor country is able to reduce its external debt burden, while also allocating funds for domestic spending (in conservation) that create local employment rather than debt servicing. When there is a high risk of sovereign default, encapsulated in a heavily discounted bond price, it may be beneficial for creditors to liquidate their holdings to a conservation-oriented distressed debt acquirer. Conservation organizations acting either as international donors or local implementers may have the funds to further their conservation mission. If the debts are purchased below face value and redeemed by the debtor government at face value, conservation organizations end up with more funds than they would have if they had chosen to pay for in-country conservation directly.

A swap where an NGO purchases the debt at discount from a commercial bank is referred to as commercial debt-for-nature swap. However, these swaps do not necessarily have to go through an NGO. In some cases, the swap is effected between two governments in a bilateral transaction, where the creditor country forgives a portion of the debt in exchange for conservation commitment from the debtor government. These are referred to as bilateral debt-for-nature swaps. The United States, Canada, Finland, and France are among the first countries to participate in bilateral debt-for-nature swaps with indebted developing countries (Cassimon, Prowse, & Essers, 2011).

Since 1987, debt-for-nature swap programs have generated over $1 billion in funding for conservation in developing countries (Sheikh, 2018), although this is miniscule compared to the total developing country external debt of $6.7 trillion as of 2015 (World Bank Group, 2017). Other international organizations active in debt-for-nature swaps include the Nature Conservancy, the Global Environment Facility, and the Leonardo DiCaprio Foundation. Throughout the 1980s and 1990s, approximately five agreements were negotiated between national governments and international conservation organizations every year, but the number had since decreased to two per year (Sheikh, 2018). This decline is a result of a decrease in the discount at which commercial debts can be bought on the secondary market (Cassimon et al., 2011). In the earlier decades, debts could be purchased at deeply discounted rates, but other debt restructuring and relief mechanisms such as the one under the heavily indebted poor countries (HIPC) initiative contributed to reduced default probabilities and lower debt discounts.

Debt-for-nature swaps have been criticized for not supporting local workers, and instead benefitting local elites from the debtor countries. The success of the conservation projects ultimately depends on the capacity of the local conservation organizations to carry out the operation, which in turns would hinge on their management capabilities, relationships with local communities, and various government agencies. Without supportive government policies and institutions, it would be difficult to achieve meaningful conservation targets. It has also been observed that sometimes debt relief revenue does not go to their intended use.

Conservation-Related Taxes

Taxes are often the primary source for government revenue. Taxes can be raised from various sources and usually the recipients of tax revenue do not have any connection to the source of the revenue. Countries can earmark certain taxes for conservation to provide a stable revenue source for conservation activities. The hunting and fishing tax created under the Federal Aid in Wildlife Restoration Act, also known as the Pittman-Robertson Act passed in the United States in 1937 is an example. Under the Act, a 10–11% federal excise tax is levied on firearms and ammunitions for hunting, sport fishing, outdoor recreational equipment, and motor boat gasoline (World Wildlife Fund, 2009). The revenue from these taxes goes into wildlife conservation and restoration, such as maintaining fish populations, expanding habitat, training hunters, as well as marine conservation. A similar legislation, the Federal Aid in Sports Fish Restoration Act, or the Dingell-Johnson Act was passed in 1950. The two Acts generate $1.1 billion in annual funding toward state conservation, and more than $20 billion since they first passed (U.S. Department of the Interior, 2018).

Large Government-Sponsored Programs

Alternatively, large government-sponsored programs aimed at paying for the ecosystem services of biodiversity conservation and environmental protection more broadly are common. Forests and wetlands are essential regulators of water flow and quality, yet they are under constant pressure to be converted into farm and settlement land. Due to the serious threat of deforestation which partly contributed to the Yangtze River flooding in 2008, China developed the Natural Forest Protection Program (NFPP) and the Sloping Land Conversion Program (SLCP; also called 'Grain for Green') for conservation and restoration of forest and grassland in order to reduce natural disaster risks and help with poverty alleviation. The former is aimed at protecting natural forest and controlling deforestation, and the latter is focused on reforming land-use systems and creating new forest.

While NFPP is enforced by the government, SLCP is a voluntary system with built-in market incentives for participation. For example, farming on lands steeper than 25° is illegal, but many farmers nevertheless farm on steep slopes in order to supplement their meager income. With SLCP, the government provides incentives to limit farming. Under the program, farmers are compensated for a number of years after the planting of trees suitable for erosion prevention on a slope, before the trees become financially viable. With a total commitment of 800 billion yuan (US$115 billion) between 1998 and 2020, these two programs are the largest government-sponsored conservation and restoration programs in the world (Wu, Liu, Li, Zhao, & Zhao, 2009).

According to the first national ecosystem assessment (2000–2010), the national conservation policy including the above two programs were successful in increasing ecosystem services such as food production, flood mitigation, carbon sequestration, soil retention, sandstorm prevention, and water retention, but have not been successful in increasing the provision of habitat for biodiversity (Ouyang et al., 2016). One reason could be that in order to further the highest reforestation rate in the world, many of the trees planted were for expediency and were not native to the regions and hence may not survive in the long run for lasting biodiversity. There were other conservation programs implemented around the same time, such as Combating Desertification Program around Beijing and Tianjin and the Wildlife Conservation and Nature Reserve Protection Program (Delang & Wang, 2013).

Other Government Instruments

When there is broad legitimacy for the use of proceeds in conservation, governments around the world have multiple ways to raise revenue for this purpose. In the past, premiums for specialty postal stamps and car license plates have been allocated to ecosystem services. More recently, a number of jurisdictions where carbon pricing has been instituted have allocated a portion of the proceeds to conservation activities. Apart from taxes, governments frequently issue green bonds to generate immediate funds for biodiversity conservation (see Chap. 14 for more on green bonds).

Philanthropic Capital

A government budget allocation largely depends on national priorities which can be volatile, creating unfortunate inconsistencies for the long-term endeavor that characterizes the nature of the conservation process. Toward the second half of the twentieth century emerged the second phase of the conservation movement, which was characterized by a mix of philanthropic and government capital in funding for land acquisition, conservation easements, and advocacy programs for environmental protection (Huwyler et al., 2014). Philanthropic organizations including environmental foundations established through government and private donations may have to contend with the interests and timeframes of diverse donors which may not always align with scientifically proven priority regions for conservation (World Wildlife Fund, 2009). In addition, there are environmental NGOs that not only raise money but also leverage their technical expertise and other resources in conservation activities.

Conservation Trust Fund (CTF)

Conservation trust funds, also called environmental trust funds, have been established in developing countries with high biodiversity to provide financing for nature conservation. With steady investment income streams (if managed well), a CTF is considered a more stable and long-term solution to biodiversity conservation. The CTFs are independent legal entities. However, they do collaborate with national governments and work toward national goals, as well as international conventions such as the UN SDGs, the UN Framework Convention on Climate Change, and the Convention for Biological Diversity.

The first CTF was created in Bhutan in 1991 as a collaboration between the national government, WWF, and the Global Environment Facility (Guerin-McManus, 2001). The mechanism was attractive because Bhutan did not have substantial foreign debt to be able to participate in the previously discussed debt-for-nature swap. As of last year, there are over 90

CTFs globally. Of these, some 38 CTFs participated in a conservation trust investment survey conducted by the Wildlife Conservation Society and the Conservation Finance Alliance in 2012, with a total of $853.2 million under their management (Mathias & Victurine, 2017).

Most CTFs manage funds that are *endowment* funds, *sinking* funds, *revolving* funds, or a mixture of the three. With an endowment fund, the revenue from investments is disbursed to finance grants and projects, but not the capital which is intended to last in perpetuity. For a sinking fund, investment income and a portion of the principal is spent every year leading the fund to eventually drop to zero in a pre-determined time frame, usually 10–20 years. A revolving fund in theory continuously receives and spends new revenue, but in practice, most of the revolving funds under management by CTFs get filled and depleted quickly, usually in less than a year (Mathias & Victurine, 2017). In 2016, on average CTFs returned 5%, which rebounded from a year earlier, as shown in Fig. 13.1. As a comparison, the S&P 500 returned 11.96% for the entire year of 2016. However, CTFs performed much better if compared to the performance

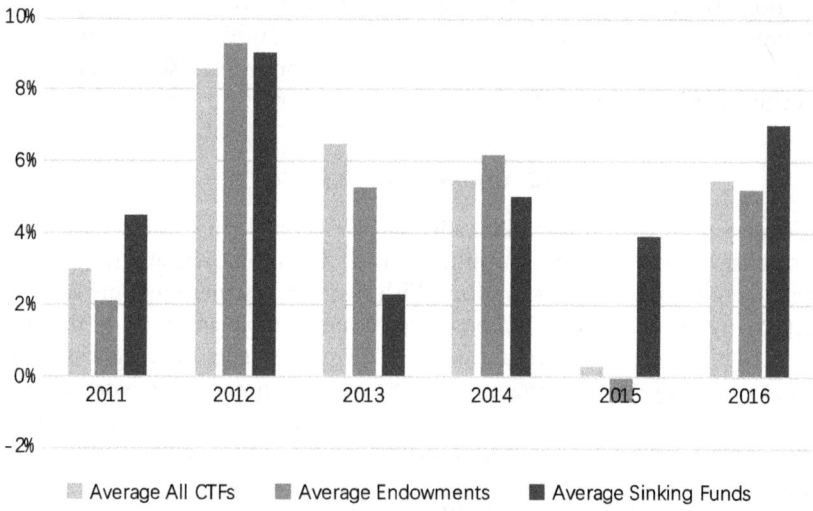

Fig. 13.1 Average nominal annual returns, 2011–2016. (Source: Adapted from Mathias & Victurine (2017), Conservation Trust Investment Survey for 2016. Note: Based on 38 surveyed CTF participants, who allocated 35% on equities, and 65% on fixed income and cash, on average)

of university endowment funds, which generated a negative return (−1.9%) for fiscal year 2016 (Commonfund Institute, 2017). The best performing year was 2012 with returns around 9%.

Despite the benefits of providing a reliable funding source for the management of protected areas and employment opportunities in rural areas, CTFs have been criticized for a lack of effort in measuring impact against their goal of maintaining biodiversity or other related outcomes (Bonham et al., 2014). Their more recent work on monitoring and evaluating the effectiveness of their grants and funded projects has been largely anecdotal and lack scale.

There are also direct loans from multilateral agencies to fund conservation projects. These agencies may include the World Bank, the United Nations Environment Programme (UNEP), the United Nations Development Programme (UNDP), and regional development banks which typically fund projects with large geographical scope. The regional development banks sometimes provide loans to governments instead of giving out project grants.

Even just to achieve the previously outlined target of $300–400 billion (which could be low as previously mentioned) for conservation finance, current levels of funding need to increase 6–8 times. While governments and philanthropy still dominate the space, it is unrealistic to expect dramatic increases in donations, grants, and government budget allocation to close the gap. Instead, the hope is placed on consumers who are the beneficiaries of ecosystem services to sufficiently compensate service providers, and on investors increasingly viewing conservation finance as an asset class which might generate competitive economic returns. Consumers and investors often work with governments and environmental NGOs in constructing innovative financing instruments that create win-win outcomes for all parties involved.

Payments for Ecosystem Services (PES)

Payment to ecosystem services was conceptualized in the late 1970s, when it was referred to as payments for environmental services (Gómez-Baggethun, De Groot, Lomas, & Montes, 2010). The ecosystem provides many services to mankind, such as goods, fuel, minerals, carbon sequestration, water storage, wildlife habitat, as well as esthetic, recreational, and educational services (Millennium Ecosystem Assessment, 2005). While some ecosystem services and goods are already provided in well-functioning markets with clear direct use value (water and logging), others (biodiversity and carbon storage) have imperfect property rights and exhibit public or CPR characteristics. While the various PES instruments work differently, they all aim to commoditize the ecosystem services by forming a market/quasi-market and compensate the owner/steward of the ecosystem for the benefit it provides, which otherwise is often subject to free riding.

Following a pure market approach, private parties would be able to negotiate a contract among themselves to overcome an externality. A well-known example is that of Nestlé, a private water bottling company, reaching an agreement to pay local farmers in France to change their farming practices in order to prevent nitrate contamination in aquifers. According to the famous Coase Theorem (Coase, 1937), a privately negotiated contract in the context of externalities is feasible and efficient if transaction costs are low and property rights are well-defined. However, PES practices following the Coasean principle, where the beneficiary pays the provider of ecosystem services directly and voluntarily are actually rare, given the very problem of imperfectly defined property rights which besets many CPRs. Alternatively, other types of PES involve the government who either pays or forces others to pay, through taxation and subsidy. This approach follows the work of Arthur Pigou (Pigou, 1920), who formulated environmental tax and subsidy in internalizing negative environmental externality. The SLCP in China follows this approach with the government subsidizing the farmers in planting trees on steep slopes rather than farming. Lastly, there are also markets for ecosystem services (MES) that have been developed, where people can trade and the price of the ecosystem service/good is determined by supply and demand. Examples include the various carbon markets around the world and mitigation banking in the United States (see below). There is some debate surrounding the definition of PES and the boundary between PES and MES can be blurry (Sattler & Matzdorf, 2013), but broadly speaking MES utilizes market-based instruments to set prices for conservation, whereas PES refers to any situation where the provision of an ecosystem service is rewarded monetarily.

Carbon Finance

Within conservation finance, especially as it relates to payments for ecosystem services, carbon finance has certainly received the most attention. Forest conversion has contributed to 12.5% of anthropogenic carbon emissions from 1990 to 2010 (Houghton et al., 2012), as well as causing soil degradation, loss in biodiversity, and regional climate change (Robinet et al., 2018). A market for carbon can go a long way in pricing carbon and provide funding to preserve and restore forests and promote sustainable land-use practices.

Carbon markets can take on either of two forms: the compliance market which is derived from a statutory cap and trade system, and the voluntary market where buyers and sellers trade freely according to a voluntary carbon standard. Under the cap and trade system, overall levels of emission are fixed and each company would have to purchase pollution permits in order to emit at a level that complies with regulation. In effect, the system encourages regulated companies to either install emission reduction technologies such as scrubbers or switch to cleaner energy sources with lower emission levels. Alternatively, companies can purchase allowances (permits). The public revenue generated from auctioning permits could potentially be used for forest conservation. Instead of purchasing permits, companies may also decide to spend on conservation activities that can 'offset' their emissions. Both of these approaches could in theory help generate revenue for conservation and emission reduction activities.

However, the European Union Emission Trading System (ETS), which is currently the largest compliance market, does not allow carbon offsets from reforestation or afforestation. Among major emission trading systems, New Zealand and California allow carbon offsets from afforestation projects generated domestically. Instead, most forest carbon credits— worth $74.2 million are traded on the voluntary market, where for example companies purchase them to meet their internal emission reduction targets, compared to $41.9 million on the compliance market (Hamrick & Gallant, 2017). In addition, $36.5 million has been paid to REDD+ (reducing emissions from deforestation and forest degradation, and the Role of Conservation, Sustainable Management of Forest Carbon Stocks in Developing Countries) programs (Hamrick & Gallant, 2017). The '+' refers to conservation, sustainable forest management of carbon stocks, which was later added, and are in relation to reforestation and afforestation. Payments to REDD+ projects are only to developing countries for maintaining their forest stock, and the carbon offset projects under the program are not tradable in any carbon market.

Despite their promise, forest conservation projects funded through carbon markets and REDD+ remain underwhelming. The supply of carbon forest offsets has been reported to far exceed demand on the carbon markets (Linacre, O'Sullivan, Ross, & Durschinger, 2015). Not all compliance markets allow carbon offsets to be used. Even among those that do, many have restrictions against forest and land-use projects, over doubts that carbon sequestered by tree planting may not be permanent in the event of forest fire and other unplanned loss. Also, oversupply of forest offsets is a concern which can cause the carbon price to collapse, in comparison to installing domestic rooftop solar or capturing landfill methane. Through REDD+, carbon finance is supposed to offer unprecedented funding at a scale of billions of dollars from donor governments in developed economies for forest conservation, eventually reaching $30 billion per year when fully operational (Phelps, Webb, & Koh, 2011). However, most of funding so far has gone into REDD+ readiness programs such as building government capacity and technical capabilities for participating countries instead of actual payments for forest carbon projects (Fletcher, Dressler, Büscher, & Anderson, 2016), and of the $2.9 billion already pledged from international donors for payments for REDD+, only $218 million have been disbursed (Hamrick & Gallant, 2017).

Mitigation Banking

As a result of the Clean Water Act passed in the U.S. in 1972, which gives power to U.S. Army Corp of Engineers (USACE) to issue permits to developers who will damage wetlands and streams with their development work in exchange for a commitment for creating or restoring a similar or larger wetland with comparable ecosystem functions and value in another area. This provision created a market for wetland mitigation banking, and the newly created or restored sites are the mitigation banks, which offer credits for anyone to purchase in order to offset the loss in wetlands and streams in the process of their commercial developments. The banks have to be approved and regulated by USACE and the U.S. Environmental Protection Agency.

In addition to wetland banks, there are other, albeit smaller mitigation banks, such as conservation banks that offer credits to offset the loss of endangered species and habitat as well as water quality banks. Depending on the type and region where it is located, the price of wetland can vary wildly, ranging from $36,000 per acre of riparian wetland in North Carolina up to $653,000 per acre of tidal wetland in Virginia (Sakyi, 2009). Altogether, there are over 100 mitigation banks in the United States, and the market value for mitigation credits in United States would exceed $100 billion (Coleman, 2015), with an annual transaction of

$1.3–4 billion (BenDor, Lester, Livengood, Davis, & Yonavjak, 2015). According to Eco-Asset Solutions & Innovations, a California-based consulting firm specializing in the U.S. mitigation credit valuation, the overall market value today is approximately $200 billion.

As a pioneer of this mechanism, the United States has by far the largest and most developed mitigation credit market. While often called compensatory mitigation in the United States, it is more commonly referred to as biodiversity offsets elsewhere in the world. As of 2015, there are over 50 countries that have regulations that require biodiversity offsets to compensate losses in wetland, species, and habitat (Barnard, Davies, McLuckie, & Victurine, 2017). Although mitigation banks are evaluated by an inter-agency team with representatives from federal, state, and local governments, who is also responsible for approving the number of credits the banks can earn, it is still challenging for the regulatory agency to correctly assess the ecological loss of any given ecosystem and to convert that loss into a monetary value. Also, most mitigation banks own wetland sites far away from the impact area, when ecological impacts may differ across regions, and may have subtle differences between artificial and natural systems which only manifest over a long period.

Payment for Watershed Services

Short of creating a market (cap and trade and offset), the beneficiaries of an ecosystem service can pay a direct fee to the provider for the flow of the service. The most prominent example for ecosystem fees is payment for watershed services that may include flood control, erosion control, water purification, water regulation, and recreation. The transaction mechanism involves water users downstream paying upstream landowners for sustainable land use in order to maintain the quantity and quality of the water flowing downstream. Such a mechanism can either be voluntary or government-mediated.

Payments can come from local governments, water utility, private farms, tourism companies, NGOs, and individual water users. For example, instead of building a costly water treatment plant, New York City devised a plan to pay local farmers around the Catskills-Delaware catchment (where water quality declined because of intensive agriculture and urbanization) for pollution control investments. Overall, 93% of the landowners voluntarily signed up for the program which was higher than the 85% threshold required for effective pollution reduction and the government was successful in preserving the source of quality drinking water for city residents at a fraction of the cost of a water filtration plant (Bond & Mayers, 2010). In total, 419 projects that conserve or rehabilitate green infrastructure were operational in watersheds in 62 countries around the world, with transactions worth $24.7 billion in 2015 (Bennett & Ruef, 2016). However, privately or user-funded watershed payment schemes are still limited while large scale programs are dominated by governments who may be more susceptible to ignore variations amongst people and places, leading to inefficiency.

Nutrient Trading

Another recent development is nutrient credit trading in the United States. Through what is also called water quality trading, farmers voluntarily install small artificial wetlands which serve to reduce nutrient runoffs from their farms and naturally remove excess nutrients that are polluting waterways. The nutrient reductions that are generated from building wetlands are treated as 'credits', which can then be bought by companies and municipalities who have to meet regulatory nutrient reduction requirements. Since purchasing the credits are usually cheaper than building cleanup facilities, the nutrient trading system can potentially create a market that yields win-win outcomes for the polluting entities and farmers in a way that also minimizes environmental damages.

Nutrient trading schemes have been proposed with feasibility studies being conducted in areas including the Chesapeake Bay, the Big Bureau Creek Watershed, and the 'dead zone' in the Gulf of Mexico. While there are clear benefits such as the additional source of revenue for conservation through unleashing market forces, providing flexibility for regulatory policies, and additional income for local stakeholders, the instrument remains an untested concept. Similar to the many other financial mechanisms intended for conservation, rigorous and scientific evaluation of the intended environmental outcomes is often difficult to conduct—many ecosystem co-benefits such as the biodiversity improvements are not easy to quantify. In addition, inter-watershed trading could lead to improved water quality in one waterway at the cost of severely lowering the quality in another. In general, this trend is likely to exacerbate environmental justice concerns. It has therefore been proposed that such a trading scheme should be structured only within the same watershed (Dennison, Helfrich, Michelsen, Pritzlaff, & Tutman, 2012), although such limits on market size necessarily reduce liquidity and market depth.

Tourism-Based Revenue

The tourism industry is one of the largest industries in the world. Directly and indirectly, the tourism industry contributes approximately 10% to world GDP. Nature-based tourism including parks, hunting, fishing, hiking, birdwatching, and nature photography requires conservation and sustainable management of wildlife and natural habitat targeted for tourists. However, if not properly managed, excessive tourism can deplete the wildlife and damage the habitat, which eventually also diminishes the tourism experience. Financial instruments such as fees charged for entry into protected areas, species-related user fees, voluntary contributions from tourists and tour operators, and resort fees charged by hotels and airports located in areas with high conservation values can go a long way in promoting nature and biodiversity. These types of direct payments are considered user fees for access or use of biodiversity.

However, in some countries, the fees collected for entry into protected areas are not earmarked for conservation and go instead into government coffers for other purposes. Other countries use a tiered pricing model, which charges visitors according to their 'willingness to pay'. For example, in Tanzania, the entrance fee was raised because they discovered that the demand for a number of northern national parks is quite inelastic, so a higher fee would lead to more revenue without damping visitation. In Mozambique, the government implements a system where foreign visitors are charged a higher fee than domestic visitors for national parks, because international visitors are found to be willing to pay a much higher fee to enter into protected areas than local tourists. Belize charges a conservation fee on top of its departure tax at its airports. There are other types of recreational license fees such as diving fees, hunting fees, and special access fees that put a value on ecosystem services species and generate a revenue which can be used for biodiversity conservation.

There are other indirect market mechanisms trying to link the value of ecosystem services to existing markets, such as fisheries, agriculture, and timber. These mechanisms aim to generate revenue by charging a premium for certified timber, agriculture, and fisheries which are produced with environmental-friendly methods. The additional price paid by consumers can be viewed as compensatory revenue for the green commodity producers to engage in sustainable use of ecosystem services that maintain biodiversity. Given the approximately $190 billion certified market for agriculture and timber, $10–30 billion annually could be generated from the premium pricing to compensate the producers to engage in sustainable practices (Parker, Cranford, Oakes, & Leggett, 2012).

A significant problem with PES systems is *policy risk*. Since prior to any PES project a relevant market has to be established, weak government institutions, regulatory instability, or short-term policy will significantly impact the success of PES projects. Difficulty with establishing property rights over land or underlying ecosystem assets is a prominent example. In addition, demonstrating additional benefits associated with PES projects has been challenging. While we have been showcasing a number of PES schemes which have worked, one cannot be certain that the positive results can be replicated in all situations. PES mechanism implementation has faced a wide range of substantial critiques (Chan, Anderson, Chapman, Jespersen, & Olmsted, 2017). Chan et al. lay out a number of challenges related to PES implementation, and design recommendations to mitigate them. The first of these is the likelihood that once a metric for success is established as a basis for payment, it will cease to function as an effective metric because actors will find and exploit loopholes that enable success according to the metric without its actual intent being achieved (Newton, 2011). PES may also create a cultural expectation that the polluter is rewarded for not polluting, which can subvert norms of ecosystem stewardship. In order to mitigate these risks, PES design needs to reward broader stewardship rather than specific actions.

An additional critique of PES in the context of Ostrom's framework for the polycentric management of CPRs is that payments by a government or by the market may *crowd out* the civic duty and self-organization that users of a CPR may have evolved. In principle, the ability to monetize conservation behavior can blunt the incentives for voluntary conservation behavior that results from local self-management. While this 'crowding out' has been demonstrated to be a problem in some cases (Frey & Oberholzer-Gee, 1997), there are other situations where it has not been an obstacle (Ito, Feuer, Kitano, & Komiyama, 2018). Frey and Oberholzer-Gee find that in a Swiss nuclear waste repository siting context, when citizens consider it part of their duty to accept a NIMBY-type project in their neighborhood, offering compensation erodes such acceptance. On the other hand, Ito et al. find that group payments for agricultural land preservation in Japan generally improved local monitoring and reduced free riding. Finally, it is important to recall that PES design is generally focused on increasing efficiency, and not necessarily on improving equity. While many PES schemes involve payments from higher income populations to lower income ones, thereby advancing equity as a side effect, making it an explicit part of mechanism design is likely to improve legitimacy and adoption.

BIOPROSPECTING

Biodiversity prospecting or bioprospecting refers to the search for new genes, chemical compounds, microorganisms, and others in ecosystems that can yield economic value. Because majority of the biological wealth is in the developing countries and the technology and wealth are in developed countries, bioprospecting agreements usually take place between international pharmaceutical companies and developing country governments. Pharmaceutical companies usually pay governments an upfront fee in exchange for the exclusive right to screen the ecosystem for valuable compounds. In case any new pharmaceutical compound is discovered and developed into commercially successful drugs, the host country will share the profit, which together with the upfront payment can be utilized for conservation purposes.

Given the significant scale of the market for pharmaceutical products globally, it was initially hoped that bioprospecting would help generate valuable finance for conservation. It has been estimated that the value of bioprospecting to pharmaceutical companies could reach close to $2 billion annually (Costello & Ward, 2006). However, given myriad difficulties, only the National Biodiversity Institute (INBio), an NGO in Costa Rica which signed agreements with biotechnology companies and research institutions, was well documented. The collaboration between INBio and various research institutions and companies was allowed by the government to conduct biodiversity prospecting in protected areas in Costa Rica, and 70% of its $6 million operating budget came from contracts with companies and research institutes, and it was agreed that 10% of the research budget and half of the future royalties be given for conservation (2009).

The process of bioprospecting is time-consuming. It would require 10–12 years of research and development after any discovery of commercially valuable biochemical or genetic information in natural resources. The process is also highly technical and requires expertise from multiple stakeholders including the business sector, the host country governments, academics, and the local community to conduct necessary exploration, extraction, and later development of natural resources. While the concept remains appealing, the effort and finance needed for such a process perhaps is the reason for the paucity of cases for bioprospecting agreements. Even INBio, after its initial success, was taken over by the government. However, proponents argue that while the direct benefit remains modest, the indirect benefits such as those connected to rural development in the host developing countries can be substantial. For example, the prospecting process can help improve the technology and scientific capacity of the local population who can become more aware of the economic value of their resources.

Environmental Impact Bonds

Discussed in Chap. 11 on Impact Investing, social impact bonds allow investors to invest in socially beneficial projects and are paid a return out of the savings achieved by the project's successful implementation. For example, projects aimed at reducing childhood obesity and improving substance abuse treatment may generate significant savings to the healthcare system, and part of that saving can be used to pay the projects' investors. Social impact bonds can be structured in a way that part of the initial investment is guaranteed by a private foundation, and the foundation is only required to deliver on its guarantee if the project turned out to be unsuccessful.

Borrowed from the concept of social impact bonds, an Environmental Impact Bond (EIB) aims at private capital to fund interventions that can promote environmental conservation and sustainable development. Potentially, an environmental impact bond can bring a 'win-win-win' situation, where the government wins from cost savings, the private investors win from return on their investments, and the public wins from preserving the long-term benefits of ecosystem services which may not be otherwise guaranteed (Balboa, 2016). As with a social impact bond, an environmental impact bond is not technically a bond. It is a pay-for-success/pay-for-performance contract from the government, which only pays if the funded intervention is successful in delivering pre-determined environmental outcomes, unlike an ordinary bond or a typical green bond which merely ensures that proceeds are utilized for an environmentally beneficial purpose but does not guarantee any specific outcome.

Outcome-dependent environmental impact bonds relieve governments of execution risk and transfer it to private investors. The investor assesses the strength of the causal relationship between an intervention and its outcome and then evaluates the potential for resultant cost savings. The investor determines whether there is a decent chance of generating a favorable return. Figure 13.2 helps demonstrate the working mechanism of environmental impact bonds.

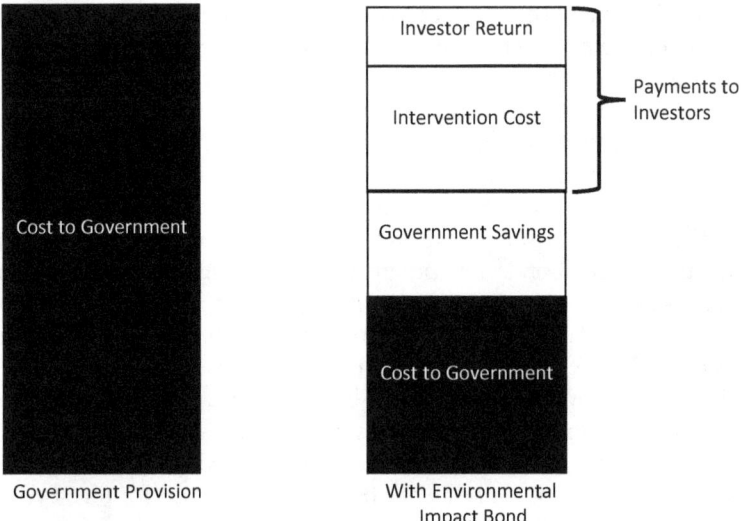

Fig. 13.2 How an environmental impact bond works. (Source: Adapted from Werneck and Havemann (2013))

DC Water (formerly the DC Water and Sewer Authority) of Washington DC was the first to issue an environmental impact bond, which raised $25 million from Goldman Sachs Urban Investment Group and Calvert Foundation in 2016 to fund urban green space which would absorb water naturally and reduce stormwater runoff. In five years, if the green infrastructure is successful in reducing stormwater runoff by between 18.6% and 41.3% from an established baseline, then the investors are compensated at annual interest rate of 3.43% and repaid their principal (Environmental Protection Agency, 2017).

If the goal is exceeded (with reduction greater than 41.3%), the investors will be rewarded with a $3.3 million bonus payment, and if the system underperforms (with reduction smaller than 18.6%), $3.3 million is clawed back from investors (Environmental Protection Agency, 2017). In this sense, the DC Water's environmental impact bond is an actual bond with a fixed interest payment and full repayment of principal at maturity, and only the bonus/penalty is dependent on performance. It is designed to share the risk between DC Water and investors in testing an innovative environmental solution. If the green infrastructure is effective, then DC

Water could expand the system across the district and avoid building costly new sewer systems which would be disruptive to local residents. The public also gains by having more beautified neighborhood and benefitting from improved water quality and reduced stormwater and sewage overflow.

Building on the popularity and its innovative approach, other cities such as Baltimore and Atlanta with similar problems of combined sewer systems (stormwater and raw sewage handled in the same pipes) and polluted runoff are in the process of issuing environmental impact bonds. In addition, environmental impact bonds can potentially be leveraged for environmental conservation and restoration. For example, Louisiana's Coastal Protection and Restoration Authority has partnered the Environmental Defense Fund and Quantified Ventures, an impact investing consultancy to explore the feasibility of an environmental impact bond in funding for coastal and wetlands restoration in Louisiana, which is dealing with severe land loss and sea level rise. The U.S. Forest Service has also been working with multiple partners in developing a forest resilience bond, a form of EIB for forest restoration in the western United States.

Governments are often criticized for their relative inability to experiment and innovate, and for prioritizing the delivery of environmental and social services over efficiency and effectiveness of those services. When governments find it hard to finance unproven projects, such as green infrastructure, environmental impact bonds can facilitate experimentation and stimulate innovation. In principle, an EIB, which is predicated on the success of an intervention instead of the merely delivery of an intervention, is also consistent with the new norm of public management (Behn, 2001). Because of this potential 'win-win-win' structure, environmental impact bonds, despite their recent arrival, have garnered widespread interest as holding much promise in leveraging private finance for the impactful provision of public goods.

Because of difficulties defining and measuring outcomes, social impact bonds have been more appropriate for areas where project goals are more identifiable and quantifiable, and where historical data and evidence of success has been more abundant. These include recidivism, preventive health care, and homelessness, among others. For these reasons, some argue that social impact bonds have been following well-established models and have not been able to lead to significant innovation in delivering social goods as was promised by the initial design of the instrument (Arena, Bengo, Calderini, & Chiodo, 2016; Gustafsson-Wright, Gardiner, & Putcha, 2015). Environmental impact bonds, on the other hand, rely on outcomes suggested from environmental science which is more exact and hence easier to define and quantify, which may relieve them of some of the challenges faced by social impact bonds.

To date, there have only been a handful of EIBs issued. While the concept in achieving win-win outcome is tantalizing, we have to be clear-eyed in waiting for more program data to emerge and to understand the fitness of the instrument for different communities and environmental problems. For example, it is reasonable to assume that the instrument may work well in attracting investor interest in larger cities and for projects that generate steady revenue streams, such as with a water utility. On the other hand, benefits from wetlands and coastal restoration could be much harder to monetize, such as in Louisiana, especially in the absence of a fee or a regulatory structure, as could be the case for certain environmental conservation and mitigation projects.

The selection of metrics that can accurately reflect environmental outcomes is never easy. Although environmental outputs and outcomes should be easier to standardize and quantify than social metrics, the lack of historical data on green infrastructure is still a significant obstacle for potential investors to conduct their due diligence, especially when investor return is contingent upon the performance of these metrics. Gray infrastructure projects have been deployed for decades, but green infrastructure has a much shorter track record, in terms of its financial cost, environmental outputs, as well as other technical aspects (Zimring, Hallstein, Blumberg, Kiparsky, & Downing, 2015). In addition, natural infrastructure varies more in performance across regions and over time than gray infrastructure (Cunniff & Schwartz, 2015), making risk assessment and replicating green projects doubly challenging. To its credit, an environmental impact bond employs rigorous monitoring and external evaluation to assess impact, a feature that differs starkly from many traditional financial instruments.

Given its short history, the jury is still out on whether environmental impact bonds can scale. The transaction cost resulting from monitoring and evaluation can be much higher than for example traditional green bonds, so higher returns would be needed to justify more issuance. However, for impact and other mainstream investors who increasingly demand social and environmental returns in addition to financial returns, social and environmental impact bonds can be an enticing concept that meets that demand.

Concluding Remarks

The earliest forms of conservation were funded by government revenue, followed by a mixture of government and philanthropic capital. While government funding continues to dominate the space, it is far from sufficient to bridging the financial gap. The third phase of conservation finance started around 25 years ago with more targeted private capital involvement, first in the United States and then in developing countries. However, the presence of the private sector, especially that of institutional investors in conservation finance remains minimal, except perhaps in green bonds.

It is a recurring theme in this book that many investment programs targeting environmental impact remain in the early stages with limited scale and standardization. Such investments remain too speculative and risky for institutional investors and the dispersed citizen investor. In addition, high transaction costs associated with small projects and the difficulties of conducting impact evaluation are common obstacles. Therefore, in order to unlock private capital, public investment in experimental programs needs to increase and be sustained to guide the project past the pilot stage. Governments also have to create the right conditions, such as sound institutions, and partnerships to incentivize private sector funding, like the ones we have reviewed with establishing carbon pricing and partnering with private investors in constructing the novel environmental impact bonds.

References

Ando, A. W., & Shah, P. (2016). The Economics of Conservation and Finance: A Review of the Literature. *International Review of Environmental and Resource Economics, 8*(3–4), 321–357.

Arena, M., Bengo, I., Calderini, M., & Chiodo, V. (2016). Social Impact Bonds: Blockbuster or Flash in a Pan? *International Journal of Public Administration, 39*(12), 927–939.

Asiedu-Akrofi, D. (1991). Debt-for-Nature Swaps: Extending the Frontiers of Innovative Financing in Support of the Global Environment. *International Lawyer, 25*, 557–586.

Balboa, C. M. (2016). Accountability of Environmental Impact Bonds: The Future of Global Environmental Governance? *Global Environmental Politics, 16*(2), 33–41.

Barnard, F., Davies, G., McLuckie, M., & Victurine, R. (2017). *Options and Financial Mechanisms for the Financing of Biodiversity Offsets* (White Paper). Conservation Capital.

Behn, R. D. (2001). *Rethinking Democratic Accountability*. Washington, DC: Brookings Institution Press.

BenDor, T., Lester, T. W., Livengood, A., Davis, A., & Yonavjak, L. (2015). Estimating the Size and Impact of the Ecological Restoration Economy. *PLoS One, 10*(6), e0128339.

Bennett, G., & Ruef, F. (2016). Alliances for Green Infrastructure: State of Watershed Investment 2016. *Forest Trends*.

Bhattacharjee, S. (2017). Forest Conservation and Management Practices among the Ahom Rulers of Pre-Colonial Assam: An Historical Assessment. *Journal of North East India Studies, 7*(2), 1–17.

Bond, I., & Mayers, J. (2010). *Fair Deals for Watershed Services: Lessons from a Multi-Country Action-Learning Project* (Natural Resource Issues No. 13). London: IIED.

Bonham, C., Steininger, M., McGreevey, M., Stone, C., Wright, T., & Cano, C. (2014). Conservation Trust Funds, Protected Area Management Effectiveness and Conservation Outcomes: Lessons from the Global Conservation Fund. *Parks, 20*, 89–100.

Cassimon, D., Prowse, M., & Essers, D. (2011). The Pitfalls and Potential of Debt-for-Nature Swaps: A US-Indonesian Case Study. *Global Environmental Change, 21*(1), 93–102.

Chan, K. M. A., Anderson, E., Chapman, M., Jespersen, K., & Olmsted, P. (2017). Payments for Ecosystem Services: Rife with Problems and Potential—For Transformation Towards Sustainability. *Ecological Economics, 140*, 110–122. https://doi.org/10.1016/j.ecolecon.2017.04.029

Coase, R. H. (1937). The Nature of the Firm. *Economica, 4*(16), 386–405.

Coleman, W. (2015). *Nine Steps Towards Doubling the Value of the US Mitigation Markets. Opinion Piece, from Ecosystem Marketplace, a Forest Trend Initiative*. Retrieved from: https://www.ecosystemmarketplace.com/articles/opinion-nine-steps-towards-doubling-the-value-of-us-mitigation-markets/

Commonfund Institute. (2017). *2016 NACUBO-Commonfund Study of Endowments Results Released*. Retrieved from: https://www.commonfund.org/news-research/press-release/2016-nacubo-commonfund-study-of-endowments/

Costanza, R., de Groot, R., Sutton, P., van der Ploeg, S., Anderson, S. J., Kubiszewski, I., … Turner, R. K. (2014). Changes in the Global Value of Ecosystem Services. *Global Environmental Change-Human and Policy Dimensions, 26*, 152–158. https://doi.org/10.1016/j.gloenvcha.2014.04.002

Costello, C., & Ward, M. (2006). Search, Bioprospecting and Biodiversity Conservation. *Journal of Environmental Economics and Management, 52*(3), 615–626.

Cunniff, S., & Schwartz, A. (2015). *Performance of Natural Infrastructure and Nature-Based Measures as Coastal Risk Reduction Features*. Washington, DC: Environmental Defense Fund.

Delang, C., & Wang, W. (2013). Chinese Forest Policy Reforms After 1998: The Case of the Natural Forest Protection Program and the Slope Land Conversion Program. *International Forestry Review, 15*(3), 290–304.

Dennison, W., Helfrich, M., Michelsen, E., Pritzlaff, R., & Tutman, F. (2012). *Nutrient Trading Preliminary Investigation: Findings and Recommendations.* Retrieved from https://19january2017snapshot.epa.gov/sites/production/files/2015-07/documents/nutrient_trading_final_report.pdf

Ellis, E. C., & Ramankutty, N. (2008). Putting People in the Map: Anthropogenic Biomes of the World. *Frontiers in Ecology and the Environment, 6*(8), 439–447. https://doi.org/10.1890/070062

Environmental Protection Agency. (2017). *DC Water's Environmental Impact Bond: A First of Its Kind.* Retrieved from https://www.epa.gov/sites/production/files/2017-04/documents/dc_waters_environmental_impact_bond_a_first_of_its_kind_final2.pdf

Fletcher, R., Dressler, W., Büscher, B., & Anderson, Z. R. (2016). Questioning REDD+ and the Future of Market-Based Conservation. *Conservation Biology, 30*(3), 673–675.

Frey, B. S., & Oberholzer-Gee, F. (1997). The Cost of Price Incentives: An Empirical Analysis of Motivation Crowding-Out. *American Economic Review, 87,* 746–755.

Gómez-Baggethun, E., De Groot, R., Lomas, P. L., & Montes, C. (2010). The History of Ecosystem Services in Economic Theory and Practice: From Early Notions to Markets and Payment Schemes. *Ecological Economics, 69*(6), 1209–1218.

Guerin-McManus, M. (2001). Conservation Trust Funds. *UCLA Journal of Environmental Law and Policy, 20,* 1.

Gustafsson-Wright, E., Gardiner, S., & Putcha, V. (2015). *The Potential and Limitations of Impact Bonds: Lessons from the First Five Years of Experience Worldwide.* Washington, DC: Global Economy and Development at Brookings.

Hamrick, K., & Gallant, M. (2017). *Fertile Ground: State of Forest Carbon Finance 2017.* Retrieved from Washington, DC. www.forest-trends.org/publications/fertile-ground

Houghton, R. A., House, J. I., Pongratz, J., Van Der Werf, G. R., DeFries, R. S., Hansen, M. C., … Ramankutty, N. (2012). Carbon Emissions from Land Use and Land-Cover Change. *Biogeosciences, 9*(12), 5125–5142.

Huwyler, F., Käppeli, J., Serafimova, K., Swanson, E., & Tobin, J. (2014). *Conservation Finance: Moving beyond Donor Funding Toward an Investor-Driven Approach.* Zurich, Switzerland: Credit Suisse, WWF, McKinsey Company.

Ito, J., Feuer, H. N., Kitano, S., & Komiyama, M. (2018). A Policy Evaluation of the Direct Payment Scheme for Collective Stewardship of Common Property Resources in Japan. *Ecological Economics, 152,* 141–151. https://doi.org/10.1016/j.ecolecon.2018.05.029

Levitt, J. N. (2005). *From Walden to Wall Street: Frontiers of Conservation Finance.* Washington, DC: Island Press.

Linacre, N., O'Sullivan, R., Ross, D., & Durschinger, L. (2015). *REDD+ Supply and Demand 2015–2025.* Washington, DC: United Stated Agency for International Development/Forest Carbon, Markets and Communities Program.

Linebaugh, P. (2008). *The Magna Carta Manifesto: Liberties and Commons for All.* Berkeley, CA: University of California Press.

Mathias, K., & Victurine, R. (2017). *2016 Conservation Trust Fund Investment Survey.* Retrieved from New York, USA. https://www.conservationfinancealliance.org/news/2017/12/1/2016-conservation-trust-fund-investment-survey-now-available

McFarland, B. J. (2017). *Conservation of Tropical Rainforests: A Review of Financial and Strategic Solutions.* Cham, Switzerland: Springer.

Millennium Ecosystem Assessment, M. (2005). *Ecosystems and Human Well-Being.* Washington, DC: Island Press.

Newton, A. C. (2011). Implications of Goodhart's Law for Monitoring Global Biodiversity Loss. *Conservation Letters, 4*(4), 264–268. https://doi.org/10.1111/j.1755-263X.2011.00167.x

Olson, M. (1971). *The Logic of Collective Action: Public Goods and the Theory of Groups.* Cambridge, MA: Harvard University Press.

Ostrom, E. (2010). Beyond Markets and States: Polycentric Governance of Complex Economic Systems. *American Economic Review, 100*(3), 641–672. http://www.aeaweb.org/aer/

Ouyang, Z., Zheng, H., Xiao, Y., Polasky, S., Liu, J., Xu, W., … Rao, E. (2016). Improvements in Ecosystem Services from Investments in Natural Capital. *Science, 352*(6292), 1455–1459.

Parker, C., Cranford, M., Oakes, N., & Leggett, M. (2012). *The Little Biodiversity Finance Book.* Oxford, UK: Global Canopy Programme.

Phelps, J., Webb, E. L., & Koh, L. P. (2011). Risky Business: An Uncertain Future for Biodiversity Conservation Finance through REDD+. *Conservation Letters, 4*(2), 88.

Pigou, A. C. (1920). *The Economics of Welfare.* London, UK: Macmillan.

Roberts, P., Hunt, C., Arroyo-Kalin, M., Evans, D., & Boivin, N. (2017). The Deep Human Prehistory of Global Tropical Forests and its Relevance for Modern Conservation. *Nature Plants, 3*(8), 17093–17093. https://doi.org/10.1038/nplants.2017.93

Robinet, J., Minella, J. P., de Barros, C. A., Schlesner, A., Lücke, A., Ameijeiras-Mariño, Y., & Govers, G. (2018). Impacts of Forest Conversion and Agriculture Practices on Water Pathways in Southern Brazil. *Hydrological Processes, 32*(15), 2304–2317.

Sakyi, A. M. (2009). Mitigation Banking: Is State Assumption of Permitting Authority More Effective. *William and Mary Environmental Law and Policy, 34,* 1027.

Sattler, C., & Matzdorf, B. (2013). PES in a Nutshell: From Definitions and Origins to PES in Practice—Approaches, Design Process and Innovative Aspects. *Ecosystem Services, 6*, 2–11.

Sheikh, P. A. (2018). *Debt-for-Nature Initiatives and the Tropical Forest Conservation Act (TFCA): Status and Implementation.* Retrieved from https://fas.org/sgp/crs/misc/RL31286.pdf

U.S. Department of the Interior. (2018). *Secretary Zinke Announces More than $1.1 Billion for Sportsmen & Conservation.* Press Release. Washington, DC: U.S. Department of the Interior.

Werneck, F., & Havemann, T. (2013). Social Impact Bonds: An Overview. *Clairmondial.* Available at http://www.clarmondial.com/social-impactbonds-an-overview/

World Bank Group. (2017). *International Debt Statistics 2017.* Retrieved from Washington, DC. https://data.worldbank.org/products/ids

World Wildlife Fund. (2009). *Guide to Conservation Finance.* Retrieved from Washington, DC: http://awsassets.panda.org/downloads/wwf_guide_to_conservation_finance.pdf

Wu, L. J., Liu, Q., Li, L., Zhao, X., & Zhao, T. Z. (2009). Progress Overview of the Slope Land Conversion Program in China. *Forestry Economics,* (9), 37.

Yi, C.-H. (2012). Sylvanic Trees Institutionalized in the Ancient Northeast Asia: Cultural and Environmental Significance of Dan-Tree and Sa-Tree. *Forest Policy & Economics, 22*, 28–39. https://doi.org/10.1016/j.forpol.2012.01.005

Zimring, M., Hallstein, E., Blumberg, L., Kiparsky, M., & Downing, J. (2015). *New Prospects for Financing Natural Infrastructure.* San Francisco, CA: The Nature Conservancy.

CHAPTER 14

Financing Clean Technology Innovation and the Transition to Renewable Energy

The existing energy system does not currently meet global needs. In developing countries, 1.1 billion people still lack access to electricity (International Energy Agency, 2017a). Improving energy access is a widely recognized development goal, framed as SDG 7 of achieving "universal access to affordable, reliable, sustainable and modern energy services" by 2030. Almost 3 billion people without access to clean cooking facilities rely on burning charcoal, kerosene, and wood, which generate local pollution that poses significant health hazards, especially to women and children. Even in developed countries, the energy system lacks resilience, often failing temporarily due to disruptions caused by extreme weather, natural disasters, and an over-reliance on single sources of electricity. The Paris Climate Change Agreement aims to limit greenhouse gas emissions from fossil fuel energy generation in order to mitigate the rise in global temperatures and to arrest the catastrophic effects of global warming. Researchers estimate that in order to keep global temperature from rising above 2°C by 2050, 88% of known coal reserves, 35% of oil reserves, and 52% of gas reserves cannot be utilized (McGlade & Ekins, 2015). In addition, coal, oil, and natural gas products are the primary feedstocks for plastics manufacture. Reducing the pollution resulting from unrecycled single-use plastics is a key component of SDG 14 (Life below water).

The transition to a low-carbon economy is an essential component of the sustainability agenda, and investments in clean technologies have the potential to facilitate the transition without hampering economic growth and

© The Author(s) 2019

S. Bose et al., *The Financial Ecosystem*, Palgrave Studies in Impact Finance, https://doi.org/10.1007/978-3-030-05624-7_14

affordable access to energy. In a comprehensive analysis of the global energy system, Bradford (2018) demonstrates that the worldwide growth in energy use in the last two centuries is approximately related to the increase in gross domestic product during that time.[1] In physical terms, energy can be defined as the capacity to perform work (which is defined as the transfer of energy). The definition of gross domestic product (GDP) aims to measure the amount of 'work' done in an economy in a given period, though 'work' in this context has a somewhat different meaning.[2] If global GDP is to continue to increase, then energy demand will grow in both developed and developing countries. If carbon emissions are to be reduced while facilitating such improvements in global welfare, the proportion of renewable electricity in the energy mix will need to increase significantly. In addition to investments in renewable electricity, the range of planetary boundaries suggests the need to invest in innovation that reduces material usage in many manufacturing processes. For example, in Chap. 5, we discussed the need for innovation to reduce the use of cobalt in energy storage technologies.

Challenges of Financing Cleantech R&D

Financing the research, development, and deployment of new clean technology is inherently more risky than financing incumbent technologies. By definition, new technologies do not have long operating histories that can reduce the perceived risk of investment.[3] A significant obstacle to financing the transition is the technological lock-in and path dependency of traditional fossil fuel technologies (Polzin, 2017). The supplanting of fossil fuel energy generation by renewable technologies will require large and persistent investment and likely seismic change in existing production processes, ways of life and the cultural and business environment. Incumbent technologies are easier to finance in the short term than new technologies because they are more widely adopted. Investments in renewable energy and waste prevention do not benefit from the ancillary investments in infrastructure, a finely evolved ecosystem of complementary intermediate processes, myriad downstream applications and the distributed knowledge (in a Hayekian sense) that sharply reduce the marginal cost of production in the hydrocarbon energy generation and related chemicals sectors. Nevertheless, as Bradford notes, investment choices based on the tools of marginal analysis (such as an evaluation of marginal cost) are not appropriate in the context of dynamic and complex disruptions to existing systems (Bradford, 2018). In the context of potentially stranded fossil fuel assets, maintaining the repeatability of welfare flows from abundant energy sources requires investment in renewable energy technologies so that they can constitute a much larger share of the generation mix. In this chapter, we examine the potential of existing and new forms of financing to provide the cash flows necessary to fund the transition to a low carbon economy.

STAGES OF CLEAN TECHNOLOGY DEVELOPMENT

Clean technology (cleantech), also called green technology refers to products, services, and production processes that reduce the environmental impact of economic activity. Cleantech can include a range of technologies relating to (1) the generation and storage of renewable energy, (2) environmental protection activities such as the building of green infrastructure (natural and cost-effective management of storm water) and green transportation (using renewable and regenerated energy), and (3) energy and materials efficiency such as through recycling and waste treatment. Investment in clean technology, particularly in renewable energy has increased dramatically in the first two decades of the twenty-first century. Gaddy, Sivaram, Jones, and Wayman (2017) develop a classification of cleantech companies into five categories, ordered with the longest development cycles listed first:

1. Companies that develop new materials, processes, or chemicals—for solar, biofuel, battery, lighting, and other applications (e.g. development of new battery storage technology).
2. Hardware integration companies for commercializing new ways of integrating existing hardware components (e.g. manufacture of electric vehicles by Tesla).
3. Cleantech software companies which analyzed energy use data and tried to improve energy efficiency by promoting customer behavioral change (e.g. statistical analysis of electricity usage to optimize utility deployment of generating capacity performed by Opower).
4. Deployment finance companies which provide turnkey finance to deploy projects with proven technology, such as large-scale solar farms (e.g. SunRun).
5. Other companies that included energy efficiency consultancy and waste processing companies (such as TerraCycle).

All development of new technologies undergoes six stages, from basic research to full commercialization, as shown in Table 14.1. Government funding of theoretical research institutes and universities generally facilitates basic research in Stage 1. Basic research often has no immediately obvious

Table 14.1   Cleantech research and development stages and funding sources

1	2	3	4	5	6
Basic research	*Applied research*	*Prototype development*	*Pre-commercial testing*	*Partially commercial production*	*Fully commercial production*
Sources of funding					
		The valley of death			
Government grants	Government grants	Family & friends	Angel investors	Venture capital	Private equity
	Corporate grants	Angel investors	Family offices	Private equity	Public equity
		Family offices	Crowdfunding	Public equity markets	markets
		Crowdfunding	Corporate profits	Corporate M&A	Corporate M&A
		Corporate profits	Venture capital (late stage 4)		

Source: Author adaptation from Polzin (2017) and Frankfurt School-UNEP Centre/BNEF (2018)

practical use for government or private actors. Though there is no specific mechanism to ensure the utility of basic research, it is possible to enumerate many productive but unintended eventual applications for the most arcane pure research (see box). Stage 2 consists of applied research, where the research objective generally envisages some eventual utility 'in the real world'. Applied research is typically funded by government grants. Until the 1980s, this type of research was also funded from the cash flows of large established corporations such as Xerox and AT&T (Janeway, 2018) though much of this source of funding has disappeared in the 'shareholder value' jurisdictions.

New technologies face a difficult transition between the government support of stages 1 and 2 and eventual commercialization in stages 5 and 6. Stages 3 and 4 are aptly referred to as 'the valley of death' (Frank, Sink, Mynatt, Rogers, & Rappazzo, 1996). Technology entrepreneurs must bootstrap themselves and avail an ad hoc range of funding sources, including family & friends, angel investors, family offices, and more recently crowdfunding (for relatively small capital needs). In some cases, if the technology has a chance to displace existing sources of revenue at a competing large corporation, some corporations may invest in developing prototypes with a view to substantiating a patent filing. Venture capital and other types of institutional private equity funding typically becomes available during the late stage of pre-commercial testing and later. Once a technology is partially commercially viable (for example, when the company is able to generate revenues though experiencing losses) it is relatively easy to access the public equity markets for an initial offering of equity, receive funding from creditors or sell the company to a strategic buyer.

As with other disruptive technologies, cleantech exhibits high risks related to technology and policy uncertainty, and the scaling of any new products and services may take a long time and offer low visibility. The venture capital model is premised on the expectation that many investee companies will fail and that the determinants of eventual success will not be clear *ex ante*. The model works so long as the return on the successes is sufficiently large that they more than offset the losses on the failures. The venture capital ecosystem must periodically replenish its cash reserves through sales (or 'exits') of successful businesses. If the development cycle takes too long, the venture capital ecosystem is unable to invest in new ventures since its capital is tied up in portfolio companies in stages 4 and 5. The common 'exit' strategy for venture capital funds is for the investee or portfolio company to either be acquired by a larger mature company or to publicly list its shares on a stock exchange through an initial public offering (IPO).

Unintended Consequences of Government Funding of Basic Research
Government funding of pure science became institutionalized in the United States during the Second World War and continued during the Cold War (Hart, 1998). The funding of basic scientific research, with no obvious immediate use for government or private sector actors, sometimes has to be clandestine, occluded even from the funders. 'Dynamic programming', a branch of mathematics devoted to the formulation of multi-stage decision problems as functions of stationary Markov processes, was conceived and developed by Richard Bellman (Bellman, 1952), a Stanford University mathematics professor while he was at the RAND Corporation. RAND was funded by the US government to provide research and analysis to the US Air Force, among other defense agencies. In his autobiography, Bellman subsequently stated that he invented the term 'dynamic programming' because he needed a label that would not raise the ire of Charles Erwin Wilson, who as Secretary of Defense, was the ultimate boss of his project at RAND. Bellman thought that Wilson in particular and the Air Force in general would be hostile to basic mathematical research: he wanted a name that "not even a Congressman could object to" (quoted in Dreyfus (2002)).[4]

Dynamic programming subsequently became a critical computational tool with applications in industrial engineering, statistical estimation, supply chain management, pattern recognition and artificial intelligence, resource conservation, groundwater and agricultural crop management, optimal bidding strategies, and option pricing, among other fields.

Angel Investors

It is often in the spaces where traditional banking and finance are absent that wealthy families and angel investors have historically searched for promising investment opportunities. The need to transcend the challenges of information asymmetry in the context of people finance creates an essential role for the close personal relationships between funder and innovator that characterize angel investments. Angel investors fund early-stage startups, perform careful due diligence on applicants, and provide valuable advice and networks to investees. Angel investors, who invest on their own behalf, do not create agency problems and do not charge fees that might misalign the incentives of funder and entrepreneur.

Although not institutionalized, angel investments in total represent a significant source of early-stage funding. In the United States, the University of New Hampshire Center for Venture Research maintains a survey of angel investments, estimating that $23 billion was invested in 2017, with an average deal size of $388,000 (Sohl, 2018). In a study of 13 angel groups in 21 countries, Lerner, Schoar, Sokolinski, and Wilson (2015) find that angel investors have a positive impact on the growth, performance, and survival of investee firms and their subsequent financing rounds. Intriguingly, the positive effect of angel investors is independent of venture activity and entrepreneur-friendliness of the country. This result indicates that individual angel investors and their networks represent a critical and beneficial source of funding for early-stage development even in jurisdictions where venture capital is not institutionalized.

The importance of angel investors and their ability to transcend information asymmetries and agency problems make them a promising institution to help finance certain aspects of the transition to a clean energy economy. The Organization for Economic Co-operation and Development (OECD) has identified a broad range of policy measures to encourage the scale and maturity of angel investments (Wilson, 2015). These include entrepreneur and investor training, the establishment and development of angel investor networks, investments in incubators and accelerators, and the development and maintenance of crowdfunding platforms.

Venture Capital Funding

Structurally, venture capital (VC) funds are a type of private equity (PE) investment. PE funds are investment funds with capital from outside investors (technically limited partners) managed by a general partner. The general partner earns fees amounting to approximately 2% of invested capital, 20% of profits and may receive other fees and expense reimbursements from limited partners and investee firms. PE funds generally buy and restructure private or publicly traded companies. In common parlance, the term PE is distinguished from VC by the special strategies of VC funds relative to other traditional PE funds. Traditionally, PE funds buy controlling stakes in large mature companies in all industry sectors, while VC funds tend to acquire minority stakes in smaller companies that are in their early stages of development, typically in high R&D sectors such as technology and healthcare. PE funds are able to utilize non-recourse debt through leveraged buyouts to finance the majority of their purchases since their investees have relatively stable cash flows. VC funds generally finance their purchases with equity. VC funds are often structured as ten-year partnerships: investments are made in the first five years in a range of start-up companies (typically 10–20) which are then sold in the latter five years. While PE and VC have been important sources of funding for cleantech innovation, the former is involved in funding late-stage, turnaround, and expansion activities that are typically characterized by lower risks and lower return, while the latter is focused on funding early and growth stage enterprises with a high-risk and high-return characteristic.

Both VC and PE source their funds from institutional investors such as pension funds, insurance companies, sovereign wealth funds, foundations, and endowments, as well as family offices that manage the assets of wealthy families. Family offices, along with angel investors represent significant contributors to early-stage funding in their own right. Due to their need to match assets to long horizon liabilities (see Chap. 10), some institutional investors such as pension funds and insurance companies do have the ability to invest in the cash flow profiles of cleantech innovation. However, the largest asset owners have a relatively large minimum threshold for a particular investment, say $25 million, which cannot represent more than say 15% of the overall capital needs of that investment. The combination of these two rules implies that the largest asset owners must generally eschew investments in the smaller emerging opportunities in renewables and cleantech.

VC funds typically invest during multiple stages of development of a company. The 'seed' stage involves an investment typically below $1 million. Subsequent stages referred to as the 'A' or 'B' rounds of funding amount to approximately $10 million, while a final or a growth round late in the trajectory can amount to above $100 million. Regardless of funding round, VC funds expect to exit in three to five years and may write off their investments if the investees cannot avail a meaningful exit strategy during this period. Consequently, VC funds gravitate toward start-up companies with short development cycles. This tendency has caused the VC industry to concentrate its investments in a very limited set of sectors. Lerner (2012) notes that the proportion of VC investments going to the computer and telecommunications sectors rose from 35% in 1974 to 79% in 2000. Lerner attributes this to the shorter innovation cycles in these sectors relative to healthcare, retail, energy, and transportation categories.

The share of cleantech in venture capital deals increased from 1% in 1996 to 10% in 2010 (Cumming, Henriques, & Sadorsky, 2016). In 2007, John Doerr, a prominent Silicon Valley investor claimed that "green technologies—going green—is bigger than the internet. It could be the biggest economic opportunity of the 21st century". In addition, governments around the world enhanced incentives for adopting clean energy. For example, the US Congress offered tax credits to many renewable energy sources, such as wind and solar. Germany and China also provide substantial incentives for renewable energy. Many cleantech companies were focusing on technologies that are not yet viable commercially but had benefitted from public research and development funding. Venture capital appeared to be an appropriate vehicle to bridge this gap. However, VC funding of cleantech start-ups has been volatile. Funding first peaked prior to the 2008 financial crisis, perhaps due to increasing public awareness of climate change as well as sharply rising fossil fuel prices (Fig. 14.1).

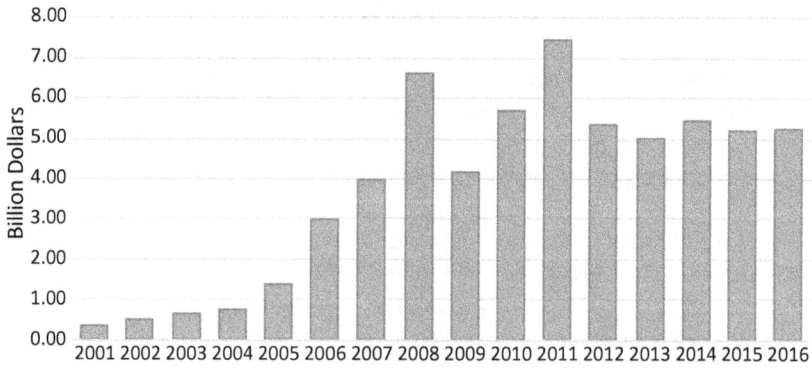

Fig. 14.1 Venture capital investment in Cleantech in the United States. (Source: Adapted from Saha and Muro (2017))

As a consequence of the credit tightening during the financial crisis, VC funding declined sharply in 2009.

Although VC funding in cleantech rebounded and peaked again in 2011, many of these start-ups, especially those in renewable energy such as solar failed to scale because the fracking revolution significantly lowered the price of natural gas. The economic model envisioned by venture capitalists where the price of fossil fuels would keep rising, making renewables increasingly competitive never materialized. The price of natural gas—which generates less than half the pollution from coal—was continuously rising and peaked at $13 per 1000 cubic feet in 2008, but then reversed the trend to drop to $3 in 2012 and has remained around there since (US Energy Information Administration, 2018).

It was difficult for cleantech companies to compete in the short term, especially those trying to develop alternative solar photovoltaics because of the advent of cheap PV cells made of silicon as well as low oil and gas prices. For example, Solyndra, the once innovative solar PV start-up touted by former US President Barrack Obama as 'an engine of economic growth', filed for bankruptcy in 2011, only six years after its founding. The credit crisis and IPO drought effectively closed avenues to refinance or exit cleantech investments.

More importantly perhaps, VCs for the first time realized that energy companies do not operate on their preferred timeline—delivering results in three to five years. Clean disruptive technologies are usually asset-heavy—in contrast with asset-light software and internet startups. It usually takes more than a few ingenious engineers and a garage to build the physical infrastructure necessary to develop renewable technologies, making funding obstacles more profound in the cleantech sector. Furthermore, in the wake of lower oil and gas prices, cleantech start-ups (which in principle are disruptors to the fossil fuel energy sector) were not attractive acquisition targets for oil majors. Compared to medical start-ups which are more likely to be acquired by pharmaceutical companies, few large energy companies acquired promising cleantech startups.[5] Conversely, VC investors were likely to fund cleantech software solutions rather than hardware and material ventures. For example, Opower, a software as a service provider founded in 2007, received multiple rounds of financing between 2007 and 2010 and was publicly listed in 2014. Compared to biotech and software companies, VC investments in cleantech performed significantly worse, in terms of the failure rate and returns to capital. In the United States, these factors contributed to the decline of VC funding from its peak in 2011 (Fig. 14.1). In the aftermath of 2011, early-stage VC of cleantech almost disappeared. Among the funds that remained, many shifted to fund late-stage enterprises with lower risk (Gaddy et al., 2017).

Globally, China commands the largest proportion of VC investments in cleantech, with 53% in 2017, while the United States comes second with 32% (Fig. 14.2). Despite some successes, such as one achieved by Tesla (which raised $7.5 million in 2004 and $13 million in 2005 and exited with an IPO in 2010 that valued the company at $1.6 billion) (Crunchbase, 2019), many forms of the cleantech start-ups may not be very suitable for venture capital. In response to the diminishing appetite of venture capitalists to invest in early-stage cleantech companies, the Paris Agreement emphasized the importance of financing early-stage renewable energy technology. Bill Gates, along with other billionaire investors started the Breakthrough Energy Coalition to pool their money in funding early-stage ventures in clean technology. Recently, a $1 billion fund (Breakthrough Energy Venture) was launched to helping cleantech companies achieve scale.

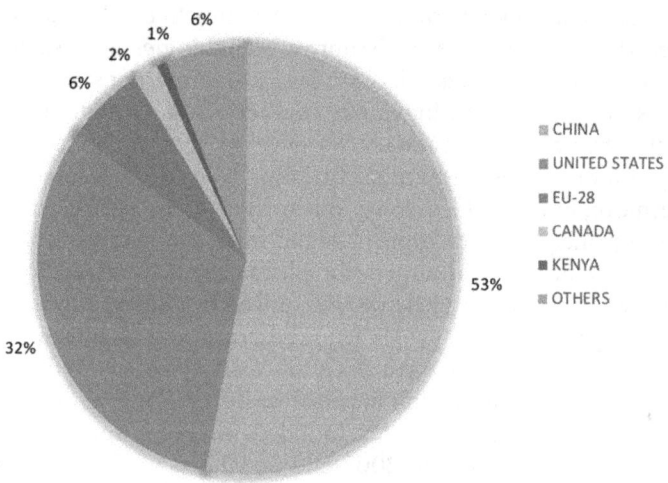

Fig. 14.2 Cleantech venture capital investment by region, 2017. (Source: Adapted from NEXT 10 (2018). Original data source: Pitchbook, LLC)

The Role of Government Incentives

While angel investing and venture capital can fund upstream enterprises that are characterized by high risk and low capital intensity, deployment of downstream innovations in renewable energy would require capital at a scale that is too large for venture capital and too risky for traditional banks (Mazzucato & Semieniuk, 2018). Renewable power plants would fit this description. Because of the constraints and difficulties faced by venture capitalists, other private sector investors who are less prone to the need for short-term returns and who have more capital can take over and invest for longer-term gain. The lesson is not to try to conform to the VC model that gravitates toward cleantech software but rather to find ways to encourage other forms of capital into funding the much-needed material and processes that are crucial to the green transition. Institutional investors such as pension funds, insurance companies, sovereign wealth funds, and even family offices that are more tolerant of the longer horizons have to be involved in funding clean technology deployment. The trick to involving these asset owners will be in developing low-cost methods of due diligence and mentorship, which are too expensive for the largest asset owners to perform.

A case can be made for direct government investment in renewable energy, a sector that is asset-heavy and would need substantially more capital to scale than available from VC or PE. While public funding is important, governments tend to be inefficient at due diligence and investment selection, lacking the experience and culture that is necessary for the proper exercise of judgment and assessment of market discipline. Short of direct government funding or ownership, 'market pull and technology push' policies which include financial and innovation policy instruments can be utilized to influence innovation and investment in the cleantech industry (Migendt, Polzin, Schock, Täube, & von Flotow, 2017).

For example, the government use instruments such as cash rebates, feed-in tariffs, loan guarantees, and subsidies to increase the demand for innovative clean technology products, which may spur cleantech innovation. Many governments subsidize renewable energy, with subsidies in the form of feed-in tariffs and loan guarantees frequently dwarfing private sector investments. For example, the US Congress offered production tax credits to many renewable energy sources, such as 30% for wind and solar (Internal Revenue Service, 2018). Solyndra received the first loan guarantee from the US Department of Energy totaling $535 million in 2009, which later became an indictment of the program after the high-profile case went bankrupt (Department of Energy, 2009). The same program also extended Tesla with a loan of $465 million in 2010, which allowed the company to expand its production facility and successfully launch its Model S sedan (Department of Energy, 2010).

From 2006 to 2014, subsidies to renewable energy in Germany have quadrupled from 5.8 to 21.4 billion euros (Böhringer, Landis, Reaños, & Angel, 2017). In addition, China, which has the world's highest renewable capacity, has provided subsidies ranging between 34% and 52% of the feed-in tariffs for solar in 2018 (Moody's, 2018a, 2018b). The credit line extended to renewable companies in China often dwarf the loans to US companies. Local governments in China frequently offer tax breaks and cheap land to support clean technology development. The national government, through feed-in tariffs, requires the state-owned utility companies in China to purchase electricity from renewable sources including solar, wind, and waste-to-energy, at above-market rates to offset their high costs. In addition to directly funding innovation, government procurement programs can fill the void left by the exit of early-stage VCs.

The International Energy Agency estimates that the subsidies for fossil fuel (including oil, coal, and natural gas) and electricity remain higher than renewables (Fig. 14.3). In 2015, fossil fuel subsidies totaled $330 billion (down from 2012 due to drops in oil prices), which was still more than twice the $150 billion subsidies for renewables (International Energy Agency, 2017b). Most of the fossil fuel subsidies occur in developing countries; advanced economies such as the United States do not subsidize fossil fuel consumption (but the United States supports energy production through tax credit and loan guarantees). Rising from $62 billion in 2004 to $360 billion in 2014, global investments in clean energy are increasing fast. However, that growth has slowed in recent years, down to $334 billion in 2017, which was only 19% of the global energy investment of $1.8 trillion (International Energy Agency, 2018).

While subsidies can be instrumental in encouraging early innovation, they are inevitably temporary and unsustainable. With rapidly increasing capacity in renewable generation, subsidy budgets are likely to be strained. Conversely, firms are reluctant to plan long term if they believe that subsidies will be transitory. For example, a generous subsidy in Spain, once a leading country in the development of solar power, led to a solar capacity that is ten times what the government had initially planned. When tariff support was abruptly ended after the 2008 financial crisis, many solar

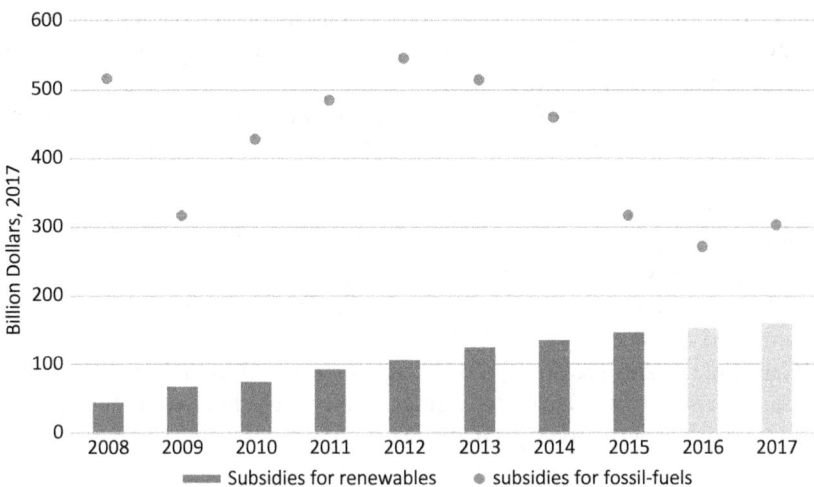

Fig. 14.3 Global subsidies for renewables and fossil fuels. (Source: Adapted from International Energy Agency (2016 and 2018))
The World Energy Outlook estimate covers subsidies to fossil fuels consumed by end-users (households, industries, and businesses) and subsidies to the consumption of electricity generated by fossil fuels. Light green columns are the most aggressive estimates for renewables subsidies by the IEA. (Color figure online)

companies collapsed (Webb, 2011). Significant decreases in costs due to innovation in renewable technology can compound these problems, making subsidies less effective and very costly. In the long term, carbon taxes and carbon trading, which we discussed in Chap. 13, could be more effective in catalyzing innovation in renewables that are conducive to their long-term competitiveness. Government subsidies can over-incentivize the renewable industry leading to overcapacity.

Government grants and favorable tax treatment of R&D investments can help push for more technological breakthroughs (technology push). Early research is costly while bearing no direct link to short-term profitability, hence it tends to be underfunded by private sector actors. This is also consistent with the economic theory of externality, which can be very substantial for technology research in the early stage. The benefits of basic research underlying cleantech technology are widely accessible, blunting the incentive for companies to invest directly. A key public intervention that fosters the adaptation of basic research for commercial decarboniza-

tion technologies in the broader economy is the variety of legal requirements for energy efficiency, conservation, fuel switching, and electricity
decarbonization (Gerrard & Dernbach, 2018).

Lastly, innovation policies can target institutional investors. For example, the initial development of VC in cleantech is closely related to the
'green wave' initiative by the California State Government in the United
States In 2004, the State Treasury called on the California Public
Employees' Retirement System (CalPERS) and California State Teachers
Retirement System (CalSTRS), the second and third largest pension funds
in the country at the time—among other 'green' investments—to invest a
combined $500 million in PE, VC, and projects in the cleantech sector
(California State Treasurer, 2004). This occurred at a time when the
cleantech sector was at an early stage, which greatly encouraged investments from other market participants.

Asset Finance

Significant technological advances have been made in hydropower, wind
power, solar PV, and energy-efficient appliances and lighting equipment.
These advances help cut production costs and drive down price. Globally,
the price of utility-scale solar PV declined two thirds from 2010 to 2015,
and the cost of onshore wind plants has fallen 30% during the same period
(International Energy Agency, 2015). With more mature technology and
competitive pricing, investments made into scaling up and rolling out successful projects, mostly through the debt markets have been very significant. For example, asset financing for renewables had reached $216 billion
in 2017 (Frankfurt School-UNEP Centre/BNEF, 2018).

At a macro level, foreign direct investment (FDI) has channeled significant funds into building nuclear power plants, manufacturing solar panels
and wind turbines, as well as building advanced battery production facilities. FDI is a direct investment in one country by a company from another
country. As such, FDI has been viewed as instrumental in transferring
valuable capital, technological and managerial expertise, as well as environmental and social standards from one country to another, and is usually
favored by the host country. In 2016, 10% of global greenfield FDI went
into renewable energy, which totaled $77 billion.[6] If other clean technolo-
gies are included such as energy efficiency, energy storage, and energy
services (e.g. carbon markets), then annual FDI in cleantech is estimated
to be around $287 billion (GreenInvest, 2017).

Asset finance refers to borrowing against the balance sheet assets of a company. Since companies have to develop to a mature stage in order to maintain a stable asset, which they can then borrow against, asset finance is the most relevant to companies in the scaling-up and rolling-out stages of development. We will review in this section a number of financial instruments these companies use to fund their continued development.

Energy Investment Partnership (Green Banks)

Energy investment partnerships are often referred to as green banks, which we discuss in some detail Chap. 12 in the context of energy efficiency securitization. Green banks are public or quasi-public institutions that aim to leverage public fund for private investment in clean technology development. Green banks use tools that differ from traditional government incentives. For government grants, once the money is offered, it no longer comes back to the public coffer, whereas for green banks, loans made will be repaid, which will allow public funds to replenish and go further in helping the development of clean energy. As detailed in Chap. 12, green banks utilize a process of capital curation to leverage public funds with private capital using co-investment, credit support, and securitization, among other methods. Through these mechanisms, green banks can help reduce the risks faced by private investors and fill their financing gaps, as well as offering the reliability of a government or semi-government partnership. Because green banks utilize public funds, they tend to invest in mature technologies, such as solar. They primarily aim to lower market barriers for increasing scale, hence do not focus on start-up technologies that are in early stage of development. While still a relatively new concept, the number of green banks has been on the rise in the United States, especially when federal level support in the United States could be lacking.

Green banks are formed with varying structures and strategies. For example, established in 2011, the Connecticut Green Bank was the first to adopt the name in the United States and it works directly with individual customers, offering them loans for their solar needs. In total, it has deployed together with the private sector over $1 billion in capital in funding clean energy projects. In 2013, New York State formed the New York Green Bank, a $1 billion entity underwritten by the State and the largest in the United States. It only works with financiers and developers on large-scale projects, and it has collectively created $1.6 billion in clean energy investment by the beginning of 2018 (United States Climate Alliance, 2018).

Green banks have been established at the national level in Australia, Japan, Malaysia, Switzerland, and the United Kingdom, at a state level in California, Connecticut, Hawaii, New Jersey, New York, and Rhode Island in the United States, at a county level in Montgomery County, Maryland, the United States, and even at a city level in Masdar in the United Arab Emirates (Connecticut Green Bank, 2019). Green investment banks tend to be created in countries without a national development bank, because development banks can overlap somewhat with the functions of green banks in leveraging public funds for private investment for green infrastructure projects.

Green Bonds

Green bonds are fixed-income debt instruments that are issued to finance or refinance green projects that have climate and environmental benefits, an innovative way to channel capital into helping the transition to sustainability, such as in renewable energy, sustainable infrastructure, sustainable transportation, energy efficiency, and responsible waste management. Green bonds are typically asset-linked and are backed by the balance sheet of the issuer. The issuer would have to generate enough cash flow to repay the principal plus interests over a preset period of time, similar to traditional bonds. Green bonds in certain jurisdictions have favorable tax treatment, which make them more appealing than taxable bonds. However, the planned beneficial environmental impact of the use of proceeds of green bonds have to be verified in a 'second opinion' provided by an environmental rating consultancy such as Sustainalytics or CICERO. The second opinion provider merely verifies that the intended use of proceeds would be beneficial, according to the guidelines formulated in the Green Bond Principles. The issuer is obliged to report on the eventual impact of the project, but no verification is required post-issuance.

The European Investment Bank (EIB) issued the first ever green bond for $800 million in 2007, labeled a climate awareness bond. Proceeds are earmarked to match disbursements to EIB lending projects in the renewable energy and energy efficiency sectors. By the end of 2018, the EIB has raised a total of €23.5 billion in climate awareness bonds (European Investment Bank, 2018). The World Bank followed up in 2008 to issue the very first bond under the 'green bond' label, and the institution has remained one of the major issuers of green bonds ever since. In fact, only international development banks issued any green bonds until 2012, when the first corporate green bond was issued. Since then, the green bond market has experienced dramatic growth (Rosembuj & Bottio, 2016).

Green bonds can be issued by governments, corporations, and multilateral institutions. Unfortunately, green bonds are not viable financing sources for cleantech activities in stages 1 through 5. Essentially, green bonds can be issued by issuers that already have access to the public bond market. In this sense, they do not significantly increase the capital available for cleantech innovation, though they do reduce the cost of capital for late stage fully commercial enterprises.

There are four main types of green bonds: (1) green use of proceeds bonds, (2) green asset-backed bonds, (3) green project bonds, and (4) pure play bonds. The use of proceeds bond is issued with recourse to the issuer in the case of a default. The proceeds are earmarked for green projects and are often backed by the entire balance sheet of the issuer. The climate awareness bond issued by EIB is an example of the green use of proceeds bond. The asset-backed bonds are usually collateralized by a pool of smaller assets, with recourse only to the assets, such as the mortgages for energy-efficient homes and leases for rooftop solar PVs, and the revenues from which will serve as the first source for bond repayment. For example, Tesla Energy (formerly SolarCity, the biggest solar installer in the United States) issued green bonds backed by residential solar PV leases. Green project bonds are issued for typically large green projects, such as a wind park or a solar farm, and are backed by these projects with or without recourse to the issuer. The assets and any profit generated from these projects are used to finance the bond and the investors have direct exposure to the projects. Any bond issued by companies that are already in the 'green' sector, such as PV producer, turbine manufacturer, and waste management plant, is going to be labeled a green bond since the revenue for these companies will be generated from the 'green' sector of business anyway.

Global issuance of green bonds reached $173 billion in 2017, a 70% increase from 2016 and up from only $0.5 billion a decade ago (Fig. 14.4). A major contribution to the growth is Chinese issuance, amounting to $33 billion in 2016 and $25 billion in 2017. While the growth moderated slightly for 2018, it is still forecasted to increase to close to $200 billion (Moody's, 2018a, 2018b), especially as fixed-income investors adopt environmental, social, and governance (ESG) integration. Despite the fast growth, green bond issuance still counts for only 2–3% of total global bond issues, and an even smaller proportion of the total fixed-income asset under management (Climate Bonds Initiative, 2017).

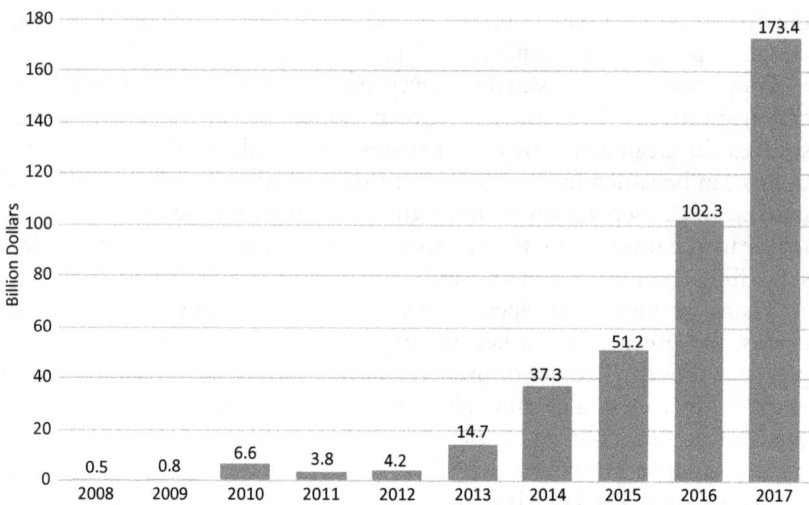

Fig. 14.4 Green bond issuance, 2008–2017. (Source: Adapted from UNEP, Frankfurt School & Bloomberg New Energy Finance (2018))

There are many upsides for green bonds. An issuer such as a government, a multilateral institution, or a private company can generate capital from environmentally conscious investors who may not otherwise invest. Green bond would also help demonstrate and improve the issuer's sustainability bona fides. It sends a positive signal to the market that may serve to reduce long-term risk, and it could form a competitive edge for the organization and help promote a 'green' brand. At the same time, the investors of green bonds can equally claim that they are environmentally conscious and are actively supporting the transition to a sustainable future.

There are also noticeable problems associated with green bond. The cost of capital with green bond issuance could be higher than a traditional bond issue (Millet, McGeachie, Harris-Ngae, Villemain, & Rhodes, 2016). For example, defining, monitoring, and maintaining green projects and proceeds can both be challenging and costly, while the issuers would have to generate as much return as a conventional bond. The 'green' label is what distinguishes a green bond from a regular bond; hence the transparency with which the proceeds are used is of paramount importance. If anything, the verification process for green bond qualification would cost time and money.

In addition, many of the activities to be funded by green bonds are going to be funded anyway, whether through taxation in the case of governments, or various corporate borrowing mechanisms for private organizations. For example, high-speed railway projects will be financed through bank loans, and environmental protection projects of any government will be financed either through taxation or government borrowing in the traditional approach without the specificities of a green bond. Therefore, unless additional capital can be raised with green bonds, on top of what would be raised anyway through traditional methods—the evidence of which has not been documented, green bonds cannot be said to produce 'additional' environmental gains.

In this vein, green bonds can lead to greenwashing rather than concrete benefits—in particular when there is not a third-party authority that can conduct independent evaluation and ensure continued compliance, except the certification of the 'green' status at issuance. Green bonds can trade at a higher premium than non-green bonds (Clapp, 2018). Instead of the voluntary frameworks used to gain the green label, credible and independent rating systems are critical.

YieldCo

Another form of innovative finance for renewable energy is the 'YieldCo', which became popular in 2013 when the first YieldCo went public. Very similar to a master limited partnerships (MLPs) or real estate investment trusts (REITs), a YieldCo is also a yield-based investment vehicle under which a public company that is formed to own operating assets typically in renewable energy, such as a wind farm or a solar farm that generates stable cash flow. Unlike MLPs, YieldCos do not face restrictions on the type of income they can generate. Separating out the operating assets from development assets would demonstrate a proven history to potential investors than the perhaps more volatile assets that may still be under development.

YieldCos grew very fast in 2013 and 2014 through initial public offerings and collectively raised more than $14 billion from 2013 to 2015 in North America and Europe (Frankfurt School-UNEP Centre/BNEF, 2016). A flurry of new listings in a relatively short period of time eventually flooded the market that halted the rise of the stock prices of YieldCos which led to the high-profile bankruptcy of SunEdison in 2016. More recently, YieldCos are beginning to see a revival with many of their stock prices on the rise. While still far from the highs achieved in 2015 and no one is promising double-digit growth in dividends any time soon, YieldCos may still have potential to serve as a way in raising relatively cheap capital for clean energy companies from the equity market.

Asset-Backed Securities (ABS)

As already discussed in Chap. 12, the market for asset-backed securitization or ABS is very large, with $1.5 trillion outstanding in the United States alone (Securities Industry and Financial Markets Association, 2017). The most well-known ABS is of course the mortgage-backed securities, with their lower-rated sub-prime mortgage securities the primary culprit for the 2008 global financial crisis. ABS extends beyond home loans and could also include car loans, student debt, credit card debit, and many others such as intellectual property and film that generates steady stream of cash flow.

Particularly in the United States, solar developers started to raise capital through the securitization of pooled leases or loans for residential and commercial solar installation. Termed as solar or solar energy backed securities, its market value reached $1.3 billion in the United States in 2017 (Feldman, Margolis, & Hoskins, 2018). Traditionally dependent on tax incentives and subsidies, securitization offers solar providers a low-cost alternative to corporate debt and affords them better cash flows to scale up the market. Given pension funds, mutual funds, and other institutional investors' large presence in securitized products, solar backed securities offer another way for institutional investors to invest in clean energy which they would find difficult to invest in smaller doses.

Asset Finance versus People Finance

The six stages of cleantech development vary in the net cash flows produced by the development activity. While the activities of scientific research rarely produce significant revenue, fully commercial business activities are financially self-sustaining. An alternative way to view the continuum between stages is to recognize that in general, later stages require investments in widespread asset deployment while earlier stages require paying salaries of highly skilled individuals. The difficulty with financing the activities of individuals is that there is no way to ensure that the output of such activities will be marketable to others. Conversely, the assets intended for widespread deployment are generally valuable to a wide range of potential buyers. In this sense, funding research and development is a little like funding student loans, insofar as the familiar challenges posed by moral hazard and adverse selection need to be addressed. Moral hazard arises if researchers become too comfortable with their current salaries, reducing the incentive to put effort into further innovation. Adverse selection may arise because the funder cannot identify good researchers *ex ante*. Since the funder is forced to offer low salaries to new researchers (so as to increase their incentives for effort), many potential researchers with higher alternative salaries in other sectors will eschew research. This was a widespread problem for researchers in mathematics, computer science, and physics in the 1980s when newly minted PhDs in such fields could command substantially higher compensation in asset management and derivatives trading than in scientific research (Derman, 2004).

It is a truism in finance that assets are easier to finance than people. Since assets can serve as collateral while people cannot, the simplest methods of banking and finance can generate funds to purchase assets, so long as they are recognizably valuable to others. It should therefore not be surprising that the scale of funds available through debt markets for asset financing dwarf that available for early-stage research and the incubation of start-ups. Indeed, the bulk of investment in clean technology has gone to renewable energy generation, reaching $280 billion in 2017, most of which was used for asset finance (Frankfurt School-UNEP Centre/BNEF, 2018).

Corporate VC Investment in Early-Stage Cleantech

Perhaps promisingly, many of the major international oil and gas companies which chose to divest from renewable energy after the financial crisis are once again making investments in the renewable sector. After announcing in 2009 that it would not invest in wind and solar, Royal Dutch Shell has recently invested $1–2 billion annually on renewables and cleantech such as electric vehicles (Shell, 2018). British Petroleum (BP), which exited the solar market in 2011, invested $200 million in Lightsource, the largest solar power developer in Europe in 2017 (Ward & Thomas, 2017). Oil and gas companies are also beginning to fund crucial early-stage development and research. Corporate VC refers to direct minority equity investments by established corporations in privately held entrepreneurial ventures. The French energy company, total—traditionally the major oil and gas company that spends the most on renewable energy and clean technology—has established a corporate VC fund of $160 million that has funded 20 start-up companies in a range of cleantech industries (Chatsko, 2018). Statoil also pledged a venture capital fund (New Energy Investment Fund) of $200 million for renewable initiatives beyond wind power (Statoil, 2016).

While it is conceivable that major oil and gas companies are investing in a cleaner energy future, it is also possible that these investments provide relatively cheap exploratory initiatives for oil majors. Corporate VC investments are a means of quickly, cheaply and flexibly accessing the knowledge base of innovative new ventures and the R&D ecosystem in the sector (Basu, Phelps, & Kotha, 2011). In a study of the voluntary disclosure of corporate VC investments by large corporations, Mohamed and Schwienbacher (2016) show that corporations use disclosure of their investments in innovative startups in a strategic manner. Large corporations have an incentive to disclose R&D to signal their leadership in the sector, but this incentive is blunted by the risk of giving away information about future competitive strategy. In this context, voluntary disclosure of start-up investments can signal R&D leadership without revealing very much about internal R&D priorities. Faced with investor pressure, oil majors may receive disproportionate signaling value from disclosures of R&D investments in cleantech firms.

It is also possible that many upstream oil and gas investments, such as onshore North American projects still offer more attractive returns than solar and wind investments. If this were true, it would explain the gap in renewable investments between European and American oil majors. In Europe, where companies have limited access to cheap oil sources, and where they face greater pressure from governments, consumers, investors, and other stakeholders have invested more in renewables. Janeway (2018) has argued that the dominant positions of large industrial firms make it unlikely that their R&D investments can compete with the profits from the existing business. He cites the example of Xerox PARC, when none of the innovations could compete with the profits of the entrenched patent-protected photocopier business.

ExxonMobil has been allocating a relatively small $1 billion a year to low-carbon technology research (Chatsko, 2018), such as working with FuelCell Energy to develop fuel cells that capture and store carbon dioxide (Eisler, 2018). Carbon capture and storage technology could be essential as the Intergovernmental Panel on Climate Change (IPCC) suggests in their latest report that limiting the global temperature rise to 1.5°C would require both greater emission reductions and the removal of carbon already released in the atmosphere (IPCC, 2018). Investments by multinational oil and gas companies into cleantech will positively affect the likelihood of early exits for VC/PE investments.

In addition, some US electric utilities such as Xcel Energy and PPL, perhaps driven by investor pressure such as through the Climate Action 100+ initiative, have started the transition from fossil fuel to low carbon by shuttering coal and building out gas as an intermediate phase.[7] US states such as New York and California have set carbon-free electricity targets for 2040 and 2045, respectively (Brown, 2018; Cuomo, 2019), which will put additional regulatory pressure on utility companies to switch to clean energy.

Despite their recent investments, major oil and gas companies still own less than 2% of the operating solar and wind projects globally (Heggarty, 2018). They are also devoting a relatively small proportion of their capital expenditure on renewables: Shell spent $200 million on renewables out of a total of $80 billion and still treats cleantech investments as medium to long-term projects (Zhong & Bazilian, 2018).

Cleantech Financing Needs

A significant obstacle to the transition to a clean energy economy is the paltry amounts of available financing of clean or low-carbon technology relative to the estimated needs. Large sums of money are needed—hundreds of billions of dollars—for investments into the technologies that can help reduce emissions, especially in developing countries (World Bank, 2010). Given the range of existing investments—$300–400 billion annually, some researchers estimate that an additional $800 billion a year would be needed for the next 30 years in order to finance the scaling of projects in energy efficiency and low-carbon energy that would be consistent with the 2°C target (McCollum et al., 2013). The latest IPCC report puts that number around the lower boundary, and suggests based on a range of studies that as much as $3 trillion additional investments a year in energy could be needed to limit warming to 2°C (IPCC, 2018). The International Finance Corporation estimates that approximately $23 trillion of investment in 'climate-smart' investments will be necessary for emerging markets between 2016 and 2030. This amounts to $1.6 trillion per year (International Finance Corporation, 2016). Fortunately, a significant portion of this investment needs consists of infrastructure and asset financing, rather than research, development, and deployment. For example, the IFC estimates that \$16 trillion (70%) of the \$23 trillion will be needed for investments in buildings, which are not typically recipients of funding intended for research and development. The financing need for all renewable energy is \$1.8 trillion, or approximately \$117 billion per year. While this is significantly larger than current investments in renewable energy generation in emerging markets, it is far more manageable. If existing methods of financing building infrastructure in jurisdictions with developed asset finance markets can be adapted to emerging markets, then climate financing needs can conceivably be addressed by a combination of cleantech innovation finance and asset finance.

Concluding Remarks

Technology innovation has emerged to become the single most important driver for economic growth. To transition to a sustainable development model, our best hope is on the continued advancement of clean technology. Significant capital has been invested, but substantial gaps still remain, not just to fund research and development of new technology, but also the manufacturing and scaling up of mature ones.

This chapter has surveyed myriad financing options, many of which are relatively new and are aimed at overcoming the barriers posed by the peculiar nature of the cleantech industry, which could be characterized as asset-heavy, high-risk, low-return, and with a long investment span. Traditional energy, which is still being heavily subsidized by governments around the world, remains a significant competitive threat. Finance is not the only problem to transition to renewables. Corporate short-termism is a major obstacle, as is renewable intermittency associated with solar and wind that may slow down the transition. Although innovation has driven the cost of some renewable energy generation to levels competitive with fossil fuels, the cost of addressing intermittency[8] can rise sharply when these renewables transition into a dominant role in electricity generation, whereas in smaller shares they can be cheaply backed up by redundant dispatchable generation (Bradford, 2018). Filling the gap with other stable energy sources would solve the problem, but would add additional costs of integration, which would be much higher with higher levels of solar and wind deployment. Storage is another solution but remains prohibitively expensive.

Given the recent rapid expansion of the cleantech sector, we have reason to be optimistic. Yet, our optimism is tempered by a belief that governments play an essential role in funding and enabling early-stage investments in R&D. For example, while funding for wind and solar has been steadily increasing, the funding for geothermal energy has declined in recent years, with only $1.4 billion invested for an additional capacity of 700 MW in 2017 (Frankfurt School-UNEP Centre/BNEF, 2018). Although it is not available everywhere, geothermal is much more stable than other renewables such as solar, wind, and hydro, and could be an important source of clean energy for countries such as Iceland and Kenya, where 66% and 45% of their energy demands, respectively, are supplied by geothermal (Kenyatta, 2019; National Energy Authority of Iceland, 2014). The Western United States and countries in the South Pacific are abundant in geothermal reserves, which could serve as an important source of clean and affordable energy. However, the upfront costs associated with exploration, and the high risks of failure makes it unsuitable for debt financing, and the high capital expenses for exploration and drilling are not typical for a VC portfolio. As a result, direct funding from government or facilitating policies to activate private capital investment becomes crucial in the development of geothermal energy.

Governments not only have to be more aggressive in funding directly the research and the early development of clean technology, but they also have to be more innovative in designing policies and regulations to encourage institutional and private investments, and more proactive in partnering with the private sector in developing new funding solutions. In addition, funding will need to be enhanced by angel investors, VCs, and public markets. In the financial ecosystem, it is likely that there is a key role for many actors to provide capital, tailored to the particulars of cash flow expectations, maturity, volatility, and other sources of both financial and climate risk for the range of cleantech innovation activities. Our next chapter is devoted to a fuller investigation of the need to address energy access and provide inclusive growth.

NOTES

1. See Chapter 1 of Bradford (2018) for a detailed explanation of and historical perspective on this approximate equivalence.
2. The difference between the physical definition of work performed (application of force over a distance) and the economic definition of work (the output of goods and services) can be traced to the value placed on non-physical activities in the economic measurement of work. Value in economics is rooted in the interaction of consumer preferences and supply. If a

change in consumer preferences were to lead to a higher valuation of activities with low physical work, then GDP could increase without additional physical work being performed.

3. See Chapter 8 of Bradford (2018) for an outline of the comparative difficulties of financing renewable energy versus incumbent energy generation technologies.

4. In their textbook on artificial intelligence, Stuart Russell & Peter Norvig note that Bellman must have mis-remembered some details since his initial article on dynamic programming was published in June 1952, six months before Wilson became Secretary of Defense (Russell & Norvig, 2010).

5. More recently, there has been a change in attitude toward renewables by major oil and gas companies, which we will return to later in this chapter.

6. Greenfield FDI refers to investments into new business instead of merging with or acquiring existing business in a country. It is also worth noting that while $77 billion is a significant figure for renewable energy, more money ($121 billion) still went into fossil fuel exploration and extraction.

7. The Climate Action 100+ is an initiative by more than 300 of the world's largest investors with $32 trillion assets collectively under management to engage 100 large emitter companies to reduce their emission and improve their governance.

8. Intermittency is a type of resource availability risk for kinetic energy sources such as wind, solar, and wave energy because these resources are not consistently available.

References

Basu, S., Phelps, C., & Kotha, S. (2011). Towards Understanding Who Makes Corporate Venture Capital Investments and Why. *Journal of Business Venturing, 26*(2), 153–171. https://doi.org/10.1016/j.jbusvent.2009.07.001

Bellman, R. (1952). On the Theory of Dynamic Programming. *Proceedings of the National Academy of Sciences of the United States of America, 38*(8), 716–719.

Böhringer, C., Landis, F., Reaños, T., & Angel, M. (2017). Economic Impacts of Renewable Energy Promotion in Germany. *Energy Journal, 38*, 189–209.

Bradford, T. (2018). *The Energy System: Technology, Economics, Markets and Policy.* Cambridge, MA: MIT Press.

Brown, E. G. J. (2018). *Governor Brown Signs 100 Percent Clean Electricity Bill, Issues Order Setting New Carbon Neutrality Goal.* Retrieved from https://www.ca.gov/archive/gov39/2018/09/10/governor-brown-signs-100-percent-clean-electricity-bill-issues-order-setting-new-carbon-neutrality-goal/index.html

California State Treasurer. (2004). *State Treasurer Phil Angelides Launches 'Green Wave' Environmental Investment Initiative to Bolster Financial Returns, Create*

Jobs and Clean up the Environment. Press Release. Retrieved from https://members.e2.org/ext/doc/20040203CATreasurer-PR-GreenWaveLaunch.pdf

Chatsko, M. (2018). *Big Oil Is Investing Billions in Renewable Energy. Here's Where and How.* Retrieved from https://www.fool.com/investing/2018/06/04/big-oil-is-investing-billions-in-renewable-energy.aspx

Clapp, C. (2018). Investing in a Green Future. *Nature Climate Change, 8*(2), 96.

Climate Bonds Initiative. (2017). Green Bonds Market Summary: Q3 2017. *Green Bonds Initiative Update.*

Connecticut Green Bank. (2019). *About Us.* Retrieved from https://www.ctgreenbank.com/about-us-2017/

Crunchbase, I. (2019). *Tesla Funding Rounds.* Retrieved from https://www.crunchbase.com/organization/tesla-motors#section-funding-rounds

Cumming, D., Henriques, I., & Sadorsky, P. (2016). 'Cleantech' Venture Capital Around the World. *International Review of Financial Analysis, 44,* 86–97.

Cuomo, A. (2019). *Governor Cuomo Announces Green New Deal Included in 2019 Executive Budget.* Retrieved from https://www.governor.ny.gov/news/governor-cuomo-announces-green-new-deal-included-2019-executive-budget

Department of Energy. (2009). *Obama Administration Offers $535 Million Loan Guarantee to Solyndra, Inc.* Media Release. Retrieved from https://www.energy.gov/articles/obama-administration-offers-535-million-loan-guarantee-solyndra-inc

Department of Energy. (2010). *Secretary Chu Announces Closing of $465 Million Loan to Tesla Motors.* Media Release. Retrieved from https://www.energy.gov/articles/secretary-chu-announces-closing-465-million-loan-tesla-motors

Derman, E. (2004). *My Life as a Quant: Reflections on Physics and Finance.* Hoboken, NJ: Wiley.

Dreyfus, S. (2002). Richard Bellman on the Birth of Dynamic Programming. *Operations Research, 50,* 48–51. Catonsville, MD: INFORMS: Institute for Operations Research.

Eisler, M. N. (2018). *Fuel Cells Finally Find a Killer App: Carbon Capture.* Retrieved from https://spectrum.ieee.org/green-tech/fuel-cells/fuel-cells-finally-find-a-killer-app-carbon-capture

European Investment Bank. (2018). Climate Awareness Bonds. *Investor Relations.* Retrieved from http://www.eib.org/en/investor_relations/cab/index.htm

Feldman, D. J., Margolis, R. M., & Hoskins, J. (2018). *Q4 2017/Q1 2018 Solar Industry Update.* Retrieved from https://www.nrel.gov/docs/fy18osti/71493.pdf

Frank, C., Sink, C., Mynatt, L., Rogers, R., & Rappazzo, A. (1996). Surviving the "Valley of Death": A Comparative Analysis. *The Journal of Technology Transfer, 21*(1), 61–69. https://doi.org/10.1007/BF02220308

Frankfurt School-UNEP Centre/BNEF. (2016). *Global Trends in Renewable Energy Investment 2016.* Frankfurt am Main, Germany: Frankfurt School of Finance & Management.

Frankfurt School-UNEP Centre/BNEF. (2018). *Global Trends in Renewable Energy Investment 2018.* Retrieved from Frankfurt-am-Main: https://www.greengrowthknowledge.org/resource/global-trends-renewable-energy-investment-report-2018

Gaddy, B. E., Sivaram, V., Jones, T. B., & Wayman, L. (2017). Venture Capital and Cleantech: The Wrong Model for Energy Innovation. *Energy Policy, 102,* 385–395. https://doi.org/10.1016/j.enpol.2016.12.035

Gerrard, M. B., & Dernbach, J. C. (Eds.). (2018). *Legal Pathways to Deep Decarbonization in the United States.* Washington, DC: Environmental Law Institute.

GreenInvest. (2017). *Green Foreign Direct Investment in Developing Countries.* Retrieved from Geneva: http://unepinquiry.org/wp-content/uploads/2017/10/Green_Foreign_Direct_Investment_in_Developing_Countries.pdf

Hart, D. M. (1998). *Forged Consensus: Science, Technology, and Economic Policy in the United States, 1921–1953.* Princeton, NJ: Princeton University Press.

Heggarty, T. (2018). Oil & Gas Majors in Renewable Energy: The Hunt for the Best Returns. *Market Report.* Retrieved from Wood Mackenzie: https://www.woodmac.com/news/editorial/renewable-energy-hunt-for-best-returns/

Internal Revenue Service. (2018). *Business Energy Investment Tax Credit.* Retrieved from http://programs.dsireusa.org/system/program/detail/658

International Energy Agency. (2015). *Medium-Term Renewable Energy Market Report.* Retrieved from OECD/IEA Publishing, Paris: https://www.iea.org/publications/freepublications/publication/MTRMR2015.pdf

International Energy Agency. (2016). World Energy Outlook 2016.

International Energy Agency. (2017a). *Energy Access Outlook 2017.* Retrieved from Paris: https://www.iea.org/publications/freepublications/publication/WEO2017SpecialReport_EnergyAccessOutlook.pdf

International Energy Agency. (2017b). *Tracking Fossil Fuel Subsidies in APEC Economies: Towards a Sustained Subsidy Reform.* Retrieved from https://eua-genda.eu/upload/publications/untitled-86781-ea.pdf

International Energy Agency. (2018). World Energy Investment 2018. Paris: International Energy Agency.

International Finance Corporation. (2016). *Climate Investment Opportunities in Emerging Markets: An IFC Analysis.* Retrieved from https://www.ifc.org/wps/wcm/connect/59260145-ec2e-40de-97e6-3aa78b82b3c9/3503-IFC-Climate_Investment_Opportunity-Report-Dec-FINAL.pdf?MOD=AJPERES&CVID=lBLd6Xq

IPCC. (2018). *Global Warming of 1.5°C.* An IPCC Special Report on the Impacts of Global Warming of 1.5 °C above Pre-Industrial Levels and Related Global Greenhouse Gas Emission Pathways, in the Context of Strengthening the Global Response to the Threat of Climate Change, Sustainable Development, and Efforts to Eradicate Poverty. Intergovernmental Panel on Climate Change, Geneva, Switzerland.

Janeway, W. H. (2018). *Doing Capitalism in the Innovation Economy*. Cambridge, UK: Cambridge University Press.

Kenyatta, U. (2019). *Kenya on Track to Achieve Full Transition to Renewable Energy by 2020*. News Release. Retrieved from http://www.president.go.ke/2018/12/04/kenya-on-track-to-achieve-full-transition-to-renewable-energy-by-2020-president-kenyatta/

Lerner, J. (2012). The Narrowing Ambitions of Venture Capital. *MIT Technology Review, 115*(6), 76–78.

Lerner, J., Schoar, A., Sokolinski, S., & Wilson, K. (2015). *The Globalization of Angel Investments: Evidence Across Countries* (NBER Working Papers: 21808). National Bureau of Economic Research, Inc. Retrieved from http://www.nber.org/papers/w21808.pdf

Mazzucato, M., & Semieniuk, G. (2018). Financing Renewable Energy: Who Is Financing What and Why It Matters. *Technological Forecasting and Social Change, 127*, 8–22.

McCollum, D., Nagai, Y., Riahi, K., Marangoni, G., Calvin, K., Pietzcker, R., ... van der Zwaan, B. (2013). Energy Investments Under Climate Policy: A Comparison of Global Models. *Climate Change Economics, 4*(04), 1340010.

McGlade, C., & Ekins, P. (2015). The Geographical Distribution of Fossil Fuels Unused When Limiting Global Warming to 2 C. *Nature, 517*(7533), 187.

Migendt, M., Polzin, F., Schock, F., Täube, F. A., & von Flotow, P. (2017). Beyond Venture Capital: An Exploratory Study of the Finance-Innovation-Policy Nexus in Cleantech. *Industrial and Corporate Change, 26*(6), 973–996.

Millet, T., McGeachie, S., Harris-Ngae, M., Villemain, S., & Rhodes, C. (2016). *Green Bonds: A Fresh Look at Financing Green Projects*. Retrieved from Canada.

Mohamed, A., & Schwienbacher, A. (2016). Voluntary Disclosure of Corporate Venture Capital Investments. *Journal of Banking & Finance, 68*, 69–83. https://doi.org/10.1016/j.jbankfin.2016.03.001

Moody's. (2018a). *Global Green Bond Issuance Rises in Second Quarter of 2018, but Growth Continues to Moderate*. Retrieved from https://www.moodys.com/research/Moodys-Global-green-bond-issuance-rises-in-second-quarter-of%2D%2DPR_387338

Moody's. (2018b). *China's Release of 7th Batch of Renewable Energy Subsidy Catalogue Is Credit Positive for Renewable Operators*. Retrieved from https://www.moodys.com/research/Moodys-Chinas-release-of-7th-batch-of-Renewable-Energy-Subsidy%2D%2DPR_385338

National Energy Authority of Iceland. (2014). *Direct Use of Geothermal Resources*. Retrieved from https://nea.is/geothermal/

NEXT 10 (Ed.). (2018). *California Green Innovation Index* (10th ed.). San Francisco, CA: NEXT 10.

Polzin, F. (2017). Mobilizing Private Finance for Low-Carbon Innovation – A Systematic Review of Barriers and Solutions. *Renewable and Sustainable Energy Reviews, 77*, 525–535.

Rosembuj, F., & Bottio, S. (2016). Mobilizing Private Climate Finance – Green Bonds and Beyond (English). EMCompass no. 25. Washington, DC: World Bank Group. http://documents.worldbank.org/curated/en/510581481272889882/Mobilizing-private-climate-finance-Green-bonds-and-beyond

Russell, S. J., & Norvig, P. (2010). *Artificial Intelligence: A Modern Approach* (3rd ed.). Upper Saddle River, NJ: Prentice Hall.

Saha, D., & Muro, M. (2017). *Cleantech Venture Capital: Continued Declines and Narrow Geography Limit Prospects.* Brookings Institution Report.

Securities Industry and Financial Markets Association. (2017). Statistics on U.S. ABS Issuance and Outstanding. Retrieved from https://www.sifma.org/resources/research/us-abs-issuance-and-outstanding/

Shell. (2018). *Shell Energy Transition Report.* Retrieved from https://www.shell.com/energy-and-innovation/the-energy-future/shell-energy-transition-report.html

Sohl, J. (2018). *The Angel Market in 2017: Angels Remain Bullish for Seed and Start-up Investing.* Retrieved from https://paulcollege.unh.edu/sites/default/files/resource/files/2017-analysis-report.pdf

Statoil. (2016). *Statoil Launches USD 200 M New Energy Investment Fund.* Retrieved from www.statoil.com/en/news/launches-usd200m-new-energy-investment-fund.html

U.S. Energy Information Administration. (2018). *United States Natural Gas Industrial Price.* Retrieved from https://www.eia.gov/dnav/ng/hist/n3035us3m.htm

United States Climate Alliance. (2018). *Green Banking.* Retrieved from https://www.usclimatealliance.org/greenbanks/

Ward, A., & Thomas, N. (2017). *BP Warms to Renewables with $200m Stake in Solar Developer.* Retrieved from https://www.ft.com/content/f2ca752e-e0d9-11e7-8f9f-de1c2175f5ce

Webb, T. (2011). *Spain's Financial Crisis Claims Another Victim: The Solar Power Industry.* Retrieved from https://www.theguardian.com/world/2011/mar/30/new-europe-spain-solar-power

Wilson, K. (2015, June 24). *Policy Lessons from Financing Innovative Firms* (OECD Science, Technology and Industry Policy Papers, No. 24). Paris: OECD Publishing. http://dx.doi.org/10.1787/5js03z8zrh9p-en

World Bank. (2010). *World Development Report 2010: Development and Climate Change.* Retrieved from Washington, DC: http://documents.worldbank.org/curated/en/201001468159913657/World-development-report-2010-development-and-climate-change

Zhong, M., & Bazilian, M. D. (2018). Contours of the Energy Transition: Investment by International Oil and Gas Companies in Renewable Energy. *The Electricity Journal, 31*(1), 82–91.

CHAPTER 15

The Cooperative Movement and Social Enterprise

Earlier chapters have described the benefits of broad societal legitimacy for corporate activity. As we noted in Chap. 3 in tracing the origins of the corporate form, the earliest occupational guilds and civic organizations that simultaneously conducted trade were created for social purposes in ancient India (the *sreni*) and Rome (the *municipia* and the *collegia*) as far back as the first millennium BCE. In this sense, the first enterprises were social enterprises. In Chaps. 4 and 9, we discussed the critical role of social capital in validating the collective purpose of sustainable economic activity. In Chap. 11, we described impact investing as derivative and particular form of investing, which developed partly from forms of social enterprise. In Chap. 12, we outlined the special role of financing local public goods.

THE COOPERATIVE MOVEMENT

In the eighteenth century, when the early joint stock corporations in Western Europe functioned as elite-controlled state enterprises focused on imperial expansion, a self-consciously democratic kind of local commercial venture arose in the form of *cooperatives*. Fire insurance cooperatives were formed in England in the early 1700s to pool capital in order to indemnify members against losses from fire, and around 1750, a number of French cheesemakers joined with clients to form perhaps the first consumer cooperative (Williams, 2007). In the second half of the eighteenth century, many more local cooperatives were formed by artisans, food producers, horticulturalists, and by those seeking fire insurance in France, Austria, England, Spain, Italy, the United States, and Mexico (Zamagni, 2017).[1] Benjamin Franklin founded one of the first cooperatives in the United States, the Philadelphia Contributory, a fire insurance mutual society, in 1752. In 1824, Robert Owen, a Welsh draper, who had accumulated capital in textile manufacturing and instituted the eight-hour workday in his mill, traveled to the United States and invested much of his wealth in a short-lived cooperative utopia in New Harmony, Indiana. He subsequently returned to the United Kingdom and became known as an advocate for trade unions and the cooperative movement. In 1844, a group of 28 weavers in Rochdale, England, who had been dismissed from their jobs in a manufacturing corporation for striking, established a small cooperatively owned store that sold flour, butter, sugar, and oatmeal. The cooperative formulated the Rochdale Principles of Cooperation, which continue today (after amendments) as the Principles of the International Cooperative Alliance. The principles include open and voluntary membership, democratic governance, limited return on equity investment, member ownership of surpluses, and a commitment to educate members on cooperative management principles as well as to cooperate with other cooperatives. An essential financial aspect of cooperatives is their constraint on the financial return generated on invested capital, which protects the capacity of the cooperative to reinvest surpluses.

At the end of the nineteenth century, the International Cooperative Alliance (ICA) was founded in the United Kingdom. The ICA defines a cooperative as "*an autonomous association of persons united voluntarily to meet their common economic, social, and cultural needs and aspirations through a jointly-owned and democratically-controlled enterprise*" (International Co-operative Alliance, 2018). By the 1930s, consumer cooperatives represented some of the largest retail establishments in northern Europe. Today, cooperatives are widespread, in developing and developed countries alike. According to an ICA survey, the 300 largest cooperatives globally had annual revenues of $2.2 trillion in 2012 and are concentrated in insurance, agricultural production and marketing, wholesale and retail trade, and banking.

European cooperatives are particularly prevalent in France, Spain, Italy, and the Scandinavian countries. The most extensive system of cooperatives in Europe are the Mondragón cooperatives in northern Spain, which comprise over 100 consolidated firms in high-growth and high-technology sectors. The Mondragón cooperative is the largest cooperative in the world with revenues of €12 billion and over 80,000 'owner-employees'

(Mondragón, 2017). The cooperative's business is divided into four areas: finance, industry, distribution, and knowledge, and it currently ranks as the 10th largest company in Spain (Mondragón, 2019).

In the twenty-first century, the United Kingdom has witnessed a renewed interest in cooperatives after a post-war lull in activity. A prominent UK example is the John Lewis Partnership, the largest of over 300 employee-owned businesses in the United Kingdom. The partnership of 83,900 employee-partners owns John Lewis & Partners department stores and Waitrose & Partners supermarkets with revenues of £11.7 billion (John Lewis Partnership, 2019). As co-owners, employees in cooperatives tend to be more committed to the success of the company and are more entrepreneurial. The more open and participatory decision-making process also leads to greater community engagement and corporate social responsibility.

There are also many cooperative examples in the United States, such as credit unions (financial cooperatives co-owned by their members), agricultural cooperatives (e.g. Sunkist and Ocean Spray), consumer cooperatives (many independent grocery stores, e.g. Equal Exchange, a well-known fair trade and organic food distributor, which is equally owned by its 120 workers), and housing cooperatives. In developing countries, such as Kenya, there are 22,000 registered cooperatives with 14 million members ranging from all sectors including finance, agriculture, and transportation (Steven, 2019). India's cooperative movement is currently the largest in world, with over 400,000 cooperatives with 166 million members (Williams, 2007). China and the former Soviet Union had their own form of state-sponsored cooperatives, which were transformed into post-reform local enterprises.

In the 1960s, in Italy, a new kind of cooperative, the *social cooperative*, was established and eventually institutionalized by Italian Law 381 in 1991 (Thomas, 2004). The social cooperative grew out of the need to provide care to the sick and elderly and training and assistance to the socially marginal unemployed in a manner that was more efficient and variegated than could be provided by the welfare state and more concerned with beneficiary welfare than could be expected of the private sector. The social cooperative differed from cooperatives insofar as it incorporated non-member beneficiaries and other stakeholders such as volunteers and providers of capital, and enshrined their rights and responsibilities within a multi-stakeholder governance structure. Social cooperatives earned the bulk of their revenue from the state, receive capital from *lending* or *funding members*, receive the donated time of *volunteer members*, are managed by *technical* or *administrative members*, and provide services to *beneficiaries* or *user members*.

With the few exceptions described above, the cooperative movement was generally small and isolated throughout much of the twentieth century. The diffusion of cooperatives is not well suited to the structure of the post-war industrial corporations, with their high capital intensity, standardized production procedures, rigid assembly lines with semi-skilled labor, and hierarchical chains of command (Zamagni, 2017). Perhaps due to the eclipse of manufacturing corporations as dominant employers in the waning years of the twentieth century, there has been renewed interest in commercial cooperatives and a related though different form of activity, known variously as *social enterprise* and *social entrepreneurship*.

Social Enterprise

There are many competing and overlapping definitions of the social enterprise sector and a consensus over its boundaries remains elusive. Social enterprise has been characterized as the public sector adoption of business skills, businesses focusing on social ends, and the voluntary and non-profit sector adopting entrepreneurial approaches (Leadbeater, 1997). The UK government defined social enterprise as "*a business with primarily social objectives whose surpluses are principally reinvested for that purpose in the business or in the community, rather than being driven by the need to maximize profit for shareholders and owners*" (Department of Trade and Industry, 2002). Most agree with the primacy of social value creation for social enterprise and that revenue generation is a secondary (albeit necessary) condition—primarily to maintain financial viability (Mair & Marti, 2006). The organizational form of social entrepreneurship blurs the boundary between for-profit and non-profit enterprise, and its typology has evolved over the years. It started with the spectrum of orientation from Dees (1998) that classified social enterprise as a blend of philanthropic and commercial orientations. For Dees, there are mission-driven enterprises—which are the charitable and non-government organizations, as well as the traditionally profit-driven businesses, and the hybrid of the two can be classified as the social enterprise business model. Either under the spectrum conceptualization or the definition by the UK government, social enterprise can in theory take on many hybrid forms, which inevitably culminates in a 'business with social purpose' (Billis, 2010).

In terms of the distinctive types of organizational hybrid, the consensus is that social enterprise includes some charitable trading activities, cooperative and mutual enterprises, and some socially responsible businesses (Cornforth, 2003; Ridley-Duff & Bull, 2015). Various researchers use different names for the similar configurations, such as entrepreneurial non-profit, social businesses and the afore-mentioned social cooperative (Defourny & Nyssens, 2017; Spear, Cornforth, & Aiken, 2009). As such, social enterprise can evolve from charitable, non-profit, non-government organizations, as well as traditional for-profit businesses.

For example, many social enterprises in the US emerged from charities and foundations starting to earn income (Bull & Ridley-Duff, 2018), where the transition hinged on the scope of revenue generation. Traditional non-profit and philanthropic organizations served social missions, with revenue generation typically a small part of the overall operation. Whereas a non-profit organization might focus on fundraising from donors, a foundation-turned social enterprise is likely to engage in genuine business operations to generate sustainable revenue in order to cover costs. For a non-profit organization to be considered a social enterprise, revenue generation has to go beyond fundraising activities and have a strategic long-term orientation with measurable targets (Saebi, Foss, & Linder, 2019). In other words, revenue generation has a function beyond financial sustainability: it is a signal that the service provided generates value for users and is not just a pet project of donors. If recipients of the service are willing to pitch in funds for its provision, then one can assume that its usefulness has been validated by those for whom it has purportedly been provided. This validation of value generation by the broader social network is a key differentiator of social enterprise from both government welfare and charitable activities.

The transition to social enterprise does not have to be initiated only from non-profit organizations with the goal of making below-market return; well-known social enterprises such as the Grameen Bank in Bangladesh and the Sekem in Egypt began as business incarnations that generated millions in profits. Different from traditional businesses which aim to maximize profit, the mission of the social enterprise is to drive social progress. A significant portion, if not all profits, is expected to be retained within the enterprise for the purpose of developing new products and services and for growing the business in order to achieve greater impact. Social entrepreneurial activities are also different from traditional corporate social responsibility (CSR) initiatives. While embracing social values, CSR nevertheless defers to the primacy of profit maximization for shareholders. In addition, CSR initiatives are not typically linked to entrepreneurship or innovation—a key hallmark for social enterprise, but rather focus on engagement of community organizations or stakeholder relations (Shepherd & Patzelt, 2011).

THE SOCIAL ENTREPRENEUR

The term 'social entrepreneur' was coined by Banks (1972), who critiqued the Marxist notion that social movements were primarily the result of historical determinism and instead emphasized that social change had to be led by inventors, adopters, and advocates. Banks cited the example of Robert Owen as an entrepreneur who had applied his managerial skills to the purpose of social change. The literature defines social entrepreneurship either at the individual level by the behavior and characteristics of the entrepreneur, or at the organizational level by the social mission of the enterprise. Both types of definition characterize the social entrepreneur as a type of entrepreneur (Martin & Osberg, 2007). Martin and Osberg cite the nineteenth-century French economist, Jean Baptiste Say, as the first to coin the term entrepreneur, defining it as someone who creates value by shifting *"economic resources out of an area of lower and into an area of higher productivity and greater yield"*. In the twentieth century, the Austrian political economist, Joseph Schumpeter, added innovation to the functions of entrepreneurs by writing that *"the function of entrepreneurs is to reform or revolutionize the pattern of production"*. Contemporary management theorists largely follow the Say-Schumpeter tradition in defining entrepreneurship. For example, Peter Drucker, widely viewed as the father of modern management, amplifies Say's value creation thesis to stress the ability of entrepreneurs to recognize and exploit value-creating opportunities (Drucker, 2014), which has become the central element of modern entrepreneurship terminology.

Gregory Dees, who taught the first course on social entrepreneurship in the American academic context at Harvard University in 1995, defined the basic characteristics of a social entrepreneur as follows:

- *Adopting a mission to create and sustain social value (not just private value),*
- *Recognizing and relentlessly pursuing new opportunities to serve that mission,*

- *Engaging in a process of continuous innovation, adaptation, and learning,*
- *Acting boldly without being limited by resources currently in hand, and*
- *Exhibiting a heightened sense of accountability to the constituencies served and for the outcomes created* (Dees, 1998).

One may wish to add an additional component of risk taking—social entrepreneurs are often expected to accept above-average risks in trying to generate social value in places where market conditions are less than ideal (Peredo & McLean, 2006; Tan, Williams, & Tan, 2005).

Difference Between the Cooperative Movement and Social Entrepreneurship

There is an important contrast between the concept of the social entrepreneur and the principles of the cooperative or social enterprise. Though enterprise and entrepreneurship sound similar and denote similar things and we sometimes use the words interchangeably, they carry different connotations. The American vision of social entrepreneurship emphasizes the creative Schumpeterian individual and is more likely to use the term social entrepreneurship rather than social enterprise or social cooperative. Both are concerned with disrupting existing social constraints, filling unmet social needs, and involve significant localized and distributed decision-making. However, Say and the Austrian economists, such as Schumpeter, von Mises, Kirzner, and, to a lesser extent, Hayek, who perhaps were most vocal in articulating the creativity and alertness of the individual entrepreneur, lauded the subjective vision of the individual who recognized the value-creating opportunity. The literature on social entrepreneurship remains deferential to the individual entrepreneur. The cooperative movement, conversely, is rooted in an egalitarian ethic of mutual aid, emphasizing the pooling of resources by equals with intersecting interests, all of whom have some entrepreneurial ability (Trincado, 2018). The European vision of the social enterprise is more likely to emphasize the multiple classes of stakeholder rather than individual founders.

Innovation is considered an innate feature of social enterprise. Social entrepreneurship is said to refer to *"an effort to solve intractable social problems through pattern-breaking change"* (Light, 2008). It *"doesn't solely refer to spreading an idea that is powerful enough to spill over borders—it also means 'shifting the frame' within which a problem is struck"* (Schwartz, 2012). These descriptions emphasize that innovation is at the core of social entrepreneurship, which is supposed to involve entrepreneurs surveying the world to understand the root cause of a problem, and then reinventing the norms or finding new ways to engage the population that has traditionally been excluded from the market or the public space. For example, lack of access to financial capital is a well-documented problem for those without collateral or centralized credit histories in both developed and developing countries. Other sources of capital such as friends and family or loan sharks are either limited or predatory. Group-based lending in microfinance is a key innovation developed by Mohammad Yunus at the Grameen Bank to address this population. Today, many microfinance institutions screen and monitor groups of borrowers on the online social enterprise crowdfunding platform Kiva. Kiva enables individual lenders to fund microloans to poor entrepreneurs around the world without charging interest. Lenders donate their interest in the form of charitable giving, but are able to reuse the funds to lend to others upon repayment. The overall repayment rate on Kiva loans is 98.8% (Dorfleitner & Oswald, 2016).

Social entrepreneurship is shaped by institutions, both informal ones such as values, norms, and traditions, as well as formal ones such as regulation, law, and incentive mechanisms. As a result, social entrepreneurial activities are different in countries with different institutions. One can imagine that developing countries with more social problems ought to attract more social entrepreneurs, but, in fact, most social enterprises are based in developed countries. Merely having more social problems is not enough to attract social entrepreneurs, as government institutions may be weak in places with severe social issues. While formal institutions—socioeconomic status and the level of development—are not strongly linked with the prevalence of social entrepreneurship (Puumalainen, Sjögrén, Syrjä, & Barraket, 2015), cultural dimensions—power distance, individualism, masculinity, and uncertainty avoidance as first proposed by Hofsteds (1980) are identified to strongly affect entrepreneurial activity (Hayton, George, & Zahra, 2002; Licht & Siegel, 2006; Thornton, Ribeiro-Soriano, & Urbano, 2011).

Often, cultures, where the general population are more empowered and politically involved, are more receptive to social entrepreneurship, as many social enterprises are aimed at decreasing power inequality through reducing social exclusion. In addition, societies that share collectivist values tend to attract social entrepreneurs. Social entrepreneurship naturally is more connected with collective values, and individualistic societies would find it hard to identify entrepreneurial opportunities for generating social impact. Higher levels of social entrepreneurial activities are also associated with less masculine societies, where assertiveness, heroism, and material reward are not emphasized. Lastly, risk taking is important for any form of entrepreneurship—societies with lower uncertainty avoidance, more relaxed attitude, and flexible belief systems (pragmatic vs. principled) are conducive to entrepreneurship in general, including the social form (Puumalainen et al., 2015).

In the twenty-first century, in many countries, social enterprises have outstripped the number of traditional commercial businesses (Kistruck & Beamish, 2010), and they are viewed as an innovative approach to blend economic and social value creation, such as in empowering women, alleviating poverty, and promoting inclusive growth (Saebi et al., 2019). Their recent rise is related with the erosion of public funds for social welfare in Western Europe and Latin America (due to fiscal austerity and the Great recession) and the failure of the public sector and international development agencies to address global social challenges in developing countries. Along with the other mechanisms outlined in preceding chapters, the insights from the cooperative movement and social entrepreneurship are essential tools to mobilize much-needed capital into solving the world's social and environmental challenges.

The overall number of social enterprises globally is hard to estimate, but Social Enterprise UK has estimated that there are currently 100,000 social enterprises in the UK alone, which employ 2 million people and contribute £60 billion to the economy (Social Enterprise UK, 2018).

Social Enterprise and Poverty Alleviation

Social enterprise promises to be an important tool in global efforts to alleviate poverty. Just as the first social cooperative in Italy emerged out of the failures of bureaucratically administered welfare, so social enterprise in developing countries is expected to correct for the failures of multilateral development aid. Some development economists such as Jeffrey Sachs are vocal advocates for development aid. Sachs argues that the poor who simultaneously lack many forms of development capital are often stuck in a poverty trap from which they can only escape with external grants (Sachs, 2006). He maintains that substantial development aid is necessary to make up for the lack of human capital and physical infrastructure, which would be difficult to accumulate without sufficient local resources. Large-scale development aid was first used under the Marshall Plan and was largely successful in rebuilding post-World War II Europe. Nevertheless, there is widespread critique of this view by other economists. William Easterly argues that after the failure of decades of large-scale external aid in alleviating poverty worldwide, significant poverty reduction cannot depend on rich country governments and multilateral organizations but must be built upon unleashing local ingenuity to come up with innovative and locally adapted solutions (Easterly, 2006). The role of grassroots entrepreneurs in serving local social needs by exploiting market opportunities is critical and can be crowded out by the externally conceived, capital-intensive, and rigidly hierarchical solutions of development experts.

The notion that entrepreneurship can help alleviate poverty is not new. Entrepreneurial activities create jobs and generate economic growth. However, profit-driven businesses from industrialized countries may find it difficult to navigate markets in poorer regions characterized by market frictions—inadequate protection of property rights, industries dominated by monopolies and special interest groups, and opaque and insufficient business information, to name a few. In addition, foreign profit-driven enterprises are unlikely to reinvest much of their profits in the local economy. Conventional economic theory suggests that governments should take over production or impose regulation in the face of market failures. However, governments often lack the resources, expertise, or will to intervene—leaving room for charitable and non-governmental organizations to step in and help. Social entrepreneurs, as an amalgam of philanthropic organizations and for-profit business, can fill the gap between what the government can provide and what the market is willing to produce. Unconventionally, social entrepreneurs cannot simply import what is successful from the advanced countries. They often have to bring something new to the table—a new technology, practice, or a theory that can effect change locally.

Social entrepreneurs, as a new form of entrepreneurship, tend to think outside the box and are more open to new possibilities. Social entrepreneurs are also more willing than traditional businesses to cross international borders and venture into areas where the potential social benefits may be high, but financial returns uncertain (Seelos & Mair, 2004). Many begin from traditional foundations with a culture that is more willing to fund higher risk social start-ups in smaller jurisdictions where revenue generation usually takes longer. The ability to expand the time horizon gives social start-ups a better chance of success.

Entrepreneurship or even social enterprises are not panaceas. Social enterprise, while innovative and important, has been in existence since the 1960s, almost as long as external development aid programs. An in-depth analysis of the particular conditions of the poor throughout the world notes the variety in adoption of surplus-creating entrepreneurial opportunities (Banerjee & Duflo, 2011). Banerjee and Duflo emphasize that many poor actors, even with easy access to microfinance and entrepreneurial 'opportunities,' do not avail themselves of these mechanisms. The poor are generally quite rational and the reason to eschew entrepreneurship and microfinance may involve the limited benefits they can provide for most people compared to the significant costs in time and effort that entrepreneurship requires.

It has been a theme of this book that the financial ecosystem values multiple tools. It is impossible for social enterprise, traditional business, government, or charity to solve problems on their own. Poverty is a complex social phenomenon and will need all the stakeholders to align their understanding and resources in order to address it collectively. Properly conceived, social enterprise is a multi-stakeholder collaboration. It can avail broad legitimacy by being embedded in social networks in a manner that neither for-profit commercial corporations nor bureaucratic government agencies can access. The focus on the single social entrepreneur and his creativity and innovation, while important, nevertheless de-emphasizes the social capital that social enterprises depend upon. If it were just individual creativity and vision, then entrepreneurship alone, as described in the Say-Schumpeter tradition, would be sufficient. Social enterprise is characterized by collaboration between beneficiaries, volunteers, government agencies, foundations, non-profits, community, local, regional, and global development finance institutions, and commercial businesses. As we have argued elsewhere in the book, placing any one of these stakeholders, such as the investor or the plutocratic donor or the social entrepreneur on a pedestal necessarily detracts from a holistic understanding of this ecosystem. To end poverty, charities, religious organizations, NGOs, international development agencies, governments, and even celebrities have all tried to contribute. We may disagree on the motivations and merits of each player, but no one would doubt that collective and collaborative effort is essential to achieving that goal.

SOCIAL ENTREPRENEURSHIP AND SUSTAINABILITY

Sustainable development is often associated with environmental sustainability. While many still view sustainability as a broader concept for environmental protection, nature preservation, and energy efficiency, sustainable development is increasingly becoming an all-encompassing term that underlines a development model that is economically efficient, socially inclusive, and environmentally sustainable. In this sense, social enterprise that strives to achieve social value creation is very much aligned with the central tenets of sustainable development.

Many social and environmental issues are interconnected. For instance, the reduction in energy intensity and transition to cleaner energy would require changes in the general attitude and behavior of the population. It is also important to understand the energy need of the marginalized population, who would wish to have the same right to energy consumption and economic development. The very definition of sustainable development— *development that meets the needs of the present without compromising the ability of future generations to meet their own needs* (Brundtland, 1987)— combines intra-generational and intergenerational equity.

Sustainability is also context based. Using a bottom-up approach, social enterprises usually respond to social and environmental imperatives of the local population by experimenting with grassroots-level innovation. For example, there are social enterprise projects that develop affordable solar lighting products for people in Kenya who have been relying on kerosene lights which pose both safety and environmental hazards. This type of initiative is meeting the social needs of the local population while promoting renewable energy and the transition to sustainable development. Similar initiatives also take place in the food industry, where locally produced and organic food products are seen as sustainable alternatives to industrial food production. Socially conscious consumers have demanded that global consumer brands adopt fair trade practices that ensure adequate pay and working conditions for local producers. The oft-mentioned microfinance institutions are increasingly offering green microfinance products to encourage eco-friendly projects of grassroots entrepreneurs.

Many social entrepreneurs are grassroots entrepreneurs running small- or medium-sized projects, and they are keenly aware of local needs and constraints—ones that may be difficult for outsiders to understand. Equipped with local knowledge and expertise, they try to deliver eco-friendly products and services—energy, food, healthcare, and education that are not only social necessities but also improve sustainability. In the face of resource scarcity, social entrepreneurs are Schumpeterian in disrupting existing production processes, market structures, and consumption patterns (Schaltegger, 2002), and they are trying to meet the development need of the poor without the energy intensity of past generations.

Closely related to social entrepreneurship, but an even more novel conception is sustainable entrepreneurship. Sustainable entrepreneurs embrace a triple (economic, social, and environmental) bottom line through balancing economic return with social equity and environmental resiliency. By embracing financial and social bottom lines, social entrepreneurs often create environmental impact, albeit sometimes unintentionally. Sustainable entrepreneurs on the other hand are dedicated to the triple bottom lines and are interested in coming up with innovative and environmentally friendly solutions to daily problems.

SOCIAL ENTREPRENEURSHIP AND LOCALIZED INNOVATION

Innovation can be an afterthought in developing countries which are keen to copy the technological advancement of the industrialized nations. More recently, however, scholars and practitioners are noticing that the number of innovations originating from developing countries has been rising. The innovative capacity of less-developed countries may even be greater considering the enormity of their markets, which are also less saturated. Because of resource constraint, many innovations originating from less-developed regions are variants of existing technologies used in new ways and in a more affordable manner.

The Earthenware Refrigerator

Mansukhbhai Prajapati, a potter from the State of Gujarat in India, developed an affordable and natural refrigerator made of clay that uses no electricity. Due to the lack of reliable electricity and the high cost of modern fridges, many in his community find it difficult to store food and cool water in the sweltering Indian summer. It may not seem obvious at first how a 'poor man's fridge' could break into the larger market, but the success with the fridge allowed Mansukhbhai to found Mitti Cool, a business that also produces other clay-made cookware and water pots that either use less or no energy. These locally produced and eco-friendly products enabled the business to tap into the expanding green market.

Mitti Cool sources from local material and hires local workers. Its success not only contributes to the local economy by satisfying consumer needs, but also helps alleviate social problems by generating employment opportunities. Such affordable inventions are not comparable to their high-tech equivalents in terms of sophistication and functionality. They are rather the reengineering of preexisting technology that may appear as frugal adaptation but are actually new concepts and products. It is important to realize that these indigenous inventions are significant upgrades to whatever the local previously had and they are no less ingenious than the advanced technology developed elsewhere. They are also disruptive, and disruptive innovation is usually characterized by its increased simplicity which is crucial to scalability, particularly for the left behind, to whom convenience, affordability, and simplicity are key. By 2017, Mitti Cool had sold 9000 clay refrigerators in India, and it hires 35 employees and is expanding its sales globally (Mitticool, 2017). Clay refrigerators in India parallel the interest in earthen root cellars amongst homesteaders in North America, which uses the natural humidity and temperature-regulating properties of clay and mud.

There is a widely held assumption that emerging economies would evolve the same way as industrialized economies once did, especially with the diffusion of knowledge and technology from global trade. Globalization also created massive multinationals that dominate many industries internationally, leaving no room for smaller countries to chart their own development course. However, the world is quickly evolving and the problems faced by less-developed countries are materially different from those in the past. For instance, countries like China and India are under severe environmental and resource constraints, which compel them to embrace sustainability, more so than the industrialized nations. Grassroots innovations under these conditions, if adapted locally and taken to the global scale, may have the potential to evolve into new development and social change models that can uproot the globalization process, one that relied heavily on outsourcing instead of letting developing country subsidiaries innovate and on management practices based solely on western principles.

CHALLENGES AND OPPORTUNITIES

Despite some of the large cooperatives we have mentioned (such as Mondragón and the John Lewis Partnership), most social enterprises remain small in scale. Scaling is a common bottleneck for social entrepreneurs who are constrained by scarce resources and decreasing returns to scale. A large number of social enterprises are funded by seed money from foundations or sources that are capable only for small scale startup funding and who typically do not expect high financial return. A related issue is the internal sustainability of the social enterprise, especially for those whose business models rely on subsidies. It may be difficult to maintain financial viability in the long run, particularly in contexts of austerity programs and highly indebted government finances.

One of the longstanding challenges for social entrepreneurs is to attract mainstream capital from the private sector that may expect higher profit, which will be harder for social enterprises to achieve. The key is to convince corporations to start incorporating social value as an integral part of their business value system, not merely in terms of corporate social responsibility. On top of it, measurement tools have to be developed to assess social outcomes, which can eventually become part of the overall company valuation reflected in the stock market. Of course, once the goal includes social impact, the outcome becomes much more difficult to evaluate, and that makes accountability hard to achieve.

One of the great attributes for social enterprise is their inclusive management structure which comprises diverse stakeholders. Such a structure lends it a comparative advantage in understanding the needs of local consumer and resource limitations. However, the structure can be difficult to maintain when the organization grows, and the multitude of stakeholders can potentially become a hindrance in scaling up the project, as decisions may be harder to reach under a participatory governance structure.

Conditions for Entrepreneurship

Mainstream development efforts usually focus on the promotion of human capital, protection of individual property rights, and access to capital. These are all critical conditions for entrepreneurship. Human capital includes the ability to read and write—skills that can be utilized for productive work. It also includes interpersonal skills—the ability to lead, communicate, and motivate others. Human capital accumulation underlies economic growth through increased productivity, and it also drives innovation and technological improvements crucial for sustainable growth. While there have been improvements in human capital through education and training, the developing world still lacks critical resources to provide widespread and relevant education to all of its people.

Adequate property right protection gives an individual the right incentive to perform entrepreneurial activities without fear of government predation—a delicate balancing act for any government. There is a long tradition in political philosophy dating back to Hobbes and Locke, where the former believed in a strong government that can prevent war and defend the country, while the latter emphasized a limited government that is not predatory or confiscatory. While developing countries strengthened their protection of property rights through improvements in contract enforcement and business regulation, a government sufficiently strong to enforce property rights yet weak enough to not engage in state predation is a happy medium often elusive in the developing world. In addition, it may not always be preferable to imitate 'best practice' institutions from industrialized countries. Best practices based on the experience of others have to be adapted to local environment and conditions or, at least, at the beginning and then be allowed to evolve. It is suggested that 'transitional' institutions can more effectively serve developing countries—it matters more to find a path toward the goal than knowing where to end up, and it may be more important to know what is locally feasible than what is globally desirable (Qian, 2002). Under these conditions, traditional entrepreneurs may find it difficult to identify and exploit opportunities in less-developed country settings. Social entrepreneurs that are willing to take extra risks are trying to fill the gap. Perhaps an even bolder approach is to include certain class of public players that are naturally more inclined to commit to societal improvement while also exhibit entrepreneurial behavior under market-like incentives.

TVEs: Social Entrepreneurship with Chinese Characteristics

Even in finance, the salience of local geography in adapting lasting solutions has led to calls for a 'place-based' approach to investing. It is no
surprise that the cooperative movement and most social enterprises are
closely linked to particular geographies. In Chap. 12, we discussed the
municipal finance market in the US as a natural and polycentric solution
to the problem of financing local public goods.

It is well established that privately owned business engages in revenue
hiding to prevent government expropriation of profits (see Chap. 3 on tax
avoidance). However, in a developing country environment without
secure property rights, enterprises owned by local governments that are
more aligned with national government interests than private businesses
may be able to prevent or limit state predation by a central government
because such predation would erode the local legitimacy of the central
state (Che & Qian, 1998; Qian & Weingast, 1997). This is the logic of
federalism which we discussed in the context of municipal finance, which
is a natural solution for the provision of local public goods. In the Chinese
context before 1978, in the absence of private enterprise, local publicly
owned enterprises known as Town and Village Enterprises (TVEs) were
able to both limit central state predation and provide local public goods.
While local government ownership might have compromised managerial
incentives relative to private ownership, it also limited revenue hiding and
facilitated local public goods.

If any significant progress has been made on poverty reduction in the
latter half of the twentieth century, that progress is in no small part driven
by the Chinese experience. Between 1981 and 2005, China has lifted
more than 500 million people out of poverty, and its experience may offer
valuable lessons for the 1.4 billion people that are still living under abject
poverty. Many researchers and observers have attributed China's early success to the development of local government-owned enterprises such as
the vast number of TVEs (Che, 2002; Che & Qian, 1998; Chen &
Rozelle, 1999; Tian, 2000). TVEs evolved from the *people's commune* and
brigade enterprises, essentially local rural collectives, which emerged during the Chinese Great Leap Forward in 1958 (Qian, 2000). These collectives expanded and developed during the Cultural Revolution which
forced many urban students and professionals to move to rural areas and
assist in the process of rural development. Unlike the Soviet collectives,
the precursors of TVEs emerged not as a result of central government

policies, but largely from local initiatives and were tolerated because they helped solve the unemployment problem without needing much financial support (Qian & Xu, 1993). While many observers have decried the disruptive role of the Cultural Revolution, some scholars have pointed out that the period of the Cultural Revolution was associated with dramatic increases in rural education and agricultural output, driven in part by the locally owned collectives with participatory governance (Han, 2008). Unlike large State-Owned Enterprises (SOEs) that dominated industries, the numerous TVEs are small in size and are very connected to their communities. Equipped with the benefit of competing with each other and retaining their revenue for local public works, TVEs were the primary source of growth in the early period of China's economic development, which took place mainly in the rural areas and served to lift millions out of abject poverty.

Because of TVEs' proximity to their immediate beneficiaries and their relative variety, competition was intense and corruption was held in check. In the early days, TVEs combined the merits of private business functioning in a competitive free market and the public orientation of social enterprise. The early success of TVEs in China helps demonstrate that local government ownership can successfully integrate government functions—the provision of social goods—with a business incentive. A combination of the two with an emphasis on the former—which naturally comes from local government ownership—is the very definition of social enterprise.

The example of TVEs in China does not mean that publicly owned enterprises should have universal appeal, especially in the developed world, where institutional conditions are quite different. The TVEs were in fact an ad hoc solution during a time when private ownership was not tolerated and effectively served as an intermediary stage before the advent of privatization and increased economic liberalization. With intensified competition from the large number of TVEs, private companies, and international joint ventures, even successful TVEs found it difficult to recruit skilled workers in order to expand into urban areas and started to experience ownership abuses from local governments (Sun, 2002). Starting in the mid-1990s, smaller TVEs were privatized, with many larger ones being converted to joint stock companies collectively owned by their employees, community government, and other outside equity holders during a nationwide ownership restructuring campaign. From being the sole owner and supervisor of the TVE, the role of the local government became similar to that of an institutional shareholder (Sun, 2002). Nevertheless, this special form of social entrepreneurship emerging from the public end of the spectrum serves to demonstrate the importance of local solutions and that transitional institutions amenable to local conditions could credibly help increase economic efficiency and promote growth.

Key Lessons for Financial Intermediation

What can the sustainable finance practitioner learn from social enterprise? The cost of financial intermediation, of selecting the right opportunities in the right places has to be reduced. When small amounts must be invested or disbursed, per investment cost of due diligence and screening cannot be large. By tapping the tacit knowledge available in social networks, group-based microfinance constructs a natural solution to the problem of costly due diligence. In Chap. 14, we discussed the difficulties of financing people over the ease of financing assets. The cooperative movement and social enterprise are efforts to address the difficulty of financing people over assets. These socially oriented mechanisms recognize that, by and large, many humans are as motivated by peer pressure and peer approbation as they are by money. These other forms of motivation are essential to leverage, if we are to persuade people to work together efficiently. Once we can harness social nudges, the problem of determining whom to provide finance to falls away. People finance is no longer a difficult problem. This is perhaps the most globally applicable lesson that we can learn from Mohammad Yunus.

CONCLUDING REMARKS

The theory of the firm in mainstream economics is often criticized for its unrealistic assumption of 'home economicus'—economic man that is consistently rational in the pursuit of self-interest. In a systemic critique of this view, Thompson and Valentinov (2017) argue that "*homo economicus is not only inhumanly selfish and superhumanly rational, but utterly impervious to the world in which he exists*". What this boils down to is one of constrained optimization of a single variable. Oddly, the superrational individual does not attempt to modify his constraints, but settles down to solve a maximization problem. Hayek has famously ridiculed the effort to solve this maximization problem by pointing to the search for distributed information. Social enterprise is one form of aggregating distributed information in a polycentric manner.

We live in a complex world and are bound by complex emotions. In the well-known 1987 movie 'Wall Street', Gordon Gekko famously said *"Greed, for lack of a better word, is good."* He went on to explain that greed *"captures the essence of the evolutionary spirit. Greed, in all of its form; greed for life, for money, for love, for knowledge has marked the upward surge of mankind."* It is true that capitalism based on the profit-motive could not function without greed. However, if we can harness greed, why would we not harness other desires, such as the need for peer approbation or sympathy or empathy, other human attributes as innate and unavoidable as greed. Finance is too variegated and sophisticated to be based on a single human trait.

We have observed the failure of government bureaucracies in the delivery of social care and those of large-scale international aid in the endeavor to alleviate poverty. We can be hopeful that social enterprise that combines business acumen, a strong sense of social purpose, and an inherent respect for multi-stakeholder legitimacy might help to bring creative-disruptive solutions to address many pressing social challenges. As we have argued in other contexts that recognize the entire financial ecosystem, being disruptive here means being more inclusive—inclusive of local stakeholders in the decision-making process and the marginalized users and consumers of end products and services, whose quiet voices are the hardest to hear.

NOTE

1. For a detailed chronology of the cooperative movement, see Shaffer (1999).

REFERENCES

Banerjee, A. V., & Duflo, E. (2011). *Poor Economics: Rethinking Poverty and the Ways to End It.* New York, NY: PublicAffairs.

Banks, J. A. (1972). *The Sociology of Social Movements.* London, UK: Macmillan.

Billis, D. (2010). Towards a Theory of Hybrid Organizations. In D. Billis (Ed.), *Hybrid Organizations and the Third Sector* (pp. 46–69). Basingstoke, UK: Palgrave Macmillan.

Brundtland, G. H. (1987). *Our Common Future.* Retrieved from Brussels.

Bull, M., & Ridley-Duff, R. (2018). Towards an Appreciation of Ethics in Social Enterprise Business Models. https://doi.org/10.1007/s10551-018-3794-5

Che, J. (2002). *From the Grabbing Hand to the Helping Hand: A Rent Seeking Model of China's Township-Village Enterprises* (UNU-WIDER Discussion Papers). The United Nations University-World Institute for Development Economics Research (UNU-WIDER), Helsinki, Finland.

Che, J., & Qian, Y. (1998). Insecure Property Rights and Government Ownership of Firms. *The Quarterly Journal of Economics, 113*(2), 467–496.

Chen, H., & Rozelle, S. (1999). Leaders, Managers, and the Organization of Township and Village Enterprises in China. *Journal of Development Economics, 60*(2), 529–557.

Cornforth, C. (2003). Introduction: The Changing Context of Governance – Emerging Issues and Paradoxes. In *The Governance of Public and Non-profit Organizations* (pp. 13–32). New York, NY/London, UK: Routledge.

Dees, J. G. (1998). Enterprising Nonprofits. *Harvard Business Review, 76*, 54–69.

Defourny, J., & Nyssens, M. (2017). Fundamentals for an International Typology of Social Enterprise Models. *Voluntas: International Journal of Voluntary and Nonprofit Organizations, 28*(6), 2469–2497. https://doi.org/10.1007/s11266-017-9884-7

Department of Trade and Industry. (2002). *Social Enterprise: A Strategy for Success.* London, UK: Department of Trade and Industry. Retrieved from https://webarchive.nationalarchives.gov.uk/20040117014152/http://www.dti.gov.uk/socialenterprise/strategy.htm

Dorfleitner, G., & Oswald, E.-M. (2016). Repayment Behavior in Peer-to-Peer Microfinancing: Empirical Evidence from Kiva. *Review of Financial Economics, 30*, 45–59. http://www.sciencedirect.com/science/journal/10583300

Drucker, P. (2014). *Innovation and Entrepreneurship.* New York, NY: Routledge.

Easterly, W. (2006). The Big Push Déjà Vu: A Review of Jeffrey Sachs's the End of Poverty: Economic Possibilities for Our Time. *Journal of Economic Literature, 44*(1), 96–105. https://doi.org/10.1257/002205106776162663

Han, D. (2008). *The Unknown Cultural Revolution: Life and Change in a Chinese Village.* New York, NY: Monthly Review Press.

Hayton, J. C., George, G., & Zahra, S. A. (2002). National Culture and Entrepreneurship: A Review of Behavioral Research. *Entrepreneurship Theory and Practice, 26*(4), 33–52.

Hofsteds, G. (1980). *Culture's Consequences.* Beverly Hills, CA: Sage Publications.

International Co-operative Alliance. (2018). *Cooperative Identity, Values & Principles.* Retrieved from https://www.ica.coop/en/cooperatives/cooperative-identity

John Lewis Partnership. (2019). *Our Partners: Employee Ownership.* Retrieved from https://www.johnlewispartnership.co.uk/work/employee-ownership.html

Kistruck, G. M., & Beamish, P. W. (2010). The Interplay of Form, Structure, and Embeddedness in Social Intrapreneurship. *Entrepreneurship Theory and Practice, 34*(4), 735–761.

Leadbeater, C. (1997). *The Rise of the Social Entrepreneur.* London, UK: Demos.

Licht, A. N., & Siegel, J. I. (2006). The Social Dimensions of Entrepreneurship. In M. Casson & B. Yeung (Eds.), *Oxford Handbook of Entrepreneurship.* New York, NY/Oxford, UK: Oxford University Press.

Light, P. C. (2008). *The Search for Social Entrepreneurship.* Washington, DC: Brookings Institution Press.

Mair, J., & Marti, I. (2006). Social Entrepreneurship Research: A Source of Explanation, Prediction, and Delight. *Journal of World Business, 41*(1), 36–44.

Martin, R. L., & Osberg, S. (2007). Social Entrepreneurship: The Case for Definition. *Stanford Social Innovation Review, 5,* 28–39.

Mitticool. (2017, December 13). *Mitticool Success Story.* Retrieved from https://mitticool.com/mitticool-success-story/

Mondragón. (2017). *Annual Report 2017.* Retrieved from https://www.mondragon-corporation.com/en/about-us/economic-and-financial-indicators/annual-report/

Mondragón. (2019). *About Us.* Retrieved from https://www.mondragon-corporation.com/en/about-us/

Peredo, A. M., & McLean, M. (2006). Social Entrepreneurship: A Critical Review of the Concept. *Journal of World Business, 41*(1), 56–65.

Puumalainen, K., Sjögrén, H., Syrjä, P., & Barraket, J. (2015). Comparing Social Entrepreneurship Across Nations: An Exploratory Study of Institutional Effects. *Canadian Journal of Administrative Sciences, 32*(4), 276–287.

Qian, Y. (2000). The Process of China's Market Transition (1978–1998): The Evolutionary, Historical, and Comparative Perspectives. *Journal of Institutional and Theoretical Economics, 156*(1), 151–171. https://www.mohr.de/zeitschriften/journal-of-institutional-and-theoretical-economics-jite

Qian, Y. (2002). *How Reform Worked in China* (William Davidson Working Paper Number 473), Ann Arbor, MI: William Davidson Institute.

Qian, Y., & Weingast, B. R. (1997). Federalism as a Commitment to Reserving Market Incentives. *Journal of Economic Perspectives, 11*(4), 83–92.

Qian, Y., & Xu, C. (1993). Why China's Economic Reforms Differ: The M-Form Hierarchy and Entry/Expansion of the Non-state Sector. *The Economics of Transition, 1*(2), 135–170. http://onlinelibrary.wiley.com/journal/10.1111/%28ISSN%291468-0351/issues

Ridley-Duff, R., & Bull, M. (2015). *Understanding Social Enterprise: Theory and Practice.* Los Angeles, CA: Sage.

Sachs, J. D. (2006). *The End of Poverty.* New York, NY: Penguin Books.

Saebi, T., Foss, N. J., & Linder, S. (2019). Social Entrepreneurship Research: Past Achievements and Future Promises. *Journal of Management, 45*(1), 70–95.

Schaltegger, S. (2002). A Framework for Ecopreneurship. *Greener Management International, 2002*(38), 45–58.

Schwartz, B. (2012). *Rippling: How Social Entrepreneurs Spread Innovation Throughout the World.* New York, NY: Wiley.

Seelos, C., & Mair, J. (2004). *Social Entrepreneurship-the Contribution of Individual Entrepreneurs to Sustainable Development* (IESE Business School Working Paper, No. 553). IESE Business School, Barcelona, Spain.

Shaffer, J. (1999). *Historical Dictionary of the Cooperative Movement.* London, UK: Scarecrow Press.

Shepherd, D. A., & Patzelt, H. (2011). The New Field of Sustainable Entrepreneurship: Studying Entrepreneurial Action Linking "What Is to Be Sustained" with "What Is to Be Developed". *Entrepreneurship Theory and Practice, 35*(1), 137–163.

Social Enterprise UK. (2018). *Hidden Revolution: Size and Scale of Social Enterprise in 2018*. Retrieved from London: https://www.socialenterprise.org.uk/the-hidden-revolution

Spear, R., Cornforth, C., & Aiken, M. (2009). The Governance Challenges of Social Enterprises: Evidence from a UK Empirical Study. *Annals of Public and Cooperative Economics, 80*(2), 247–273.

Steven, O. (2019). *The Economic Case for Cooperatives in Developed and Developing Countries: Are There Any Special Characteristics in Particular Country Settings: A Case of Mondragon, Spain and Kenya*. Retrieved from Nairobi, Kenya: https://www.un.org/development/desa/dspd/wp-content/uploads/sites/22/2019/04/NCBA-CLUSA-UN-Presentation-26.03.pdf

Sun, L. (2002). Fading Out of Local Government Ownership: Recent Ownership Reform in China's Township and Village Enterprises. *Economic Systems, 26*(3), 249–269.

Tan, W.-L., Williams, J., & Tan, T.-M. (2005). Defining the 'Social' in 'Social Entrepreneurship': Altruism and Entrepreneurship. *The International Entrepreneurship and Management Journal, 1*(3), 353–365.

Thomas, A. (2004). The Rise of Social Cooperatives in Italy. *Voluntas: International Journal of Voluntary and Nonprofit Organizations, 15*(3), 243–263. https://doi.org/10.1023/B:VOLU.0000046280.06580.d8

Thompson, S., & Valentinov, V. (2017). The Neglect of Society in the Theory of the Firm: A Systems-Theory Perspective. *Cambridge Journal of Economics, 41*(4), 1061–1085.

Thornton, P. H., Ribeiro-Soriano, D., & Urbano, D. (2011). Socio-Cultural Factors and Entrepreneurial Activity: An Overview. *International Small Business Journal, 29*(2), 105–118.

Tian, G. (2000). Property Rights and the Nature of Chinese Collective Enterprises. *Journal of Comparative Economics, 28*(2), 247–268.

Trincado, E. (2018). The Debate Between the Austrian School of Economics and the Cooperative Movement: The Assumption of Unequal Perception Among Agents. *Revista de Historia Industrial, 27*(73), 81–103.

Williams, R. C. (2007). *The Cooperative Movement: Globalization from Below*. Aldershot, UK: Routledge.

Zamagni, V. (2017). A Worldwide Historical Perspective on Co-Operatives and Their Evolution. In M. Jonathan, R. B. Joseph, & B. Carlo (Eds.), *The Oxford Handbook of Mutual, Co-Operative, and Co-Owned Business*. Oxford, UK: Oxford University Press.

CHAPTER 16

Toward the Common Wealth and the Common Weal

The scale of global financial markets has come to dwarf governments and even whole economies. Measures of annual financial market activity count in the hundreds of trillions of dollars, which exceed estimates of global GDP or the value of natural capital services. The financial ecosystem derives its funding from the hard-earned savings of the wider global population, who is seeking capital stewardship and sustainable returns. The imperative to save comes from pressing future needs such as retirement, educational expenses, the purchase of essential capital goods, or as insurance against possible future calamities. The financial ecosystem represents a global common property resource for savers and issuers. We can choose to conserve it by eliminating the misallocation of human, natural, and financial capital and the leakage of value or we can let it be exploited by the few to appropriate the common wealth of the many.

As important as the flow of savings is to the ecosystem, even more critical is the unfettered flow of small voices that aggregate all the untraded information vital to preserving our non-financial capital. The role of decentralized civil society in keeping financial market participants honest is indispensable. To seek returns on non-financial capital, we must tap into a diversity of analytical paradigms and universal stakeholder perspectives to ensure that governments, corporations, and the financial sector are held to the highest standards of transparency and accountability that ensure the integrity of the whole system. The extensive and mutual interdependence of the public and private sectors, as underlined in the formulation of the UN

© The Author(s) 2019
S. Bose et al., *The Financial Ecosystem*, Palgrave Studies in Impact Finance, https://doi.org/10.1007/978-3-030-05624-7_16

Sustainable Development Goals (SDGs), behooves us to strive toward the possibility that savers, citizen investors, enterprises, the financial ecosystem, and society at large can align their objectives. The shared interest represents both the common wealth of global savings and the growing concern with the common good, or weal, from whence the word wealth derives.

The financial markets represent tremendous opportunity for those savers relying on the innovation and vibrancy of global economic activity to earn investment income to meet their needs without depleting capital. Those savers are as diverse in form as a postal savings bank customer in rural Zimbabwe, a retired public employee in California, or the beneficiary of a sovereign wealth fund in China, but their interest in preserving the common property resource that is the financial ecosystem is the same. Long-term asset owners and managers, investing for these savers, have the essential and formidable role of ensuring the sustainability of return. Long-term return depends on many sources of intangible value, including returns from well-conserved natural capital and consenting stakeholders. The persistence of investment income also requires healthy ecosystems, nutrient-rich soils, sources of clean water and clean air, and the absorptive capacity of the environment near industrial sites, as well as satisfied consumers, motivated employees, and investors eager to provide capital.

The financial ecosystem also presents an unparalleled opportunity for companies and issuing enterprises that are now responsible for an ever-growing share of the world economy. The scale and impact of corporate activity makes corporations indispensable partners in any effort to advance the sustainability of the global ecosystem. The twentieth-century nostrum that the purpose of corporations is above all to make profits for its shareholders, if necessary, at the expense of other stakeholders turns out to be a relatively new and hopefully short-lived concept. The acknowledgment of the value of stakeholder-focused corporate governance regimes, the advent of benefit corporations, and investor efforts to measure the environmental and social impact of corporate activity have manifested the potential of corporate efforts at sustainable impact.

Despite all our technological marvels, close to half of the world population are still living in poverty and 1.4 billion people are still fighting for subsistence. Emerging economies such as China and India that have demonstrated unimagined success in alleviating poverty are facing other no less severe problems such as social inequality and environmental degradation. In the U.S., the richest nation on earth, more than 46 million people

(15% of the population) live at or below the poverty line (Abramsky, 2013). The stated goal of the World Bank is to end poverty, as is the overarching mission of the SDGs, which recognize the importance of the private market in financing our common development goals at the broadest level. Significantly, the SDGs have been adopted by nearly 200 countries, demonstrating that, for the first time, shared ambitions are embraced across iron curtains and equatorial divides—low-, middle-, and high-income countries alike. The rapid growth in the assets under management of signatories of the UN's Principles of Responsible Investment to more than $70 trillion makes evident that investors are seeking to integrate their understanding of what sustainability demands. As this book argues, there is a growing sense of a common interest among all stakeholders in pursuing shared goals of inclusive growth, prosperity, and sustainability.

The prospect of joint implementation by the public and private sectors to realize shared or complementary ambitions animates anew the possibility of real progress in widespread sustainability. However, in the collaboration across public, private, and civil society boundaries lie many challenges. In *The Prince*, Machiavelli writes: "There is no more delicate matter to take in hand, nor more dangerous to conduct, nor more doubtful in its success, than to set up as a leader in the introduction of change. For he who innovates will have for enemies all those who are well off under the old order of things, and only lukewarm supporters in those who might be better off under the new" (Machiavelli, 1913). Barriers to cooperation, the tragedy of the horizon, conflicts of interest, and vested analytical monocultures frustrate the need for urgent progress.

The origins of the financial accounting system as a tool to help owners of firms determine whether management is an effective steward of capital limits the focus of financial accounting to the relatively narrow concerns of investors. Strong alliances within and between investor communities and NGOs are essential to new performance frameworks. Decision-makers in the financial ecosystem can view the multiplicity of frameworks and metrics as an obstacle or an opportunity. We believe an understanding of the financial ecosystem and its place within planetary boundaries enriches our understanding of the traditional role of finance within society. It allows the financial analyst to ask questions which operate at the frontier between the financial ecosystem and societal efforts to attain sustainability. There is overwhelming evidence that many measures of sustainability performance are associated with at least modestly improved financial performance, though these returns are often manifest in the fullness of time. On the contrary, there is little evidence to suggest that corporate social performance might be detrimental to corporate financial performance, which means that there is no financial justification for delaying the integration of social and financial purposes.

Discounting, cost-benefit analysis, methods to monetize the value of natural capital, a deeper engagement with the returns to human capital management, and an appreciation of the value of diverse social networks are tools at the disposal of the sustainable financial analyst. Modern portfolio theory, despite its limitations, continues to be useful as one narrative framework among others to shape our understanding of the attribution of risk and return, which remains critical to performance evaluation. The full range of such tools, despite their limitations, allow us to navigate the trade-offs between the short and long term in many routine investment decisions, and to parse the domain of prudential judgment from that of mechanistic calculation.

The essence of financial decision-making is that effective solutions are designed in a decentralized way, tailored to the particulars of specific situations, with different cash flow expectations, maturity, volatility, and other sources of both financial and ecosystem risk. It is for this reason that we have not attempted to prescribe a top-down roadmap of solutions or a prescriptive design for a new financial ecosystem that more ambitious commentators may have chosen to swing for. A roadmap or a new architecture would be useful only to those precious few global decision-makers who might have the power to re-shape the financial ecosystem. We are doubtful that any such powerful decision-maker exists. Instead, our treatment has focused on a critical explanation and evaluation of the range of tools available to expand the analytical monocultures that have come to colonize financial decision-making.

We are hopeful that an understanding of the financial ecosystem and its linkages with the global environment will allow financial analysts to identify pressure points in the existing financial ecosystem and facilitate the disciplines of risk identification and the search for opportunities. We have much to learn of value among the small but innovative advances in advancing non-financial performance in the field of impact investing. The interaction of ecosystem services and conservation finance has the potential to expand our risk and valuation frameworks to recognize the web of supportive interconnections within nature. The special problems of financing early stage sustainable innovation demonstrate the value of public and private sector complementarities in cleantech investment. The cooperative movement and social entrepreneurship point the way toward collaborative ecosystems in participatory governance and decentralized and inclusive growth. We have illustrated the possibilities of decentralized finance platforms to aggregate the wisdom of crowds in the context of corporate governance, trade finance, and prediction markets. Building on these examples, a future financial ecosystem will be able to fulfill its newly defined roles: to allocate scarce capital to its highest social value, to match investors in search of a broad range of financial, physical, human, and natural returns with appropriate risk-adjusted investment opportunities, and to generate decentralized signals of scarcity in the context of planetary boundaries.

We believe that embracing the heterogeneity of investor and stakeholder perspectives on the meaning of sustainability is essential to the resilience of the ecosystem. In that regard, the SDGs may have turned a new page in the path to a future financial ecosystem. They were built through inclusive consultation, a bottom-up approach where all UN member countries were participants. They promise to usher in a new era of cooperation and shared responsibility, with partnerships between public policy leaders, private financial markets, and civil society. There will inevitably be tensions, conflicts of interest, and differences of opinion during the iterative process for working through these partnership processes, but there is now a shared global ambition for sustainable development that acknowledges the role and the responsibilities of financial markets—grounded in our common wealth. As citizens, workers, savers, consumers, and investors, we all belong in the overlapping interest communities that collectively form the financial ecosystem. *The crux of the matter lies not in what gets decided, but who gets to decide.*

REFERENCES

Abramsky, S. (2013). America's Shameful Poverty Stats. *The Nation, 297*(14), 1–3.
Machiavelli, N. (1913). *The Prince* (N. H. Thomson, Trans.). Oxford, UK: Clarendon Press.

Index[1]

---

[1] Note: Page numbers followed by 'n' refer to notes.

© The Author(s) 2019
S. Bose et al., *The Financial Ecosystem*, Palgrave Studies in Impact
Finance, https://doi.org/10.1007/978-3-030-05624-7

CPSIA information can be obtained
at www.ICGtesting.com
Printed in the USA
BVHW040442221119
564509BV00003BA/34/P

9 783030 056230